Narrative Approaches to Working with
Adult Male Survivors of Sexual Abuse

also by Kim Etherington

Becoming a Reflexive Researcher – Using Our Selves in Research
ISBN 1 84310 259 5

Trauma, the Body and Transformation
A Narrative Inquiry
ISBN 1 84310 106 8

Rehabilitation Counselling in Physical and Mental Health
ISBN 1 85302 968 8

Counsellors in Health Settings
ISBN 1 85302 938 6

of related interest

Counselling Adult Survivors of Child Sexual Abuse, 2nd Edition
Christiane Sanderson
ISBN 1 85302 252 7

Creative Group Therapy for Women Survivors of Child Sexual Abuse
Speaking the Unspeakable
Bonnie Meekums
ISBN 1 85302 453 8

Good Practice in Counselling People Who Have Been Abused
Edited by Zetta Bear
ISBN 1 85302 424 4

Good Practice in Working with Victims of Violence
Edited by Hazel Kemshall and Jacki Pritchard
ISBN 1 85302 768 5
Good Practice Series 8

Guiding Recovery from Child Sexual Abuse
Horizons of Hope
Dave Simon
ISBN 1 85302 571 2

Psychodynamic Perspectives on Abuse
The Cost of Fear
Edited by Una McCluskey and Carol-Ann Hooper
ISBN 1 85302 686 7
ISBN 1 85302 685 9

Narrative Approaches to Working with Adult Male Survivors of Sexual Abuse

The Clients', the Counsellor's and the Researcher's Story

Kim Etherington

with Mike and Stephen and a Contribution by Sarasi Rogers

Jessica Kingsley Publishers
London and Philadelphia

First published in the United Kingdom in 2000
by Jessica Kingsley Publishers
116 Pentonville Road
London N1 9JB, UK
and
400 Market Street, Suite 400
Philadelphia, PA 19106, USA

www.jkp.com

Copyright © Kim Etherington 2000
Printed digitally since 2005

The right of Kim Etherington to be identified as author of this work has been asserted by her in accordance with the Copyright, Designs and Patents Act 1988.

All rights reserved. No part of this publication may be reproduced in any material form (including photocopying or storing it in any medium by electronic means and whether or not transiently or incidentally to some other use of this publication) without the written permission of the copyright owner except in accordance with the provisions of the Copyright, Designs and Patents Act 1988 or under the terms of a licence issued by the Copyright Licensing Agency Ltd, 90 Tottenham Court Road, London, England W1T 4LP. Applications for the copyright owner's written permission to reproduce any part of this publication should be addressed to the publisher.
Warning: The doing of an unauthorised act in relation to a copyright work may result in both a civil claim for damages and criminal prosecution.

Library of Congress Cataloging in Publication Data

Etherington, Kim/
 Narrative Approaches to working with adult male survivors of childhood sexual abuse : the clients', the counsellor's, and the researcher's story / Kim Etherington.
   p. cm.
 Includes bibliographical references and index.
 ISBN-13: 978-1-85302-818-2 (alk. paper)
 ISBN-10: 1-85302-818-5 (alk. paper)
   1. Child sexual abuse—Case studies. 2. Adult child sexual abuse victims—Case studies. 3. Adult child sexual abuse victims—Counseling of. 4. Boys—Abuse of. I. Title.
 HV6570.N37 2000
 362.76'4'081—dc21
                                                                                00-028274

British Library Cataloguing in Publication Data
A CIP catalogue record for this book is available from the British Library

ISBN-13: 978 1 85302 818 2
ISBN-10: 1 85302 818 5

Contents

	ACKNOWLEDGEMENTS	8
	PROLOGUE	9
1	Introduction	13

Part 1 The Clients' Story: The Elephant in the Living Room

2	Stephen's Story	27
3	Mike's Story	77

Part 2 The Counsellor's Story

4	The Iceberg: A Tale of Therapy	103
5	Beginnings	106
6	The Therapeutic Relationship	119
7	Transference and Counter-transference	130
8	Post-traumatic Stress Disorder	137
9	Healing Trauma	143
10	Writing as Therapy	152
11	Writing to and from the Inner Child	165
12	Bodywork	176
13	Collaborative Working	185

14	Stories Within Stories	201
15	More Stories Within Stories	213
16	Traumatic Sexualisation	223
17	What Helps?	230
18	Endings	235

Part 3 The Researcher's Story

19	The Swamp	247
20	Research Process	252
21	Ethics	261
22	Research Methods	268
23	Doing the Research	283
24	Sorting Data and Writing	295
25	Where Three Streams Meet	302

APPENDIX 1: STEPHEN'S LETTER TO HIS DEAD GRANDFATHER	306
APPENDIX 2: RESOURCE LIST	311
BIBLIOGRAPHY	313
SUBJECT INDEX	325
AUTHOR INDEX	333

This book is dedicated to Mike and Stephen – their names have been changed to maintain their privacy – but they know who they are.

Acknowledgements

The enormous contribution made by Mike and Stephen will be obvious to anybody reading this book. I am grateful for their generosity in allowing me to use their material, for the time they have given to meetings and discussions of the project, to reading and re-reading drafts, and their expressed pleasure in making their contribution that has sometimes been tinged with sadness as new realisations have occurred. But their dedication and enthusiasm for the task has never failed. I am grateful for the additional opportunity they have given me to know them better, and in a different relationship.

The less obvious contributions that have been made by the many clients, students, friends, counsellors and supervisees are also implicitly present and I never cease to marvel at the new learning I can take from each and every encounter.

I am also grateful to Jacki Pritchard who 'got me going' by suggesting that I should write this book and for her introduction to Jessica Kingsley who, even at the early stages, supported me with her 'unequivocal enthusiasm' for the idea.

I also want to acknowledge the important part Sarasi Rogers has played, both in collaborating with me in working with Mike and Stephen and in allowing that work to be included in this book. She generously gave her time and energy to reading the work in progress and to writing her part of Chapter 13. Without that it would have been only half a story.

To those other friends and colleagues who have taken the time and trouble to read the work and give me useful feedback, I am also grateful: Tim Bond, Hazel Johns, Shirley Margerison, Janet May and Jane Speedy.

Lastly, and importantly, I wish to acknowledge my ever-increasing family whose love always sustains me, especially the 'backroom boy' – David, my husband, computer 'techie', cook, shopper and general factotum, whose love, moral and physical support has kept me going when moments of self-doubt have threatened.

Prologue

One day, back in the early 1990s, I was teaching a course for counsellors on 'Working with the Aftermath of Sexual Abuse' when a man in the group asked, 'Is it the same for men who have been abused?' The discussion that followed highlighted that none of us had had much experience of working with men who had been sexually abused in childhood. There were some people in the group who found it difficult to accept that boys *were* abused. So I began to explore the literature and found a few books which acknowledged that males were abused, but almost as an afterthought. The feminist literature that encouraged women to accept their status as survivors rather than as victims vehemently placed the blame for abuse upon patriarchy and on males as abusers. At the same time there were whisperings about the possibility that sometimes abusers were female, but others argued that this was a backlash against the empowerment of women and a denial of the reality of male sexual domination of both women and children (Herman 1981; Russell 1984).

In this climate only a few brave men 'came out' as a sexual victims. Men had been well socialised into identifying themselves as 'sexually dominant'. The idea that a male could be sexually victimised meant that he had to admit to being sexually powerless, which patriarchy equated to being 'less than a man'. Feminists were right when they exposed the iniquities of patriarchy; what they failed to recognise was that patriarchy was damaging to men as well as women and children. Any man who did not measure up to the 'macho' image portrayed as being a 'real man' was considered inferior. Because being female was considered to be an inferior status, any man who displayed stereotypically 'feminine' qualities such as sensitivity, caring or feelings was dismissed along with women and children. Men who had been raped as adults – gay men, gentle, sensitive men – all came into this category. In fact, any man in a subordinate status to another man, perhaps in the workplace, might have been be subjected to patriarchal domination by a more senior man. As I write these words I notice I use the past tense. I'm not entirely convinced that this is appropriate – all this is still happening today in spite of our awareness of it.

So in 1992 I became a 'proper' researcher, setting out on a journey into relatively unknown territory. I say 'proper' because I had previously undertaken a small research study as part of a postgraduate diploma in counselling back in 1987 and had later produced a small research study for an MSc in Counselling (training and supervision). Previously my research projects had been part of a course requirement, but this time I was on my own; I decided to submit my work for a Ph.D. I didn't even know where to start. I knew nobody who had gone before from the counselling world (although I now know that some others had gone before me). This felt very different; I was in my fifties and I had only recently discovered my brain! My decision to submit for a PhD was because I wanted my research to be taken seriously and I believed that my work would need to be assessed and valued in a way that was recognised in the academic community if that were to be the case.

My interest in the topic of childhood sexual abuse had begun many years before when I faced my own history of abuse. This interest had developed as I trained to become a counsellor and later as I practised as a counsellor, working with women who had also been abused in childhood and training others to do the work.

Around the time I began to research the subject we were beginning to hear of the large-scale abuse of male children as well as female children in care, in boarding schools, in churches and other institutions, as well as at the hands of large paedophile rings. It was acknowledged that paedophiles frequently abuse boys and during their 'career' their victims might run into hundreds. So where were all these boys who by now must have become men? Women had been coming forward in their droves since feminism had allowed them a voice, appearing in mental health settings, drug and alcohol rehabilitation clinics, rape crisis centres, etc. But where were the men?

At that time I had been referred a man who had admitted to abusing his daughter. He wanted to understand his behaviour and take responsibility for changing it. He told me of his own abuse at the hands of some young soldiers at the army camp where his father had been based (see Robert's story in Etherington 1995). He had repressed the memory of this abuse until he sought help after his first episode of abusing his daughter. During his work with an acupuncturist, he had been flooded with the early memory of the distressing and terrifying abuse at the camp when he was 8 years old. But he had gone on to abuse again. His abusing did not mirror what he had experienced from the young soldiers. He loved his daughter and felt confused about what he had done to her. His abusive behaviour towards her did not involve force and had, in his view, been a demonstration of his love for her. I had read an empirically derived research study (O'Brien 1989) which indicated that abusers usually re-enact their abuse on someone of the same gender as their abuser, and that the type of abuse was often similar to what they had experienced as the victim. This didn't add up.

Gradually his story emerged. His father had been a brutish man who had beaten and terrified all his children and their mother. Robert's mother had been an 'angel of protection': 'Without her we wouldn't have survived,' Robert told me, his eyes full of tears and love. When Robert was 12 years old his father was imprisoned for sexually abusing children in the neighbourhood. Mother had needed her eldest son to comfort her and had taken him into her bed. Robert could not allow himself to interpret her behaviour as abuse. He described her sexual behaviour with him, using almost the same words he had used to describe what he had done to his daughter (Etherington 1995). Now it made more sense. Slowly and painfully Robert allowed himself to know the reality of what his mother had done to him, and as he did so he realised what he had done to his daughter.

Much of the published research had been conducted with men who were convicted offenders (Burgess *et al.* 1987; Carlson 1990; Groth and Burgess 1979; Johnson and Shrier 1987; Petrovich and Templar 1984). And here was I, also understanding abuse from an offender's point of view. What about the men who did not go on to become offenders? We had never heard from them. How valid is the research if we hear only from those who had gone on to re-enact their own abuse?

The more I read and heard, the more curious (and confused) I became. Had we denied men the right to help by dismissing the possibility of viewing them as sexual victims? It was at this point that I decided I wanted to find out for myself. So my research was led by my curiosity about questions that emerged from my practice as a counsellor and as a counselling trainer.

Much of what I had already in my rucksack was useful and even necessary, and on this journey I found out how to use some of my existing tools in a different way. I also developed new skills and learned how to use some tools I had not used before. The journey was lonely and, at times, downright distressing and fearful. Now in 1999, I can look back and see it for the valuable and important journey that it was.

After my thesis was completed my book followed and was published in 1995. Shortly after that Stephen found my book, sought me out and I began to work with him as his counsellor and later with his brother, Mike. When our work together was finished both men expressed the thought that, someday, they might like to tell *their* stories – like those they had read in my book.

Early in 1999, when I was asked to write a chapter for a book on working with the aftermath of violence (Kemshall and Pritchard 2000), I contacted Stephen and Mike to ask them if I might use some of their stories to illustrate the chapter. They both expressed pleasure at being asked. I wrote the chapter, very aware of how much more there was to say and of the need for another book, of a different kind, to help counsellors and others to feel more confident about working with male survivors of sexual abuse.

One of the books that had inspired me in an earlier stage of my development as a counsellor was *Love's Executioner* (Yalom 1989). At the time of reading it, I remember being impressed by Yalom's honesty and courage and his ability to acknowledge his mistakes and negativity. All of this made my own shortcomings and negative feelings seem more acceptable. I grew in confidence as I recognised in his work some of my own thoughts and feelings, and some of my own ways of working. If a man with such a length of experience and breadth of knowledge could allow others to see his darker side, then maybe I could too. I no longer felt I needed to be 'perfect'. Yalom and Elkin (1974) showed from diaries kept during the process of therapy that the client's perspective on the work can differ greatly from the counsellor's. Rennie (1990, 1992), Rennie (1992), Mearns and Thorne (1988) and Dryden and Yankura (1992) more recently explored and represented the client's experience of psychotherapy by taping counselling sessions and reviewing them with clients after the work was completed. I had not taped my sessions with Stephen and Mike but I thought they had both kept diaries; Stephen's had been used in his sessions.

It had been several years since I finished working with them and I wanted to find out what they had felt about it at the time and how they felt about it now. My curiosity was partly driven by my belief that we need to be accountable for what we do as counsellors and partly by my need to discover if, and how, my own competence had developed over the years.

In recent years there has been a blossoming of the culture of research in counselling and counsellors frequently set out down their own paths of discovery. I began to teach research methodologies in 1997 and enjoyed working with students at that level. I wanted to write a book for this group of students, one that was accessible and in a language that they could understand easily without necessarily having to have recourse to a dictionary or glossary of terms. I hope therefore that this book will be of help to those who are interested in knowing more about how a counselling practitioner might become a researcher and how we can go on evolving and learning through the process of doing research.

I remembered Stephen and Mike's enthusiasm and decided to approach them individually to sound out the idea of collaborating on the research for a new book. Both men responded positively and we decided to meet...

CHAPTER 1

Introduction

As I sit down to write the first words of this book I have an image of myself as a small girl standing in a hall of mirrors. The hall of mirrors is just inside the entrance to the 'Crazy House' at the permanent funfair located at New Brighton on Merseyside. My father has friends who own some of the rides/amusements and they allow me free access. The 'Crazy House' is a favourite of mine. It is scary, funny and, no matter how often I visit there, always a surprise. In the hall of mirrors I face one full-length mirror which reflects the front of my body. Behind me is another mirror which reflects my rear view onto the mirror facing me. Then the reflections go on, and on; reflections of reflections, of reflections. Other people come and stand beside me sometimes and gaze at themselves; they too are reflected and their reflections are reflected. Some pass by, not stopping but their reflections are there too, fleetingly. (Diary entry – April 1999)

This book is like that; reflections upon reflections upon reflections – mine and those of others who have passed through my life or stood beside me for a while. Those reflections carry echoes of distant pasts, as well as images of the present. They are ever-changing, alive and sometimes funny, sometimes not.

And after the hall of mirrors, there is the rest of the 'Crazy House'; sometimes the ground moves beneath my feet, backwards and forwards so that I have to hold on tight; sometimes a sudden gust of air blows my skirt above my ears and I feel exposed, embarrassed, amused. I enter rooms where the floor is sloping down one way and I find it hard to keep my balance, I am forced to run over to the wall. But I know there is a way out; and I know that if I follow the laid out route I will find the exit, and outside there will be the sunshine and ordinary life again – well, as ordinary as life ever is, and as extraordinary as most lives are. (Diary entry – April 1999)

And this book is an extraordinary story of interwoven lives. Mainly the lives of Mike and Stephen, two of my ex-clients who are brothers, and my own life. But other lives are part of the richness of this story too. The lives of Mike and Stephen's family, then and now, my own family then and now, and the lives of all the men and women I have worked with as a counsellor, trainer and researcher. In this book I use 'counsellor' and 'therapist' interchangeably.

Back in 1992 I began a study of adult male survivors of childhood sexual abuse – I studied the stories of 25 ordinary men – echoes of their stories are also here, reflected in the mirrors of time. In 1995 I wrote a book which told the stories of those men and it was through this book that I came to meet Mike and Stephen.

One day I came home and found a letter lying on my doormat. It had been forwarded by the university where I was employed part-time; it was a letter from Stephen and it said:

Dear Kim,

I apologise for tracking you down, but I think you will understand why I have done so.

I always told myself I would carry my dark secret to my grave; to protect myself and those I love from the pain involved in disclosure.

However, events have caught up with me and my secret is out. As I feared my older brother and I shared the same sort of attention from our grandfather. He has started to come to terms with what happened to him and recently talked to our parents, who are naturally devastated. As a result my mother asked me if anything had happened to me. I confirmed her worst fears and since then I have been in emotional turmoil, to such a degree that it is affecting my family, and employment. I either want to cry, or feel very aggressive.

Without my wife, who is being incredibly supportive and understanding, I don't know where I would be. Also, I have talked at length with my brother, and we have shared our common experience.

I realise I need to talk to someone who can help me survive my crisis.

Unable to find any 'self help', I was amazed to see the title of your book, in the bookshop. Although a 'text book' I am reading through it. I am identifying strongly with a lot of what I am reading, and it is helping me understand.

I also think I feel your empathy coming through, and that I could talk to you. However, I do appreciate this may not be possible. The nature of my profession makes talking to just anyone very frightening. If I could not talk to you, I feel as if I could trust you to recommend another counsellor skilled in this area, who could maintain confidentiality.

Thank you for reading this. Thank you for writing the book, and for caring about 'us'.

Yours sincerely,
Stephen

My response was instant. The letter touched me; the painful rawness of an exposed wound could not be ignored. I phoned him. We met and we went on meeting. Later I met his brother Mike. In this book you too will meet Mike and Stephen (not their real names); they want to tell you their stories. In my previous book many men told their stories of childhood sexual abuse, (Etherington 1995) describing the abuses they had suffered, and I wrote about the way I understood theory to be related to themes that emerged from their stories. Other books have been written that focus on the impact of sexual abuse on males (Bolton *et al.* 1989; Hunter 1990; Lew 1988; Mezey and King 1992). This book is different – this is a story of hope and healing highlighting the journeys made by Mike and Stephen as they struggled towards health and wholeness. Part (and only part) of that story is their experience of counselling – with myself as their counsellor, and their work with Sarasi Rogers, a body therapist. One of the purposes of this book is to offer a lifeline to men who may feel confused, hopeless, eternally damaged or trapped in the painful darkness of shame and secrecy that Stephen graphically portrays in his letter. Finding a book that included stories of men with whom he could identify was an important stage in the process of healing for him. He and Mike want this book to do the same for other men. They kept diaries capturing the process of recovery and have offered these very personal and powerful accounts in the hope that others will know that they too can heal. There has been little written about the abuse of males – there is even less written about their recovery, and especially by the men themselves.

Stephen and Mike were abused by their grandfather from very early childhood until late in their teens. All through their childhood, adolescence and young adulthood they were trapped in a fog of secrecy and silence – neither knew of the other's victimisation. It involved some of the most severe abuse and betrayal that a child can sustain – and they have survived, indeed they have done more than survive – they have flourished. They want people to know *how* they survived; what helped, what they needed, what resources they found, both within themselves and externally.

So **Part 1** of the book is **'The Client's Story'**. The first brother I met was Stephen and so **'Stephen's Story'** comes first in **Chapter 2**, although he is the younger. His story is told through his diary, over a period from 22 July 1995 to 27 October 1995: just three months during which his life was turned upside down by facing up to what had happened to him as a child and helping his family to face up to their part in that. I have not changed the content except to rearrange the wording on the page to allow the reader's eye to find the shape and patterns of his experiences at that time. The capital letters are his own. The power of his writing reflects the power of his experiences. Part of his therapy was to write a letter to his dead grandfather, his abuser. This letter written from 22.00 hrs until 04.00hrs, between 3 and 4 September, describes the betrayal and the horror of the actual abuse. For some people this letter may be too difficult to read. The diary can be read and understood without the need to read the letter so I have placed the letter in Appendix 1.

'Mike's Story' in **Chapter 3** has been written retrospectively by him, using his diaries and his memories of what seemed important at the time and still seem important now. I have added some of his letters to his story, with his permission, illuminating his text with some of his therapeutic writing. The brothers' individuality comes through in their writing. Both men have sustained the same degree of abuse, over the same time period and by the same abuser. However, their experiences were individually felt and individually dealt with – in their own unique ways – even though they worked with the same therapists. These stories speak for themselves and I have tried to join with the men and think *with* their stories rather than *about* their stories. Arthur Frank (1995) says:

> To think *about* a story is to reduce it to content and then analyze that content. Thinking *with* stories takes the story as already complete; there is no going beyond it. To think *with* a story is to experience it affecting one's own life and to find in that effect a certain truth of one's life. (Frank 1995, p.23)

So **Part 2** of the book is **'The Counsellor's Story'** – where I think *with* the stories. I have been particularly curious to know how Mike and Stephen experienced our relationship. I also wanted to discover what was helpful and what was unhelpful in the counselling process. I wanted to discover some of the significant moments for them in the work and which of the tools I used that may have contributed to their healing. I also hoped to find out something about how their stories affected my life because we are changed by stories, both as teller and listener. We rarely have an opportunity to reflect back with our own clients and learn about ourselves as workers, or learn about the process that is usually life changing for our clients and ourselves.

Using myself as my 'primary instrument' (McLeod 1994), I have written about my experience of the work. Part 2 begins with **Chapter 4** – one of *my* stories, **'The Iceberg'**, written towards the end of my first period of therapy some years ago. My story (or stories, for we have many), my values, beliefs and life experiences, my learning from research and from practice inform my work. **Chapter 5** is concerned with **'Beginnings'**, exploring the concept of 'the wounded healer' and examining how, as helpers, we can use the awareness of our own wounds to facilitate healing in others. This chapter also explores some of the issues concerning assessment – how do we know if the client is ready to undertake the work? What do we need to ask ourselves to discover if we are ready and able to offer to help others? In **Chapter 6** the focus is on **'The Therapeutic Relationship'** – and the factors that influence the process of engagement with people who have had to cope by isolating themselves, or parts of themselves, from other people. Further aspects of the relationship are examined in **Chapter 7** as I explore some of the issues concerning **transference and counter-transference**.

It is now recognised that people who have sustained sexual abuse during childhood, particularly over a lengthy period of their lives, may be suffering from a type of **Post-traumatic Stress Disorder** and in **Chapter 8** I describe some of the ways that Mike and Stephen presented with symptoms of delayed onset. In **Chapter 9** I explore how we can help people to **heal from trauma**, even when it has occurred a long time ago.

In **Chapter 10** I have explored **the therapeutic use of creative writing**. Since completing this I have discovered another book (Bolton 1999) that describes in greater detail the vast potential of writing as a tool for healing in a variety of settings. **Chapter 11** focuses on **writing to and from the 'child within'**, with some examples of how Mike used this tool effectively.

Since I was a small child I have written poetry as a way of soothing myself, and making sense of my experiences, using images, metaphor and language to express thoughts and feelings. I made up stories about horses put out to grass, crippled children or runaway orphans and wrote them down. Looking back now I realise that the stories were all about me. Nobody told me to do this; it was as natural to me as talking to myself – which I'm told I did repeatedly as a small child. As a counsellor I have always encouraged my clients to keep diaries, write stories and poems too. Sometimes they discover, by this means, a part of themselves of which they had been unaware: a creative, inventive, imaginative, feeling part of themselves. Having suggested to Stephen, early in our series of sessions, that he might keep a diary, he took full advantage of this suggestion and the first part of this book is the product of that work. Later, he went on to write poetry, an activity that amazed and inspired him. Mike also kept a diary, wrote poems and letters. All of this enabled him to construct a narrative about his life and, in particular, his therapy. Stories have an active role in constructing the person's world in the here-and-now and in the future, (McLeod 1997).

Stories can also be used as a vehicle for communicating memories. Sometimes it is easier for a person to tell their story 'as if', in the voice of a fairy story, or through a metaphor as a means by which they might draw closer and face their painful reality. In the initial stages reality might be too terrifying to fully experience. By using stories, letters or poems to create slight distance, the client might be enabled gradually to draw closer to their true experiences. Schafer (1981) says experience is 'made' or 'fashioned' and not directly encountered: 'To experience we have to imagine; imagination is consciousness struggling to gain sovereignty over its experience' (p.31). Sometimes the unconscious takes over and stories are told that symbolise the person's reality which might only be known intuitively, tacitly or perhaps carried within the body.

Telling our story is a way of reclaiming ourselves, our history and our experiences; a way of finding our voice. In telling my story to others I am also telling it to my 'self' – and my 'self' (who is the audience) is being formed in the process of telling. So there are witnesses to my story, the 'other' to whom I recount my story (which is what clients do with us in therapy), and the self who is growing within me as I hear my story retold as I speak or write it down. Frank (1995) recognised that 'repetition is the medium of becoming' and in the process of research we go a step further. When we use our own stories, or those of others, for research, we give testimony to what we have witnessed; and that testimony creates a voice. There is power in having a voice. McLeod (1997) says;

> Being powerful requires the willingness of other people to listen, to hear, to be influenced by what that voice has to say. There are many people in the world who possess little power of this kind, who are effectively 'silenced'. (McLeod 1997, p.93)

Even those who are powerful in one sphere of life may carry intimate personal stories that are never heard. Stephen and Mike are two such men. Mike is an inner city GP and Stephen has returned to orthopaedic nursing since leaving the Prison Service where he was employed when I first met him. They are members of a powerful profession, both historically and in modern life – the medical profession. You will hear from them how their membership of such groups added to their difficulty in telling their stories. They believed that membership of and acceptance by such powerful groups was dependent upon them behaving in a way that conformed with the norms that underpin patriarchy. Those norms deny the possibility of male vulnerability. This too was a means of silencing them. However, both men faced up to the fear of rejection by others by choosing to tell their stories, after discerning who was able to hear them. They also chose to collaborate in the writing of this book as another means of breaking the silence and encouraging other men to give voice to their stories too.

During the last five years my practice has developed and changed as I have developed and changed. My practice is influenced by my own therapy – experiential learning about a variety of approaches. Most recently I have experienced the powerful effects of working through my body, using massage and breathing to connect with myself physically. I have become more and more inclined to believe that therapy for people who have been abused *needs* to include work with the body; for men particularly, working through the body seems to be a powerful healing tool. Abuse involves the whole person; body, mind and spirit and healing needs to occur in all those spheres. **Chapter 12** explores some of the ways the body carries our hurt and describes **body therapies** that have evolved over time. Because of the nature of sexual abuse, which also involves physical and emotional abuse and often neglect, clients may need careful preparation to allow themselves to trust their body to a stranger.

Just before I met Mike and Stephen I had begun to work collaboratively with Sarasi. Sometimes clients work with both of us concurrently and sometimes the bodywork comes after they have finished their work with me. Many counsellors would decline to work with a client who is also concurrently working with another therapist. However, in our postmodern world 'collaboration', 'integration' and 'working systemically' are buzz words of the present era in counselling. My **collaboration with a body therapist** is related in **Chapter 13**, as well as my own experience of being a bodywork client. Mike, Stephen and Sarasi also comment on how our collaboration was experienced by them.

It takes courage and honesty for us to expose ourselves and our work to the outside world. Many people express fears and anxieties about counselling; the lack of access to what happens behind the closed doors of the counsellor's room creates a mysterious space into which fantasies can be projected. Body therapy takes us even further into an unknown world – the world in which we fantasise about the use of massage, touch, nakedness, sexuality – all holding their potential for 'abuse'. The experience of working on myself in that way has allowed me to know what actually happens when we do that work; the power, the potential, the healing that occurs at the deepest level of being. Alice Miller (1990) has said that we can only go with our clients to where we have been able to go with ourselves:

> Only therapists (helpers) who have had the opportunity to experience and work through their own traumatic past will be able to accompany patients (clients) on the path to truth about themselves and not hinder them on their way...for they no longer have to fear the eruption in themselves of feelings that were stifled long ago, and they know from their own experience the healing power of these feelings. (Miller 1990, p.316)

My fear of working through my body took a long time to overcome; I think it is the memory of that fear which allows me to work patiently with clients to encourage them along the same route. I would like to share some ideas about working this way with male survivors and for the reader to draw their own conclusions. The task of writing about these changes will allow me to reflect on what I think has proved to be good practice, and maybe what has not.

In **Chapters 14 and 15** I have attempted to highlight the **stories within their stories** that I believe stem from their socialisation as males within a patriarchal society and creates additional burdens for men who have been victimised during childhood. **Chapter 16** focuses on **traumatic sexualisation** as an outcome of childhood sexual abuse and how this is particularly manifest in sexually abused men. **Chapter 18** deals with **endings** – a particularly powerful process when we have worked with clients at a deep and meaningful level.

Counsellors tell me they do not feel confident about offering counselling to men who have been sexually abused. My hope is that they will feel more confident after reading Part 2 of this book. Stephen saw me in total 27 times over a period of eight months with my annual two-week holiday and the Christmas holiday intervening. Mike had a similar number of sessions. Both men worked with Sarasi for about twenty sessions concurrently. So I am not describing long-term work, although in both cases there may have been some additional value in spending longer in the process. However, there are very few services for adults working through the effects on their adult lives of childhood sexual abuse, and fewer for men than women. So private counselling can become too costly in the long term and we need to consider these restrictions when offering our services. To give prospective clients the idea that they will need to spend years in therapy before any benefits can accrue may prevent them from seeking help at all.

There are some similarities in the work with women who have been abused, and there are some differences. There are excellent recent books dealing with good practice when working with adult survivors in general (Bear 1998; Sanderson 1995). I have tried to highlight some of the issues that are particularly pertinent when working with men. But I am just one counsellor, working in my own way, and I do not attempt to say that there is only one way. What I hope to show is that the basic relationship of respect, genuineness and warmth is, as ever, what matters most to our clients, including male survivors (Rogers 1951). If we feel confident and willing to face the pain and suffering, then we can help.

Practitioners are less frequently researchers. My research is practice based – I can only tell what I know and I constantly seek to know more; the more I learn, the more I realise how little I know. Over the years I have had the opportunity, mainly through writing my previous book, to work with many men. Of course, all their stories are unique and I do not aim to generalise. However, back in 1961, Carl Rogers, the first major figure who called himself a counsellor, wrote that 'what is most personal is most universal' (Rogers 1961, p.26). Meaningful connections are made when we are able to find our unique personal centre and experience a sense of belonging that can cut through apathy and reach the deeper currents of the life in which we participate (Nouwen 1994). In telling the stories of just two men and myself as their counsellor, I believe that others will find connections for themselves.

So the third and final part **(Part 3)** of the book is **'The Researcher's Story'**, which begins with **Chapter 19, 'The Swamp'**, a 'quest' story (Frank 1995) based on my experience of myself as a novice researcher into the field of male sexual abuse back in 1992. Currently I co-ordinate and tutor on an MSc in Counselling at the University of Bristol. During the course, my colleagues and I enable students to discover the researcher within themselves and support them through the production of their own research in the form of a dissertation. Students often complain about the density of the research literature, which leaves them feeling confused and disempowered. I have attempted, with Mike and Stephen, to bring some of the theory of research alive, and used the process of planning and writing this book to illustrate the ethics and values that underpin such a research project and the methodology and methods that were used; and to demonstrate that research can be reported and understood in everyday language. I would like to think that this part of my book might be used as a 'rough guide' for counselling researchers. I do not attempt to cover the vast range of the growing body of literature but to provide a limited overview and add another voice.

Many counsellors, like myself, have come to the work in middle age, as a second career. The majority are women, part-time workers – often working freelance and sometimes in a voluntary capacity. Few – very few – are in full time academic posts that allow paid time for doing research. That culture is often an alien one. Back in the early 1960s I married someone who was a full-time research biochemist and I was therefore familiar with the culture of scientific research – albeit as a 'camp follower'. We packed the children into the car and travelled around the world to attend conferences that had 'women's programmes' to accommodate the reality of the wife's place in the order of things. Although I had benefited from the grammar school system throughout the 1950s – there were still limited expectations of us as females. I can remember thinking I would like to be a social worker but I had no idea how I might realise that dream. I did know that I would need to go to university and that seemed entirely beyond me (and most of my peers). The convent grammar school I attended expected us to go on to teacher training college, nursing training or secretarial college. I broke the mould when I announced that I had obtained a place at the College of Occupational Therapy. Looking back now, my choice was motivated by wanting to be different; knowing it was a three-year, full-time course (at the time teacher training was for two years and I wanted to postpone facing the world for as long as possible); and that I could attend my local OT college while living at home and taking care of my mother (an expectation placed upon me by my family as the only daughter). I think my own experience is not dissimilar to many counsellors who are facing the idea of becoming researchers. Even those who are younger than I am probably need to overcome societal messages about gender roles that exclude them from what might be seen as the masculine scientific world.

Counselling research is still comparatively new and unformed, although that is rapidly changing. Traditional psychological research has largely adopted methods from the natural sciences; measurements, statistics, experiments, by taking the stance of the objective researcher. Carl Rogers also attempted to pioneer systematic scientific research into counselling and its outcomes. Counselling training is now coming of age and people who are experienced practitioners are returning from the field to attempt to make sense of and build on their knowledge and practice through additional training in research and completion of a dissertation. Many of these courses, like ours, take place in universities, which are the traditional seats of learning and scientific research. Counselling research students struggle to fit the image of the traditional, objective researcher with the relationship-based, subjective, ways of knowing with which they are familiar. There is rarely a comfortable fit. But we do not have to fit into the traditional paradigms – there are new paradigms (Denzin and Lincoln 1994; McLeod 1994; Moustakas 1990, 1994; Reason and Rowan 1981, 1988; Strauss and Corbin 1990) that are increasingly recognised as credible, rigorous and valid (Black 1994; Blaxter 1996; Boulton and Fitzpatrick 1997; Mays and Pope 1995; Seale and Silverman 1997). Even in the 'hard science' field of medicine there is a growing recognition of the value of patients' stories as topics for research into the management of people's illnesses (Frank 1995; Greenhalgh and Hurwitz 1999; Kleinman 1988).

Another task I set myself in writing this book is to show how I have applied the learning from research to my practice. Few of us really think about how research might inform our practice, although there are some researchers now asking those questions of counsellors. In general, it seems that counselling practitioners rarely see themselves as researchers – even when they are doing research and writing books informed by their research (Speedy 2000). I hope to show how my research has enhanced the service that I am able to offer as a practitioner.

Chapter 20 is about the **research process**, philosophical considerations that guide our choice of methodology. I have described how my own methodological choices have developed over time as I have increasingly come to value the use of reflexive and overtly subjective approaches to research. **Chapter 21** deals with some of the **ethical issues** this kind of methodology raises, and issues related to using our own clients or ex-clients as research participants. It may be that readers will have begun to wonder as they begin this book about how it came to be written, about how much say Mike and Stephen had in the process; how issues of power were addressed; and about the ethical issues involved in using clients in research. If that is the case I suggest beginning with **Chapter 22**. In Chapter 22 I show one of my ways of **collecting data** and how I obtained truly **informed consent.** I have tried to be as transparent as possible by reproducing (with some editing because of length and readability) the first conversation I had with Mike and Stephen right at the beginning of the process, before the shape of the book had formed.

In **Chapter 23** I document the **order in which the research progressed** and the timing of the tasks along the way. In **Chapter 24** I explain my thinking about **sorting out and writing up the data**; about whose voices are being heard, who is the audience and how I think about validity.

Finally, **Chapter 25** is where the three streams join and form a creative synthesis as Mike and Stephen and myself meet to look back over the research process and the writing of this book. I have called the last chapter of the book **'Where Three Streams Meet'** – the three streams are the client's story, the counsellor's story and the researcher's story. In this book all three come together, merge, overlap and flow into one another forming a deeper, wider pool of knowledge. I invite you to walk gently, dipping in your toes, feeling the cool water as it rises against your ankles – slowly allowing yourself to become immersed. Do not dive in quickly, headfirst, for at times the water is deep and turbulent. The water is also cleansing and healing if you take the time to float gently with the current; and it flows on and on to form a wide and beautiful river, flowing out to meet the sea, the ocean and beyond.

Throughout this book you will come across stories of all kinds and if you are sitting comfortably I will begin with one written by Mike and Stephen for this book.

Once upon a time there lived two little boys, in a little house, in a little village, outside a little town. They lived with their mother and father and were very happy. Nearby lived several aunts and uncles, and all their little cousins, and best of all, their grandfather. He had a jolly, red, round face, and a mop of white hair. He told lots of funny stories, and made everybody laugh. And everybody loved him.

Gramps was always ready to look after the children and had plenty of sweets and treats to please them; and he loved to take them on holidays with him. The two little boys had a very good time when they were with their grandfather because he let them stay up late and do things they were not allowed to do at home.

Gramps was very proud to be head of such a large, happy family and the mother and father, aunts and uncles were very grateful.

The two little boys were very good and tried always to do as they were told. Like all brothers they squabbled sometimes, and were, in many ways, very different from each other. However, unbeknown to one another, they shared a very special secret.

For sad to tell, their jolly grandfather was really a wicked paedophile. He was clever and skilful and used his attention, sweets and treats to entice children, who were too young to understand, into doing rude and wicked things. He even did this to his own children and grandchildren.

Amazing to recall, the little boys and all of the other children, each thought they were the only one to receive this special attention. Grandfather had told them how special they were and when they were with him, they felt special.

Astonishing to recount, because of the children's shame, fear and guilt, the wicked paedophile kept his secret till his dying day; and to the whole world he was, right to the end, the proud and respected head of a large and happy family.

(Written on 22.3.99)

PART ONE

The Clients' Story
The Elephant in the Living Room

To be ourselves we must have ourselves – possess, if needs be re-possess, our life stories. We must 'recollect' ourselves, recollect the inner drama, the narrative of ourselves. A man needs such a narrative. (Sacks 1985, pp.105–106)

CHAPTER 2

Stephen's Story

1966 to 1978
From the age of 7 years (or earlier), to 18 years
I was sexually abused by my
'Grandfather'.

May 1992
He died – aged 84 years.
After the funeral I was relieved he had died and not given away our secret.
I could bury the past and get on with enjoying life

August 1992
Memories flooding back.
I partly disclosed this to my wife.
MY DARK SECRET,
partly out, for the first time ever,
after 26 years.
I'm very, very
SCARED.
I love her deeply
and don't want to lose her.
I'm afraid she will find me disgusting and perverted, and be angry that I had been dishonest.
Thank God she is fantastic.
She is very shocked but reassures me, puts me at my ease.
I feel much better, relieved. I can now bury the past
FOREVER.

But I have not told her
THE WHOLE SORDID TRUTH
only that I had been abused as a child, up to about 15 years old. So the lid is back on the past,
but it is still simmering away.

Easter Day 18th April 1995
Mum tells me what happened to Mike.
'Nothing happened to you did it?'
I tell her it happened to me as well.
Very matter-of-fact.
She is shocked.
I tell her I'm OK, and that it hasn't affected me – to try and save her pain.
She doesn't believe it
'You seemed to get on so well with him – how could you, after he'd done that?'
It doesn't make sense to her. I feel worse.
I feel I have betrayed her. I feel guilt and shame, not only for what had happened
but for
LIVING A LIE.

27th July 1995
Tell Mike I think we have something from our past
'in common',
a legacy from our grandfather.
He knows immediately what I mean. We are unable to talk but arrange to meet
having 'disclosed' very briefly to each other.

3rd August 1995
Mike and I meet at the motorway service station for four hours and tell each other what happened to us but I don't tell him how old I was when it finished.
I feel bad about this because Mike's had continued as mine had done.
This 'takes the lid off'.
His story sounds much worse than mine.
it makes me
VERY ANGRY.

5th August 1995
Disclose everything to Stella including when it stopped. Felt relieved to do so. She is again fantastic in her support and reassurance, encouraging me to face up and work through it.

Moved HIS clock and the wedding picture out of the lounge.

7th August 1995
Stella shared it with her friend, Margaret.

14th August 1995
In trouble: since talking to Mike the flashbacks have begun;
his cock; my cock,
his mouth next to my face; his dentures.
All very realistic.
Visions, smells, tastes: not seeing his face

just his cock.
Afraid of what is happening. I look for information/self help.

It's all unbearable. I'm not coping at work. I need help, but from where?
Too risky to talk to anyone;
they might know me.

I go to a bookshop to find some self-help, of the kind Mike has given me.
Couldn't find anything until I found a book called
'Adult Male Survivors of Childhood Sexual Abuse' by Kim Etherington.
I read it quickly, realising others had suffered worse and gone through similar
consequences.
I need to talk to someone like Kim who can understand
and not be
shocked.

Rang
CHILDLINE
they tell me they are only for
children

15th August 1995
Met Mike at motorway services again for four hours.
Told him when it stopped. Shared more memories and feelings.

17th August 1995
I am scared of what is happening; I cannot cope.
This gives me more courage to take a risk and I write a letter to Kim Etherington.

Remove all HIS possessions from display, put them away in a bag.
Start to remove HIM from all our photos.

21st August 1995
Take away all his possessions and give them to a charity shop
(except the clock and 2nd World War dispatch rider's case).
It feels good.
PHONE CALL from Kim Etherington. We arrange to meet.

24th August 1995
Meet Kim 10.15–11.30. She is like the book felt. I feel safe, I trust her.
It's painful, scary risky BUT I am BURSTING to unburden myself.
The time closes too quickly.
She helps me to realise the situation I am in; suggests that I should not go to work
when my two-week holiday ends in three days time.

I PANIC,
what can I do about work?

I can't tell them; I can't trust them;
I will lose my job.

Talk to Stella. She helps me decide to take a very
BIG RISK
and go and tell John (my senior) what is happening to me.

He is what I dared not hope he would be.
He is understanding, kind, generous
and tells me to take time off – as long as I need.
PHEW!
But he says I must see my GP and tell him about it, and get a certificate

29th August 1995
<u>Kim:</u>

Talk about

FEARS

OF

DISCOVERY

about talking to Dr Bailey
about confidentiality
and
PRIVACY

ME – HOMEWORK
Use big pens and card to explore my feelings

ME – ROLLERCOASTER

Ashamed		Exhausted		Disgusted
Tense	Afraid			Can't relax
Revolted	Hard to sleep	Sick		
Can't breathe	Nauseated			Libido low
Out of Control		Self-conscious		Guilty
Afraid of company	Stupid		Paranoid	
Dirty	Preoccupied		Used	
Obsessed	Vulnerable		Tearful	
Embarrassed			Headaches	

ALL OVER THE PLACE

NOW LACKING IN:
Self-esteem
Strength

Confidence
Judgement
Security
Responsibility for family
Tolerance
Concentration

AFRAID FOR:

Pressure on Stella, Mike, Mum, Dad, In-laws, etc.

Other victims

Work, job security, colleagues, coping again, finances
Disclosure vs Privacy?

FLASHBACKS

Real
Increasing
More – memories
Details – Situations

I AM WHAT I FEEL

ANGER
    HATRED
        VIOLENCE
            REVENGE
                BETRAYED
                    LET DOWN
                        CHEATED

                                                    Sad

For the loss of

Childhood
Innocence
A real grandfather
Normal sexual development (perverted 1st ejaculation)

Sexualization – a habit
The past being destroyed
Honesty
Pride
What I should have been doing instead

ANGRY

WHY?

IT WAS WRONG
I TRUSTED YOU
YOU TOOK ADVANTAGE
LOOK WHAT YOU LEFT BEHIND YOU

You were so BLATANT

HOW COULD YOU DO IT?
YOU'VE MESSED UP MY BROTHER AND GOD KNOWS WHO ELSE
I'M GOING THROUGH PAIN – NOW
DID IT HAPPEN TO YOU?
DID YOU KNOW IT WAS WRONG? – you must have

WHAT ABOUT YOUR:

WIFE
SONS
DAUGHTER

GRANDCHILDREN

GOD

30th August 1995
Dr Bailey at 9.15.

He ALSO is kind and understanding! – off sick for a month at least!
HELP that's SCARY!
Throw out all porn because of association with the past.

31st August 1995
Kim.
Went to see Bob and Jane.
Gave Stella permission to talk to Jane.
Uncomfortable.

1st September 1995
After much fear and pain
give permission for Stella to tell her Mum and Dad why I'm off sick.
Go and see Wendy (old friend).
Disclose frankly except for 'flashbacks';
amazed I do not cry but stay
calm,
in control.
Show her 'homework'
amazed at how open I am – I think it's because she is open, and shares her own pain
with me.
Feel 'better'; even elated.
Wendy has raised my self-esteem. I think I am making progress;
the flashbacks fade away.

2nd September 1995
Bang, crash; that didn't last long.
Back to square one.
Feel terrible;
flashbacks return. I am full of energy.
Joe (son) pressing me to go for long bike ride – he gets one! 35 miles there and back
home again.
We are late back, but I don't mind,

because Stella's Mum and Dad are coming for tea.
Feel guilty because Joe went so far – he is proud of himself.
They are 'fine' the subject is avoided as arranged, but I still feel
<u>very awkward.</u>

Mike rang: He sounded sad. I am worried about him – has he got enough support?
I am *so, so* lucky to have Stella. I suggest he needs to talk to someone like Kim; or to
Kim.
I want her to take care of him, show him the way, as she is doing for me.

3rd September 1995

Well I get on with the work Kim has suggested.
It's not easy, I can't get started.
I draw my family tree for her. That's easy
BUT FRIGHTENING.
Who else?
Now I am going to write HIM a letter!
I can't get into the mood. BUT I look at the slide of him and me aged about 7 years
old.
I start to cry; I'm back there;
the words POUR out onto the page. I can't stop writing.
I persuade Stella to go to bed as she is exhausted. It's after 10 o'clock.
It continues to pour onto the page. It's so powerful, I feel driven, compelled; no longer
embarrassed or inhibited.
Every sordid detail comes out,
I amaze myself. I even feel able to do the bit I was trying to
forget about.

I start to draw the flashbacks. These images
DARK, INTIMATE, REAL, and REPULSIVE.
I put them crudely down on paper.
I FINISH
its 4.30 am.

I sleep.

4th September 1995

I get up at 7.30 with Stella and the children. I am exhausted, and I want to show it to
Stella, BUT I'm anxious, it's very frank, intimate and disgusting.
BUT – I must show her – NO MORE SECRETS.
She reads; I re-read over her shoulder, it's very scary. We look at the pictures together. I
explain them. THIS IS FRIGHTENING.
Will she ever want to touch me again?

Even after seeing all that, she is still very loving, caring, reassuring.

STEPHEN'S STORY

<u>I AM A VERY LUCKY MAN, A VERY LUCKY MAN.</u>

We cuddle and cry. She lets me rest my head on her breasts; I feel enveloped by her womanliness;

SAFE.

We caress and fondle each other.
We do not make love; it still doesn't feel quite right.
I feel I cannot let myself go, with those thoughts and images so close that they may spoil it.

5th September 1995

Kim:
I am very anxious about Mike,
Kim is seeing him tonight,
She reassured me she will try to help him – I feel relieved.
I want her to read the letter, BUT it's very frightening.
Some of those things I've written about myself – will she be offended as a woman?
Then I think of her book.
She suggests I leave it with her to read later. BUT I can't, she must read it, I need her to.
She asks me to read it aloud!
HELP!
I don't know if I can say those things out loud. The crude language – will she mind?
I can't look her in the eye until I've finished. I feel naked, indecently exposed, embarassed.
I struggle to keep my voice; the tears come a few times.

Now I am able to cry in front of Kim; I feel safe to do so.
We hug at the end; I feel unburdened.
Kim has been there with me, now she will help me to

LEAVE IT BEHIND.
I remember when she hugged me before, I didn't respond. I was too tense;too much pain.
I feel as if I am beginning to get somewhere.
Kim again tells me I seem to find it easier to be
GUILTY than ANGRY.
Can I express my anger to relieve my guilt?
When I get home, I put a picture of him on top of all the pillows. A picture of him when we were on holiday in Scotland,
DOING THOSE THINGS.
I feel silly at first,
BUT THEN I PUNCH AND PUNCH; HARD; HARDER.

I want to scream but I can't, because of the neighbours. I throw the picture away; it hardly needs tearing up; it has practically disintegrated!
YES I will go and see the body work lady. I need to really let go
PROPERLY.

I feel 'lighter'
UNBURDENED
I have done something significant?
YES,
I think I must have done.

That night we go to bed; we cuddle for comfort. I soak up Stella's comfort, love, and her sexuality.

I become aroused, for a long time.
The flashbacks have gone away at the moment.
Is it safe? Should I let go? I'm worried, but it feels right, different than for the past few weeks.
I am aching with
LOVE,
and I feel I want to
EXPRESS our love by MAKING LOVE.
Stella gives me the option of stopping if I want to. We make long, passionate caring, loving love.
We are so close.
I feel good, fantastic, we both do. We hold each other, to savour the moment.

A flashback starts to creep into my mind but it goes away very quickly.

<u>When I think about what we have just been doing. I thank my lucky stars.
I am a very lucky man.</u>

6th September 1995

I feel more active,
RE-ENERGISED
in a sorting out mood. I have a strong compulsion to SELL the clock,
and German dispatch rider's case.
Last week I asked Stella to do this for me;

BUT NOW I FEEL AS IF I CAN DO IT FOR MYSELF!

I don't care if I only get 1p for each of them – it feels symbolic.

YES, I've done it! £5 for the case, and £10 for the clock;

YES, that feels GOOD. Is it vengeance? Spite? Yes, I think so and I don't care.

Finished sorting out the slides. I feel like I've achieved something.

GOOD.

Mike rang. I hold the phone so tight; it hurts my hand and elbow! MY old broken finger really HURTS. I am so anxious about Mike, and how he got on with Kim.

RELIEF, he has seen her; he is very impressed!

Thank goodness. He praises me for tracking her down. He feels up, 'good', at the moment and he puts it down to having seen Kim, but he is afraid it won't last!

We talk about Dad. I tell him I feel I have to talk to him very soon. He says this is OK; that he understands I need to.

I feel better. I am still getting the odd flashback, but it's not freaking me out like it was. Instead I am preoccupied, obsessed with the 'subject' or my predicament.
I am very worried about the consequences of what I have DONE, AND what is going to happen with DAD.

Sam from work rang from his home. It was good to speak to him. Says everyone is wondering what has happened to me, and why I'm not at work. He is going to call in and see me. I want to see him but what am I going to say?

Sally also rang from home. She was very warm and concerned, but didn't quite know what to say to me. But it felt good that they care.

It made me feel like crying.

7th September 1995

This started out as a neat chronological list of events BUT again I can't stop writing! I hope this is a positive sign?

20.45 hrs. Dad rang on their way back from holidays. Sounded bright, cheerful. Normal chit chat.

NOW I FEEL PANIC, ANXIETY, HELP.

21.30 hrs: a very old memory has just come into my head. I remember HIM taking me to Blackpool, must have only been 8 or 9.
Long coach journey, illuminations, funfair, circus, boarding/guest house;

him sucking me in a small bedroom.

22.00 hrs. Stella has just voiced her unspeakable thoughts that I have also been pushing to the back of my mind.
Is Joe's behaviour like it is because of anything Dad has done?

NO, NO, IT'S UNTHINKABLE. WE'RE BEING PARANOID – MIKE TRUSTS HIM WITH
ROB AND JUDY.
THAT I COULD NOT COPE WITH
No; it's not likely
is it?

8th September 1995

Have woken up feeling very low, sad, and overwhelmed. I think I can see things in a clearer light now, and am reassuring myself how unlikely last night's fears are.

I am copying 'the letter' into this diary.
It has dragged up another early memory.
I remember him when he was still working, telling me what he thought was a funny story.
He told me he had played a good trick on one of his workmates by creeping up on him.
He had his first two fingers bent at the knuckle,
dampened them with his saliva and then touched them on the unsuspecting man's face, making him jump as he thought it was somebody's knob.
He thought that was very funny.
I found it a bit frightening. DOES this mean he was sexually familiar with men where he worked?
He did also say he preferred men to be circumcised? So did he have that preference from experience?
YES,
I expect he did.

Kim: We explore how my life has been affected in many ways. How I have always been afraid of anger, and seen it as a negative force.
This may be contributing to Joe's problems. I need to be able to show my children and myself that anger is OK and can be positive.
It's also OK to cry, and show them that it's OK to be sad.
I must be more

AUTONOMOUS

decide and act for myself, and not be worried what others will think,
or how they will be affected (that sounds selfish?). These sound more likely reasons for Joe's problems, rather than the fears of last night.

<u>I am making progress</u> – Kim tells me so as well as I still need to check. I feel much better after the session, which again only seemed to last
15 minutes.

Rang body therapist Kim has recommended and leave a muddled message on her answerphone.

She rings back, sounds nice, easygoing, relaxed.
I ask to see her a.s.a.p. and will do so in four days for one-and-a-half hours.

YES I AM MAKING PROGRESS.
I could never have contemplated seeing someone to 'let go' even two weeks ago!
I have always avoided being open and honest with myself
BECAUSE
of what happened, and with others because I have never learned to
TRUST

properly.
Have done it now – rang Mum and Dad. Told Mum (eventually) that we were coming over Sunday evening, without the children to discuss
'what we have been talking about'.
Mum asks me if I'm sure that it's the right thing to do, and that I might not get the response I'm looking for.
I apologise for the consequences she will have to deal with, but I tell her that it may well help things in the long run.
Had another memory come back. As a small child I used to attend a clinic because I wet the bed.
Used to get a star on my card if I had a dry night.
Now I know why
I used to wet
the bed.

22.00 hrs. Phone call from Mike. Sounded positive. Told him about speaking to Dad.
Very supportive.
Talked over today, he identified with some of the things I said.
He felt nervous about the idea of 'letting go' with the body therapist too. Told him this was just how I felt until a few weeks ago!
Talked to him about the 'Joe' issue – he thinks it is very unlikely.

9th September 1995
Mum rang lunchtime.
Worried that Dad will suss something wrong if she says we are coming over in the evening without the children.
Tell her we will come over in a few hours' time.
Get a babysitter.
A few hours of building tension, but I still feel I MUST talk to him.
In the car on the way over we discuss the possible outcomes; rage, rejection, running away, not talking, heart attack.
Acceptance and understanding is what we hope for.

We get there and Mum is OUT seeing a neighbour!
So we have to make painful

small talk

for what seems ages.
She returns after half an hour. More

small talk.

At 17.20
I
tell
them
'I've been off sick today; in fact for the past two weeks.
I've been having counselling twice a week as well.'
Dad looks awful; I ask him,
'You can probably guess why?'
Dad says,
'Oh no, not you as well'
and starts to have angina attacks, and using his spray.
'Why now? Why not before? Can't cope now.'
I ask, 'Did you not wonder about me after you knew about Mike?'
He says Mike he can understand, his behaviour fits,
'BUT YOURS DOESN'T.'
Says he hasn't slept properly for a year thinking about Mike and his father. Tells me that's why he fixed up a weekend away in November; <u>to tell me about Mike.</u>
Says he wished he had known about it before his father died so that he could have 'helped him on his way'.
He tells us that he did die in absolute agony, right to the very end,
'I was there, I know,' he said. 'Perhaps that's why.'
Then he said, 'Don't tell Helen [his sister],
she doesn't
know.'

I put it over
as strongly as I could that I love them
BOTH
and do not BLAME them for what happened.
I did such a good job of concealing it; they could not have realised.
Dad says,

'It's MY FAULT, I FEEL GUILTY.'

He says it was his job to recognise these things in children BUT he still FAILED us.
More angina attacks,
asks for glass of water. We're worried he's going to have a heart attack.

We talk openly, frankly, with pain and understanding.

I try and explain how it happened.
I tell them about some of the incidents. Dad seeks clarification, I tell him
'He had his hand over the side of the settee, playing with my penis, while you were all in the room; I was paralysed for fear of discovery.'
They are shocked;
he keeps tapping his fingers on the chair,
looks awful.
At some point he goes out to the kitchen and takes a tablet.
Stella and I both fear he is going to take an overdose. He asks me to stop; he can't take any more.
Says when he heard about Mike he was wishing himself to have a heart attack.

We pause for a while.

He says:
How did you let me take Joe away for the weekend? You must have been worried!!
I tell him it's because I trust him,
And don't associate him with abuse.
He says
He has even wondered if I've been abusing Joe because of the way he is!
Then I spilled out 'YES, these last few days I've wondered about YOU abusing Joe as well.'
He replies that he has not and never would.
I believe him and say 'Good,
<u>'cause I would have killed you if you had.'</u>
<u>He accepts this and says how since he heard about Mike he has been afraid of getting too close to his own grandchildren.</u>
I feel relieved, I have put the
BIG QUESTION
and I
believe him and so does
Stella.
I ask him if he was abused, or any of his brothers or sister.
He says he's sure the first four were not, but he is not sure about the youngest brother,
Dave.
I say I fear this may be a possibility.
He says: 'No, Mum was alive.'
I say: 'Yes, but Mike's abuse started BEFORE she died, and possibly mine too.'

He wants to know if Mum knew about this. He is angry towards her.
I tell him how difficult it has been for me, and Mum to talk to him about this, because we knew the effect it would have on him.

He asks who else knows.
He's upset that Wendy knows about it.

I try and be positive, to say that we must try and move forward, and to help each other.
I say the positive things that have happened,
about Stella and I being closer,
and Mike as well.
I plead with them to talk to each other, help each other, and to get some help from whoever they wish.
I leave Kim's number, and explain how she has helped me.

He is dismissive:

'I've always sorted things out and made my own decisions since I was 15.'
I say to him that we all need help sometimes, that it's too much for them to bear on their own. I also tell them he has my permission to talk to the family
if he wants to.

He offers to pay for the counselling, and not to worry about the £200 we owe.
He is <u>insistent</u> he wants to help, so I say that to forget the loan would be a big help BUT please use the money they would spend on me, on HIMSELF and MUM getting some help.
HE THEN SUGGESTS THEY TAKE US OUT FOR A MEAL NEXT WEEK
to celebrate the fact that their mortgage is paid up.
This is a hand of
ACCEPTANCE
and
UNDERSTANDING,
MORE
than I could possibly have hoped for. I ask if it's still OK for us to come over tomorrow with the children. He's not sure, will ring and let us know in the morning.
We say we would like to.
We then return to

small talk.

Although they are both shocked and
DEVASTATED
and I fear for the wider implications for all of us, I feel relieved.

I HAVE DONE THE THING I FEARED MOST.

As soon as I get home I ring Mike, he is amazed!

10th September 1995

a.m. I talk to Dad on the phone. He sounds very down and miserable, but agreed we can go over with the children.

On the way over more memories return. I remember playing truant for the day, aged 7, from the infant school. Hid in the bushes all day.
Then aged about 12, I did the same but cycled to Shrewsbury – miles away, <u>ran away from home.</u> Ended up ringing Mum and Dad to fetch me!
The day went well. They were both shattered.
Dad was cheerful with the children;

we didn't talk about it at all.

Stella managed to talk with Mum, who came up with the horrifying thought that my grandfather was once a live-in caretaker at a private boys' school following the war.

<u>She wondered why he left that job?</u>

Still feeling relieved when Mike rang when we got home. He has just spoken to Dad on the phone.
He feels even more <u>rejected</u> now as Dad told him

he didn't want to talk about it.

I feel rotten and selfish as I have got so far which must make Mike feel even worse.
I tell him the same
He now feels the ball is back in Dad's court and does not want to talk to him unless invited.
I feel very
SORRY and SAD
about this and
ANGRY
towards Dad.

11th September 1995

Kim:
Read over last week's events.
Kim says: I have made such big steps. Dad needs some space now before Mike talks to him.
What I did was a very important step in HEALING our family.
We discuss my anxiety about Mum. She is an adult and must make her own decisions about him BLAMING her and riding roughshod over her feelings. She can talk to friends and get some help of her own
if she needs it.

I need to say to Dad that I feel ANGRY with him for rejecting Mike and dismissing Mum's feelings. I am still afraid of him being angry with me.
I MUST NOT BE.
I have made rapid progress.
I am looking forward to tomorrow and 'letting go'.

12th September 1995

It's hard to put into words what happened today

I

feel

FLAT,

exhausted, stupor-like.

I spent over an hour telling Sarasi what had happened to me.
She was very direct and frank, very quickly, which was scary. But by being like this, she took away my inhibitions,
so I was able to be open and frank too.

Then there was only 20 minutes to 'let go'.
Sarasi said I should try a practice run, I couldn't start.
I felt embarrassed, silly, stuck, wanting to let go but unable to start
and conscious of the time.
I looked at the pictures of

HIM,

and Sarasi repeatedly pummelled the back of my shoulders until I think I became
irritated
at first with her, and

THEN WITH HIM.

I hit his photos on the chair with the pillow, as she had asked.
Part of me still felt a bit silly, but then I started to hit them,

HIM,

really hard, then harder. Then it didn't seem to be a game any longer. I felt like
collapsing into the floor, hiding in it.
Sarasi then told me to lie on the mattress, and hold onto a pillow,
and imagine the pillow was

Me

as a small boy.

I then pictured me, the first time I remember being in his bed and him showing me his
erect cock, and sucking me.
Then I travelled back as me, an adult now, to rescue me as <u>an innocent child.</u>
Then I picked me up and carried me away to a safe place. This was hard to do because
of his
POWER and HIS FACE.

Sarasi told me to come away, leave the memory behind, but I couldn't,
I had to put little me somewhere safe, and

GO BACK AND KILL HIM

before he could do any more damage and for what he has done to us.
I tell him he is a
PERVERT, a CHILD MOLESTER
And

RIP

Off
His
balls and cock,
and stuff them in his mouth, choking him.
Then I kick his head HARD, HARDER, until it is smashed.
Then I strangle him to make sure he's
DEAD.
Sarasi tells me to leave now and think of that place as warm. I can't and he's there in
the bed. I must push him down the drain,
FLUSH
him into the sewers where he belongs.
Then I set fire to the place, to burn away the memory,
the PAIN.
Then come away slowly to pick little me up again, and bring me back
SAFE
before it started, an

INNOCENT
BOY
to here
and
now.

13th September 1995
I am exploding with ENERGY and RAGE.
I walk flat out to the swimming baths in 12 minutes then swim 22 lengths, 6 without
stopping.
I am exhausted and need to stop after 10,
BUT
I keep going I want to keep going for a few more but the common sense part of me
tells me to stop. I am staggering when I get out, my body is
BURNING.

I am physically exhausted, doze for 20 minutes in the afternoon. That night I am tired
BUT wake after two hours, only half asleep the rest of the night. My mind is RACING
over everything.

14th September 1995

09.40 Dad rang. He was friendly, light. Said he hadn't forgotten us, or the meal, but his money wasn't through yet.

I asked if they were both alright.

He replied: 'Not really, but that's understandable in the circumstances.'

I agreed.

It's a great relief to receive some positive contact after four days of wondering.

Visit to Sarasi:

10.30–12.00.

We talk about Tuesday's session. How I felt before, during and after.

Then I show her the pictures I've drawn! I feel awkward, embarrassed, and want her to hurry up and finish looking at them.

I am very tense.

I am shocked and scared when she asks me to undress down to my underpants!

Thank goodness they are a new pair, and not gaping or anything.

I am embarrassed, self-conscious,

feel naked

and

SCARED

of what she might do.

She reassures me

she isn't going to do anything sexual to me.

I lie face down on the couch, she stretches my legs. I am tense at first, but soon let my body go.

Then

she climbs on my back and tells me she wants me to imagine she is HIM,

and I must try and throw her off,

with all my strength.

I must hit, punch, kick the couch (HIM) as hard as I can.

This is difficult.

She is only tiny. I am scared that I will seriously hurt her, or break the couch.

She convinces me she is okay and safe, so I start to do as she says, kicking, thumping, throwing her off with my power.

She asks me to shout and scream, but I can't, my voice won't come out,

only quietly

without feeling.

We move to the mattress where I feel a bit more secure.

Then I soon get into it,

SMASHING, KICKING, PUNCHING <u>HIM</u>
and trying to throw
HIM
off.
Sarasi gives me a pillow to put over my face as I am afraid someone will hear me shout
and scream.
She tells me to tense my buttocks, as though
FUCKING him
I am angry, that's not right because

FUCKING IS GOOD
with him it was
BAD
I do as she says

BUT I AM ANGRY
it tips me over the edge.

I SHOUT AND SCREAM. YOU FUCKING PERVERT,
CHILD MOLESTER
YOU SHOULDN'T have done that to me; I WAS AN INNOCENT CHILD.
I RAGE
Until
I
am
EXHAUSTED
and can go no more. I am breathless
my body
is
BURNING.

Then I have to lie on my back, bring my knees up, heels together, and move my knees
slowly outwards, downwards on the bed until they shake.
Then I have to thrust my hips upwards, as I breathe out, as if I'm fucking.
When I recover Sarasi tells me to think of a way of coping with these thoughts if they
should return.
I say I will use something positive from my past.
I think of my other grandmother, my mother's mother, of her

LOVE and GENUINENESS.

She loved me and I loved her
I miss her. I cry tears.
I think of my love for Stella and the children and I think of THEIR love for me.
I keep thinking of it,

SAYING IT
Sarasi is rubbing my chest, my heart, filling me with their
LOVE, HEALING ME
I feel
GOOD
I hug her, she holds me and hugs me.

Sarasi tells me to
RECLAIM
my own body. I hold myself, my arms, my legs hug myself hold my balls, my cock.
I reclaim me for
MYSELF
to use and value, and to share with Stella.
Then I hold a pillow; it is
ME
as the innocent child. I tell this child I am
SORRY
it shouldn't have happened to him.
I'm sorry I shouldn't have let it happen to him.
BUT I COULD NOT HELP IT, IT WAS NOT MY FAULT.

I tell my Gran I am sorry and if where she is, she knows what I did will she forgive me. Sarasi asks me what my Gran would say to me. I say – she forgives me, loves me.
I am crying.

Sarasi leaves me covered with a blanket and puts on some relaxing music.
I am FREE from him;

I NO LONGER FEEL GUILTY.
I still feel angry but a different angry. Anger towards him for what he did to me as

A SMALL CHILD

I now feel

LOATHING

and

PITY

towards him

I lie there totally relaxed, I am crying real tears, tears of RELIEF.

I walk in the rain across the Downs to meet Stella. I feel GOOD, relieved,
UNBURDENED
RELEASED

It's difficult to put into words but Stella can tell I seem different.
Wendy meets us there. She can see the difference as well. It's good to tell two people who love and care about me,

MY GOOD NEWS.

Then I go and see KIM.
The session feels different than before, somehow lighter, more a review and check of what has happened;

MY PROGRESS

YES

I feel I have now left my

GUILT behind me, LET GO, and RECLAIMED my body for myself.

When I think of HIM now, I don't see his penis, I now see his *face*. It doesn't trouble me though.

I still feel rage, but now loathing and pity as well. I feel a new anger at what he did to me, now I see it more objectively

<u>WITHOUT THE GUILT</u>

I feel <u>SAD</u> at what he took from me, from us.
We talk about my 'voice'. Sarasi and Kim say maybe it is so quiet because he stole it from me.
That is why I am too shy to sing.
I must use my voice
more now.

Kim feels I need more time off to convalesce, to recover, and to put myself back together again.
She says again that I have been through
'post-traumatic stress disorder'
that I should look it up, that I will recognise my symptoms. She says it's like I've had major surgery and that I should not be afraid to take enough time off to recover.
I find this scary, being off sick.
She agrees to talk to my boss if necessary.

Night of 14–15th September 1995

I sleep better, for longer.
I wake but manage to fall back to sleep. Then I wake in the end of a dream.
It's 5.45 am.

I feel like going back to sleep, then I remember Kim suggested I wrote down my dreams.

Then I realise

BLOODY HELL

what have I just been dreaming about. It's what has just happened to me yesterday,

the past few weeks.

I can't believe it, and even though I am so tired I am compelled to write down what I can remember before it is lost.

Then as I write, the whole dream is very clear, ALL

the details

COME BACK.

I have captured them all. I feel myself crying as I write the dream down. It's a very powerful dream, it's

SYMBOLIC

of what has been happening to me.

05.50: 15.9.95

I am walking on the north coast of Devon or Cornwall.

Mum, Dad, Mike, HIM and loads of friends are there. I am a young adult. The walk is very long and arduous with very steep hills. The people at the front are going much too fast; they are being a bit silly. I am worried because people are not staying together, but are too far apart, and they may get lost or have an accident. Dad is struggling to keep up as he has a bad knee, which means he is NOT in charge, in control and leading as he usually is.

We get halfway up, a pub/hotel. It's time to set off again. Dad comes to see and says awkwardly that he can't go any further because Mum's TIRED; but I know it's because of his knee. I say okay and dash off through the hotel to catch up with the group before they rush off without me. Then I bump into HIM on the stairs. I tell him he ought to stay behind as he won't be able to keep up. I don't want him to come but I make an excuse that the terrain is too rough, and he won't be able to keep up. I see his face, he wants me to help him keep up; to look after him. He wants me to feel guilty about leaving my old grandad behind.

THEN I decide not to worry about hurting his feelings. I say NO, I'm going on, on my OWN, and stride off fast, leaving him BEHIND with the others who have dropped out. He looks <u>upset</u>, <u>hurt</u> BUT I DON'T CARE ABOUT HIM ANYMORE.

I stride off, there's a very steep hill. I've fallen behind, the others who are near the top are all lost. I know the way. I've done the walk before. I CATCH UP and TAKE CONTROL, 'FOLLOW ME, I REALLY KNOW THE WAY. IT'S VERY DANGEROUS IN SOME PARTS, YOU MUST FOLLOW ME.' Then the rest of the group chooses to follow me and we all get back safely.

On the way back we are on an open top bus, driving very fast, too fast, on winding sharp cliff roads. I'm sat at the front, on the top. Mike is sat next to me. He looks exhausted, but I don't remember him being on the walk. He is dressed in black and looks sad. I tell him 'YOU MUST HOLD ON LIKE ME. LOOK, HOLD THE SIDE OF THE BUS, HOLD ON TIGHT!' He holds on, we're close together, holding on, It's hard to survive, but we are managing to stay on the bus.

Now one of last night's dreams is coming back. It's only a faint memory. I remember its FEELING rather than details or its content. I am upset, I am a young adult, I rush off from home and go and visit my Gran. She is pleased to see me, welcomes me in as always. I spend some time with her. I feel SAFE. I know she loves me and I love her. Now I cannot stop my tears.

15th September 1995

I carry on and get the children ready for school.
I am
ENERGISED, ELATED, BURSTING.
I RIP up the landing carpet and squash it into the dustbin.
I have now cleansed the house of everything to do with HIM.
As I no longer need the photos of him, I save a few for Mike to use. The rest I put in a box, pour barbeque lighter fuel on them
And
BURN
them in the garden.

It feels the right thing to do.

Mike rings. I share my joy with him. It's his day off. I ask if we can meet.
So we meet at the motorway services and drive to Longwood Forest. I tell Mike what has happened to me but I am careful not to give away any details of what I did with Sarasi, only the
RESULT!

I let him read my dream!
He is pleased for me. We review what has been happening for both of us.
I share some of my 'work' with him; the letter, pictures and meeting with Dad.
I feel I want to share these with him as we are <u>survivors</u> together. We share more details of what he did to us, and realise just how much we have in common.

Mike has written a letter to Dad saying all the things he would like to say to his face.
It's powerful stuff.
It very frankly tells Dad about what happened to him

'I find your attitude hard to swallow as I did his penis and semen!'

Most of all Mike expresses his anger and sadness about Dad's continued rejection of him.
He asks me should he post it.
I say: 'Yes, it will hurt Dad, but we must now both CONQUER our fear of his anger. I think he must face up to the fact that we are also victims!'
We both understand the devastating position he is in
BUT HE MUST NOT FORGET ABOUT US.
Stella reminded me that when I disclosed to him, he had said:

'You will work through this but I never will.'
We part on a positive note, closer now than ever. When I get home I am overwhelmingly

EXHAUSTED.

My bubble has burst now, but my guilt is
GONE.

I sleep better but am still restless and dreaming a lot. I remember dreaming I was floating, and effortlessly flying over the earth below.

16th September 1995

I enjoy a lie-in with Stella. I still feel

EXHAUSTED.

I make an effort and take Joe and the dog for a walk. We walk a long way.
It's a good walk BUT I bump into Andy from work! I don't know what to say! We talk about dogs.
I have to catch Joe on his bike.
Andy tells me, with feeling, to look after myself.

On the way home I feel drawn to Gran's grave. I tidy the grave, and while Joe has a look round, I spend some quiet moments thinking of her,
and how she has been in my thoughts <u>helping me</u>, even though she is gone. I talk to her, tell her
I love her and miss her.

Then I drive to Mum and Dad's, I feel drawn there.

I am upset that Mum hasn't rung me at all since Saturday. They are out. I wonder where they are.

17th September 1995

I can wait no longer.
At lunchtime I ring Mum. She quickly becomes very upset
She hasn't rung me as she doesn't want to burden me with her problems.
She gets more upset.
Dad has gone out and not told her where he was going.
I tell her I will come and fetch her. I drive over, give her a big hug and bring her home.
I leave a note for Dad saying I have taken Mum back for tea,
please come and join us.
She tells me how Dad is angry, blaming her for everything and not listening to anything she says. I tell her this isn't right, but that she is the only one who can do anything about it.
She agrees she has made the problem worse over the years, by putting up with his behaviour to avoid confrontation, but at this stage of her life

she can see no
way
out.

I try and tell her my positive news about losing my guilt. I don't think she comprehends the importance of this to me.
We talk over the past
She says it must have been awful for us while it was going on.
I tell her that we both enjoyed it at the time.
She is SHOCKED, so I try and explain. We get home, and she unloads onto Stella while I cut the grass.

Sam from work rings! Is friendly, concerned, choosing his words carefully.
He puts over that I haven't been forgotten at work, but that nobody knows what is going on.
I tell him I am dealing with personal issues,
but that I am making good progress.
I tell him John knows the full reason, then ask him if he knows. He says he doesn't but that I might want to tell him when I'm ready!

He does however tell me not to rush back, but to get fully sorted first.
'Perhaps you should drop in for a visit to see everyone before you return?'
Asks me if I do intend to return, so I tell him:
'YES,
I want to when I'm ready.'

Dad comes over. When we are alone he asks me if I am back at work! I tell him
NO,
and not for another few weeks yet.
I ask him if he has told anyone. He says he's been thinking about it and does not think it is a good idea! 'Why spoil their memories, you've got to think of the consequences, you don't know how difficult it is for ME.'

I tell him Mike and I do appreciate the terrible position he is in,
BUT
that
WE are victims as well!

He does not seem to LISTEN, he is more concerned with his feelings rather than mine or Mike's!

He is afraid of other people knowing. 'How am I ever going to talk to Stella's Mum and Dad again?' Tells me:
'Counsellors are a waste of time – their own lives are usually a mess – they need counselling themselves – Mike agrees you know – he told me that last time we spoke on the phone.'

Rang Mike to tell him how angry I am at Dad for being so

SELFISH.

He is more concerned for his own feelings, and the consequences for himself of our actions!

Why are we being parental to our parents?
Mike <u>has</u> posted his letter, we must wait for the bang, <u>or</u> no response.
Says he may well go and talk about the letter with Ellen (wife). Then perhaps Mike and I should go and be honest with Mum and Dad. Talked about how and if we should tell the rest of the family?

18th September 1995

A good night's sleep at last although I still feel tired.
Thinking about Mike's letter arriving and I am feeling symptoms of ANXIETY about it.

Jane calls in. I feel okay with her and able to talk about my progress.

KIM: Tell her all that has been happening!
I am still positive and my guilt is definitely behind me now.
Read her my dream, which she agreed was amazingly symbolic for me. Then we talked over my increasing <u>new</u> set of fears, and that I was no longer on a high!

Talked about Mike's letter, Mum and Dad, the 'family', 'work'
and the tears
rolled.

Kim reminded me how far and fast I had come, and done some very tough things. Now I have removed my guilt I will be able to face up and deal with the inevitable increasing 'mess'. Talked about fears of what might happen.
Shared a mantra she uses:
'I am here, I am now and I'm OK'
and to remember
to breathe.
She reminded me how I have been disorientated in time, and gave me a
book to read about post-traumatic stress disorder.
This enabled me to feel less anxious about taking more time off.
Kim is away now for a few weeks. I will miss her, she has guided me through so much.
I tell her I will be OK until she comes back!
AND I WILL.

Return home drained; message to ring Mum.

She's in a terrible state, hardly able to talk because she is crying so much.
Says she has rung Mike and he is angry with her
blaming her for everything.

Dad's had the letter but won't show it to her.

They have been talking!

She can now see Dad's point of view and how hurt he is! BUT he had walked off in the rain hours ago, didn't tell her where he was going

ONLY THAT HE IS SUICIDAL.

'They're not going to Cornwall with their friends "because of all this".'

She still has **not talked** to ANYONE, still has no support!

I calm her down, but I support Mike's message and tell her she *must* get some support. Dad comes back in so I wind down the circular conversation. I feel too shot away to be worried.
Stella is angry and anxious. I'm more worried about this.

Then Mike rings.
Mum has not listened (again) to all he said. Yes, he was angry towards her, BUT he also put over lots of positive things, which she has not taken in.
Exhausted we go to bed and I sleep well.

19th September 1995

Fetch carpet from Evelyn's. I am comfortable enough to sit and have a cup of coffee and a chit-chat.
Mike rings in the afternoon, worried he has overdone it!
Feels he has let some of the anger go but is now worried about the consequences, and about me.
I reassure him I'm OK, but think he should ring Mum to reinforce the positive aspects! This he intends to do. Says he is working through his agenda and moving closer to seeing Sarasi!
I give him her number.
15.20 Mike rings back, having just spoken to Mum and Dad.
Dad angry about the letter at first but things improved to the extent that he offered to pay for Mike's counselling.
He said: 'Before you say it, no I don't want to spend the money on getting counselling for myself!'
He spoke to Mum and restated all the positive things he said last night. BUT the most important thing Dad said was that he has
SPOKEN TO UNCLE GEOFF
and intends

to speak

to his other brothers and sister.

This is amazing news! I'm so glad <u>he has done this for us</u> rather than leave us with no option but to do it for ourselves. And things are now improved between him and Mike, and Mum and Dad, from the situation last night.

20th September 1995

My senior, John from work, rang. Wanted to know how I was and what I had been doing. Was concerned to know that I was progressing?

I told him I was and that I had lost my guilt. He couldn't understand why I had been guilty! Told him I had been told that I had been going through PTSD.

He was worried about how much money I had been spending. In order to make sure I'm OK, that I've been spending my money wisely (!)

And because of sickness policy, I agreed to see an occupational health doctor.

I told him I have had to be persuaded to take time off. He reassured me to take as long as it takes.

Enjoyed a walk around the park. Rang Mum and Dad.

Mum went over the same old stuff – told me about Adam and how hurt they both are by Mike's letter, and having to tell the family.

Dad told me it all could have been better managed if we had told him before Gramps died.

I explained that would have been impossible for me at the time, as it was repressed; I was afraid of discovery; afraid of the consequences for me and for DAD.

He said it would have been easier to deal with it then, so I replied:

'What, with us going to the police; him in prison getting beaten up?'

'Uncle Adam agrees with me,' he says. He goes on and on about the consequences of what we had now started,

'the ripple effect'

'pulling the carpet from under people's ordered lives'

etc., etc.

So I asked him if it would have been better if we had kept quiet?

'Oh, no,' he says, 'but by telling loads of other people like Wendy, Stella's Mum and Dad you have left me with no choice but to tell everyone else on <u>my</u> terms.'

Also he says that he and Mum are now talking seriously about separation. I ask if that is my fault!

'Oh, no BUT if all this wasn't happening'

etc., etc.

Then he tells me he's not allowed to get angry. There's things he wants to say to me but won't because they would hurt me too much!

I tell him we need to be honest so could he please say them now. No, he says: it's up to him to use his judgement whether to say them or not!

I tell him its ridiculous to say that and then just leave it.
A classic Dad ploy to have the last word and think he's in control!

He would, of course,
deny it

but I got the FEELING that he was blaming me for the mess HE now finds himself in; losing his father and his sons, the family; and for the break-up of his marriage; that it would have been better for me to keep quiet or, at the very least, hand over complete control of the situation to him to deal with how he felt best suited
HIM.

This feels like blame from my father BUT I know I am not guilty. Even so, it hurts; I am close to tears.

Sam from work rings. Can he call in and see me?
YES please!

Then Mum rings – tells Stella she's on her way over! Oh no, I can't cope!

Mike rings to see how things are! I can't hold it together anymore; end up crying and inconsolable. I don't want Mike to worry but I feel

OVERWHELMED with EVERYTHING.

He says he will ring back later.

I go and have a good cry. Then Mum arrives! Talks over and over about how hurt she is and Dad and quite rightly so; Mike's letter, the family, your

POOR FATHER

etc., etc., etc.

I have to ask her repeatedly to stop talking about Mike, as I can't cope with it all! She doesn't listen. She says she wants to find someone who will take

RESPONSIBILITY

for all this.
I ask, 'Do you mean ME or Mike?'

'Oh, no,' she says.

I tell her: 'There's only one person responsible this, isn't there?'
She says: 'Your Grandfather, but he's dead.' She goes on and on about the consequences for the family.

I ask her:

'Would you rather I had kept quiet?'
She says: 'No but…'

etc. etc.

Sam from work calls. It's great to see him. We go out of the way into the roof.

I tell him everything in general terms.

He is very supportive, understanding; he discloses something very personal he has never told anyone before.
We talk for one-and-a-half hours. It is very good to see him. He leaves loads of gifts! And promises to call back again.

Feel better. Drop Cheryl off at Brownies, and then take Mum back home. Don't go in as I can't take any more!

On way over Mum goes over and over the same issues. She does however promise me she will ring a Vicar from Church tonight and
talk to him.

Mike rings to see if I'm OK. I tell him I am. He has had a horrendous day. Two people have disclosed to him this afternoon, and he has had problems with Judy and Ellen (daughter and wife), and me as well! But he sounds OK and has felt stronger to cope than before. We talk over the day.

It's good to talk.

22nd September 1995
Sarasi: Tell her my guilt has GONE, thank her again and read her my dream.
She says it is very powerful and gets me to talk about and
REPEAT
the feelings it left me with of being unburdened, free and energised.
She tells me how to recapture that feeling when I need it, by touching my leg.
She points out my incongruous laugh, when I tell her something painful or meaningful. Points out that it leaks energy from the power of what I am saying.

I tell her of my feelings of hurt and anger provoked by Dad. We talk about his bullying over the years of everyone.

We talk about my fears now, about the family finding out.
She asks me to consider how I feel now, and how I might have ended up if I had continued in repression. She feels the part of the dream, where I take control, could symbolise that I should tell the family and not leave it to Dad!

I must be autonomous, act for myself. Being afraid of hurting his feelings is being afraid of him. I do some bodywork to release my anger and frustration towards Dad.

When I get home Dad has rung Stella and has invited us over for lunch on Sunday. That sounds positive. That evening I get silly over a disagreement with Stella, and behave

JUST LIKE MY FATHER

riding roughshod over her decisions and feelings. I regret that very much now, and wish I hadn't been so stupid.

I have no excuse except I might have still been aroused by today's session, and used my anger on the wrong person.

23rd September 1995

We all enjoy a trip to the museum, on the train. Then, as arranged, Mike and Ellen drop Judy and Rob off while they go over to see Mum and Dad.

Mike has previously told Mum and Dad that he and Ellen need to get 'angry' with them!

As a consequence Mum and Dad are all steamed up for a confrontation! About an hour later they return. Mike with broken glasses and a swollen and bruised eye, and visible bruising to his throat!

They explain that Ellen had been talking calmly to them when Dad started pointing a finger into her face. Mike stood between them, so Dad grabbed his throat and then fists were flying. Then, as they were leaving,
Dad stood on Ellen's foot and pushed her.

Ended up with Mike and Ellen holding Dad on the floor and Mike telling him, among other things, that he reminded him of Gramps,
and Ellen telling him his angina was
a sham.

They were both shaken up, telling us what had happened when the phone rings.

It's Dad telling me he is leaving Mum and that could I do something as she was in a state!

When I arrived with Mike, Dad is putting his bags in the car, preparing to leave. I tell Mike to stay in the car, and go and see if they are OK.

Dad has bruising under his eye and Mum is sobbing uncontrollably. I go and sit with Mum and try and console her,
VERY aware that Dad may start up with Mike again!

(Is this what Kim meant by convalescence?)

Dad shuts the front door and starts going on and on about Mike and Ellen.

I tell him I don't want to hear it, and ask where he is going.

Says he might call on Adam or Wendy or go on to Jack at Oxford.

Ask him if that's a good idea, to drive all that way, in his present state of mind, and where is he going to stay if they are all out?

Says he's going anyway so I write down Mum and my phone numbers and ask him to keep in touch.

Put my arm round him and tell him to take care, but he doesn't want a hug! Asks if that's Mike in the car and tells me not to let him into his house.

'You owe me that.'

The last thing he says is for me to make sure my children have good memories of him if we don't ever see him again!

Then he drives off into the night. I go and fetch Mike, tell him what happened, and then we both go in and console Mum for the next few hours.

Mike and Mum seem to have a better understanding of each other. She doesn't want to come back with me for the night so I tell her I'll come back in the morning.

NOT
a happy night.

Dad could crash or kill himself and Mum is in a desperate situation.

24th September 1995

As I'm ringing Mum's doorbell at 8.25 Dad pulls up!

Mum says: 'Oh, no' when I tell her he's arrived.

He's OK. He's been to see Jack and **told him.**

Then they seem to be back to 'normal'. Mum expressed an opinion he doesn't like and he threatens to leave again! I tell him that's unfair.

I ask him if he's staying, as I'm worried about Mum, and I thought he'd left home. Tells me separation isn't as simple as all that! Then he goes on and on about the family and Mike and Ellen. Last night's events happened because Ellen is jealous of the attention Stella and I and the children get.

Now I know things are back to ABNORMAL and I go back home.

26th September 1995

Saw Dr Bailey as certificate running out. Asked me how long I wanted off!

I suggested I go back in two weeks' time. I think, hope, I am making the right decision.

Rang work, John not there, so spoke to Sam, who was very supportive. Said I can change my mind if I want to, and stay off longer.

2nd October 1995

Feel OK, but waiting for something to happen! My Aunt Helen (Dad's sister) and Uncle Clive (Dad's brother) are back from France now so Dad may have spoken to them.

3rd October 1995

a.m. Dad rang to invite us over on Saturday. I asked him how he was and if he had spoken to Helen and Clive yet. He said he hadn't yet because it was Clive's birthday, so he didn't want to spoil it for him.

Told me people he had spoken to also thought it was
not a good idea to tell other people!

BUT

he now had no choice, he said.

I reminded him that he did have a choice and he had chosen

to speak

to the family.

18.05. Mum rang: 'Well its over,

they know.'

She had come home to find Clive and Helen, and (their partners) Sue and Jim, and Adam (other brother) in discussion.

Mum says: 'You were right. We're all together on this. You weren't the only one's either, there are two others as well. They're all going back to ask their children now.'

Dad comes to the phone. I tell him I am pleased to hear the family are supporting each other. He doesn't see it like that, STILL thinks it would have been

better not to involve the rest of the family!

He says that Jim was not surprised, was very angry, cursing and swearing in the garden.

Helen is devastated.

Clive is upset and very drunk
Sue seems strong and is handling it very well.

Adam is going home to tell Gwen (his wife).

Dad tells me:

'YOU WERE RIGHT AND I WAS WRONG;

it's hard for me to say that but I admit it.'

Says two others were abused as well but can't tell me who. Tells me he has known about one of them for over a week. Also tells me Jack is very ill with angina.

I tell him I think he has done the right thing in telling them although things will be very painful now, they will be able to support each other.

He says he doubts this!

Tells me I must let him pay for my counselling, that he wants to.

20.50: Aunt Helen rang sounding very upset. Asked how I was, that she was sorry about what happened to me.

Told me she is a victim as well.

Told her how sad I was to hear that but not surprised. Said she didn't know how she felt at the moment. I told her how I felt after I'd first talked with Mike; rage, guilt, fear, confusion.

She recognised these feelings.

She asked me about guilt, so told her about my guilt and how I had to lose it before progressing.

She told me she had taken down all the photos in her house. Told her how I had done this too, and about the clock.

She says she doesn't know how she is going to cope with work tomorrow.

I advised her to go off sick, and told her what had happened to me.

She suggested we should get together for a chat, so she can give me a hug. I agreed and apologised for the pain she is in now, but that she needs to talk to, and get some support from those she loves and to get some professional help if she needs it.

She asked if Mike would appreciate a phone call and I said YES, he would.

21.30 Rang Mike who had just been talking to Aunt Helen who was very supportive to him.

She told Mike a few more things.

Jack was a victim as well.

When she and Jim were courting, Jim stayed the night during which Gramps made a sexual advance to him, which he rejected.

We talked about the implications and I reassured Mike he had been right to disclose to Mum and Dad,

And

that I now felt stronger for working through it.

4th October 1995
A poor night's sleep.

Went to see Helen and Jim. Hugs all round, concern and support from us to them and for us from them, even though they are in a crisis.

They said their son Matthew was not a victim but they were worried sick that their other son Bill might be. Matthew had flown to Spain to ask Bill if anything had happened to him. Bill rang them while we were there to tell them he was not a victim, but asked Helen why she had let him go on holiday when she knew what he might do!

Helen very wounded by this.

Talked with them about repression and that I understood why she hadn't said anything.

Dad then arrived with Adam! Dad said loads of stupid things:

'It's important we get back to normal!'

'Jim your mother

doesn't need to know.'

Adam looked very white. He was very supportive. Has told his wife Gwen who is very shocked.
He said,

'Looking back, things are falling into place.'

After more hugging with Helen and Jim we left. Called in on Uncle Clive and Sue but they were out so left a note.
Then called in to see Mum who didn't even know where Dad was!
She looked better, relieved but still saying BUT! Dad came home, many 'yes buts' listed; says

the family will be divided

etc., etc., etc.

I put over the opposite view, but with no effect! I think he fears not being in control and working to his own agenda.

Gave me a cheque for £200.

17.10 Uncle Clive rang, very distressed, voice trembling. Expressed his deep sorrow about what had happened to me and Mike. Asked how I was now, how the family were, etc. I asked him how he was, if anything had happened to him,

He said 'Yes,' he supposed it had, but it was a long time ago, just after the war and he just wanted to

put it behind him.

I told him I did as well but that perhaps it needed to be dealt with before it could be put behind us.

He said if there was anything he could do to help to let him know, Mike as well. I suggested we could get together for a chat and thanked him for ringing.

Got back from seeing KIM early. Stella told me Uncle Jack's son James was coming to see me at 22.00 hours, as he would really like to talk to me.

He was pleased to see us; wanted to say how relieved he was that it was all **out in the open now.**

Said he always hated Gramps and was relieved when he died. Had taken a lot of flack from his parents for not going to visit him like his other cousins,

Mike and me!

But couldn't tell them why he didn't want to go. Had also been very confused about his sexuality in his teens, and had tried to pass off what had happened to him as

'a normal thing that happens to everyone'.

Some of his friends had told him 'No, this was not normal.' Also very relieved to be able to sort out his feelings before his first child arrives in April. Fear was in the back of his mind wondering if is something that is passed on through generations.

When James was 8, and Uncle Jack's son Barry was 9, Gramps took them to Spain. James described this as a

nightmare holiday

from which he couldn't wait to get home. Gramps started to touch their genitals, under the pretext of rubbing on suntan cream, before going swimming,

even though it wasn't sunny.

James and Barry both told him to keep off and leave them alone. Aunt Sue kept asking James why he didn't like his Gramps.

He eventually told her he just didn't like him, that he was a bad sort. After the funeral Sue asked him again why he didn't like him and James told her:

'He's dead now, it's past.'

James feels guilty now that he didn't speak up and is worried his brother Gerry may be a victim as a result. Gerry says nothing happened but James is not convinced.

Told him how I also feel guilty about that, we probably all feel it may have changed things if we'd spoken out about what was happening to us, but that was impossible at the time.

Told James about Uncle Clive's phone call saying he had been a victim too.

He wasn't surprised, had guessed as much from his Dad's behaviour and comments. Talked of very similar communication difficulties with his Dad, about sex being a taboo subject, of being sent to fetch coal whenever anything to do with sex came on TV.

Offered our support to himself and his wife and with what might happen with Clive and Jerry. Asked if he would ring Mike and have a talk with him.

While James was there Stella answered the phone to Ellen. She is worried about Mike who had rung Dad seeking reconciliation. Dad has rejected him again telling him their relationship is finished.

Ellen is very worried as Mike is out and very upset. Asked if I would ring him.

Rang Mike. He is very hurt by Dad's rejection. Says he realises he tried too soon. Mike asked him how he was to which he replied that Mike had to take back what he said about him looking like Gramps

Mike tried to explain that's how he felt on the night.

That was it.

Dad told him he never wants to see or speak to him again; the end; finished. Mike now full of doubt about if he was right to start all this off.

I tell him loads of positive reasons why he was right, and about all the other people that care about him, Helen, Jim, Clive and James. Tried to persuade him to go off sick but he doesn't think he can. We agree to talk tomorrow.

Later ring Mike but he's not in yet so have a long talk with Ellen who's still worried about him and angry and upset herself.

Mum rang them at 7.30 am and told Ellen it was all her fault, and she had no right to be angry with them; that she had

no right to tell

her parents about what had happened to Mike or about the fight!

Ellen understandably told her if her Dad didn't live so far away he would have been round to put one on Dad!

22.10 Rang Mike whose phone had been engaged for ages. As I hoped, he had been talking to James, and had felt a lot more positive as a result.

James had told them both all he had told us, and is going over to see them as well.

Good for James! Mike says he is feeling much better, and coping OK. They are pleased we've invited them over on Sunday and hopefully will feel less isolated.

4th October 1995

PHEW what a few days! My worst fears are coming alive. I am very sad for all the pain my family are in BUT there is only one person responsible for that and it's not me or Mike.

It's a good job he was cremated and has no headstone.

If he had I would add to LOVING FATHER, HUSBAND, GRANDFATHER;

PERVERT, PAEDOPHILE, CHILD MOLESTER,

and
PISS

on his grave.

Despite all this, I am sure it is right for all this to come out, and hope and pray that everyone will progress to be free of <u>his</u> legacy. I am still scared that something terrible will happen though.

I am looking forward to going back to work and see it as an important step.
I am much better,
STRONGER.

KIM: It is really good to see Kim as I am longing to tell her how much better I feel and show her how much weight I've lost.

She is impressed! Then I tell her why I have needed to feel better, stronger. When I finish reading her the traumatic events of the last 18 days she gives me a big hug – tells me not only have I been able to cope for myself but for everyone else as well!

PHEW.

We talk about how far I have come in so short a time and that I need to take care. Agrees I can start work but to be aware of my limitations to start with. We discuss what I might say to people at work, that I can be honest BUT maintain my

PRIVACY.

Discuss my problem of trusting Sam. Kim agrees I can be direct and honest. Discuss Dad. Kim says she would chat to him (not counselling) for no charge if I wanted her to. We recognise a probability that he may be a victim himself. Talk about the Vicar who told Mum he couldn't understand why we wanted to rake up the past – that we should have kept quiet.

Kim is angry when I tell her what he said! Offers me a number of a sympathetic clergyman who has been on one of her courses, IF Mum would like it.

We discuss my fear of worst case scenarios in my family – someone dropping dead or killing themselves – that it would not be my fault.

Someone likely to take that option might be one of my relatives who had perhaps become an abuser themselves.

HELP!

An awful thought that has crossed my mind but that I have suppressed.

Go straight round to Mum and Dad's. We talk with Mum who goes on and on, she can't take any more, she's reached a decision. She's finished with Mike and Ellen.

'They've gone too far'

etc., etc., etc.

'Your poor father'

etc., etc.

I'm very direct and remind her of what has happened to Mike, that she is his mother and needs her. More 'yes buts' about Ellen telling her parents and what her Dad said.

I tell her I agree with Ellen telling her parents and what her Dad said about 'putting one on him'.

This upsets her.

Agrees that maybe one day she might change her decision, but not for a while yet.

I can see the discussion is going nowhere, so go into the kitchen and talk to Dad.

He's not as bad as Mum. Doesn't agree with Mike's version of the phone call; Mike got funny because he did not ask how he was. Dad upset because Mike is not retracting his comment about Dad looking like Gramps

I explain that he may have been saying how he felt that night; that he should have listened to the rest of what he was going to say.

I remind him of what Mike has gone through and how devastating it has been for us; that he should remember this before rejecting him.

Tells me how the family want to keep 'it' quiet and are terrified of discovery.

That Helen and Jim want to move away from where anyone knows them.

I tell him I know, and he knows this feeling well. Says James is coping well because he works on building sites and is used to taking hard knocks!

He's not interested in Kim's offer; says he can't let go and <u>lose control</u> and shout and cry. I tell him I think he needs to and remind him of all the symptoms of stress he has told me about.

Overall I feel more positive about Dad's attitude than Mum's. However, it's all unresolvable for a while and I feel Stella and I must hang back and look after ourselves for a while.

As we leave Mum seems colder towards me. She told Stella she had hoped I would have understood and supported her more.

7th October 1995
Awake since 5 am.

My mind turning over. Ring Sam and let him know I've heard nothing from staff health. After checking with John at home he says I can start work Tuesday but will have to see staff health

a.s.a.p.

Mike rings about 21.00. I tell him about yesterday. Kim and Mum and Dad feelings.

He sounds more positive!

23.00 hrs. Mum rings, sobbing, very angry with me:

'How could I do that when she has enough to cope with already.'

Tells me Ellen has just been on the phone shouting at her and she can't take any more. It's my fault 'cause I told Ellen about what she said yesterday. I tell her I spoke to Mike, that I was explaining her feelings, just as I had tried to explain Ellen and Mike's to her. Tells me

'there's no point to anything'

and she is walking off into the night!

Dad calls out and asks her if she wants him to talk to Mike! She says no, then repeats herself:

That she thought I understood.

Sunday 8th October 1995
Our twelfth wedding anniversary and Ellen's birthday. Mike, Ellen, Judy and Rob all come over for tea. All goes well, I am able to have a long chat with Mike; and we all chat together.

Monday 9th October 1995
Helen rang wishing me luck for starting work tomorrow, which is very kind of her. Says she is OK but afraid to go out and of discovery. Is off work with anxiety/backache after argument with her GP.

Ring Mum. She is no longer angry, sounds terrible. Says no one understands the position she is in, so I offer her the number of the clergyman Kim suggested. Says she might ring it or Father Damien.

Says she has smashed up the kitchen, that Dad can't understand why; she has broken the door glass. Apologises for forgetting to give us an anniversary card!

Tuesday 10th October 1995

BACK TO WORK, after six weeks, two days sickness and two weeks holiday! A big step as I started to get ill nine-and-a-half weeks ago, after talking with Mike at the service station on 3rd August.

Hardly slept! Up at 5.40 am and off to work.

It went OK, everyone pleased to see me; staff and inmates, especially BM.

Only a couple of staff probed at what had been wrong with me, so I told them I had been dealing with a personal problem and left it at that. Saw John and thanked him again for his support and understanding.

It was a quiet shift but seemed to go on for EVER. Felt like it was time to go home at 10.30 am! Felt good to get through the shift but I was very tired when I got home.

After I fetched kids from school, fell asleep for half an hour!

Dad rang to see how I had got on at work, was supportive and pleased to hear things went OK. Told me of his difficulties and about Mike and Ellen again! Says he has written to Mike.

Mum still sounded terrible. Has not spoken to anyone – might do so tomorrow! Has written Mike a letter as well – 'If Ellen doesn't tear up it up before he gets it'.

Rang Mike – he has just seen Kim, sounds very positive.

Wednesday 11th October 1995

At last – a good night's sleep!

Back to work for the late shift. During handover was asked to take Will M. home – he had apparently had a bad angina attack.
He was very frightened and shocked. I found out why when I returned; he had just been suspended but had not been able to tell me.

Then I sat down to talk to Sam K. He was warm, friendly, pleased to see me. I thanked him for his help and support during the phone calls. When I asked him, he said that all John had told him was that I had 'psychological problems'.

I explained to him that I would like to be able to tell him about what had happened to me but that I was worried that he might have a laugh and a joke about it later, as I had seen him do with other people's problems.

He laughed nervously, said he hoped he knew when to be serious and confidential. Assured me that what I said would go no further.

Then I told him some of my story.

He was very supportive and pleased that I had come so far. I was able to tell him that although I felt much better, I realised I might have some limitations. He accepted this and reinforced the positive aspects such as greater understanding of our work.

I felt relieved and supported having talked so honestly with him,

and perhaps we may get on better now.

Then enjoyed being an escort, to a ten-pin bowling alley!

Thursday 12th October 1995

Mike rang in the morning to see how I was and to tell me he had plucked up courage yesterday and rung Helen. He was relieved that she did not reject him.

As with me she did express her concern about Mum and Dad, but in a balanced way even though she had only heard their side of the story.

Mike enlightened her about his rejection, being strangled, etc. She has offered to try and mediate between them.

Mike wants to ring Mum and Dad but is afraid of being rejected again. He and Ellen have written a reply to Mum's letter, but doesn't know whether to post it or not.

Get to work. Only five staff on and no one can take charge except me. I ask Sam K. if one of the others can be in charge when he gets back from break but he jokes he would rather I did it.

I feel nervous, I only know three of the inmates well.

Otherwise
I'm out of touch.

I just about remember how to do the paperwork and allocation. We have to have someone supervising a painter, an inmate on close observation, and another one is out on escort!
A lot to think about.

At 15.30 HJ requests the door to the garden open, so he can go for a walk with HP. I open the door and watch them through the window.

One of the others is in the lounge with Terry B. I then have to go to the toilet, but I forget to tell anyone where I'm going. Approx. one minute later the alarms go off.

I run out of the toilet and Terry tells me he has just seen DK running away from outside of the perimeter.

It transpires there was no one in the garden when he climbed the fence, so as I opened the door

I carry the can.

I get sent out to search the locality.

The consequences of my mistake begin to sink in. I don't know the inmate but he is a serious offender and in a bad state.

He has a history of violence and may harm others, or himself. He is only wearing jeans and a T-shirt so he might die of hypothermia. John knows what has happened and is livid. Later he walks by in the distance and doesn't approach me.

In retrospect I fully realise how stupid I am for
(a) not following them out into the garden, as per policy;
(b) not telling anyone else I was going to the toilet;
(c) coming back to work before my powers of memory and concentration were back to full power.

Sam K. is not angry when I tell him it's my fault.

In fact he is very supportive and persuades me to withdraw my incriminating statement. Feels I should wait and see what happens and for the official investigation.

All my colleagues very supportive but it's no good, I've blown it, lost what tiny bit of confidence I had. I've let everyone down, Stella, me, Kim, Mike.

Stella is worried and upset but still supportive. She was right, I did go back too early.

I am a stupid fool, I just want to hand in my notice and get a boring, simple job because I can't cope, I'm not up to it.

How can I though, I'm trapped, we need the money, now more than ever. What am I going to do? What if the escapee died or kills someone?

It will all be my fault.

Ring work to see if he has returned.
No news. I go to bed and cry myself to sleep.

Friday 14th October 1995
Ring work at 7.15 am.

No news – they will ring me if there is.

Feel terrible, I remember dreaming in the night that I was being lowered by a rope into a pit of snapping crocodiles.

Kim: she senses that things are not right before I start. I read her what happened.

She is upset for me.

I am very distraught and the tears are flowing.

Kim gets me to realise for myself what is happening to me.
Yes, I have made a mistake but I am slipping back into a role I've had a lot of practice as and that fits very comfortably.

I am being a <u>victim</u> again.

I have to keep hold of the progress I've made and keep the mistake in the perspective of the full circumstances.

Mike calls in. It's comforting that someone in my family is being parental!
He reinforces all Kim said and is very supportive.

Sunday 15th October 1995

Gave Sally a lift to work. Disclosed some of my story. She is very supportive and disclosed a lot of things about herself and similarities in our situations.

When I got to work I had a long talk with Sam K. who was very supportive.

Yes, there is going to be an inquiry. He suggested that I will have to decide whether or not to

'play my trump card'.

He told me he reminded John every time I rang that I needed to see the Occupational Health Doctor. Offered me the option to go and work on an easier section and I accepted.

Also told me I don't have to do any nights next month.

The shift went well – all my colleagues being very supportive – a contrast to Thursday! Everyone is very sympathetic about Thursday.

One of them pointed out that going into the garden with them is only practice and <u>not</u> policy.

Spoke some more to Sally on the way home. She disclosed a lot of personal things to me – gave her Sarasi's number after I told her what she had enabled me to do.

Rang Mike to let him know how I got on – he was relieved for me.

Monday 16th October 1995

Late shift on easier section.

Spoke to someone who was very helpful and explained about the investigatory interview on Wednesday next at 4.00 pm. Rang me in the workshop to let me know that the escapee had given himself up to Doncaster police station.

WHAT A RELIEF!

Rang Sandra who works in personnel for advice and she says she will pick me up and take me to the interview on her day off! I told her not to feel obliged but she insists, a good friend in need is a good friend indeed!

Rang Kim and Stella to let them know he's been found.

Got home and rang Mike who was very relieved. Mum rang at 23.00 hrs (phone off hook since I rang Stella) to see how I was.

So I told her of my predicament. She sounded much better.

Is going to see Kim's contact on Wednesday but doubtful it will help. Spent a long time persuading her it was a good thing to do!

Being parental again. Exhausted – off to bed.

Tuesday 17th October 1995
Early shift.

Again good staff, loads of support.

Again the day seemed never ending.

I did the medication; was nervous and cautious but it went OK.

Spoke to the escort who fetched the escapee back. He is OK. Went to Manchester a few times to see his old girlfriend. Skipped the fare on the train.

I had a bad headache from mid-morning so had a long soak in the bath when I got home.

Stella understanding that I'm very tense about tomorrow.

Dad had rung earlier to see how we were. Mum had not spoken to him about last night's call, so he did not know about my mistake!

Stella told him.

Sandra arrived at 3.00 pm; felt the notes I had made would be very useful. She had spoken to the regional officer who thought I did not have much to worry about. They both felt that I would have to explain that I had been ill.

It was great to have Sandra there. She knew some of the panel as she had been an investigating officer herself.

Although a serious, formal occasion, they all did their best to put me at my ease, being warm, friendly and calling me by my nickname. They went over the incident in great detail and asked many questions. Everything was recorded in shorthand. I was able to say everything I had prepared. I explained that I had been working through PTSD but they didn't probe any further.

The Personnel lady apologised that I had not seen the Occupational Health Doctor; that there had been a serious communication breakdown. John should have sent me a form but didn't!

They asked me if I was fit for work now. I said yes, but realised I had some limitations which I thought would quickly improve.

I explained about how long the shifts seemed. The Personnel lady then offered that, after my holiday next week, I work two three-day weeks, then two four-day weeks

OR

anything I wished so that I get used to full-time work in a gradual fashion!

All I have to do is see my GP and get a month's certificate saying

'to be rehabilitated back into work'.

That way my pay won't be so badly affected.

Said I only needed to see the Occupational Health Doctor if I wanted to. Repeated I was willing to see him but was happy with the guidance I am receiving from my counsellor.

Finished after 40 minutes. I went in worried that I was in trouble and could be suspended but came out feeling very valued, supported and wanted. Thanked them very much and told her I wished I could have spoken to her
before I had returned to work!

Will know on Friday if any disciplinary action will be taken against me but Sandra felt this would be extremely unlikely.

PHEW (I hope)

Sandra very supportive and encouraging on the way home.

Got home, Stella very relieved things are better than we expected. Dad rang 7.00 pm, relieved to hear things had gone well. Spoke to Mum who was also relieved. She has seen Kim's contact and found him very helpful; is going back Monday!

'He told me I haven't done everything wrong after all!'

I am so pleased she has got someone sensible to talk to.

Thursday 19th October 1995
Anxious before going to work on the late shift.

I've been told there will be no further action but they would like me to see the Occupational Health Doctor. Filled out the referral form that John forgot.

Told me that he could not remember Sam telling him I would rather not take charge or specifically about my limitations! Asked if I would mind discussing this with him and Sam together. Said I could refuse if I wanted to as I should really have Sandra with me. As she was unavailable and I had already been told the decision, I agreed to the 'chat'. Sam told me of his 'selective memory loss'.

Told him firmly that I did remember clearly and had written it down the same evening. He suggested that I did not make myself clear enough and should have taken him to one side to tell him!

So that's how he got out of it, covered his own back.

Then he took over the discussion and questioned me as to whether I was really fit to work and when was I going to be 100 per cent fit? How would I know? Had my counsellor given me a time scale?

He's so like Dad, like Napoleon,

'attack the best form of defence'.

He did not acknowledge any fault on his own part, instead turned it round to question my fitness.

The rest of the shift went well, rang Stella and Sandra to let them know.

Sandra thought that Sam was very defensive and that John would not take it any further as he would leave himself wide open to criticism.

Best of all they have fixed it for me to work two three-day weeks and two four-day weeks, on my return from leave.

Friday 20th October 1995

Early shift went well. The day again very long, feel exhausted but now relieved to have survived such stormy waters.

I am looking forward to our week off, and then a more gentle break back in.

Kim: Talked over last week and what a stern test that had been; the relief and exhaustion.

Talk about Mum and Dad, about what I want and need from them —being there as parents, grandparents; that I need their love as they need mine. Understanding is not what it might be from them but that's understandable!

Right now I need to stand back a little, be autonomous and not be overwhelmed by their distress.

I realise I am being unfair to Stella by wanting her to restrain her feelings towards them but now I am better, I accept this. I _have_ made some progress with them, am now able to be honest on an _adult_ basis; even my ADULT to their CHILD!

Kim asked how I felt about seeing us all together. I feel it is no longer an impossible concept and would like it to happen.

Talked about if it's time for a change of job or career! Kim thought I should extend my learning.

Mum rang to tell me they are going away for the weekend with Helen and Jim; also that Dad had taken the dog over to Wendy, our old friend, alone, which indicated to her that he was going to **talk about 'it'**.

Arranged to meet up later in the week.

Saturday 21st October 1995

p.m. Went to Mike and Ellen's. Went off with Mike who let me read his letters from Mum and Dad which were full of positive and negative things.

Swapped Joe for Judy for a few days!

Sunday 22nd October 1995

Church in the morning, walk around the park with the girls in the afternoon. Spoke with Mike and Ellen on the phone.

Ellen wanted to check Judy wasn't going to see Mum and Dad.

Went to a concert with Sandra and Bob in the evening. Enjoyed myself despite a few intrusive memories in the concert hall.

Monday 23rd October 1995

Visited some of the seaside towns nearby.

Tuesday 24th October 1995

Pet City, Old Macs. Mike came over for tea, to go to Kim's and to swap back Joe and Judy. Rang Dad and suggested we get together later in the week.

Wednesday 25th October 1995

Dentist! Feeling miserable all day for no particular reason.

Cheered up in the evening at a good gig The Victoria Inn. Sandra and Bob were able to come.

Drank three pints which helped me relax!

Thursday 26th October 1995

Up early – off to buy shoes for everyone.

Kim: Didn't read from this diary, now using it less.

Talked about how religious beliefs affected; about yesterday, feeling sad, depressed – it's to be expected I have a lot to be sad and depressed about!

Talked about being fat – what would it be like to be thin? Fears for the future, family, career, etc. It's a symptom of PTSD (i.e. fear of the future).

Homework – poetry!

Friday 27th October 1995

Day at the seaside with Mum and Dad. Went OK, didn't talk about it at all, good to have a break.

CHAPTER 3

Mike's Story

Prelude

I am 18 years old, an awkward and diffident boy, despite my height and beard. I find myself about to go to medical school, and I am scared. In the early 1970s it is still not so commonplace for someone of my background to go away to university. I'm not sure I shall cope. There is however at least one thing that pushes me on; for I see this move – away from home, away from town, away from the world I know – as a golden opportunity to rid myself of a dreadful obsession.

This obsession is buried deep, deep inside me. I absolutely refuse to visit it voluntarily, to contemplate it, to think of it at all; the shame and self-hate are too much. Yet it still rises unbidden from the depths to overwhelm and choke my will; and when it does I am consumed with urgent need to seek out my long time and very secret paramour, to have sex with him. He is a lot older than I am, he is my grandfather, and yet these are facts which are somehow unimportant or irrelevant to me at the time. All that I see, as I sicken with myself on the way home, is that my sin is twofold – to have sex, and to have sex with a man!

Now, as I walk through the wet dark streets, I make a decision. It will never happen again. This is a decision I have made many times before, but this time it is of a different quality: I am 18; the world sees me, or claims to see me, as an adult; I am moving away. This time I will succeed.

Interlude

I did succeed; I never ever had sex with him again. University life was uncomfortable, I was shy and isolated, I found few friends and all of them were women. I hovered about the other men, rather in awe, but finding no companionship – they seemed so much more adult than me. Uncomfortable it may have been, but I had managed to leave him behind.

I found an anonymous little church, approached the priest, and went to confession; I said the words, though I remember my knees nearly buckling under me, speaking and understanding only that I myself had done wrong! It seemed like the hardest thing I had ever done, but afterwards the sense of liberation was enormous. I could put down my sin and get on with my life. Here was my new start.

And so it was. I lived my new life, I achieved a degree, I started work and complained how medicine seemed to take over our lives. The medical 'system' was, I now realise, very abusive, but I wouldn't have put it that way, and of course I was ripe to be used! However I survived, when some didn't; I succeeded in my profession. I rarely thought about my childhood. I wondered vaguely if I was homosexual but as I was so awkward in the company of men I did not see how this could be put into practice! I was very lonely, I used to imagine that one day I would have a warm and loving family of my own; I remember that it was very important to me that this warmth and love would be accessible to others, that it should and could be shared. How I was to move from my loneliness to this idyllic scene was a bit of a blur!

I had proposed to a girl from home whilst still a student, but then I had broken it off, telling her that I had had a homosexual past relationship. Ironically, at the time this felt like an excuse. My 'real' reasons for breaking it off seemed to be many, and largely to do with the fact that she didn't fit in with the social expectations of others. My parents certainly didn't approve! I would not admit to myself my fear, and I saw no connection between this confused attempt at a relationship and my past. She came out of it with dignity, and perhaps a lucky escape!

After I had been working for a year or so, I met and was amazed to fall in love with my wife. She was pretty and vivacious, outgoing and demonstrative, tough and prickly, the life and soul of the party; my complete opposite. I loved to please her, to do whatever she asked of me. This time I made sure that, when things began to get serious, I told her about my previous 'sexual relationship with a man'. To my great joy it seemed unimportant to her; to my even greater joy she agreed to marry me. Within six months we were married with great celebration. Yes, surely I had put down my past: God had forgiven me, and it seemed irrelevant to my wife.

Recapitulation

Now I was surely not unintelligent, but nevertheless I did not see what happened to me in any other terms than those I have described. My sexual past had never seemed other than something for which I was responsible; even if, to my shame, I had been unable to control it. I do not believe that memory of my experiences was ever truly unavailable to me, even the fact that the beginning of my abuse was shrouded in mist somewhere in my very early childhood. I simply had no other terms of reference with which to think about it. The sexual abuse of children in general, and my own in particular, was something I simply did not think about.

This surely was not only personal, but also societal. Even professionally, in those days, it was rarely discussed. We were taught to look out for children being physically abused (euphemistically referred to as non-accidental injury); we heard mention of sexual abuse of little girls by men, but the fact that those little girls became women with problems was ignored. The fact that boys could be victims, let alone grow into adults having to cope with their past, was unthought and unspoken. No wonder I felt alone.

Da Capo

I first realised that what had happened to me was sexual abuse in my early thirties. Our daughter was nearly six and my wife was expecting our son. It was an explosive experience! As I write this I remember vividly the hot sensation that flooded over me as the truth dawned. I do not remember why or how the realisation came to me. I do remember wondering what to do with it. The difficulties in our marriage were bad enough to be hard to ignore. I felt that my childhood was implicated and that I should probably be asking for help. But from whom and from where? The only source of help I could think of was psychiatry, and that idea was instantly placed as a very last resort indeed! I could not imagine any of the psychiatrists with whom I had worked or whom I knew being able to help. After all, I had never come across such a situation in my time working in psychiatry! So as there was no help to be had, I should just get on with my life as I had before. I had lived with my past when I felt it to be my responsibility, surely it would be easier now that I had recognised it for what it was.

However, the cork was now working loose in the bottle. My wife, a gregarious person and always happy to make a large family occasion, had invited my parents and my grandfather, despite my reluctance, to spend a few days with us over Christmas. I had assumed that I would be able to endure this, as I had on so many other occasions in the past. But, at that time I had not seen the connection, but now I found myself saying to her, 'I have something to tell you; I think I was sexually abused as a child.' All that I remember of her reaction was that it was very angry, and that she was insistent about knowing who had done this to me, and what precisely. The cork seemed to be slipping faster; I could see that now I had shared this knowledge with another, I had lost control of it. This is a truly terrifying experience.

Eventually I did tell her, and of course her immediate reaction was to insist that he must not come for Christmas, and that if I did not stop him, then she would tell my parents in order to prevent the visit. Panic! Events out of my control!

Presto furioso

And so came my epic journey on a dark and wet autumn evening to confront him. Simply put, I told him that I now realised that he had sexually abused me; that my wife knew; that he had wrecked my life; that he was not to come to our house ever again; and that if he did not pull out of the Christmas visit, we would tell my parents.

As I was talking to him it came to me that once when we were children, my younger brother had told me about 'what Grampy does in bed'. I told him that I suspected that he had abused my brother too and that I wondered how many more of our cousins he might have treated in the same way. He denied any of the others, and then said he had only done what he had done to me because I enjoyed it! I remember forcing myself to say, but wondering whether it held conviction, 'But I was a child'. In the end he accepted that he had done wrong and asked me to forgive him. I told him that I wasn't sure that I could, and then left meekly at his bidding! I do not think I showed him any of my anger. I never saw him again.

He acted swiftly, arranging to move into an old people's home, telling the family that he didn't feel safe on his own any more! His children were all puzzled by this, but the Christmas visit was off – problem solved.

I began, very surreptitiously, to scour bookshop shelves for anything that could help me understand. I quickly discovered that there were books, both academic and self-help, for practically every kind of difficulty but mine! On a trip to Oxford one day I did discover two small books for women abuse survivors. I read them avidly and secretly! It was a strange experience. So much was familiar to me that it was a great relief, but the issue was dealt with in such a feminist way; women writing to women as victims of men, in a society where women expect to be victims of men. Exciting, yet desperately depressing. What about me?

Life in general seemed to carry on much as before. Then my grandfather became ill and began to die. My father couldn't understand why I did not go to visit him and I would only say that we had fallen out. When I heard he was near death I took pity and telephoned him. I spoke perhaps only two sentences; but told him that I had been trying hard to forgive him as he had asked, and that I thought I had succeeded. He died a day or so later, off the hook. The funeral was dreadful for me. However, I really felt that my problem had been buried with him. How wrong could I have been?

A few months later my parents were planning to visit us; my father told me that he had found some old home movies of my grandfather with me and the others as children and that he was planning to bring them to show us. I was mortified but said nothing at the time. However, as the days passed, I realised that I couldn't do this and that eventually I was going to have to tell them about what had happened to me from about the age of five years old.

To this day I do not know how I managed to do it, but I went to see them and could think of no way but to blurt it out, 'I don't want you to bring over the films of my grandfather.' My father said, 'OK' and seemed to shrink into his chair, but my mother asked, 'Why ever not?' So I told them, 'Because he sexually abused me from the age of about five.'

To say those words felt as if my heart was being torn from my chest. My father fled the room shouting, 'Oh no!' My mother was, at first, unbelieving. 'You must have misinterpreted.' I found myself, to my horror, explaining fairly bluntly, some of what he had done. I also told her that I thought he might have abused my brother also.

Then I could stay there no longer. I simply had to leave. My mother wanted me to help them, but I was just unable to do it.

Things seemed to close down. Little more was said. I heard hints that my parents' relationship was 'in trouble', but I had too much of my own in that department to worry much for them; the unacknowledged anger in our marriage was spiralling almost beyond belief.

Now my brother and I had never really been close. I had never understood why, but was not really surprised that we had little contact. I was conscious vaguely that I was missing something that other people enjoyed in their relationships with siblings; I had buried again my suspicions about him.

Our mother, however, had not! She would drop hints from time to time that he wanted to get in touch with me, but I tried to take little notice of this. Eventually came a family invitation to tea. I desperately tried to avoid being alone with him, but eventually he cornered me in the garden and announced that Mum had spoken to him and that he thought we had something in common. Panic! We arranged to meet and discuss it.

We met and talked for hours. I remember feeling exhausted, wanting to stop for a rest, and yet being unable to stop; the pressure of words seemed to just keep coming, first from one, then the other, and yet with many pauses to check out whether what was being disclosed was not too shocking to be said.

The facts of our abuse were very similar. However, it seemed that he had been much less aware of what had happened than I had, until our mother had asked him about it. The impact on him was much more sudden and dramatic. I was unable to suggest any help other than mutual support which we had at last been able to discover in each other. I felt guilty that I had no knowledge or idea that there was anyone to turn to. I did let him have some of the 'helpful hints' that I had culled from the books I had found.

Then came the news that he too had found a book in a bookshop, this one written specifically about adult male survivors of sexual abuse. I travelled in search of a copy. What a tremendous sense of relief. I cannot emphasise enough just how important it was. For someone in our position, searching for a book may be the most exposure one can risk in seeking help. I still remember vividly how risky it felt to be standing at those bookshelves, and how I travelled to other towns in order to be sufficiently anonymous.

When my brother, in the most tortuous way, discovered a therapist, I was pleased for him. He tried hard to encourage me to do the same but I still didn't see it as something that could practically be available to me. The fact was that my professional position rendered enormous difficulties for me in seeking help. Eventually he suggested that therapy with the same counsellor might be an option, and with great reluctance I took the plunge.

Therapy

In therapy I spoke very little about the precise events that happened to me as a child. That seems quite surprising really, but I suppose that I was ventilating that aspect of the problem in the frequent 'mutual support' sessions with my brother and in my writing of letters and my diary. Kim encouraged me to write to my father to ventilate some of my feelings – not necessarily to post it, but just to use it as a way of expressing my pain. It took a while for me to allow myself to really let go but eventually I did. This is the first letter I wrote the day after my second counselling session; I had started seeing Kim on 5th September 1995 and there was to be two weeks gap because of her holiday. She had suggested that I might begin to write as a means of bridging the gap until she returned:

13.9.95

Dad,

I've put pen to paper because I find it so difficult to address issues face to face. I'm sorry if it seems the wrong thing to do, but I have to express my feelings some way or other if I am to have any release from my pain; and I must try to have that if only for the sake of my children.

I want to acknowledge how you have helped me – especially recently when I left home (marriage home) and you had me stay 'no questions asked'. I was, and am very grateful to both of you for the house-room and for the space. Thank you.

I want also to acknowledge the effort you put into bringing me up 'awkward bugger' as I was – and I was that in both senses of the word, wasn't I? You encouraged me in learning and education and for that I'm grateful, for I'm sure that is the major way I've coped all these years.

I want to acknowledge all the hard work you put in to keep house and home together and provide for me physically – and I do remember how hard and long you worked. Also the energy you put into the marriage (I remember it wasn't easy and I know how hard that can be). Thank you.

I want to acknowledge your pain now, over the discovery of our abuse by your father. It must be terrible and I don't see any way of lessening it for you. I'm sorry for that. I know you are physically unwell also and that this last year must have made that worse. I know that times are hard financially and I'm also sad about all that.

But I feel angry with you and frightened of you – still! Even now I am shocked with how much effort and how much pain it has cost me to write that sentence.

Why? When I disclosed to you last year I was anxious about your feelings and your health and on that occasion I told you I saw your pain. I understood your rage and I was grateful for and accepted your apology for your immediate reaction. Since then you have tried very hard to be normal and friendly and I am grateful for that – indeed I feel we've got on better this last year than ever before. When I knew Stephen was about to tell you of his own abuse I was worried for you and tried to acknowledge your pain and offer support.

When you asked me to leave you alone the other day I was devastated. I felt rejected and hurt and angry. In all your distress you have never once acknowledged to me *my* pain, *my* hurt, *my* anger, *my* grief, *my* destroyed childhood, *my* ruined life, *my* spoiled marriage. This is what I feel angry about. When the other children were learning their ABCs, I was having to learn that being regularly buggered by one's Grampy was not normal and not to be discussed in the playground.

When the others were learning to let go of their parents and start independent life at school, I was struggling to distinguish between sex and affection. I didn't learn what a healthy normal affectionate physical relationship with caring adults was about. For me affection was mixed with being used for sex.

When I try to imagine myself at my son's age I see a little boy with grown-up genitals! I had learned to exchange sex for affection, sex for presents, sex for treats, sex for holidays.

Where were you? Why didn't you see? Why couldn't I talk over my troubles with my Daddy? Why didn't you understand my difficult behaviour for what it was? Why did I not have normal hugs and cuddles to compare with Grampy's to help me see that his were different?

I tried so hard to be 'manly' for you – but no, I didn't like football and fighting and so forth (small wonder I suppose); but that made you angry, didn't it? When I used to want to pop round to the girl down the road to play house and dolls with her, that made you angry didn't it?

Anger at home and sex at Grampy's! This makes me angry.

And when I was older, a teenager, and looking for help from religion, that made you mocking and angry didn't it? When I was suicidal with panic because I thought I was a 'homo', but still going up to Grampy's for my 'fix' of sex, where were you? Why couldn't I talk over my problem with my Dad like others? Why didn't you spot the distress? Why had I learned not to talk about feelings, or bodies, or sexuality at home? No, I had to go up to Gramps for that sort of conversation – and it came with strings attached!

I've just remembered that by now my 'reward' had degenerated into a purple club biscuit! I was well and truly hooked! *And* he was the only person who listened to me and that I could talk to.

Why hadn't I learned to cuddle you and talk to you? It should have been part of our relationship from the first, why wasn't it? This makes me angry with you. And fear – fear always. I was afraid of you, afraid of letting you down, afraid of not pleasing you; afraid to touch you, afraid to share with you.

I am still afraid – afraid and angry.

I want you to know that I still value our relationship, such as it is. I desperately want to build on it. It is hugely important for me that my children enjoy a good relationship with you – this must not go on down the generations.

I want to learn to love you, but you must know and understand that there is nothing you can do now that is enough to make up for what was missing – that is why I couldn't take your hand that evening when you extended it to me.

I am afraid that the only option is to start from now, from where we are in this pain – and you most certainly are not the only one hurting – and try and rebuild. I hope you will, because I'm sure its worth doing. We could be friends – we could even learn to be Father and Son.

Mike

P.S. I've struggled long and hard over whether to send this to you. A week has gone by and still not a word from you. You are my parent – not the other way around. So here goes. I still mean the last sentence of the letter (sent 16.9.95)

Later the same day as I sent that letter I wrote another to my dead grandfather:

16.9.95

Dear Bastard,

It's taken me a long time to getting round to writing this to you. I thought I'd forgiven you for what you did to me – I think I probably had, and that forgiveness cost me so much! Ha! But now it turns out that when you asked me to forgive you, you pathetic bastard, you promised me that you had never done it to anyone else – especially Stephen. I particularly asked you about Stephen didn't I? But no, you said it was only me. I wanted to believe you, but looking back on it I knew that you'd abused Stephen too. I supposed in some minor way that it hadn't really affected him!

You looked so pathetic that evening sitting in the chair in the corner – like the pathetic old poof that you were! It had taken so much courage to face you. I don't think even then I could have done it if it hadn't been for the fact that our marriage was hurting so much and I was desperate to do something to help. I drove over to see you with my heart in my mouth, gripping the wheel. I stopped by a telephone box and looked for Stephen's number. I almost rang him to ask if he would come with and support me (ironical isn't it) but I lost my bottle and didn't. What a huge pity – if he'd come perhaps we'd have beaten your brains out! Ha!

Even then I was too gentle, you old bastard. I told you I'd come to be unpleasant, ha! And to talk about child sexual abuse. 'I don't know what you mean.' Coward! 'Well it was only messing about.' Messing about! 'Well, you enjoyed it.' Well, you hit the nail on the head there, didn't you, you old bastard. Of course I enjoyed it – you'd been training my sexual responses since I was practically a toddler! I was like a little puppet; you could turn my cock on like pressing a switch on a machine – you evil twisted old pervert. You were the adult and I was the child – you were my grandfather and you did that to me – such evil, evil stuff.

Oh you squirmed didn't you, ha! You squirmed even more when I told you how it was wrecking my marriage. 'Ellen doesn't know does she?' Oh you looked frightened when I said: 'Of course she does!' 'Oh, how can I ever face her?' Ha! Probably the only reason you didn't have to was because I thought she'd smash you to pulp and I didn't want her to get into trouble. You bastard! I really enjoyed telling you that you'd have to think of an excuse not to come to stay at Christmas or I'd tell Dad!! Of course I knew I wouldn't do that but it made you think quickly didn't it? Go into a home, ha! – for your own safety – you evil old toad.

'Can you ever forgive me?' (tears – I should think so too) I didn't feel sorry for you but I said I'd have to keep trying and at least you'd asked – I suppose that was something.

And so it was done, and then this next bit makes me feel sick, really sick now that I consider it. 'I think you'd better go now' and I agreed with you and left! Bastard! I should have had that last word – and I'd gone to that house again and smelt your smells and heard your clock and seen your sickening face again.

I remember turning the car in the end of the close and feeling sick with relief – I'd put it behind me so I thought, that was that. But it wasn't was it?

There and then I drove up past Gran's's house – looking for comfort but she wasn't there was she? I nearly went to Stephen's then – if only I had!

(Oh, Gran, Gran, what a strong wave of grief came over me just now; the lost little boy looking for a grown up to love him and protect him and look after him – you were the only real parent I had, weren't you, and you died and left me alone. And I never told you I loved you did I, nor showed it as much as I should – the bastard made me like that I'm afraid. I am so sorry. You always promised me that if you could come back you'd do it, didn't you? Well, I don't think we can meet at that level, but I find comfort in the fact that you might be watching me now and I know if you are, you care and you love me. I remember you giving me that really good advice before we got married 'never let a day go by without telling Ellen you love her'; thank you, you know I try hard to abide by it. Why, oh why, didn't I tell you about the bastard – would you have understood? Perhaps it would have been beyond you, but perhaps not – anyway consider me telling you now! I do miss you so much, I can't tell it in words.)

Is this a grief I'm going to have to go through also? I obviously repressed it before like mad, but I don't mind grieving our Gran, she deserves it.

(Yours is the house with good memories, and even where he contaminated it that can't spoil it. I wish I could be there now, in your front room with the red curtains, or even the regency stripe, with the sun shining in through the windows, warm and safe and comfortable. With you always beavering away at something, cooking or cleaning; and best of all telling me stories about the old days, of your youth and your squabbles with your family, of your days in service. You had a bad life too, didn't you? Oh I wish we could meet now and share – perhaps we will one day; I do love you. Thank you.)

So I let the bastard stew, that was that, I'd 'finally laid it to rest' – but no, it wasn't was it?

I had to put up with the family saying, 'You don't see your Gramps much do you?' We had to avoid Sunday lunch at Mum and Dad's – he always seemed to be going there. And constantly they'd tell me how ill he was, and how unhappy he was, and how good Stephen was to him; and all the time I was making sure my feelings were kept deep down inside. Ellen knew – she kept saying we should tell Mum and Dad; but no – I didn't want to hurt them.

But also my own conscience was nagging at me. I felt – and still do feel – that I should try to forgive: after all I need forgiveness in my life too – 'forgive us our sins as we forgive'. Oh, how much it cost me to ring you that day from work and tell you I'd been trying hard to forgive you since we met last and that I'd decided I had. I meant it and I'm still glad I did it, and I wasn't the least bit surprised when you upped and died a couple of days later. It felt as if I'd had you squirming on a hook and let you off. All that time Stephen was worrying you were going to confess to someone, ha! Well, while he was worrying about you, you were worrying about me! Perhaps there's some justice in that!

Well, maybe I'd forgiven you about what you'd done to me; but there are some 'buts' aren't there? But you denied you'd done it to Stephen – and you had hadn't you? You bastard! So that means I haven't forgiven you for what you did to him – you evil old poof, and I haven't forgiven you for the lie.

But also my intelligence tells me that Stephen and I are probably only two among others – perhaps we'll never know, but I haven't forgiven you for that doubt either. Dad? Helen? Clive? Gerry? James? Jack? Adam? Nancy? All these spring to mind. And what about all those unknown to me – the army for instance? How much evil did you do? And Grandma – what did you do to her with all this – she was your wife, you were supposed to love and protect her, not bugger her grandchildren, you bastard!

So you see, there's a whole lot I haven't forgiven you for – I suppose I shall have to try – but not yet. I'm not ready.

And then there was Dad – I feel sorry for him now. He was so distressed by your decision to go into a home, by your illness and your struggle with death. I did wonder if you'd tell him, and if so, what you'd tell him. Ha! – some chance.

It was so hard to be sympathetic and listen to him grieve. It was so hard to explain to the children; I so wanted them to have innocent memories of you. The funeral wasn't so hard to go to – it was a 'final, final' laying to rest of the problem. Ha! Fat chance.

And then, as that old fart pronounced some gibberish over your coffin – that was hard to take! And sitting in the crematorium chapel looking around and wondering: 'who else' – I wonder.

And then quiet – the lull before the storm, I'd managed to put down the violence, but looking back on it, I hadn't managed to put down all the old fear.

And then the film – and Ellen adamant – as I was – that you shouldn't come to this house. Yet another stressful journey – to Mum and Dad's this time, sitting on that rocking chair with bowels like water and making small talk. Then: 'I don't want you to bring the film of Gramps to our house, nor does Ellen.' Interesting responses – Mum looks surprised: 'Why on earth not?'; Dad looks angry but subdued: 'OK then – if you say so.' I answer Mum: 'Because he sexually abused me from the age of about 5 or before, until I left for College.' Stunned silence, then Mum: 'You must have misinterpreted something.' 'No, believe me, I know what happened, it wasn't misinterpreted.' Dad saying, 'Why now?' and storming out. Then it's all a bit muddled. I tried to help Mum deal with it. I tried to get dates out of her. I told her I thought Stephen might also have been a victim and that possibly Dad might. All this time I was trying to help them cope.

But then deafening silence until recently and then only because Stephen approached me and I approached them!

And on the face of it what are the bare facts? You sexually abused me for years. You used me in your pathetic power, sex and secrecy games. Until recently I thought it was only me, but now I know you were ruining Stephen as well, and I'm rapidly becoming convinced we were only a small part of what was going on. It's only now dawning on me! Evil Bastard!

I don't remember the first time, it was always there. I remember sort of leaking it to my other Grampy – of course he didn't understand, but I must have been very small then. Stephen says he died in 1964 – which would make me 7 or 8 when he died. That's the first time I remember any sort of dissonance – that what was happening wasn't right. I remember telling about my sexual fantasies in the playground at primary school to a rather loud boy who told some of the others and who then shunned me – that must put it back to under seven years of age.

I believe it started way back in my very early childhood. There was that famous trip to the seaside. You know – it's a family joke about how you said it was 'miles of golden sand', and how we went on the early morning cheap excursion and had to stay 'til late to get the cheap return; and how it poured with rain all day. And we all sat under the portico – it's still there or it was when we went a few years back – and that made me feel sick I can tell you. I have a very vivid picture of sitting on deckchairs sheltering from the rain by wrapping some sort of tarpaulin over us. Grandma was handing out pickled eggs on top of the tarpaulin and you – bastard – were masturbating me under it! Mum and Dad were certainly there!

How did you get me to do it to you – I really don't remember – it just was always there; just a learned response I suppose, like Pavlov's dogs.

I remember 'coming' was a big issue wasn't it? You used to say 'I've come' and sort of hide what actually happened to you in a tissue – I just knew that was that for that day. Then you used to go on about how it would happen to me and I'd like it, 'It'll be like having a hot poultice on the back of your neck' – I didn't even know what a poultice was! You bastard! And when I did ejaculate for the first time it was on my own – you weren't there, and I didn't want to tell you about it – you were quite disappointed too – stupid old bastard.

And then how old was I the first time you said 'turn over' – that was in your bed after Grandma died. 'Why,' I said. 'I'll show you' says you – and then I really did get a surprise, something new; you tried to shove your penis into my anus. I don't think you managed it that time, but you kept on trying, 'practicing' until I let you do it. You filthy rotten old queer. I was a little boy and you were buggering your own grandson. And then one day I wanted to do it to you. You weren't so keen on that were you? I must have been a little bit older by then. I know you were always making remarks about how much bigger my erection was than yours – so I shoved it up your bum. I remember that made you squeal – I wonder if you'd done that before. You never did like that much did you? But I think by then, I was frightening you a bit – getting a bit too big to handle so safely I suppose.

Then I remember the occasion you were staying overnight at Mum and Dad's – perverted bastard. Stephen and I squabbled and squabbled about which of us was to move out of our shared twin-bedded room into the spare room so as to let you 'sleep' in one of our beds. We both wanted to be the one to sleep with you. This is giving me *very* angry feelings. Dad intervened in the end and shouted at Stephen to go and sleep in the single room, and to celebrate the triumph I made the running didn't I?

You evil bastard, I feel so angry with you. I was a little boy at junior school and you were my grandfather. You were trusted. You had me so sexualised that I was willing to do such things to you. I feel angry, sick and disgusted. The sad thing is – I can't think of myself as that child – what was I like? It seems as though I'm talking about an adult, but it's not; it's perhaps a 9- or 10-year-old. Oh my God – that such a small boy could do such things. You have an awful lot to answer for.

And the smell, the smell of the house and of the blankets on your bed – always blankets next to the skin. Thank God for continental quilts. I hate blankets. I've noticed it's something that old and dirty men have – beds with blankets that are not covered with sheets – yuck!

And I remember having 'after sex' chats – you were my only confidante weren't you and I really valued that and the affection. I remember telling you how odd and shameful I felt after ejaculating, ha! And asking if you felt the same – no, you didn't really understand did you? I remember you telling me about 'homos' who did it because they liked it with men – but you weren't a 'homo' and nor was I. You were just teaching me so that I'd know what to do with a woman. I remember my puzzlement – 'cause by then I'd worked out that that was what was happening – we were 'homos' together – the fact that it was incestuous added to the guilt but seemed only secondary. You bastard, you did that to me. You sexualised me so early, you programmed me to do sexual things for you – you used me (among others).

You took away trust, childhood, fun, my parents, and my other grandparents. You stopped me from having any real friends as a child. You evil bastard. I had no one but you.

And when I was older – during my secondary school days – a teenager; 'Mike was so good to his Grampy.' I used to go to spend evening with you, listening to classical music – so everyone thought! Well, the music was there but I was going for the sex. This is the worst part of it all – I wanted it, sought it out – it makes me want to vomit with shame and disgust.

And all this time when other boys were beginning to explore their sexuality – you deprived me of that too. What should have been a gradual awakening in my teenage years had happened to me, in its perverted, strange way, years before. You sick bastard.

So I worked at school – no sport, no fighting, but I used my intelligence as an escape. Oh, how jealous and frightened I was of the other boys who seemed to be able to use their bodies as they wanted – to run, to play rugby, to fight, to change and shower without shame. While I cowered in a corner, avoided what I could and endured humiliation of my own making when I couldn't avoid; and I got fatter.

And when I went to College, away, to London – release. I 'finally' put it down. I went to confession and confessed *my* homosexuality (as I saw it then) and my incest. How so, so, sad – but it was positive – I did feel better. I assumed I must be gay. I felt jealous of those around me who were enjoying their sexuality – of all varieties. But of course I was paralysed – it didn't apply to me. I mixed and made friends among the safe girls, Vicky and the Christian Union set – they weren't likely to engage me in any sexual feelings.

Of course I didn't really mix, I didn't live in Hall but in those sad, sad bedsits. My sex life was just obsessive, unhealthy masturbation with no release.

I had no joy from my years in London – it should have been the best time of my life. I had no fun, few friends; I was lonely, lonely, and sick of myself.

And what about Tessa – poor girl? She was my attempt at proving that I wasn't gay! I feel so sad and ashamed now. I felt sorry for her – pregnant, face like the back of a bus, strange home life. (I wonder – it's just struck me – she seemed almost as new to it as me; who was the father of her child?) Anyway – I remember going to talk to one of the curates to ask if it would be right to go out with her. He wondered why I didn't talk to my parents about it and was surprised at the vigour of my reaction! So we 'went out' – the odd kiss but otherwise very virginal! I took her home and remember Dad's horrified question: 'Should we consider her as a potential daughter-in-law?' I think it was my enjoyment of that which finally decided me to ask her to marry me!

Oh, I'm so sorry about that. I really meant it – we even had a bit of heavyish petting – which reassured me a bit. But then she came up to College (to see me in a production of Pirates of Penzanze!) and I put together the two separate parts of my life and I felt sick – so I broke it off. I told her that I was gay and we couldn't get married. She said we should work it out but I said: 'No.' I used the gay excuse, and I thought it was true at the time. Poor Tessa – I hope she's happy now. I didn't love her, but I was totally kack-handed about the whole thing.

And you did that to me you bastard! By taking away my sex life, my parents, my social skills – you spoiled me, you evil old queer.

So no College romances for me. Sexual abuse still wasn't on the agenda and I still hadn't made the connection.

In my house job I had to come out of my shell – I had to work closely with others. That was good. It was good to work with the other House Officers, it was good to be helped and respected by the staff and especially one particular physiotherapist – the one with the long hair and bubbly personality. The one who worked so hard and was such fun. The one I fell in love with and wanted – for herself, for her smile, because I fancied her like mad. The one who flattered me by wanting me in return, who got angry when I wouldn't have sex with her, who even said yes when I asked her to marry me. Strong Ellen who could do anything, face up to anyone. I was so proud – but it couldn't work – wasn't I supposed to be gay? Look what had happened with Tessa. So I told her, I told her I wasn't a virgin and that I had had sex with a man – that was enough for me to handle. She didn't reject me – I was so happy that I skipped along the Common (discreetly).

And sex with Ellen – wow – this was how it was meant to be. But you Bastard, you crept into that didn't you – read the lesson at the wedding – puke, puke. You two-faced evil old poof.

And all that evil, all that shame and guilt and stolen childhood and stolen adolescence, all those stolen feelings and lost parentage – all of that came with me into our marriage. You spoiled it, you bastard.

The fear and anger and inability to assert myself – the sheer despair – that came too didn't it? I am so angry about this. This is the real huge anger I have with you – evil bastard.

But I repressed it all away and things carried on.

Then came that day when I was towelling little Judy after a bath and she said I'd rubbed her wee-wee. Well, it was of course totally innocent but I was devastated by it – and I think it was from then that I began to realise that what had happened to me was child sexual abuse. By now it was being discussed and aired in public. But of course it was all about abusing little girls. I had to make my own connections – or rather fail to make most of them.

And of course I felt abused by Ellen as the marriage went on from bad to worse. I see that this time was an awful lot to do with my own repressed abuse. It must have been awful for her – it certainly was for me.

And so eventually I told Ellen that I'd been sexually abused as a child and left it at that. She guessed of course by whom, and was very angry – anger to fear again. You got everywhere you Bastard didn't you?

And I felt abused by medicine, the patients, the government, etc., etc. Probably to an extent I was right; but also some of it is to do with my own abuse by you – bastard.

And then more and more damage in the marriage. I blame you for 90 per cent at least – you evil old queer, you bastard – probably more. Rock bottom – could it get any worse? Back to obsessional masturbating, back to suicidal thoughts and plans – this time with all the means at hand. I even collected enough pethidine to do the job. Only Ellen saved me from that I think, as from divorce.

Then that devastating afternoon at Stephen's. My heart stood still and my chest tightened up when Stephen took me to one side and confirmed what I'd been trying not to accept for all those years. It made me so angry with you, bastard, I wanted to burst.

It was so good to be able to tell Stephen about it, although it was painful to hear his story; and especially painful to see his overwhelming reaction.

I knew things were coming to a head; Ellen was getting edgy at 'secrets'. I was so pleased when Stephen tracked down Kim, for him, yes, but also because here was someone 'safe' that I'd get round to talking to.

What a relief to acknowledge my anger towards Dad; what a relief to show Ellen that letter – the most I've done so far. What a comfort for me to have felt as I felt towards Grandma as I wrote this today.

What you did was evil, it has made me chronically angry and afraid. But I do not care anymore. You cannot hurt me unless I consent to go on being angry and afraid. I do not consent and I am going to try hard as I can to keep on this road towards healing.

I know that I need Ellen to read this one now. I'm frightened of this but I think I must do it. For I do love her and I don't think things will be right until I share this properly with her.

(I showed the above to Ellen and sat by her as she read it. I was terrified – but she was supportive – I felt guilty that I allowed myself to think that she wouldn't be.)

Thank-you,

thank-you,

thank-you

Emotionally it was electric, riding the roller coaster from numbness into pain and back over again. Years and years worth of anger came up, as I was contained and enabled (just) to feel safe with it by the therapy. As I read some of the written exercises that I undertook at the time, pages and pages of anger at my abuser, and at my father for failing to notice or provide me with healthy affection, I remember the distress of it all. We actually had a fist fight on one occasion which I describe in my next diary entry written three weeks after the last one. My father's life was exploding in his face too, as we discovered yet more of his family members had been victims of the same man, his father. This next letter was written three days before my third session with Kim on her return from holiday.

7.10.95

Well, a lot of water has passed under the bridge!

Ellen was getting angrier and angrier that I had managed to vent my anger towards Dad but that she hadn't. So with a great deal of trepidation on my part we arranged for Stephen to babysit and we went to Mum and Dad's.

Ellen had hardly begun to sound a bit angry when Dad started to wag his finger and bully – just like the old days.

To my continuing surprise I told him to stop bullying my wife; he then stood up and came towards her, finger still wagging. When I stood and confronted him, angrily telling him that I would not be bullied by him any more, he grabbed my throat and started to strangle me, then pushed me, breaking my specs and toppling me into Ellen. Again to my surprise, I landed a punch on him and then managed to wrestle him to the ground and hold him there. Eventually he seemed to calm and I let go, having promised to leave if he did.

As we went to leave he seemed to acquiesce, then slyly pushed Ellen into the door frame calling her a cow (and treading on her foot, it afterwards transpired). I made a move toward him and he actually ran from me! He was cornered in the dining room and I called him a bastard (my favourite new word!) and screamed at him that he was pathetic and that he reminded me of his father! He seemed to shrink at this and we left – bloodied and broken glasses – heading for Stephen's.

He rang Stephen and gave his version of events and to say he was leaving Mum, which was all my fault!

So Stephen and I went to try and comfort Mum – spent hours there going over and over the same old ground, i.e. Dad was bound to tell 'the family' – which was all my fault; that 'the family' would be split and divided – which would be my fault; that other families would have to go through this distress – which would be my fault; that she would be rejected by 'the family' – which would leave her with no one – and that would be my fault also.

Pointless it seemed to reiterate that if Dad chose to 'tell' that would be his responsibility and that the one person responsible for all the pain was the abuser! But we seemed to part as friends – hugs. I felt shaken and damaged, but also quite elated that I had stood up to him and even physically overpowered him – who had always laid stress on 'manly' things like fist-fighting. Ellen a great comfort – a tower of strength.

Next day we hear that he has driven down to see Jack who is terribly ill as a result – all my fault.

Has also told Adam who 'knows all about that sort of thing through counselling members of his church'. Dad has sworn him to secrecy – even from his wife! At least he is back home with Mum!

Mum rings me (!!) after a couple of days – supposedly at Dad's suggestion – an olive branch? But same old circular conversation – they just seem oblivious to our feelings.

I am beginning to feel overwhelmed by what has happened – sad and helpless.

Then Helen and Jim are back from holiday. Mum rings briefly to tell me they've had a conference and yes, two of Dad's siblings have admitted to being abused – names no names but thought I ought to know!

Helen rings – more support and concern from her in 5 minutes than ever from my parents! Candidly admits to having also been a victim and also that her fiancé (now husband) had been 'woken by advances' neither having disclosed to the other before this. Both children know within hours. All v. positive and promises of support for Mum and Dad and (warning bells) family solidarity.

Helen also names Jack as the other admitted victim.

Positive couple of days I suppose, various and varying reports coming in.

I now know of admissions of abuse or attempts at abuse by my paternal grandfather of three of his five children plus his daughter's fiancé; myself and Stephen; two other male cousins (not brothers) – one of whom witnessed the other, the second of whom is reported to have declared himself as 'in the clear'! Three other male cousins have said no, three female and one other male cousin have not been asked – so far eight admissions.

I strongly suspect Dad was a victim or knew (his ready acquiescence to my initial request and seeming knowledge that 'Gramps had let me down'; also his anger and attempts at denying (wanting to hide it).

Stephen says that Adam (for all his supposed expertise) looks deathly and is refusing to ask his children and also – he was present in the house for many of our sessions during our late teens.

I would also worry about Nancy my cousin – her angry chaotic relationships. Everyone in the 'family' is adamant that she mustn't be spoken to – 'in case her mother finds out'. That would be 11 – I wonder how many more?

I am relieved, but very, very sad at waking people to their pain.

I ring home 'spontaneously' (!) and Dad answers: 'How are things, how are you?'

'That depends on whether you retract those awful things you said.' It suddenly dawns on me how important for both of us is that likening of him to his father. Can I retract it? When I said he looked like his father he'd been 'abusing' me and Ellen, physically and emotionally. He'd been sly, he was running scared; he was cornered.

'No. That was how I felt that night.'

'So you say I'm like him – a dirty evil old man?'

'That's how it felt Dad.'

'Well, that's it – our relationship is now over.'

Mum comes to the phone. Helen and Jim are there and they agree it is to spread *no further* – keep it in the 'family'. Bang! Feeling good about Helen just burst like a balloon.

I explain that Dad has cut himself off from me, not the other way round. She says she won't be able to see our children. I insist yes, if she wants to come she will be welcome – usual circular conversation.

I am gutted. Everything is exploding in my face. Ellen is angry.

I feel that people may be right to blame me for opening all this up – although in my head I know I have acted with good intent.

Stephen a tower of strength as usual. I am worried about him taking responsibility for this mess and trying to carry people.

I come in from a call next morning to find Ellen on the phone to Mum.

'Don't tell me not to tell my parents and not to be angry.'

I take over – usual round and round. All this before work at 8 am! I must have been quite short with her.

Amazingly helpful telephone conversation with my cousin James, who has also been helpful to Ellen. Says he is really relieved that its all come out and has healthy fears about his father and brother (Clive and Jerry). Sensible, open. What a good man – wants to meet. I hope I can open up a relationship with him as I have with Stephen

And now tonight Stephen has recounted his conversation with Mum, in which she said she'd decided to have no more to do with me or my family and that she appeared to have gone over to Dad's attitude. Stephen also says he perceives a slight unbending of Dad's attitude towards him. OK. I accept this quite calmly, but when Stephen has gone I start to feel devastated again – how many more rejections can I take?

Ellen is furious – eventually rings and snaps out to Mum that in her opinion they are making victims of our children too! Good for Ellen!

Can I stand much more of this?

I suppose I had been lucky in my first few disclosures. Then the second round of people – Stephen helpful +++; James helpful +++; Helen helpful but reported to have changed. The rest of the family (uncles and aunts) anti – reportedly; the curate also anti – reportedly – that was a real downer! And old family friend Wendy reported to agree with Mum – worse!

I suppose I'm still lucky. When I write it down the balance is not bad. But this is my fear all along – fear of rejection and blame. I am frightened of it still. I do feel isolated.

But when you look at it logically I wasn't on more than nodding terms with any of the family before was I? So I've gained Stephen and James. Can I have lost Wendy? Probably not, but I need to speak to her to find out – dare I?

The curate – well, a downer from a churchman after trying to defend the church to Stephen (and potentially to Kim). I suppose he always was a bit of a reminder of Dad! A victim or abuser? Possible I suppose. School for sinners not rest home for saints!

How much evil did this man cause? I am still angry with him, but in a calm and historical sort of way. My present and ready anger is for my parents, my father in particular, and the 'family'. This latter is probably still quite unreasonable – it's new to them, they must be in a severe panic about discovery – OK. I think it all comes back to Dad (and Mum).

They've had this for a year now – and have offered me *no* support at all. It's apparently my fault that Dad has told his siblings, my fault that he, and now Mum have cut themselves off from me and mine. Where is their much valued love and support which I am supposed to be rejecting?

This makes me feel angry, and very sad, and very, very lonely. Also it makes me frightened of disclosing again – it's made me realise how much it opens me up to hurt!

I was sexually abused, I do not consent to let him hurt me any more.

I am angry at all the damage it's causing.

I am angry that he has obviously abused others.

But all this is minor compared with the anger I feel towards my parents for their rejecting behaviour now. I try to understand and it must be hard for them, but I was their son, my children are their grandchildren (!).

In a way, now that I've written that I feel more at peace. If my parents have cut us off, so be it – we start from there. God is good. I have to acknowledge my own imperfections and continue to work at life.

I love Ellen and the children very much and I am so sorry that my anger spills over onto them. I love Stephen and I am so grateful for his support. I hope some good will come of the pain for everyone. I believe it will.

The next letter was written between sessions 6 and 7.

12.11.95

Time goes by, but I don't!

I was feeling better – things calm. Mum and Dad quietly out of the picture and myself quite calm and accepting of that.

Tired working long hours and weekends on call. One partner off sick with a hernia repair.

Kim challenging – 'I may have worked through my anger but haven't really started on my fear.' I don't want to hear this. She, like Stephen, wants me to watch that TV programme called 'The choirmaster' which is a documentary about boys abused by a choirmaster. I don't. I am afraid. I don't want to give up my sense of being in control.

So yes, I admit I am afraid.

I watch the film when everybody is in bed. I am frightened as Julian walks into the cathedral and starts his story. I feel really scared. As the programme progresses I feel so, so sad.

Sad at the pain of those men they interviewed – but strangely I find it difficult to see the pain of the boys. Why is it so much easier to be sad for others? So sad, that those young adults have such pain, admiring that they are so open, and afraid, afraid for myself – could I ever be like that?

Angry at the Dean who says 'things like this happen' – here is the curate's attitude again.

Angry and very frightened at how much the abuser looks like me! How can I stand this, I want to get off this ride now.

And then I am filled with pain at the supportive remarks of the bereaved father (his son committed suicide as a result of his abuse) Why can't I have this from my father?

So I watch it again, *twice*! Lingering on the pain of the young adults and skipping over the scene of the abuser. Fear and pain – this is what I am left with.

Kim is right – I don't show my pain – ironically Mum has said it too now. How can I learn to do it?

Over the next few days, fear comes more and more to the fore. I really am shit scared and have been for years. Why must I live my life in fear?

I feel quite pressured by all this. But still I don't show my pain. I'm just at the point of taking time off but pull back from the brink after the practice meeting! So much trouble for the others, but still fear for me! I can't see it working without all of them knowing.

I try to plug away at monitoring my feelings and transactions – it's not very easy.

I am trying to say how I feel and take responsibility for it myself – the others are a bit non-plussed but we're surviving so far. I am trying to keep on with the Adult–Adult transactions with Ellen. I'm not sure about Judy – probably I'm too much Adult–Adult and not enough Parent–Child. She still ends up as the butt of people's angry but misplaced feelings. I must try to persevere.

I must try to make time for this without sacrificing quality time with Ellen, Judy and little Rob. I was sexually abused as a child. I am determined to face up to this. It has left me angry – which I think I have partly worked out of me – although not that regarding my parents. It has left me chronically afraid, so scared. I have yet to work this through. It has left me hurting and in pain. I am so good at hiding all this. I have to make a conscious effort to notice my feelings and express them. This is new to me. God help me to persevere.

So the problems that I took to therapy were, as I remember, mostly about present difficulties with present relationships – with my wife, my children, my parents, my colleagues, my patients, my parents-in-law, my self and my God.

At an intellectual level it was a cause of huge wonderment that all those ideas that I had pecked at in my reading of psychology could seem real and applied to me! It was a truly blinding revelation to be led to see that I had been truly unable to recognise, quite apart from express, my own feelings. It sounds so simple and yet it represents so much blood, sweat and tears for both my therapists and me.

In parallel with the counselling I was doing bodywork. It sounds so ridiculous to speak of hitting cushions and wrestling with blankets, shouting, raging in a room until the windows were steamed up, but it has been a vital part of my recovery. Here I was also able safely to express the anger I felt towards my wife, recognising how mutually abusive our relationship had been.

And the sadness: I was mourning for my childhood, my spoiled relationships, for the all-pervasive loss in my life, for all the love that I needed and yet had never felt. Thirty years' sadness in a few weeks, that's a pretty tough endeavour. I wrote this poem with my therapist's encouragement:

Plea

Love?
What is love?
How do I know,
Who can show me?

The child strangled, tangled, wrung and wrought in wrong.
Where is the child?
Who knows?
He is where? He is where he is, there in the lap of evil.

Who cares but himself,
And where is himself, where is he, where?
Who can love this strange bewildered thing, this thing, this plaything of sin?
Who knows what is love for such a twisted spoiled
and frightened piece of human flesh?

What is love,
What is there,
Where is what is,
How can he be free?

O my son, my son what has been done to you is done.
I love you now as I always did,
Since the moment you were and came to be.
And who made it so, that you came to be,
And came to what you came to and came to know?
I made it that you came to be, and my creation was despoiled by wrong,
But my making was not wrong.

I too know pain my son.
You and I with tears to shed,
And will they be seen, and will they be heard?

I know of beautiful beginnings shamed, creation marred,
I know betrayal,
I know of love's waste.
I know what it is to be used and discarded.
Let me introduce you – 'my son, my Son'.

To ask me to trust is inordinate.
How do I know these angels to be yours?
Only by trusting, risking.

But my son, love is here nevertheless,
available.
I am love known through pain.
Can you grasp the hand?
It is enough, it will have to do.

And then of course, the fear; I still remember vividly the session in which gently, I was led to understand just what was meant by existential fear, and to own it for myself.

The fear had a very practical consequence. I was desperately in need of taking time out of work in order to deal with my past, yet how does a doctor 'go on the sick' while retaining privacy from his colleagues? There is too a culture of 'grin and bear it' among the medical profession which is far from healthy for us, or for our patients, although it seems expected of us by society at large. Well, after much soul searching, and nagging by my counsellor, I did take the plunge and allow myself some space. The courage it took to implement will only ever be known to me.

At the time I justified so much hard emotional work as being a gift to my wife and my children, in so far as I was trying to save the marriage. Well it was that, but as I look back, now that my wife and I have separated, it was of course for me; although certainly our children have received a huge benefit from it. Perhaps that may seem selfish for an adult to spend so much energy on himself, but I was working to recover what I should have done and received as a child.

Postlude

Putting down therapy was quite hard, a bereavement in a way, but it was also like growing up and leaving home. Life has been a lot richer, more exciting, more real, since then. It has not been pain free.

I now have a very close relationship with my brother; it is great to have recovered that from the ruins of our childhood. I have never felt closer to my parents, especially my father. They have been able to proffer, and I have been able to allow, much support and parenting.

What has really amazed me is the number of adults whom I come across in my day-to-day practice of medicine, who have also been victims and are survivors of sexual abuse. Men as well as women. It seems that I have added to my task; for if you are open to listen and accept, then people will tell of their pain. It is a rewarding, if painful, part of my work; but who am I to deny them what was denied me for so long (I hasten to add that I do undertake supervision).

A word of thanks to all who have helped me. I know my therapists are reluctant to accept my characterisation of them as angels, but so I believe they have been for me – messengers of hope on the journey of life.

Coda

I was sexually abused by my grandfather from a very early age; I can give a terminus ante quam of five years. The abuse was always in a 'caring' context, and involved masturbation, oral genital contact and anal penetration. He manipulated this into mutuality when I was about six years old. I was unable to break free of this until my late teens. He rewarded me with affection and the small treats of childhood; he rewarded himself by taking me on special holidays with him. He was, to the world at large, a caring and respected member of the community. My brother and I have counted at least eight other members of our extended family of both sexes who have disclosed some sort of abuse by him. We can think of several more family members with whom we have lost touch who fit into the category of 'probable', not to mention the many others with whom he had contact. And we each thought we were 'special'.

PART TWO

The Counsellor's Story

My wound evokes your healer. Your wound evokes my healer. My wound enables me to find you with your wound where you have the illusion of having become lost. (Remen 1993 quoted in Frank 1995, p.83)

CHAPTER 4

The Iceberg
A tale of therapy

Once upon a time, in a place at the end of the earth, there lived an iceberg. The iceberg was quite a small one; part of a much larger one from which she had broken away and floated free in the cold water.

Sometimes she found herself bumping up against other icebergs but she learned to steer clear after a particularly painful bump during a patch of stormy weather. On the whole she managed to stay out of trouble, watching the weather carefully and adjusting her course to suit the conditions. She was weary and lonely and wanted to find a place where she could be with other icebergs who wouldn't hurt her and where she could relax a bit.

Now we all know about icebergs and how the part that shows above the water is only a very small part of the whole. This particular iceberg was bright on the surface and when the sun shone on her, she sparkled and twinkled and danced about on the water, bobbing up and down as if she didn't have a care in the world. This was the part that showed above the water, but below there was a great weight of ice into which lots of debris had become frozen. All the flotsam and jetsam of her own and other people's lives had become entangled and was firmly lodged into this heavy submerged part; it was slowly dragging the shiny tip of iceberg right under the water. Steering herself had become more and more difficult and dangerous.

Then one day the iceberg found a small sheltered bay on the edge of the land and she floated into it without even realising where she was going. She just felt she was safe at last and able to stop worrying about bumping into other icebergs for a while. She rested herself and basked in the warmth of the sun that shone on her. When night time came she thought that tomorrow she would find that she had floated out again into the dangerous waters and every new day, when the sun came out again, she marvelled at it and wondered if it could possibly last. And it did.

After some time, she really began to trust in the constancy of the sun and found that she didn't need to worry about it any more. Sometimes a cloud passed in front of the sun but it soon passed and afterwards the sun seemed all the warmer by comparison.

The longer she stayed in the sheltered bay, the warmer the water became, and then a strange thing began to happen. The edge of the ice beneath the water began to melt, freeing *some of the debris trapped in it. Every day the sun shone and the ice melted a little more. The iceberg watched in amazement as bits floated to the surface; she realised that these were parts of herself that had been submerged for a long time, causing her to feel so heavy, dragging her down. She began to understand why things had been so difficult for her and she was glad to watch the rubbish drifting away into the wider waters.*

The sun's warmth had also changed the bit of the iceberg that showed above the water. The great deep jagged clefts etched down her sides had been smoothed away by the great rivers of water that streamed down her as she watched the debris floating to the surface. The tip of the iceberg, instead of becoming smaller, had actually become larger as more of herself showed above the water, freed of the entanglements.

This affected the iceberg in different ways. At first she found it hard to recognise herself and she wondered if the other icebergs would know her, or if they would notice a change in her. She wondered if her new size would cause her problems when she went back into the wider waters and if she would be able to steer clear of the other icebergs in quite the same way. But then she realised that now that she was bigger she would not need to be so fearful of being bumped or hurt and being free of the debris she would be able to steer more easily and have more choice about the directions in which she moved. She was less likely to be dragged down or tipped over, even if she did occasionally bump into other icebergs. She began to feel more whole, as though the part below the water was less separate from her.

Although there were still some bits of rubbish frozen into her submerged parts, at least she knew they were there and how they might affect her and that in time they too might work free and float away. Now it may seem that all this happened a little too easily but it was not so. Whilst the iceberg basked in the sun after first finding the sheltered bay, there was a lot of turbulence beneath the surface and the iceberg was very anxious, not knowing exactly what was going on down below. At times she was frightened of the degree of agitation in the waters and wondered if she would be able to maintain her balance. But all the time the sun kept shining and that reassured and comforted her and made her feel that whatever was going on beneath the waters, all was still well up above.

When the ice had melted enough to free the debris, the disturbed particles began to hurt as they broke free and the pain was worse as the icy numbness dissolved away. The iceberg was dismayed when she recognised some of the debris that had floated to the surface; bits she didn't want to see; bits she had forgotten she had picked up on dark and stormy nights; bits she was frightened about and with which she had wished she had never come into contact. But she had to admit, they were all parts of her, whether she liked them or not. And the sun still shone.

The sun shone on the good bits and the sun shone on the bad bits; somehow that made the iceberg feel as though things couldn't be so bad after all. Some of the bad bits didn't belong to her at all, but were parts of the larger iceberg from which she had broken away. As the debris floated in the water around the iceberg and the sun shone on them, she was able to look at them more closely and see how they had been harming her. She allowed herself to feel angry about the bits that had been attached to her by others and that she had thought were hers. She had always realised something was there, weighing her down, but she had not known what to do about it. Some of the rubbish might even be quite useful, like lots of flotsam washed up on the shore; useful at another time, in another place. It had made her the shape she was and now her shape had changed to something that was much more her own.

The iceberg looked out towards the wider waters and wondered if it was time to risk herself out there. She knew the sun that warmed her would still be shining down on her and that it did not only shine on the sheltered bay. She still needed the sun and the wind and the rain in order to be fully aware of living, experiencing and growing.

She felt the breeze stirring around her, tugging gently at her and she let herself go, with new hope and courage, out into the wider waters.

(Written in 1987)

CHAPTER 5

Beginnings

The Wounded Healer

Even now as I read 'The Iceberg' I am put in touch with the powerful feelings I experienced as I lay in bed writing it. It was after a period of illness that had kept me bed-bound during an intensive period of working with my first counsellor. Our relationship was ending. My body had carried my repressed memories and dissociated feelings for 47 years and throughout those years the only way I had known how to allow myself to rest or be cared for was by becoming ill. It was easier for me to say: 'my body is hurting' than it was to say: 'my heart is breaking'. But I had begun to remember – to reconnect with myself – and I was disorientated, vulnerable and in the fragile process of changing.

I had never before allowed myself to experience the warmth and love of 'unconditional positive regard' or been in a relationship in which I felt accepted and challenged with respect and understanding. Looking back I realise that I *had* been loved for who I was (by my husband and children), but I had never allowed myself to *experience* that love. I had built a wall of ice around the painful memories of my childhood – that wall was successful in numbing my pain, but had kept me from allowing in the warmth I needed from other human contacts. I had become very good at presenting a 'false self' – a self that I believed was acceptable to others but was of great cost to my real self. I was very confused! I had believed that if somebody knew the *real* me they would reject me; and in my counselling relationship that hadn't happened. I had thought that if somebody did not like my behaviour towards them, they would not be able to like any part of me; that hadn't happened. I had thought that if somebody became angry with me, then I would disintegrate entirely and I would lose them forever; and that didn't happen either.

But I was about to lose my counsellor. The relationship was ending and it was not of my making. How would I cope with losing somebody who had become so important and so precious to me? I coped with the intolerable feelings in the way that I knew best – I became ill.

But this time it was different – during that illness I began to heal myself. I had let go, surrendered my control and opened myself to the possibility that crisis could be a source of change and growth. Deep down I began to know, to experience and accept myself. However, I still did not know how to communicate any of that, either to myself or to those around me and least of all to my counsellor. So I wrote about an iceberg.

Metaphors can be powerful means to healing (Frank 1995). I have never forgotten the power of that story and the important part it played in my journey. Looking back on that day I have understood that, during the writing, I was touching an unclear 'felt sense' by 'focusing', as Gendlin describes it (1996), and experiencing the creation of meaning. I had gone inside my body to a space that had been created by my illness, to a place of 'tacit knowing' (Moustakas 1990) – the source of my 'self' that had guided me, almost blindly, through my life, to this place and time. I had reached within and found the potential to heal myself. I had found and integrated an experience of 'self'. Only then was I able to experience real healing. Bays (1999) says:

> Once you learn what the disease or physical block has to teach you and you finally let go of the emotional issues stored in the cells, then, and only then, can real healing begin on all levels – emotional, spiritual and physical. Only then does the body go about the process of healing itself naturally. (Bays 1999, p.45)

It was only recently, through reading Campbell's description (1972) of the hero's journey, that I discovered that I had travelled a well-documented route, with a sound narrative structure. Such a journey is made to find out the *nature* of the journey one is making. He describes three phases of the journey:

1. The departure – which is characterised in 'The Iceberg' by the drifting away from the larger iceberg at the beginning stage of letting go of denial and the first steps to awareness that something is not OK.

2. The initiation – which may only be recognised on reflection at the journey's end, when we have come to the beginning again and are now prepared to know the place (T.S. Eliot). This stage tells of transformation and the receiving of a 'boon' – something that the traveller has been given by undergoing the journey, such as an insight that may be passed on to others.

3. The return – the storyteller is no longer 'ill' but still carries the mark of the 'illness' and has new knowledge. The 'hero' is not characterised by slaying dragons but rather through the initiation phase of awareness of their own suffering, and an integration of the experiences that have caused the suffering. The 'hero', in that process, strengthens their sense of being 'at one' with themselves, with the world and with 'its principle of creation' (Frank 1995).

Returning to the world from which we have been separated can be frightening – we might wonder if it is possible to go back in our changed state and still feel part of it. These fears are expressed in 'The Iceberg' and are echoed in Stephen's story, when he wonders how he might respond to work colleagues on his return to the workplace. They will want to know about his absence. How can such a journey be explained superficially and understood by others who may not have travelled such a road?

This process of suffering and 'atonement' is not always recognised by 'significant others' as something to be celebrated. The 'boon' may be hard to recognise by those nearest and dearest who may find they are caught up in the change process – unwittingly and unwillingly. Stephen's story too is a 'quest narrative'. His time out during the three months he describes in his diary marks a period of fundamental change. In an interview with me, as we reflected back over his diary, he says:

> 'It's been a long journey – lots of things have happened; going through the healing process has changed me dramatically. I think I am more alive, more feeling and understanding – more of a whole person – a lot more tolerant of others. I think I am less staid, less rigid. Life's better in lots of ways, but it's more difficult in lots of ways, because changing so drastically has coloured relationships. I still feel I'm on the journey, I'm not at the end of it and I think I never will be.'

Having returned, and having accepted the 'boon' of knowledge and insight, we desire to pass this on to others. Others need the boon for the journeys they will undertake. In passing it on we bear testimony to our journeys, through writing, speaking or telling our stories. We reach out in order to be there to guide and support others upon their way.

My own journey continues. Almost eight years after writing 'The Iceberg' and after years of further therapy of different kinds, further training, research and experience of working with abuse, I met Stephen and Mike. So I came to this work with an awareness of my own wound – no longer hurting in the same way, but 'bearing the mark'. I came also with my 'boon' to offer and to pass on to others as encouragement. The awareness of my wound resonated when I read Stephen's letter and made it possible for me to empathise with his raw pain; the 'boon' was my ability to bear his distress and walk steadily alongside him on his journey.

The concept of the wounded healer is familiar to many of us who enter the field of counselling. Nouwen (1994a) suggests that what we offer others is a form of hospitality. Hospitality, he says, is the ability to pay attention to the guest: 'It requires first of all that the host feel at home in his own house, and secondly that he creates a free and fearless place for the unexpected visitor' (p.89). Those who choose to visit us need to come to us on their own terms – without our need to impose ourselves upon them with 'intrusive curiosity':

> When we have found the anchor places for our lives in our own center, we can then be free to let others enter into the space created for them and allow them to dance their own dance, sing their own song and speak their own language without fear. (Nouwen 1994, p.91)

And it is from this centred place that we may truly *meet* another and make an assessment that will help us to form a therapeutic relationship.

Client Assessment

My assessment began when I read Stephen's letter. There are certain questions I ask myself when considering working with a client on issues related to sexual abuse. The most important questions are about readiness and the availability of other support. It was very clear from Stephen's letter that he was ready. But he may *not* have been ready before Mike's disclosure to their mother and his mother's subsequent question, 'Did it happen to you too?' which catapulted Stephen into a state of crisis when he was forced to face up to his traumatic past. So, yes, he was ready to ask for help and support, but he may not have been ready to work on the abuse. I would have to wait and see. Working with people in crisis usually consists of 'holding' and 'containing' them, until such time as the underlying issues can be worked with. To push somebody into the work at this stage is unhelpful and even, in some cases, harmful. Although Stephen mentioned that he felt 'in crisis', I was also aware that he was able to articulate his thinking clearly and that he displayed considerable insight into his condition. He also spoke of the support that was available to him from his wife and his brother.

Working through sexual abuse, or any childhood trauma, is usually painful and for a while disorientating. Without support the client may open up the past with insufficient resources to deal with it. Part of the assessment must take into consideration the external and the internal resources we perceive in the client's world. Stephen mentioned his work in the letter, giving me an impression that he was probably in some sort of supportive professional role; he used words like 'empathy' that indicated a certain understanding. He wrote about his search for self-help material, giving me the impression that he was somebody who was willing and able to take responsibility for himself. He also indicated a mature acceptance that what he was asking for may not be on offer, and that he would be able to manage my inability to work with him without taking it as a rejection. There seemed to be sufficient available 'adult' for the creation of a working alliance.

This is not to say that I would not work with people who did not display all of the characteristic shown by Stephen; but at the time he contacted me there were certain conditions within my own life that meant I could not guarantee long-term or open-ended work. My assessment therefore also took into consideration the resources I had within myself that I could offer to him.

Self-Assessment

At the time I met Stephen I had recently moved into a flat to live alone for the first time in my life. The last of my three sons had left home, I had spent three years deeply engaged on my research for a Ph.D. and had written the book that had led Stephen to me. I was at a crossroads in my life. As a young woman I had gone straight from my family home into marriage. I had not 'left home' to go to college like most of my contemporaries, but had gone to a local college so that I could remain at home and take care of my mother. Looking back now I realise how ludicrous that was, as she was still in her fifties and perfectly capable of looking after herself. But there was no discussion in the family – just an unspoken expectation that, as the only girl in the family, that was my role. My father had died when I was 15 years old. Most of my older brothers had gone into the Forces and travelled abroad, married and visited home occasionally. Another had gone into the priesthood after completing National Service. I had two younger brothers who left home shortly after I married. And at the time I met Stephen and Mike, 33 years later, I was still very much married to the same person. I needed to find out what it was like to live alone. My family thought I had taken leave of my senses – everybody viewed our marriage as rock solid; my sons were appalled at what I was doing to their father and their own sense of security. But it was the very solidity of my marriage that made it possible for me to do what I needed to do. My marriage had always been a solid container for my growth: a 'secure base'.

I had spent my life surrounded by men. I had seven brothers, a husband and three sons. I had been brought up in an Irish Catholic household where I was trained to meet everybody else's needs at the expense of my own. I had been angry at a society that had indoctrinated me to believe that being a woman was second best. But my research had been very healing of my attitude towards men in general. I had listened to their pain and realised that the same system that had abused me had abused them too. Strict gender roles had cost men dearly, as well as women. Most of them had fathers who were absent, physically and emotionally. Those whose fathers *had* been present did not like what they had known of them; they had been abusive, aggressive and domineering – just as mine had. The men's concepts of what it meant to be male had been damaged and they wanted none of it.

I had listened to the men in my study as they struggled to identify themselves with a maleness in which they took no pride. One participant said:

> 'My father didn't work for me as a role model; if this was what it meant to be a man then I didn't want to be a man. To be abused by other men meant that I didn't know what it was really like to be a man. I did not know what men were, what they were like, and if these three persons were indicative of the adult male then I didn't want to be a man.' (Etherington 1995, p.88)

So when I started working with Stephen, and shortly after with Mike, I was in a state of transition. For the first time in my life I had a bedroom I could call my own. I was able to eat baked beans on my lap in front of the TV if I wanted to, to dance naked to my own choice of loud music if I wanted to, to come in and go out when I wanted to, to answer to nobody. It was terrifying and wonderful, but I did not know how long it would last. I had decided to stay with the chaos and find out what I really wanted for myself.

(20/6/99: I had a dream last night in the middle of writing this section, and when I thought about its meaning, I realised that I had excluded something important about why I needed to live alone at that time. I had spent several years deeply immersed in 25 men's stories of childhood sexual abuse, which is what I needed to do if I was to present a phenomenological study that successfully communicated the experience of abuse for those men. Although I had an academic supervisor, I had no arena in which I could offload some of the distress I felt about the horrific abuses those men had undergone. My own therapy was spent dealing with the events in my personal life at that time. Consequently I believe I suffered 'secondary post-traumatic stress'. I was frequently left with images that intruded into my dreams and even during the day I found myself daydreaming and thinking about some of the painful stories to the exclusion of other thoughts. In qualitative research the researcher needs to become immersed in the work. I began to understand why so little research had been done into male abuse. I was familiar with women's stories but I felt there was a different quality about those told by the men. The other factor was that, as a researcher, I had no way of intervening. If I had been listening to the same stories as a counsellor, I would have been able to stop the client and help him connect with the feelings attached to what he was saying; thereby not taking his disconnected feelings into myself. Many of the men were completely dissociated from the feeling quality of their material; I was not working with a clinical sample, but with ordinary men from all walks of life. Some of them had been in therapy and in those cases my stress was less severe. As a researcher it was not within my remit to make counselling interventions – the stories followed one after the other like an uncontrollable torrent. I had set aside a period during the three summer months to interview the men – this fitted in with my availability as my teaching and client work was reduced at that time. I have asked myself since why I 'abused' myself in that way.

My dream last night helped me to realise that I may also have been re-enacting my childhood role of taking care of my brothers at the expense of not taking care of myself. I believe I was also unconsciously attempting to connect with and heal my wounded 'masculine aspect', my animus (Stevens 1990), which I had not wanted to acknowledge as part of me – my experience of masculinity having been so negative. I believe that many of the men in my study were also attempting to heal their animus)

All this distress undoubtedly affected my personal relationships and, in retrospect, I believe I needed a space in which there was no male energy – at least for a while.)

So my assessment needed to take all that into consideration: could I offer them what they needed in terms of commitment, time, energy, and emotional availability? Was I prepared to admit male clients into this space? I had a room in the flat that was dedicated for the purpose of seeing clients and I decided that I would see Stephen there – at this time I did not know that I would later work with Mike.

Mutuality

Assessment is an ongoing process and not an event; although the assessment began with his letter, my assessment of Stephen went on during the first few sessions of our meeting. Assessment is also a two-way process – clients make their own assessment of us right from the start. I asked Stephen, in an interview for this book, what some of his impressions were when we first met and how he decided I might be the right counsellor for him:

Stephen: Well, there'd been a very frightening process of building up to trying to find somebody to give me some help. At that time I was really worried that if I went to see just anybody it might be somebody I knew and finding your book made you nice and anonymous. It seemed that you obviously knew about the subject, so I was lucky to track you down and then I was just desperate to find you as quickly as possible really, 'cos I don't think I could have carried on much longer. I was on the verge of not functioning, so it was a relief to find you. I was ready for you to refer me to somebody else, because I figured that you might be too important or too high up, having written a book, and being at the University, to have the time – I trusted your judgement that you would tell me somebody to see. I was also quite pleased that you were going see me yourself – so that was a relief as well. I don't think I was really nervous. I was quite in turmoil – my overriding impression when I first saw you was that it was just such a relief to start. I remember that first session going by in what seemed about three minutes – there was so much waiting to come out. I remember the little room and [laughs] the box of tissues.

Kim: What did that feel like when you saw the tissues?

Stephen: I was on the verge of tears anyway, so that sort of gave me more permission – but up to that point I had been someone who didn't really cry. I didn't show any emotion before then. I was all boiling and simmering up to that point really – there was a hell of a lot of stuff waiting to burst forth. I actually felt the endings were quite sharp at the beginning, and I wanted to carry on sometimes – it seemed to go too quickly especially the first ones – there was a few times when we did go on a bit and then it wasn't so bad...

Kim: Yes, and it was really important that you had more at that earlier stage?

Stephen: Yes, once a week would have been too far apart at that stage, definitely.

Kim: So how did you feel when I ended the session when you still felt you wanted more?

Stephen: Erm, I was a bit frustrated, I wanted to carry on 'cos it felt really important to do so – it was making me feel better to spill it out. I was a bit nervous to start with, obviously now and then are two different times and places – I'm a different person now. Then I was embarrassed to talk about such things – I know you're not – but then – it was still very intimate and embarrassing for me to talk about these things, but very quickly I felt at my ease with you.

Kim: How did you manage to feel at your ease so quickly?

Stephen: You put me at my ease.

Kim: How did I do that?

Stephen: By showing empathy and understanding. I felt that you weren't shocked by what I said – I figured from what you said in the book that you had probably been through something similar yourself – so you were coming from the right place. I remember thinking that you could have empathy rather than just sympathy – it was important.

Kim: That is something I'm curious about – if the fact that you think somebody has themselves been a victim – that it makes it easier...?

Stephen: Makes it easier – I don't think it's crucial – I think I would still have carried on if it hadn't been the case. The most important thing that shone out from your book was the fact that you were dealing with men. There was so much written around about female victims and all they seemed to do was decry men even more – blame men for everything, some of them – which made me feel more uncomfortable again. And at the time the fact that you were a woman, not a man, was important as well.

Kim: Why was that important?

Stephen: I didn't really think about it at the time – but I think the fact that the perpetrator in my abuse was a man for a start – I think I find it more comfortable to talk to women about more intimate things...

Kim: Something about trusting women more...?

Stephen: Possibly, yes, yes, or feeling uncomfortable perhaps because the only man I've ever spoken very intimately to was HIM. There is a discomfort about talking to a man. I think I could now, more so than then.

Kim: So the fact that I was a woman, the fact that I seemed to understand – partly because you sensed that I might have also experienced something like it, but also, I seemed to be more aware of how men felt and that I didn't see men only as perpetrators?

Stephen: Absolutely, and also, in my work I had seen quite a few interviews / counselling sessions – the part of me that was still in gear, the bit of my brain that was still working, liked the way you were talking to me, listening – actively listening, not interrupting, being non-judgemental – that made me feel more comfortable. I was saying to myself 'Hey this person is not so bad after all' – 'cos I have seen some really bad things in my time unfortunately.

Kim: So you had that standard in place – that ability to judge...

Stephen: Yes – that fear that I might get somebody terrible who was going to make it worse...

Kim: And you knew the difference? So even though you were so needy then – almost like anybody would have done – there was a part of you that was able to say – 'no just anybody won't do – it has to be the right person'.

Stephen: Yes, that is what drove me to the extent of looking through the bookshop really; the fear of knowing somebody and the fear of it all going badly wrong and making everything worse. I knew it very easily could; and I was on a slippery slope and I was trying to hold on somewhere. Yes, it's a habit of a lifetime I suppose – being cautious and not being found out – not wanting things to go wrong – fear of failure. Yes, the tranquillity of the place you saw me – crossing the Downs – the setting was important – it felt safe and it felt different – all that was very important.

Contracting

The above clearly demonstrates the client's ability, even when in a severe state of distress, to assess the counsellor's suitability for the work, including the sex of the counsellor, her emotional and behavioural style, the safety of the context, the skills and the competence of the counsellor. All these issues had been addressed by me in the first meeting while setting the contract. I had invited Stephen to ask anything he needed to know about me. I asked about his feelings about me being a woman; spelled out my qualifications and training; issues around the limits of confidentiality; and the approach I used in the work, including some of my beliefs and philosophies that underpin my approach.

I see this contracting stage of the counselling process as similar to the stage of informed consent in the research process; the client needs to be informed, as far as it is possible, about what the work entails and the ethical issues that might arise from it. As a humanistic helper I see this as part of an attempt to redress, as far as it is possible, the imbalance of power in the relationship. I noted early on in the assessment process how Stephen had a tendency to attribute power to me, in his perception of what it meant to work in a university and be the author of a book. This became an issue for the work – his self-effacement and his projection of his own power onto others. Being aware, even in the letter, that this might be the case made it all the more important for me to return his power to him from the start and constantly work with myself to be aware of the seductiveness of the power he handed over to me.

Diagnosis

It was clear when I met Stephen for that first session that he was suffering acutely from post-traumatic stress disorder; he met all the diagnostic criteria which I outline in Chapter 8. Stephen described himself as in a 'crisis'. Crisis usually refers to ways in which people respond to certain life events (Murgatroyd and Woolfe 1982). These crises can create danger or an opportunity (the Chinese symbol for the word 'crisis' includes the symbol for danger *and* the symbol for 'opportunity'). If we back away and close down when faced with a crisis, we miss the opportunity to grow and develop through to maturation. But Stephen had no choice; he was faced with a situation that took over his life for several months. This is more accurately described as an acute phase of post-traumatic stress disorder than a 'crisis'.

Friedrich (1995) describes his mental images of the sexually abused boys he treats as 'thin-skinned containers, ready to burst. Sometimes I do not get them until fragments are flying all over the room' (p.116). This is a very good description of how I experienced Stephen when I first met him. Another equally valid image of an abused boy Friedrich uses is 'a walled-off, over-controlled, highly defended, and unavailable boy' who is 'expending a great deal of energy…in order to maintain these brittle barriers' (p.116). This is an excellent description of how I perceived

Mike to be when I first met him. He described himself to me in an interview as 'the walled-in, hermetically sealed client'.

Stereotyping

My assessment of Mike came later, and by that time I had some of knowledge of him through his brother; they had become close through sharing their stories of abuse. I had heard that Mike was supportive, caring, in pain and finding it very hard to ask for help. I knew he was a doctor, a married man and a father. I carried many of the societal expectations of doctors and some mixed personal feelings in response to my experiences of years of ill health and of feeling misunderstood, not listened to, humiliated by, disempowered by and generally uncared for by hospital doctors! However, I also had the experience of having a dear friend, my GP, who had always treated me with love and respect – against which to set all those negative experiences. Some years earlier I had been deeply moved when I read *The Wound and the Doctor* by Glin Bennet (1987), himself a doctor, who wrote honestly about the burden inherent in the assumptions and expectations that society places on members of his profession.

However, in the moment of meeting Mike all previous assumptions fled out of the window. I saw a man in pain, his eyes darted to and fro, unable to meet my gaze, frozen fear etched on his face. All my motherly instincts flooded through me as I led him into the safety of my little counselling room, which he seemed to fill. His body was taut – his voice surprisingly gentle in such a big man. I found myself making a formal assessment – much in the same way as he might take a patient's history. I sensed he needed the familiarity of that routine to feel in control (as much as he could in these circumstances). His language indicated his preference for cognitive communication; he said he needed more than anything to *understand* what was happening to him. He expressed little feeling. He was clearly uncomfortable to find himself in the 'patient's' chair. As the hour went by, I sensed a growing ambivalence – he both longed to be cared for and hated the thought of allowing himself to show any degree of need.

First Impressions

He told me firmly that he had dealt with his abuse and was here to sort out his relationships, particularly with his wife and parents. I sensed a 'keep out' message. I realised I must be about the same age as his mother – something to keep in mind for the future when transference issues might emerge. He had had some experience of family therapy – when his wife and daughter were having difficulty in their relationships, so he had some preconceived idea about therapy. I felt a momentary anxiety about what he might expect of me – I thought my humanistic stance would probably be very different from that which he had experienced. Would he be critical

– expect me to be 'a blank screen'? He used some jargon that seemed to indicate that he had read psychology books – what attitudes might he have about what 'should' and 'shouldn't' happen in therapy?

He was very, very polite to me but underneath I sensed a huge anger, rage, even aggression – not towards me, but carried in his body. He was a big man, I am very small – could I contain him as he began to feel? I know that I am frightened when I sense unconscious, disowned anger; when it is owned and expressed I do not need to fear it. But there was also the matter that I was now living alone – would I be safe? After completing my research study I realised that, at times, I had left myself in unsafe situations; meeting men who were strangers for interview in circumstances that, on reflection, exposed me to potential danger (Etherington 1996). With this new awareness I could be more cautious. Early in our sessions it emerged that my sense had been correct – Mike had been aggressive and even violent on occasions – this behaviour was something that concerned him and he had begun to change it. How could he express his anger assertively and healthily when he was not consciously aware of any feelings?

During childhood sexual abuse the abuser projects his own unbearable feelings of helplessness, humiliation, pain, rage, guilt and terror onto his victim, who then becomes a container for them. It is then the victim who feels helpless, disgusting and dirty; not the abuser. If the victim identifies with these projections they become part of his unconscious life. So getting in touch with his anger will also put him in touch with the internalised abuser. This identification with the abuser may explain why victims often feel no anger towards them. The anger is turned in onto the self or, in turn, projected onto others – often the very others whose support is most needed (Raine 1999).

Readiness and Motivation

However, I recognised that Mike really wanted to work; it had been his efforts that had dispensed with secrecy; and his willingness to face up to the pain of acknowledging the past, in spite of the cost of opening the cupboard full of family skeletons. He had less support than Stephen in that his marriage was difficult and his parents seemed more inclined to expect support *from* him than to offer it *to* him. He wrote of his parent's response when he first disclosed to them:

> To say those words felt as if my heart was being torn from my chest. My father fled the room shouting, 'Oh no!' My mother was, at first, unbelieving. 'You must have misinterpreted.' I found myself, to my horror, explaining fairly bluntly, some of what he had done. I also told her that I thought he might have abused my brother also. Then I could stay there no longer. I simply had to leave. My mother wanted me to help them, but I was just unable to do it.

Even at his moment of greatest need they had wanted him to put their needs before his own. This was something that escalated as time went by.

In a later interview with Mike I heard that he too had been making his assessment of me during our first meeting:

Mike: *And I had read your book.*

Kim: *Yes – so that meant you knew something about me?*

Mike: *Well yes, I suppose I did – erm – but somehow – this is going to sound condescending so I'm sorry about that, but it somehow lent respectability – the fact that you were in print and that you had letters after your name.*

Kim: *Yes, I understand that. So at least you felt you were trusting yourself to someone who had a degree of recognisable competence.*

Mike: *Remembering all the time that I had this fairly heavy load of 'doctors against counselling' type of thing. 'It's all a load of nonsense' – that sort of thing... I don't want to tar the whole profession with the same brush but I had naturally gravitated towards hearing that sort of opinion... because of where I was.*

   [Shared laughter]

Kim: *Because it suited you?*

   [Laughter]

Mike: *Yes – except I look around now at the sort of people who still express it and I think: 'Yes, you believe that because it suits you – not because it's true.'*

Kim: *So what did you feel about me when you met me?*

Mike: *I remember feeling struck by how little you were. I don't think that reflects your physical size, but the fact that emotionally – although I wasn't recognising it – in my fantasy, you had been a huge, parental authority figure that I was going to come to and be a little child with. I'm looking all the time retrospectively aren't I – this is how I now interpret it.*

Kim: *Sure – this is your **now** construction of **then**.*

Mike: *That's right. So I was almost shocked to find that I was a lot bigger than you, which is a bit stupid anyway because – given my size – I'm likely to be larger than most women I would meet.*

   [Laughter]

Kim: *Yes, so that was the first impact – 'Oh gosh she's only little' – so what did that mean to you? I was wondering, if you had this fantasy were you disappointed that I didn't measure up – so to speak.*

Mike: *I think at the time – my fantasy was to have a very parental, large figure who would hold it all for me, so it was a bit scary that you were almost frail, shall we say. And I remember when you disclosed to me, there was a bit more of that frailty – although it was terribly helpful – in the initial stage I thought: 'I wonder if she's big enough to deal with all this.'*

Kim: Yes, and that of course would immediately hook your 'I'd better take care of her or protect her'?

Mike: I know that crept in as time went by – I used to worry about you. But initially... I was much more selfish – much more – I had a feeling my guts were about to come out and I needed somebody there to put them back... So I think that was all about my fear – 'will she be up to it?' I guess it may well have been after the first session – I know there was a point when I thought 'she knows about this' and that in itself giving me a huge sense of relief.
And I guess that first time, we must have talked mostly about me and Ellen, but surely we must have touched on the abuse – and I think you did it very tactfully – the odd sentence dropped in here and there – that's how I remember it.

Kim: I can imagine that's how I would do it with somebody who had 'Keep Out' signs on them [laughter] I would be wanting you to know that it was OK to talk about that here, but I wouldn't have wanted to frighten you off by focusing on it too quickly – but to follow where you were leading.

Mike: Yes and so – I guess it was probably after that first meeting that I thought 'at last' – although I felt I had a huge mountain to climb at least I was in the right place... And with that goes that dumping of my feeling in control.

Kim: Dumping of feeling in control – that you didn't have to be in control?

Mike: No that's not what I mean but erm – [long pause]. It felt very suddenly that I'd gone into being a little boy and that you were the parent who was going to look after me.

Ongoing Evaluation

Assessment becomes evaluation as the process continues. Evaluation allows the client to take his share of responsibility for the process and creates an ongoing structure that ensures that his needs are being met by the counselling. It also enables the empowerment of the client by checking out with him: 'How is this going?' 'What is helpful?' 'What is not helpful?' 'How are you experiencing me in this relationship?' The counsellor has a chance to give direct, intimate feedback about 'How am I experiencing you in this relationship?'

This leads me on to the importance of establishing a therapeutic relationship at the start of the work that becomes the main vehicle for the counselling process.

CHAPTER 6

The Therapeutic Relationship

In this and the following chapter I would like to focus on the relationship. In every relationship there are at least two people and each of those people has many parts to bring to the relationship. We also bring aspects of past relationships into our present relationships. In Chapter 7 I will reflect on transference and counter-transference as it impinges on our 'real' relationships in the here-and-now. In a previous chapter I have written about my own therapeutic journey which played an important part in the formation of myself as a counsellor. My personal journey and my professional journey are inextricably linked, just as my personal self and my professional self are inextricably linked. Who I am in the relationship with my clients is who I am – and whatever is happening in my life cannot be ignored if I am to be fully present for my clients. That is not to say that my own life necessarily intrudes upon the work I do with clients. I believe that the more I am in touch with what might intrude, the less likelihood there is of intrusion. Kaufman (1996) offers an important guideline:

> In my therapeutic relationships, I share only relevant and appropriate aspects from my own life that are already resolved, and only for the client's need, never my own. When a therapist shares current, unresolved conflicts, it burdens the client and misdirects the flow of the relationship. Therapists need to be emotionally available for their clients and not the reverse, just as parents need to be freely giving and genuinely responsive to their children and not the reverse. (Kaufman 1996, p.161)

And who is the client – how did they become the person I meet in the relationship? What developmental factors have influenced how they might relate to me? What do I need to think about in order to attempt to help them form a therapeutic relationship?

Empathy

There is common agreement among workers in the field that the relationship between the client and counsellor is the most important factor in successful outcomes of counselling. Over thirty years ago Truax and Carkhuff (1967) described vital elements in any counselling relationships as accurate empathy, non-possessive warmth and genuineness. These echoed the earlier work of Carl Rogers (1961) who regarded the 'necessary and sufficient conditions for therapeutic change' being concerned with helpers having an attitude of 'unconditional positive regard' towards the client, as well as the client's perception of the relationship as helpful. It is therefore not enough for the counsellor to be empathic, understanding and genuine – the counsellor also needs to be able to communicate those qualities to the client. For communication to occur between two people, both 'selves' need to be present. Rogers (1961) quotes a study based on a behavioural approach in which the therapist 'permits as little of his own personality to intrude as is humanly possible' (p.47) and he explains the ineffectiveness of the work being related to that: 'To withhold one's self as a person and to deal with the other person as an object does not have a high probability of being helpful' (p.47).

So when a client comes to tell his story to a counsellor, he needs to feel empathically understood – to feel that the counsellor is able to imagine something of what it is like to be living his life and can respond to him with empathy. Empathy is not a psychological or emotional experience, nor a psychic ability to get inside the mind of another person, but it is an openness to and respect for the personhood of another (Levasseur and Vance 1993). It is a position we adopt in relation to another that stems from an openness and respect for our own personhood. Frank (1995) quotes a famous passage written by Albert Schweitzer after a period of illness resulting from his internment during World War 1: 'Whoever among us has learned through personal experience what pain and anxiety really are must help to ensure that those out there who are in physical need obtain the same help that once came to him' (p.35).

Empathy is different from identification, which is when we take on the other's pain as if it were our own. Empathy means that we experience the expressed emotion as the *listener*, so that we might accurately understand. In identification those emotions might burden or bias us, but if we cultivate a capacity for curiosity and resonance, we are more likely to be remain sufficiently object and reliable (Halpern 1993). Empathy helps us listen and understand better and therefore enhances our skills of assessment; empathy allows us to disentangle ourselves from some of the emotional reactions that might otherwise threaten our helping role.

Freud rarely referred to empathy in his early works – on the contrary he recommended (Freud 1912) to early psychoanalysts that they should remain 'emotionally cold' and put aside feelings and even human sympathy. However, by 1955 he was recommending that empathy was 'the mechanism by means of which we are enabled to take up any attitude at all towards another mental life' (Freud 1955, p.110). Jung accounted for empathy in terms of projection, when we merge with another and feel their feelings as though they are our own. However, other psycho-analytically oriented therapists began to recognise the healing power of empathy and de-emphasised the importance of gaining insight and understanding (Kohut 1984). Self-psychologists began to recognise that clients' suffering was caused by deprivation and by something going wrong in the course of their development. So the goal of the work became 'mature interdependence' nourished by 'empathic intunement' between the self and the sustaining aspects of the counsellor (Kramer 1993, p.177)

Rogers (1975) described empathy as 'entering the private perceptual world of the other and becoming thoroughly at home in it...you lay aside the views and values you hold for yourself in order to enter another's world without prejudice. In some senses it means you lay aside yourself' (p.2). My view is that we do not lay aside our 'selves', but rather that we have sufficient self-awareness that we can recognise that which belongs to us and that which belongs to the client – thus being able freely to enter into the client's experience without the threat of over-identification.

However, empathy may have its darker side. There may be an appealing, even an addictive quality about intimate attunement with another person (Kramer 1993). This allure often draws people into the helping role whose earlier life experiences have trained them in the ability to a sensitive attunement to underlying cues (I recognise myself in this description). Clients and colleagues alike often describe how, at an early age, they developed the ability to sense atmospheres or moods before they were made explicit. This heightened awareness of things not yet spoken, or even known by the other, may create situations where we might cause excessive discomfort to clients who are not yet ready to know what we may have perceived, or made known to them, in an empathic response. Clients' defence mechanisms may be over-ridden too quickly, causing them to be flooded with exposed negative feelings (Modell 1986). However, we can recognise well-used empathy by the client's response – it may elicit new material for the work and allow the unfolding of deeper levels of communication. Empathy may not always be soothing; sometimes the client will benefit from the challenge and stimulation such responses can evoke, when the challenge is balanced with caring.

Power

Devereux (1967) wrote about the conscious and unconscious motivations underlying the topics we choose to research, and the importance of being aware of and understanding our motivation so as to eliminate unconscious bias. Most counsellors would agree that their motivation for becoming a counsellor was, at least partly, an unconscious way of vicariously seeking self-care; others have written of the unconscious motivation of power seeking in the helping role (Bennet 1987). I would suggest that many people who enter the helping professions are responding to an unmet need of some sort within themselves. Both Stephen and Mike have become helpers – being the helper, as opposed to the one in need of help, may be a way of denying feelings of helplessness and powerlessness. Both of them have cared for those who are ill and those who are old or very young, people they can have a degree of control over and are unlikely to be controlled by. Stephen worked in the prison service when I first met him, caring for and containing people who were considered a danger to society. Inadvertently both men had ended up in potentially abusive systems – something they came to recognise during therapy.

Issues of control and power are likely to be central to the formation of the counselling relationship. A man who presents himself for counselling is potentially handing over power and control to another. He is asking for help, allowing somebody else to be the helper; the potential for abuse is clear and terrifying. And what about me as I accept that power and control and the potential for abuse it brings with it? I have known the passive side of the power dynamic for myself – the potential of the opposite polarity is within me, for every child who has been abused has learned both roles. Will my anger at my male abuser, and the patriarchal society that has formed me, activate the abuser within me? Or will my fear of that possibility hold me back from using my authority and power for the benefit of my clients? How can I help the men to become the powerful people they can be, reclaim their autonomy and recognise power as useful energy that they can choose to use for good or evil – once it is accepted as part of being human?

Trustworthiness

So I enter into the relationship aware, but also not knowing. I need to believe myself to be trustworthy and to have a belief in the ability of my client to be trustworthy. I do not believe I can expect, or should expect, my clients to trust me. People who have been abused in their early years have usually been damaged in their ability to trust. That damage may manifest itself by an inability to trust anybody else, or it may have resulted in their inability to discern who is to be trusted and who is not. The danger in the first position is that they might never allow anybody close enough to care for them, or form an intimate relationship; the danger in the second position is that they may be over-trusting and indiscriminately expose themselves to further abuse. Thus reinforcing their belief that 'people are not trustworthy'.

If I give a client the covert message that I need him to trust me, I am likely to recreate a situation in which he takes care of my needs. A more useful message to give might be that it is not necessary for him to trust me, it is only necessary that I behave in a trustworthy fashion. Honesty and openness are essential elements of trust building, which is part of the recovery process (Sgroi and Bunk 1988). So adherence to contracts made and keeping promises, which are important elements in responsibility and accountability, will also help the development of trust within the relationship.

A child develops trust through attachment with its earliest caregivers. But when that trust is betrayed by those caregivers, it may be more advantageous for the child to deny the pain in order to survive – the greater the degree of dependence, the greater the betrayal. Humans, as social beings, are dependent on relationships and trust. Betrayal violates the basic ethic of human relationships. Although we may recognise betrayal when it occurs, that recognition may be stifled for the greater need for survival (Freyd 1996). A sexually abused child is in a double bind; he needs to trust the caregiver, but to allow himself to 'know' about betrayal is to put himself in danger. To 'not know' is to align himself with the abuser and therefore ensure survival.

Thus we blind ourselves to all sorts of everyday betrayals; we sever our relatedness in order to have relationships. Gilligan (1991) notes that this behaviour is so common that perhaps it is acceptable – even healthy. However, ultimately being separated from parts of ourselves diminishes us (Freyd 1996).

Attachment

It is therefore no wonder that 85 per cent of abused boys (and girls) are 'insecurely attached' (Karen 1994) and, as insecurely attached adult men, they come for help defended against forming intimate attachments which are both threatening and longed for. Bowlby (1969) saw attachment as a biological, instinctive bond with the caregiver. Remaining close to the caregiver is important for survival – the parent needs to be a 'secure base' from which the child goes out into the world. The child develops what Bowlby (1973) called 'an internal working model' that forms the basis of his personality. This model is created by the child, over time, in response to his repeated experiences in attempting to form attachments. The model is cognitively formed in the child's mind in response to questions about himself such as 'Am I worthy of support or not?' and about the caregiver 'Can I rely on this person to provide the care I want or not?' The model guides the child's future relationships with others and his attitude to self. The child learns to interact in predictable ways that are shaped by his expectations of his caregiver (Friedrich 1995).

So a child is securely or insecurely attached. A securely attached child has been able to develop an internal working model from his experience of having caregivers that have been consistent, supportive in times of distress and attuned to his needs. Insecure attachments generally fall into three categories; resistant/ambivalent, avoidant and disorganised (Alexander 1992). Insecurely attached children have usually experienced caregivers as inconsistent, not attuned to their needs and unable to soothe them in times of distress.

Resistant/avoidant children behave in ways that indicate they want and seek out contact from caregivers, while at the same time behaving with angry resistance. Such children can seem to be clingy and needy while at the same time creating distance by their behaviour from the very person they seek to be closer to. Caregivers often respond to such children by seeking care from the child rather than vice versa.

Avoidant children often appear to snub or avoid their caregivers. They become guarded in their interactions with others as a result of having caregivers who were emotionally unavailable, who disliked any sign of the child's need for them and who encouraged them to become independent before they were developmentally ready.

Disorganised attachment is seen in children who do not consistently demonstrate any pattern of attachment but may flip from one to the other. This seems to be related to the fact that the caregiver is both the source of the child's distress and the child's comforter. This pattern can be seen in children who have been abused by someone such as Stephen and Mike's grandfather who, while severely abusing them, also gave them a sense of importance, pleasure and being cared about. As described in their story, Gramps was a frequent carer of the boys – taking them on holiday, spending time with them and generally paying a great deal of attention to them. Their own father, Gramps's son, was unapproachable, angry and domineering during their childhood, no doubt as a consequence of his own parenting by a father who used children to satisfy his own needs. Gramps had abused several of his own children, as well as his grandchildren.

Specific attachment-related features originating from insecure attachments and frequently found in families where sexual abuse occurs include rejection, role reversal/parentification and fear/unresolved trauma (Friedrich 1995). In forming my relationships with Stephen and Mike I was very conscious of all three aspects. My belief is that the problems experienced by both men stemmed from their early experiences within a sexually abusive family and the 'internal working model' they had developed throughout their childhood and adolescence, which was still in operation for them as adults. By providing them with a relationship of warm acceptance, empathic understanding and respect they have an opportunity for growth and healing. In providing a different kind of relationship, which may not fit their perceptions or expectations of what relationships are, I can make a difference to their experience of self in relationship with another.

So an alliance is formed between us when we agree to work together. A successful alliance depends upon how well I can create a therapeutic space characterised by safety. Stephen's first contact with me emphasised his lack of safety and his need to be able to trust himself to another human being in order to repair the damage caused by his early life. He wrote of the need for confidentiality as part of that safety and the need for somebody who could empathise with him in his distress – his fear of judgement, rejection and exposure all came through his words: 'I...feel your empathy coming through, and that I could talk to you...talking to just anyone (is) very frightening...I feel as if I could trust you.'

Mike described his need for safety and the lengths he went to in order to maintain his anonymity; 'I still remember how risky it felt to be standing at those bookshelves, and how I travelled to other towns to be anonymous enough...'

Self in Relationship

Stephen came into the relationship with me in a state of severe distress. His sense of self had suddenly and dramatically become endangered. He had managed his life up to then by compartmentalising his abuse into a whole portion of his identity from which he had dissociated. He had been pretty successful, one way and another, at living his life out of just part of himself – the part he trained to ignore his abuse and his negative self-beliefs about what his experiences meant. Outwardly Stephen was sociable and friendly, always seen as someone who was kind and caring of others. He liked to please people – thereby earning their affection and goodwill. The cost of this to Stephen was that his own needs were squashed, hidden and unmet. His dependency needs had been met by allowing others to depend on him. His grandfather had trained him well in the art of meeting other people's needs and this had become so fixed as part of who he believed himself to be that he felt no burden in it. On the contrary – his self-esteem was strongly based upon his ability to meet other people's needs. But the reality was that Stephen, like anybody, had needs of his own: a need for care and love, for attention, for validation of who he really was. So Stephen had formed a 'false self' (Winnicott 1965) which had helped him to counteract his sense of unworthiness, shame and badness by living to serve others, while feeling empty inside.

Friedrich, Einbender and Luecke (1983) describe a very telling study. Pre-school boys who had been sexually abused were asked to draw a picture of themselves. He observed that not only was the developmental quality of the drawings lower than their non-abused counterparts, but the boys drew themselves *upside down* – for the examiner's ease of viewing. These boys had already become 'other directed' in their need to please.

A child's sense of self usually begins with a sense of the physical self, which progresses on to the social self and the psychological self, which includes the child's emotional and cognitive self (Friedrich 1995). A consolidated sense of self usually emerges in infancy and forms the basis for the development of a sense of autonomy. When a small child is sexually abused he might cope by dissociation and denial; both are strategies which interfere with his ability to experience or articulate who he is, what he can do and what he cannot do. Stephen had a memory of himself as a very small child and he reminds his dead grandfather of this in his letter (see Appendix 1):

> I didn't like it that time when I was younger, when you were rubbing my cock when Mum and Dad were in the same room. I was playing with my toys, laid on the floor. You had your hand over the side of the settee rubbing my penis.

Stephen spoke of this incident several times in our sessions. It was by no means the 'worst' abuse his grandfather perpetrated upon him, but there was something about it that deeply affected him at a very early age. Mike describes a similar episode:

> I have a very vivid picture of sitting on deckchairs sheltering from the rain by wrapping some sort of tarpaulin over us. Gran was handing out pickled eggs on top of the tarpaulin and bastard was masturbating me under it! Mum and Dad were certainly there!

My understanding of this is that Stephen and Mike felt that they were not in charge of their bodies. The power their grandfather wielded by touching them like this, reinforced the message that there was no help for them, that Gramps had complete ownership of their bodies and nothing would change that – not even the presence of their parents.

As the self continues to develop, a healthy child will be able to integrate both positive and negative aspects of himself. A child who has dissociated the negative aspects of the abuse, in order to survive psychologically, is unable to think about even the positive aspects of himself. He may fear that it is best not think about himself at all for fear that he may have to think about the abuse. Thus the child does not know how to describe himself or who he is. His thinking is about others – not about himself.

Adolescence is the time when sexuality comes to the fore. The boy who has been abused seeks the meaning of the abuse in terms of his sexual identity. Stephen and Mike both describe their preoccupation with their concerns at this time about their confusion about sex – wondering if they were in some way abnormal or deviant. Stephen tells of his feelings at this period in his letter to his grandfather: 'I'm thirteen now and I'm feeling guilty, disgusted, ashamed of what we do. I've got my own magazines now, and I wank myself stupid, trying to reassure myself I'm not queer.' Mike was confused:

> I wondered vaguely if I were homosexual, but as I was awkward in the company of men, I did not see how this could be put into practice… I was surely not unintelligent, but nevertheless I did not see what had happened to me in any other terms… My sexual past had never seemed other than something for which I was responsible; even if to my shame I had been unable to control it.

A boy who has dissociated parts of his experience will have less cognitive powers available with which to process the victimisation. At the stage of adolescence both boys were unaware that they were being victimised – their grooming had been so successful that it was impossible for them to consider themselves anything but equal partners in the sexual activities. Sadly, this view is still one that is widely held within a society that equates the status of 'male' with 'power and control'. Both boys had internalised this societal attitude which further complicated and prolonged their period of abuse.

Neediness

The degree of neediness in a client is usually proportional to the extent of the deprivation they have experienced. In most cases the needs of people who were sexually abused within the family were ignored, denied and abused. For some children whose parents also experienced deprivation in childhood, the child is used to meet the parent's needs. Stephen and Mike were used to meet their grandfather's needs, an impossible task. The child adopts a schema for himself that goes something like, 'I only deserve to live if I meet other people's needs but no matter how hard I try, I can't do this. Therefore I have no right to exist.' The child learns to withhold requests for his needs to be met and eventually denies that he has any needs to be met.

In the therapeutic relationship the counsellor aims to provide 'good enough' parenting while at the same time enabling the client to take responsibility for himself. This balancing act is often precarious. Both Stephen and Mike had learned to take responsibility for others long before they were developmentally ready for that. This left them deeply needy but in total denial of their needs. Indeed their neediness was so painful that they became quite fearful when the awareness began to emerge in the counselling relationship and this created a degree of resistance. Stephen describes this in his interview with me for this book:

Stephen: As time went on... [long pause] I got very attached to you but I knew that it would have to end... and you were quite mysterious in some ways but that was good – you had to be – you had to be quite anonymous for me to be able to tell you all the things I was telling you. If I'd known you I couldn't have told you all those things... I didn't know anything about you, but that was OK because it needed to be that way. It was a good counsellor/client relationship – we were very close but there was also a boundary as well – just about in the right order, the right quantities – looking back on it.

Kim: So you were aware of getting attached?

Stephen: Yes, I was aware that it would have been easy to get too attached.

Kim: Too attached?

Stephen: Yes, too dependent upon you – it would be nice to see you every week for ever and just come along, have a chat and tell you all my problems [laughs gently].

Kim: Yes [laughs gently].

Stephen: It would be good to have you there all the time – 'cos you're so nice and you cared – but I knew that it wasn't reality – I couldn't do that for ever – I think that went OK – the parting. Yes.

Much of the counsellor's work will be to give the 'child' within the adult examples of 'good enough' parenting: 'not to meet their needs, not to comfort, not to assist the client, too often merely duplicates the hurt and neglect of his childhood instead of teaching responsibility' (Vasington 1989). Clients who have worked with therapists who withhold comfort and assistance often describe this as shaming.

The skill seems to be in finding ways of fulfilling a client's need in order to re-pattern the past. We can never make up to the client for their past abuse or neglect, but we can help them bear the pain of experiencing it while receiving something different in the counselling relationship. Stephen talked about the extent of his neediness and frustration when he first came to see me; the sessions were too short and too infrequent for his degree of need at that time. So in the beginning we arranged to meet twice a week. Later, as his need lessened, we went to once a week, then fortnightly and finally there was a month's gap between the penultimate session and the last one. So in ending the session after an hour his needs were slightly (and I hope sufficiently) frustrated in order to help him take responsibility, but in offering the extra sessions at his neediest stage I attempted better to meet his needs. This gave him an opportunity to experience feelings he may have experienced as a child when he did not get his needs met and allowed him to differentiate needs from wants.

The additional difficulty for me with Mike and Stephen was that both men were inclined to want to pay attention to my needs rather than their own, so when I did hear them eventually express their needs I was drawn into wanting to meet them rather than frustrate them. Mike always began sessions as if I was a patient visiting him in the surgery; he would ask with fatherly concern, 'How are you today?' It was a difficult habit to break. He spoke to me in an interview about his decision to allow himself to be needy:

Mike: *It felt very suddenly that I'd gone into being a little boy and that you were the parent who was going to look after me.*

Kim: *So once you felt that this person knew what she was doing and was not frail in the sense of being able to deal with this, you could actually let go.*

Mike: *And I dare say that didn't show, but it feels as if it was very sudden – as if I was sitting on the edge thinking about it and then sliding down.*

Kim: *Mmm and that felt quite early on for you?*

Mike: *Yes, although I remember still feeling all shut in as a little helpless boy – but all shut in as the little boy, not as the suspicious, aloof doctor...*

Kim: *So once you'd established enough trust you were able to be your needy child.*

Mike: *Yes, that did happen almost immediately.*

Although Mike experienced that letting go so early in our meetings, my experience was that, at the start of most sessions, there were several minutes while he wrestled with his acceptance of his role as the one being cared for. Stephen spoke in a research interview about his own struggle with being cared for:

Stephen: *I used to worry about you.*

Kim: *Did you?*

Stephen: *Yes – you used to say to me about it at the time – most days I used to worry about what it would do to you, having to listen to all that stuff...*

Kim: *Oh, yes. I think I knew you used to worry about me on that level.*

[Pause]

I used to worry about me too.

[Laughter]

In responding in this way, which was how I would have responded in the client–counsellor relationship, I am being open and honest. At the same time I am giving Stephen the message that I can do my worrying for myself and relieve him of the need to worry for me.

CHAPTER 7

Transference and Counter-transference

Transference

In the previous chapter I am proposing an empathic therapeutic relationship that is based on openness, honesty and trustworthiness, that takes into account attachment patterns which may be repeated by men abused as children and that have left them with deep and unmet needs – a 'real' relationship. It is the meeting of two people for the purpose of enabling and empowering the client's healing which may occur through a process of 're-parenting'. This involves providing a 'reconstructive' relationship that entails 'living out a corrective emotional experience' (Kaufman 1996). Clients need to be able to identify with someone and for clients to be able to identify with us, they need to 'see' us as real people.

However, what about transference? Transference can be understood in different ways. Sometimes clients transfer feelings, or ways of relating towards people in their earlier lives (often parents), directly onto the counsellor. However, this phenomenon occurs within everyday life for most of us and is not unusual in itself. The therapeutic setting, in which the client seeks help from the counsellor, reawakens feelings from childhood when the child seeks help from the parent. Clients will sometimes re-enact those scenes as if the counsellor is the parent and will expect (and maybe evoke) reactions from the counsellor that replicate the way the parent reacted towards them as children.

Just coming for help can evoke transference before the client and counsellor have actually met. Mike describes how he stood for the first time on my doorstep, struggling with the reality which clashed with his fantasy: 'I think at the time – my fantasy was to have a very parental, large figure who would hold it all for me.'

Normally I disclose information about myself if it seems to be helpful to the client. Mike acknowledges that my disclosure was helpful (to his adult self) but may have felt unwelcome to his 'child' self. However, because I do not work psychodynamically, preferring to be in as genuine a relationship as possible with my clients, I usually disclose my own status as a survivor in order to bring as much equality into the dynamic as I can. Internalised shame and stigma can cause clients to want to reject such information but I believe by my modelling a lack of shame or sense of stigma clients can internalise different emotions concerning their own abuse. At a later stage in the process I will usually ask clients to talk about how they felt when I disclosed to them.

Kaufman (1996) states that clients need a 'security-giving' relationship that directly fosters identification. He describes such a relationship as allowing 'dependence as well as independence, identification as well as separation/ individuation. It means communicating honest, caring and respect, not in words alone, but by living them out over time within the therapeutic relationship. A security relationship is mutually wanted.' (p.160).

However, fostering a security-giving relationship does not preclude the occurrence of transference; neither does such a relationship make the process less effective. On the contrary, it is my view that the 'blank screen' approach fosters insecurity and often creates more hostility in the relationship than is helpful. It may also re-create feelings of shame and loss of self-esteem.

When transference occurs it can be useful in allowing the counsellor to engage the client more deeply in the process. I believe that clients can be helped by understanding what is happening in their relationship with the counsellor. If knowledge helps us as counsellors, so too it can help clients. Knowledge is power (Foucault 1980) and if we work to enable client's empowerment, we also need to share knowledge.

The following extract from an interview about the counselling process with Mike deals with some of these issues. Mike is talking about how he trusted me like a little child and we go on to talk about recognising and naming transference:

Mike: *Mmm. But I did that to you [trusted me like a child]. And as I say, I wouldn't have expressed it in that way, but I can't imagine the process having worked without me doing that.*

Kim: *So that positive transference was actually very important?*

Mike: *Oh – I think so. Given that I was stuck as a tiny child emotionally, I can't see how you could have 'brought me up' as it were, without that to start with. And I dare say you started to talk about it at some stage.*

Kim: *About the transference? My memory is that it was you who often referred to it; almost as if you were nervously reminding yourself that 'this is what they call transference'. It seemed as if you were using intellectualisation – almost as a defence against allowing yourself to know the dependency you felt – because it would have been so painful, I imagine, if you'd let yourself know the depth that you felt it. That was my sense of it.*

Mike: *Yes, that makes sense. I had to keep reminding myself that it wasn't real, because that made it alright somehow or other – it made it safe.*

Kim: *Yes. You used to keep saying 'I mustn't get into this transference thing' and I would usually sense at that time that you were feeling quite scared.*

Mike: I remember you asking me if you reminded me of someone, and I remember being quite puzzled by the question, but then when you started talking about transference, using the word, I remember being relieved, I suspect because it gave me that defence that you've just mentioned.

[Laughter]

I can't remember the context we were in at the time – either you were the good wife or the good mother at the time – one of those – the good wife I suspect – I don't know why you asked the question when you did. It was relief because you gave me permission to do it – maybe that's not what you intended.

Kim: I don't remember what I intended at the time – but I know that I would always try to make transference conscious. I would acknowledge it, understand it and share that understanding – almost as a way of avoiding taking too much power. In giving you information about the process, I was engaging in some way with your adult, and not keeping you trapped in this child who didn't know what was going on – whilst at the same time...

Mike: Allowing me to...

Kim: ...Giving the child permission to be there in a way – 'this is what happens and it won't last for ever'.

Mike: Yes. I think I had a sense of it almost being a criticism at the time.

Kim: Did you? Now that explains that to me. I often used to feel when you referred to it – it was almost – not an excuse exactly – but it felt like you were saying 'Oh it's that transference thing – don't worry about it.'

Mike: Almost an apology.

Kim: Yes, or 'it's not real, it's alright – I know what's going on'. [Laughter.] But I used to worry a bit about it **sounding** like an apology and I didn't ever understand that – isn't it interesting. So you heard it as a criticism?

Mike: Yes, there was me having an emotional dependence on you and you were reminding me that it wasn't real.

Kim: Yes, yes.

Mike: 'This is a relationship that – I must be careful not to let it get out of hand' – or something.

Kim: Yes, a bit of guilt or something?

Mike: Yes.

Kim: Guilty about being dependent?

Mike: As you said just now about you bringing the transference into consciousness – I may have seen that as a way of protecting both of us – and maybe I was receiving something about you needing to be protected from the transference.

Kim: From you – and your dependence on me?

Mike: Yes.

Kim: Mmm. That really helps to explain what was happening when you used to say that. I used to feel a bit anxious – 'it sounds like he's telling me that to reassure me'.

Mike: Yes, that's what I was doing. I was trying to reassure you that I wasn't going to fall in love with you – maybe it wasn't as strong as that – maybe I had the feeling that you were protecting yourself against that.

Kim: Against what you might have felt as the doctor when the patient fell in love with you?

Mike: Yes. Except at the time, I think we were much more in a dependency than... So maybe I was trying to reassure you: 'It's alright. I'm not going to sue you. I'm not going to come knocking at your door – write love letters...' [laughing].

It was during this interview that Mike reiterated that what he had needed more than anything was a 'real' relationship and the hope that gave him for future relating. I had commented to him that he had said comparatively little about the abuse during his work with me – most of his work had centred around relationships. I asked him what the counselling had meant to him and invited him to think of a metaphor to describe the process:

Mike: Scary...[long pause]. Sometimes it felt like a flower opening and sometimes it felt like someone trying to break into a walnut... And actually a quite a powerful part of it is the ...ending and a sense of having, or beginning to have, a more adult relationship between the two of us. I know that was a bit rocky and up and down – that's the prominent part in the centre – a bit like having a teenage child grow up – so growing up – yes, actually that's what the whole thing was really – the part of me that hadn't grown up – growing up.

Kim: Yes, yes – a process of growing up – I really understand that.

Mike: And I felt – yes, the 'keep out' sign you referred to – saying 'I've come to talk about my relationship' – I know exactly what you mean – but it was the relationship that was at the forefront of my consciousness. The problems in my relationship.

As the interview progressed Mike and I spoke more and more about our relationship and what an important experience that had been. Towards the end he referred back again to this point:

Mike: [Laughter] It felt – maybe this is a bit corny – there was almost a sense of 'I've now had a real relationship with somebody and its come to its natural conclusion – that's interesting – I've never had one of those before'. There was that level of it, although of course it was a strange relationship, but there was a sense of 'well if I've done that once I can do it again'.

[Pause]

...I was very much alone before you and I met. Lonely, alone and, for all that now I'm on my own, I have so much less loneliness than before when I was with someone. It's the isolation. [Pause.] That's not very organised is it?

Kim: It's very powerful. It sums everything up, doesn't it? How, when that happens to a child, they are cut off – from everything: from themselves, other people, their feelings.

Mike: Thirty odd years. That's...that's...

Another form of transference can be experienced when the client, instead of transferring his feelings towards others in past relationships onto the counsellor, plays out the role of the other internalised person (such as mother or father) and behaves towards the counsellor in the way the parent behaved towards him as a child. So the counsellor experiences, first hand, what it was like to be the client at that time. She might feel 'not good enough', deskilled, victimised – just as the client had felt as a child. If we can understand transference for what it is, it can be a powerful way for the client to communicate his story to us. We can thereby use our own feelings to mirror back to the client what they might have felt and enable them to articulate and express those feelings as a way of assimilating their experiences.

Transference can also occur from the counsellor to the client. If there are unresolved issues from the counsellor's life, they might become activated in the relationship with the client. It was the awareness of the potential for such a possibility that caused me to reflect on my own relationships with men, doctors and male authority figures as I made my assessment of my readiness to do the work with Stephen. However, transference is unconscious until made conscious and it is important that the counsellor uses supervision to process and make conscious any likely transference issues that may adversely affect the relationship with the client.

Counter-transference

As the client re-creates relationships from the past in the therapeutic relationship, the counsellor may reciprocate with feelings that are a response to those transferred onto her. As Stephen and Mike allowed themselves to become needy and childlike, I frequently found myself wanting to take care of them in a maternal way. As we spoke about the pain and resistance of the dependency in the relationship, I began to remember some of the protective feelings I had had as I watched Mike's ambivalence, which had been every like my own when I was a client:

Kim: *I remember as a client I had been very much in that position and I know how hugely rewarding that had been for me [being allowed to feel dependent]. I was aware that some of my counselling colleagues often gave me the impression that they thought clients **shouldn't** become dependent – that used to upset me a bit because I knew how valuable that had been for me – and how painful too. And bearing in mind the painfulness of it, maybe that was something I wanted to protect you from. I think I would have made it conscious anyway, because that's the way I work – but if I had appeared to do that in way that might have sounded critical I am wondering if it was some of my anxiety about the pain that you might have been feeling that was behind that.*

Mike: *So we were busy trying to protect each other.*

At other times, when Mike felt angry with me for being vulnerable myself, I felt like a 'bad mother'. He talks about his struggle to accept me as a 'real' person when he wanted me to be 'invulnerable'; he is talking again about his longing to be dependent and his resistance to it:

Mike: And the resistance...

Kim: ...and the pain that it brought up.

Mike: *That echoes – I reached a point somewhere in about the first third of the counselling, having not really thought about it before but then thinking 'Goodness me – I'm so dependent on this woman' – and being horrified by it. Thinking of all those wise old GPs who would say, 'Don't let them get too dependent on you.' What would happen if you were run over by a bus or terminally ill – and yet I was probably intellectualising it and saying 'I've made the decision – I'd better get on with it' [laughing]. 'There's no going back now.'*

Kim: *You really did disguise that very well. I think this is the first time you've ever really expressed the depths of feeling.*

Mike: *I was only letting you in as far as I could at that time. I remember one time you told me that you were at a difficult stage in your own life. I don't think those were the words you used but – about being in the flat on your own for the first time – and I remember coming away partly concerned for you – in the way that I would be – but also concerned for myself. 'If she falls apart where does that leave me?'... I don't think I was thinking 'that's really scary' but, 'what would happen – that might leave a right mess'.*

Kim: *Yes and you might have been quite angry about that.*

Mike: *Yes.*

Kim: *Yes. I remember feeling like that when my counsellor went into hospital – I was furious with her. [Laughter.] I didn't care that she was ill – I was just furious with her for not being there.*

Mike: *Oh except, that being me, my equivalent of that was being terribly concerned for you as well. But at the other level 'Oh dear, she seems such a strong person and yet even she's vulnerable and in trouble'; and that was helpful I'm sure in the long run. But at the time I had these two bits of me – 'how dare she be vulnerable – at all – she can't leave me dangling like this'.*

Not all feelings that counsellors have towards their clients are to be understood in terms of counter-transference; many feelings are those that would be expected in any real relationship. Even more confusing are those times when the feelings the counsellor (and the client) have are a mixture of both real and counter-transference feelings. Mike struggles to explain how he wanted to give me a gift at the end of our time together and he was concerned that such behaviour might be transference being acted out.

Mike: *I remember saying something to you at the end: 'I'm pretty certain that this is the adult me talking to the adult you.'*

[Laughter]

...Do you remember we had this issue – you would ask quite often about why I kept thanking you – being so grateful?

Kim: Yes.

Mike: *And I bought you that book and I really wanted to give it to you but I was really hung up with it then and I nearly didn't bring it into the room. I thought: 'She's going to think this is me being over-grateful.' I remember being uncomfortable, sitting in the car giving myself a talking to, and eventually saying, 'No, this is me being grown up.' I remember going in and making that statement.*

Some of the most uncomfortable counter-transference feelings I experienced in my relationships with both Mike and Stephen were concerned with power. Both men disowned the powerful aspects of themselves as they regressed into the dependent relationship they needed. I was frequently made aware of feeling the discomfort of my potential to abuse them. No matter how often I tried to refuse the power they handed me in order for them to know it for themselves, they worked just as hard to make sure I took it. Even in the interview for this book there was still an element of this present. During the work with Mike I had tried to help him realise the position he left himself in when he gave away his power in his relationship. He refers to this work as a powerful turning point in one session. I had talked to him about transactional analysis (Berne 1961) and particularly focused on body positions by asking him to stand on a chair while I knelt at his feet. Then we took it in turns to fully experience both positions. He remembers the huge sense of discomfort he felt and how he wanted to get down, but I insisted that I would keep him up there, no matter what, which was, of course, what he was doing in his relationship with me and with his wife.

In Chapter 12 some of the theory related to working with the body is explained in greater detail so I will not go into that here.

Kim: *So were there any other significant stages for you – or occurrences – or changing moments?*

Mike: *Yes – there was the time we got into the Eric Berne stuff. You standing up on a chair and then making me stand up on a chair.*

Kim: *I'd forgotten about that – what was that like?*

Mike: *Oh, very powerful. I remember when you made me stand up on the chair and you knelt on the floor and you said 'how are you feeling?' and I said 'I don't know, but I want to get down'...*

[laughter]

...but again – what kept me at it was you engaging me at an intellectual level and talking about the different ways of relating – showing me those pictures. Explaining it at an intellectual level was so important.

So when we work with transference and counter-transference, while at the same time finely balancing cognitive and emotional aspects of the work we can gradually work through to a more equal adult-to-adult relationship – as Mike called it, a process of 'growing up'.

CHAPTER 8
Post-traumatic Stress Disorder

History of PTSD

The acceptance of the idea that psychological disturbance occurs after traumatic experiences has only in fairly recent years become well-established. It now seems unbelievable to think that men suffering from PTSD during World War I were labelled as being of 'low moral fibre' and seen as weak; some men who tried to avoid the repetition of the trauma that overwhelmed them were shot as deserters. But even at that time there were a few enlightened neurologists like W.H.R. Rivers who tried to treat the men humanely (1918) – even if only to ensure their fitness for return to the front (Barker 1991).

'Shell shock' was the term applied to the condition that seemed to be the male version of what had previously been known as 'hysteria' when applied to women. Men developed symptoms such as blindness, paralysis and other disabling physical and mental conditions on returning home from World War I. In 1941 Kardiner wrote the first comprehensive clinical and theoretical study of war trauma which was updated in 1947 (Kardiner and Spiegel 1947). In this volume he complained about society's tendency to discredit men who exhibited symptoms of hysteria. Slowly the stigma attached to men who were considered to be suffering from a 'female' disorder was beginning to fade. However, this understanding attitude did not prevail and men's suffering went underground once more.

In recent years there has been an increase in the numbers of World War II veterans as well as Holocaust survivors who have presented themselves for treatment of the conditions that have kept the past alive in their present-day lives. It was only after the Vietnam War that 'a systematic, large-scale investigation of the long-term psychological effects of combat' was undertaken (Herman 1992). This only came about because the men themselves refused to have their symptoms ignored, unlike their fathers and grandfathers who had attempted to live up to the impossible expectations placed on men in our society; expectations of invulnerability that were an anathema to identifying themselves as potential victims of physical, sexual and emotional trauma.

Diagnosis

However, it was only in 1980 that post-traumatic stress disorder was officially classified in the American Psychiatric Association's (APA 1980) manual DSM-III (*Diagnostic and Statistical Manual of Mental Disorders*, 3rd edn). What had previously been referred to as 'gross stress reactions' and 'transient situational disturbance' were reclassified as post-traumatic stress disorder and 12 symptoms were listed providing diagnostic criteria for acute, chronic and delayed manifestations of this psychopathological response to an extreme stressor. The updated version (APA 1994), reflects an increasingly sophisticated understanding of the condition, particularly in relation to its occurrence as part of the aftermath of sexual abuse. It has been recognised that the condition exists along a continuum and that not every child who has been sexually abused experiences it; and that the effects of chronic sexual abuse are not the same as a single one-off occurrence. Terr (1991) suggests a Type I and a Type II. The former is a simple traumatic experience, whereas Type II, reflecting prolonged, repeated trauma, includes denial, psychic numbing, self-hypnosis and dissociation, and alternating between extreme passivity and rage. In DSM-IV, additional manifestations such as survivor guilt, a narrowing of social interaction, a heightened sense of ineffectiveness and impairment of affect regulation are listed (Friedrich 1995).

People who have suffered the terror of torture and abuse have been studied to enable neuroscientists to develop an understanding of the biological impact of *uncontrollable* stress on human beings. Goleman (1996) states that the operative word is 'uncontrollable':

> If people feel there is something they can do in a catastrophic situation, some control they can exert, no matter how minor, they fare far better emotionally than do those who feel utterly helpless. The element of helplessness is what makes a given event *subjectively* overwhelming. (Goleman 1996, p.204)

Mike and Stephen were small, helpless children when their abuse began. Their grandfather continued to abuse them, even sometimes in the presence of their parents. They were programmed from a very early age to understand that there was nothing they could do except accommodate the experience as part of their normality. Summit (1983) describes the process through which the child 'accommodates' to the sexually abusive experience. Sepler (1990) comments on the fact that such accommodation is well documented in female victims but:

> The depth of the accommodation and the intensity of the notion of mastery and control is a far more gender-specific response for male victims than female victims and should be expected...neither powerlessness nor violence make any sense to a male victim who has accommodated to sexual abuse by adopting a pseudo-consensual posture or by reciprocating with aggressive acts. (Sepler 1990, p.78)

Not being as tolerant of his helplessness, because of his conditioning as a male (which equates with being powerful), the boy may rationalise that this dysfunctional sexual relationship is actually positive. The danger is not only that he will accept this relationship, but keep the power of it alive in his own adulthood, through a series of similar situations in which he adopts the passive side of the power dynamic in another abusive relationship.

Any negative feelings about the abuse are repressed, dissociated and denied. The child's first and foremost concern is survival and in order to survive they adapt to their conditions. However, it was clear when Stephen's flashbacks started that the whole experience had been terrifying, disgusting and uncontrollable, and these feelings and sensations were unassimilated parts of the experience.

When Stephen arrived at my door he was in the acute stages of PTSD of delayed onset. Mike too showed symptoms of chronic PTSD, but of a very different nature. Stephen was exploding with feeling, both in his sleeping and waking hours; he had suddenly become flooded with feelings from which he had been disconnected for most of his life. He described to me in the interview how he had felt when he came for his first session and saw the box of tissues: 'I was on the verge of tears anyway so that sort of gave me more permission – but for me up to that point I was someone – I didn't really cry, show any emotion before then – I was all boiling and simmering up to that point really – there was a hell of a lot of stuff waiting to burst forth.'

Mike was extremely controlled and shut down on all of his feelings – the effects of the PTSD had been denial, psychic numbing, self-hypnosis and dissociation, and alterations between extreme passivity and rage, described above as classic Type II PTSD.

Flashbacks

However, although both men had heard of the condition, they still held on to some of the cynicism about whether or not this was a 'fashionable' label that allowed men to opt out of behaving 'like a man'. I had offered Stephen a book describing the condition shortly after we began our work together (Mezey and King 1992). I had felt it was important for him to know that he was not 'going mad' and that the symptoms he was experiencing were very understandable. I wanted to give him back a sense of control over his life, to alleviate some of his fear of being totally out of control. His lack of control was particularly related to the flashbacks. These intrusions were visual, tactile, olfactory sensations of being back in the abusive events:

Stephen: I do remember the flashbacks – they were very, very frightening obviously… It really brought it home – it was so real and frightening. At the time actually seeing it – it was as if what had happened to me was reoccurring. Details of intimate sexual abuse – seemed to be there with me, happening then and I was recalling it in detail – smells, sensations, tastes, everything — it's hard to get back there now — but I felt I was actually in it at the time. I thought I was going mad... Yes, I thought I was cracking up.

Kim: So what helped with that?

Stephen: You reassuring me that I wasn't going mad — that there was a reason for what I was experiencing — having it explained to me — reasons why...

Kim: And that it was normal under the circumstances, normalising it.

Stephen: Yes, you told me about post-traumatic stress disorder — I wrote it out in detail in my diary to reassure myself.

Kim: What was it like having that label.

Stephen: It was something to hold on to — I had heard lots of people being cynical about it — friends [rueful laugh] — but I was happy to hold on to it. Then I read about other people who had post-traumatic stress disorder who had been through things a million times worse than I had and I felt a bit guilty — having that label sometimes — that I wasn't really worthy of saying that about myself. I'm thinking of people who have suffered extremes of torture. And in a way that helped me to go on as well. Knowing about people who had suffered worse than I had — not minimising what had happened to me, but putting it onto a world scale of things and thinking that I was unfortunate but I was also fortunate — I was still alive if you like — that I'd got where I had.

Kim: And what you did with those flashbacks — what I encouraged you to do was to make them more concrete.

Stephen: Yes, to draw them — it was very scary but I did it. It took a lot of doing — drawing them. Then later when they came over me, I just learned to ignore them quite well. I said, 'Well, they're here — so what?' That was at the end of the process, after a lot pain in between.

Kim: So initially they would take over and you couldn't do anything but react to them?

Stephen: Yes, I'd feel very uncomfortable, especially dreams at night.

[Long pause]

I still get the odd one but it doesn't worry me. I feel like I've been through a process — dealing with it you know. [He thinks about it] I think it's because I expect it to go away — it comes over me and then goes back into its place.

Kim: You know that it will go and not take over and it doesn't mean you're mad.

Stephen: No — it's **understandable**.

Physiological Brain Changes

Goleman (1996) explains that such symptoms can be accounted for by changes in the limbic circuitry in the brain, focusing on the amygdala which acts as a storehouse for emotional memory. If the amygdala is destroyed or removed, the person loses all recognition of feeling, as well as any feeling about feelings. Tears are triggered by the amygdala along with another nearby structure (the cingulate gyrus); being comforted, held, stroked, massaged soothes these brain regions, stopping sobs. Without an amygdlala there are no tears to soothe.

The amygdala stores blueprints for emotional life even before a time when infants have words for their experience; so when these emotional memories are triggered later in life, there may be no words to articulate our response to them. The amygdala can react in a delirium of rage or fear, before the cortex (the thinking brain) knows what is going on, because such raw emotion is triggered independent of, and prior to, thought. The left prefrontal lobe has been understood to regulate the responses to unpleasant emotions and can normally switch off or dampen down all but the strongest negative surges of emotion (Goleman 1996).

The key changes in the limbic circuitry created by trauma are in the locus ceruleus, a structure that regulates the secretion of adrenaline and noradrenaline, the chemicals mobilised by the body in response to an emergency. The same surge of secretions stamps traumatic memories with extra strength. In PTSD this system becomes hyperactive and extra large doses of secretion are activated, even in some situations that hold no threat but are reminders in some way of the original threat (such as the sound of Westminster clock chimes, that remind Stephen of the clock in Gramps's house). The locus ceruleus and the amygdala link with other limbic structures, such as the hippocampus and hypothalamus, to form the circuitry to carry the adrenaline and noradrenaline to the neocortex of the brain, the thinking brain. However, in PTSD there is a short cut from the senses (eyes, ears and skin) to the thalamus, then to the amygdala which responds in some circumstances before the signal reaches the neocortex, thereby bypassing a route which allows the brain to initiate a more rational response via thinking processes.

In PTSD the body is alerted for an emergency that does not exist in the present. This produces symptoms such as fear, hypervigilance, being easily upset or aroused, readiness for flight or fight and the indelible coding of intense emotional memories (Goleman 1996).

Another change occurs in the brain's opioid system, which secretes endorphins that act to blunt the feelings of pain. It too becomes overactive and the effect in PTSD is that there is a general emotional numbness, which can come across as an indifference to the feelings of others, as well as their own, or lack of empathy. Pleasure, as well as pain, is blunted so that the client finds it hard to feel joy, happiness or anything positive. Indeed life may be viewed with dread and there is a sense of a foreshortened future. Another effect may be dissociation, which might include the inability to remember times associated with traumatic events, as well as the events themselves, or the feelings attached to those events. In such circumstances clients can be in danger of being re-traumatised, as their normal responses to danger are absent or dampened by the excess endorphins.

The traumatic events seem to remain as fixtures that interfere with subsequent learning of normal responses. Normally, when a person learns to be frightened of something, the fear subsides in time through natural learning, as the feared object is encountered in the absence of anything actually frightening. Repeated exposure to the images leads to reduction in affect response, but in PTSD this spontaneous relearning is blocked because the client avoids stimuli that evoke painful and frightening images.

But given the right conditions and time, this can change and healing can occur as clients are helped to face the negative feelings in a safe environment, while at the same time using cognitive processes to reappraise the events and create a more realistic view, thus changing habitual thinking. This leads to greater control and a reduction in helplessness. In the following chapter I will focus on how we can help clients heal from trauma (Herman 1992).

CHAPTER 9

Healing Trauma

The Good News

The pre-frontal cortex can learn to suppress the amygdala's commands to respond with fear. Herman (1992) suggests that memories can be transformed, both in emotional meaning and in the effects in the emotional brain. She sees the conditions necessary for healing to be:

1. Enabling clients to regain a sense of safety by calming their fears (perhaps by giving information that explains they are not going mad).

2. Helping clients to regain some control over their lives (perhaps by teaching relaxation techniques). Sometimes medication helps the client to find a 'window' of calm that allows them to regain some sense of security and control until such time as the relearning can occur.

3. Helping clients to retell their stories in the harbour of a safe relationship.

4. Enabling clients to mourn the losses created by the trauma.

Timing and pacing of these stories is crucial – if we go too quickly, the amygdala will flood the brain and clients may be re-traumatised. However, clients generally seem to have the ability to go at the pace that suits them and – providing we do not push them into facing memories before they are ready – they will reach a point of recovery in their own time. There may be periods when flashbacks and memories are frequent or even non-stop, followed by periods when none appear for months at a time.

The counsellor encourages the client to tell the story in as much detail as possible, including smells, tactile sensations, sounds, what they saw and heard, as well as their reactions of disgust, horror or nausea. The entire memory needs to be put into words or pictures in order to capture parts of the experiences that may be unassimilated. Some trauma researchers speculate that in states of high arousal of the sympathetic nervous system, which would be the case during sexual abuse, the linguistic encoding of memory is deactivated, causing the central nervous system to revert to sensory forms of memory (Raine 1999). Sensory details bring the memories more under the control of the neo-cortex, the thinking brain, where the reactions can be made more understandable and therefore more manageable: '[the neo-cortex] contains the centres that put together and comprehend what the senses perceive. It adds to a feeling what we think about it – and allows us to have feelings about ideas, art, symbols and imaginings' (Goleman 1996, p.11). All of this allows the brain to relearn that such events can be thought about without the extreme fear response that has held the client captive in the past.

Finally, clients need to mourn the losses created by the trauma. Such mourning marks the ability to let go of the trauma to some degree and, instead of being held captive by the past, the client can begin to look to the future. Sometimes a few symptoms persist, as described by Stephen – some things can still trigger off memories and feelings of being abused: 'triggers – like Westminster clock chimes – he had a Westminster clock. I remember it chiming when the abuse was occurring and whenever those chimes go, and they are everywhere, it sends a shudder down me.' However, they no longer have the same power to control the present for the client. Clients may still have the emotional responses, but they have a way of dealing with those emotions that was not available to them before. LeDoux (1992), the first neuroscientist to discover the key role of the amygdala in the emotional brain said:

> Once your emotional system learns something, it seems you never let it go. What therapy does is teach you to control it – it teaches your neocortex how to inhibit your amygdala. The propensity to act is suppressed, while your basic emotion about it remains in a subdued form. (Goleman 1996, p.213)

So we may not be able to decide when we have emotional outbursts, but we can have more control over how we respond to them and how quickly we recover, which may be said to be a sign of emotional maturity.

Stephen ended his interview about his counselling with me by talking about the place his abuse memories now held in his everyday world:

> 'It's been a long journey – lots of things have happened. Although I wish the abuse hadn't happened, going through the healing process has changed me dramatically. I think I am more alive, more feeling and understanding – more of a whole person – a lot more tolerant of other people, less rigid, staid. Life's better in lots of ways but it is also more difficult in lots of ways because changing so drastically has coloured relationships. I still feel I'm on the journey – I'm not at the end of it and I think I probably never will be. I've learned to deal with it now. I'm glad that I came to the point of seeking help. I don't know what would have happened to me if I hadn't. I think it has made me a stronger person for sure. It's good that from the terrible things that happened to me, something good and positive should come, and also, looking back now, although I said I'd never forget what happened, it does seem to have gone a little bit into the distance – a little. It seems longer ago now – seeing you seems longer ago and what happened to me as a child seems a lifetime away now; whereas before, it always seemed right there, but in the back ground.'

The Bad News

Possible Effects on the Counsellor

Listening to the detailed contents of the flashbacks and seeing the drawings that Stephen produced was disturbing and at times I found myself wanting to avoid them. He was also writing in his diary at this time – capturing in words some of the horrors of what he was remembering. He needed me to witness this work and at times I did not always want to. I think with hindsight that my reluctance was in part because I had found the experience of doing the previous research quite distressing – listening to 25 men's stories had left me feeling overwhelmed and, I believe, suffering a degree of secondary post-traumatic stress. So I too was trying to avoid stimuli of distressing memories.

As a woman, I think the abuse of males by males fed into all my worst conditioning about the darker aspects of male sexuality. Pictures of erect male genitalia that had been used to degrade, hurt, force and disempower children aroused in me the same kind of feelings expressed by Mike and Stephen – nausea, disgust, fear and anger. Because Stephen identified himself with the abuser when he first came for counselling – a defence mechanism to protect himself from feeling powerless – he drew pictures of himself as the same size as his abuser. These pictures depicted two adult males engaged in 'homosexual' acts. It was a salutary moment when he noticed this for the first time. He reminded himself then, by drawing the child (7 years old), naked, beside the full-grown man, that he had indeed been the victim and not the abuser – a very different picture. I have noticed that my decisions about what to include in this book have been coloured by my wish to protect the reader and not to become abusive in forcing others to read and see some of the same kinds of things I have listened to and seen.

As I write this I am aware that I am re-enacting my childhood role as protector and carer of others again; taking responsibility for the reader and assuming their inability or unwillingness to know; perhaps linked also with my own inability to 'know' about my own abuse, my family's and society's denial and 'not wanting to know'. Part of the loneliness and isolation I experienced when doing my previous research was that people did not want to hear about the work I was undertaking. Frequently I was asked, 'Why on earth do you want to spend your time delving around in such horrible material?' – always with the implication that there must be something wrong with me if I chose to examine such experiences and report on them. This isolation mirrors that of the abused child who cannot tell, or who tells and is disbelieved, or is told they must be wicked to have such evil thoughts about their 'Daddy or Mummy – or Grampy!

Good and frequent supervision is essential if we are working with this kind of abuse. However, I believe I may also have tried to shield my supervisor from 'knowing' at times and perhaps this was because I had picked up an attitude in her that I have been aware of in others. I have been aware at times, when discussing work with abuse among colleagues, that there is a wish to deny the centrality of the harm caused by abuse. Colleagues might say, 'Well of course we know abuse is harmful, but it's only one part of the child's experience, and I think too much is made of it.' So they may avoid focusing on abuse issues during the work. Sometimes counsellors have a resistance to asking clients if they have experienced childhood abuse (as they might ask about other childhood experiences) which may based in counter-transference.

Like society at large, a victim's family and, frequently enough, clients themselves, counsellors (and supervisors) do not want to know that the people sitting before them were violated sexually –sometimes in sadistic ways – and at a very young age (Davies and Frawley 1984). There is also fear among counsellors that if they should ask such questions they might be accused of 'putting ideas' into clients' minds and encouraging false reports of sexual abuse. However, I believe that we need to attempt to redress the additional difficulty that patriarchy creates for male survivors, who are socialised to see themselves as sexual predators rather than sexual victims. We need to invite them to consider the possibility of abuse, or even to reframe their experiences as abuse when we are able to recognise it as such. I have heard time and again that it was an external influence that helped a boy or man realise that he had been sexually abused. Sometimes that source was a book or a newspaper article; sometimes a television programme; some realised when hearing others relate their story (usually a woman).

The Walled-in Hermetically Sealed Client

However, I can also agree that for some clients it is not always necessary to focus on the abuse during counselling, providing this does not indicate some form of denial. What might be more important for them is to work with the effects of the abuse on their present lives. However, without having first allowed themselves to connect with the abuse, the later work may not be successful. Mike was clear that he wanted to work on his relationships when he came to see me. However, it was clear that his relationship problems were rooted in his early abuse. He acknowledges this in his interview with me for this book:

Mike: *And we're still talking about relationships apart from sexual abuse aren't we?*
Kim: *Yes.*
    [Long pause]
Mike: *That's the real harm it did to me. That's the real hurt... Cutting me off from my 'self'.*
Kim: *Yes, 'cos how can you have a relationship when you haven't got yourself. [Pause] So you found your 'self' – with whom you could have a relationship with somebody else.*
Mike: *Yes – and then of course found that I was in the wrong relationship... You pointed that out to me once at the beginning – that there was that risk.*

Kim: *What did that feel like?*

Mike: *Oh I think you were telling me something I already knew. Ellen and I had troubles going a long way back...[too quiet]*

Mike, who described himself as the 'walled-in hermetically sealed client', describes his first contact with feelings that had been frozen in time and how important it was that I allowed him to escape into his intellect when he felt the threat of being overwhelmed:

Mike: *As I recall it, the next huge happening was the discovery of my feelings.*

Kim: *You say 'the discovery of my feelings' like you'd found this chest full of treasure.*

Mike: *Well yes [forcefully] – that's not a bad metaphor.*

Kim: *Do you have any sense of how you made that discovery?*

Mike: *Yes. I remember sitting there feeling – erm – what word can I use that hasn't got an emotion in it – feeling very ill at ease – I mean extremely ill at ease, and you looking at me in the eyes and saying, 'You look very uncomfortable – what's happening?' You obviously could see that I was in distress and you winkled away for what seemed like ages, trying to get me to describe the physical sensation in my body – and then you saying, or getting me to say, 'this might be an emotion'. What a revelation!*

Kim: *Going in through the physical sensation – noticing your body, helping you to focus down on your body, going behind and behind and behind – seeing what kind of emotion was there.*

Mike: *It was very, very hard work I recall – on your part, with me resisting all the way.*

Kim: *Do you remember what the feeling was?*

Mike: *I was sad I think – I've got tears in my eyes now because it was such a... Well, I'm feeling sad now – but when I first started to talk about it they almost felt like tears of joy. Even though the emotion I was discovering wasn't a pleasant one. And I remember it was very top heavy with the academic, thinking explanation of why I might find it difficult to experience emotions – you had to keep me going, involving my brain – that was the way you kept me going...*

[Laughter]

Kim: *Using your intellectual strength to make that possible.*

Mike: *Yes, I think if you'd gone for the jugular and stuck to the emotion without that, I'd have probably been gone.*

Kim: *It would have been too direct, too overwhelming? But winkling away so that you could find It ....mmmm*

Mike: *Incredibly skilful.*

Kim: *Flatterer!*

[Laughter]

Mike: But I do think that was the most significant thing – I know there were lots of other things, but I do think that was the top of the list. We had to keep doing it over and over again. I suspect I'm compressing into one event what was actually several.

Dissociation

Childhood abuse is a form of chronic trauma, in which the abuser over-stimulates the child who becomes overwhelmed and his ego capacity is rendered inoperative. Young children depend not only on their own ego capacities, but also on the auxillary capacities of their parents. However, when the abuser is a close family member the child loses any ability to depend on those too. Van der Kolk (1987) sees the loss of the 'secure base' normally provided by the parents as 'the earliest and possibly most damaging psychological trauma' (p.32). The parents who fail to protect the child, as well as the abuser, are guilty of primary betrayal. Any attempt to reveal the abuse would threaten the entire family structure upon which the child depends; to a small child this represents a threat to his very existence. In his efforts to preserve any degree of ability to depend upon the parents for emotional and physical care, the child separates his ego into two parts. One part represents 'business as usual, the daytime self, the part that responds to the parent's denial by imposing its own denial. No one speaks of the other, the nightime self. It exists only as part of a dreamlike state whose very existence assumes and air of vague unreality in the light of day' (Davies and Frawley 1984, p.54).

Because the child cannot speak of these experiences, no verbal link exists between the two dissociated aspects of the self. Without language to represent these experiences, there can be no communication between the separate experiences of self. However, the body speaks it own language and that is often the way to begin.

Over the years I have come to recognise certain clients who present in the same way as Mike. Initially I have found it very difficult to 'reach' such clients and at times have noticed myself feeling bored, angry, frustrated and deskilled in their presence. I now recognise these feelings as counter-transference and, as such, they can help me to have a sense of the client's experience of themselves. Such clients are often dissociated from the feeling part of themselves and, as I try to work with them, I take on their feelings for them. If I am able to recognise when this is happening and mirror those feelings back to my clients, in time they begin to reconnect with themselves and then with me. I often need to provide a language for them; teach them to make connections between words like fear and the fluttering sensation in their stomach or bowels. I might notice red marks appear on their necks that might link with the word 'anger', or blushing that might link with the word 'shame'. However, it is important to offer these words tentatively and not impose them, because our assumptions may not be correct. Eventually the client will find the right words to describe their very personal feelings. Clients sometimes struggle to recognise that descriptions such as 'let down', 'pissed off', 'fed up' might represent 'anger'; and that 'rejected', 'isolated', 'wobbly' might represent 'fear'; that 'hurt', 'choked up', 'heavy' might represent sadness; and that 'over the moon', 'on the up', 'buzzing' might represent joy. These words indicate that he might be experiencing feelings in a bodily sense. If we can track back and back to find the emotion that connects with the felt sense there can be a true experiencing and release of emotion.

Gendlin (1978, 1996) taught his clients to tune into this felt sense through a technique he called 'Focusing' using a six-step model. He asked them to identify a word, image or phrase that was connected with the felt sense and then to ask questions of whatever they produce. A client might identify the flutterings in his guts as fear, and might ask, 'What is it about this that makes me so fearful?' Further exploration may reveal understanding that brings physical and psychological changes by connecting them with knowledge stored within the body.

I have found the model of dissociation proposed by Braun (1988a, 1988b) helpful in these situations. The model is conceptualised along four dimensions of experience: behaviour, affect (emotion), sensation (body feeling) and knowledge (BASK). As I listen to a client's story, I attempt to discover which of these aspects of experience are missing. For example, if a client describes a rape experience in a very calm manner, the dimension that is lacking is affect. Sometimes a client will describe a very strong emotion attached to an experience of assault, but will describe himself as feeling 'numb'; the missing aspect is therefore sensation. When the event is forgotten, the missing aspect is knowledge. But knowledge is multi-stranded; we can know and not know about betrayal at the same time – it is part of the human condition (Freyd 1996). A survivor of childhood sexual abuse who does not know or forgets about the abuse may simultaneously have memory and knowledge of events that surface in other ways such as specific phobias, learned behaviours or self-perceptions of 'being bad'. Behavioural components may intrude upon a client's life and become frightening, such as described by one client who would find his body convulsing, gagging and choking in the absence of apparent cause. Sometimes there is a combination of sensory and body clues (such as choking and pain in the rectum) which occur without knowledge of the source and are referred to as 'body memories'.

In sexual abuse, intense shame is the predominant affect and is accompanied by fear, humiliation, embarrassment, distress (sadness) and rage (Kaufman 1996). Mike had full knowledge of his abuse but spoke in a flat tone, without affect, as he described his situation. His body carried his fear in the form of irritable bowel syndrome, which he had suffered for many years. His facial expression was 'frozen' but his eyes darted from side to side and he found it very difficult to look at me directly for many months. Tomkins (1963) says the 'self lives in the face' and in her description of characteristic facial defences against shame, she includes 'frozen face' – like the wearing of a mask behind which the self can hide. Another facial characteristic is the 'head back look' in which the head is tilted back rather than forward. She explains this as a response to the inclination to hang the head in shame – a reversal of that position as a defence against the feeling. The third facial characteristic she names is that of 'contempt', manifest by a sneer, top lip curled — another defence against feelings of shame: 'I will shame you rather than feel my own shame.'

In Mike's case he had full knowledge of his abuse. His facial behaviour manifested his shame. His body carried the sensations of abuse indirectly through his irritable bowel and the aspect of his experience that was missing (in BASK model terms) was affect. Counselling needs to pay attention to the full range of feelings. Each must be made conscious, separated out from the others and labelled correctly. Anger is different from disgust and contempt; shame must be distinguished from fear and sadness. The client might need to be taught a language through which feelings can be expressed, something to which men and boys in our culture rarely have easy access. For instance, a man who has been socialised to believe that anger is an appropriate feeling for men, but that it is inappropriate for him to feel sadness or hurt, may respond to sadness with expressions of anger or aggression, thereby leaving sadness out of conscious awareness, unexpressed and stuck.

The 'talking cure' proposed by Freud is misleading; counselling or therapy is not a cure but a process of healing. The therapeutic value of language is undoubted, but if only language and cognition were activated, real change would not occur at a deeper level. Therapy is not an intellectual exercise. Because abuse and shame are embedded within certain contexts and scenes, those actual scenes must be reactivated directly within the therapeutic process (Kaufman 1996). The full imprint of their affect needs to be made fully conscious and for this we need to include work with metaphor, activating imagery, visualisation, stories and poetry — linking the sensory processes with cognition and feelings. Metaphor illuminates childhood scenes and communicates understanding on many levels. Perls (1969) said that the full awareness of an unwanted emotion and the ability to endure this emotion may be the main condition for healing.

So the counsellor needs to be willing to contact these scenes of shame with the client. A counsellor who is defended against her own shame, and therefore avoids these scenes, may be in danger of recreating the client's childhood family patterns. The relationship is reciprocal and to be able to bear our client's shame with them, we need to bear our own. If we can do this, the client's internalised shame is returned to the original source. A helpful example of a visualisation for returning shame to its original source (among other useful visualisation scripts) can be found in Parks (1994).

Shame has been described as 'a wound made from the inside by an unseen hand'; this wound disrupts the natural functioning of the self (Kaufman 1996, p.5). Clients who have suffered such damage often describe themselves as being 'all over the place', 'in pieces', or 'I don't know where I am' — all these phrases indicate the disintegration of the core of the self.

In the previous two chapters I have described the history, diagnosis, manifestations and experience of aspects post-traumatic stress and its impact on the development of 'self' and on my 'self' as the counsellor. In the next chapter I will describe some of the ways I have tried to engage affect, imagery and language through the use of writing with Mike and Stephen to enable them to rediscover and heal the deep wounds inflicted on the 'self' by others.

CHAPTER 10

Writing as Therapy

> The wound is a source of stories, as it opens both in and out: in, in order to hear the story of the other's suffering, and out, in order to tell its own story. Listening and telling are phases of healing; the healer and the storyteller are one. (Remen 1993, p.183)

Stories

The past cannot be reinvented or changed, but through storytelling we might shift the place our past takes in our present lives. Unassimilated fragments of our past haunt us in the present and we need to create closure of our past and continuity into the future; through narrative a sense of coherence can be restored. The abused person who turns abuse into a story transforms fate into experience. When two people like Mike and Stephen tell their stories to each other they share the common bond of suffering. Stories can heal; wounds become the source of the potency of their stories and create empathic bonds between themselves and others. Wounded people need to be cared for but 'as storytellers, they care for others' (Frank 1995, p.xii). Gergen (1991) says:

> Under post-modern conditions, persons exist in a state of continuous construction and reconstruction; it is a world where anything goes that can be negotiated. Each reality of the self gives way to a reflexive questioning, irony, and ultimately playful probing of yet another reality. The centre does not hold. (Gergen 1991, p.7)

A postmodern storyteller writes in order to discover what other selves were operating in their story; but the writer is many selves. In this book I am a writer, telling how, as a counsellor who has been a client, I became a researcher with my clients and how, as a woman, I have been affected by my clients' stories. The story I am telling you is also a story I am telling myself, thus creating a new memory, possibly for you as well as for myself. I am both the actor and the observer and as I observe I am conscious of myself as actor.

As I worked with Mike and Stephen I encouraged them to write down the story of what their lives were like at that time, while at the same time they were telling their stories orally. In doing that, they told the story of their past abuse as they reflected, in the present, on the earlier part of their lives; thus they created a new story. As they wrote their letters to their dead grandfather, they created other stories about who they now knew themselves to be. As they reflected on all of that with me for this book, they created yet another set of stories, including the 'fairy story' that they now recognised their life story had previously been. In trying to relate their experiences to others, they naturally resort to narrative; they tell stories to explain their lives to themselves and to others.

The stories we tell about our lives are not necessarily those lives as they were lived, but those stories become our experience of those lives (Frank 1995). Mike was aware of this when we met for the first time to discuss writing for the book:

Mike: One of the things that I've been almost looking forward to is, that whatever I do, even if I sit with my diary in front of me and go over it, in the end what comes out will be seen through the lens of now – the therapy and the recovery... I'm looking all the time retrospectively, aren't I – this is how I now interpret it.

Kim: Sure – this is your **now** construction of then.

Mike: ...it won't be the same as just reproducing it as it happened.

Kim: No – it's a reflection – looking back over it, isn't it?

Mike: Yes, and I suppose one interesting thing is then to compare the two – the finished product – as it were.

I had a sense that 'the finished product' he was referring to was the reconstructed 'self' that he now felt himself to be.

Telling and writing stories is a cathartic experience and can produce physiological changes that contribute to gains in health and feelings of well-being (Harber and Pennebaker 1992; Pennebaker 1988, 1993). It is often our most painful stories that we withhold and this inhibition can serve as a chronic low-level stressor, which may lead to health problems such as the irritable bowel syndrome experienced by Mike. Pennebaker and his colleagues found that research participants who showed the greatest improvements in health were those who wrote about topics that they had actively held back from telling others. The research task was to write for twenty minutes, for four consecutive days, about a traumatic event in the past. They also noted that writing about traumatic events changes over time. They cite an example of a woman who had been abused at the age of 9 by a 12-year-old boy. Initially, in her writing, the victim had expressed feelings of embarrassment and guilt. By the third day of writing she had expressed anger at her abuser and by the last day she had begun to put it into perspective. At the follow-up survey, six weeks after the experiment, she reported: 'Before when I thought about it I'd lie to myself.... Now I don't feel like I even have to think about it because I got it off my chest. I finally admitted that it happened.... I really know the truth and won't have to lie to myself any more' (Pennebaker 1988, p.243).

Pennebaker (1988) also noted that during his research participants who wrote about traumatic events (as opposed to the control group who wrote about everyday non-traumatic matters) were more distressed and reported more physical symptoms and negative moods immediately after writing. He reports a study by Lamin and Murray (1987) comparing writing therapy with a client-centred approach that found that clients were more depressed after a writing session than a live person-centred therapy session. So, in the short term, it would appear that writing about traumatic experiences is distressing. If taken on its own, writing does not allow for the concerned support of a counsellor – or a way of reconstructing the narrative through gaining objective information that might offer different perspectives (for example, when the victim has coped by thinking they are responsible for the abuse). However, as therapy progresses and clients are more in control of their responses, writing can become a kind of self-help therapy that they can use in times of need.

Writing serves several functions. It is a way of deepening our conscious awareness of inner events; it is also a way of 'putting the "indescribable" into words, calling on all of the creative capacities of the person' (McLeod 1997, p.152). Writing became a way of psychologically re-educating Mike and Stephen – a process that links emotional and cognitive intelligence. In Stephen's case his need was to re-educate the neocortex (thinking brain) to balance up the work of the amygdala, which flooded his brain and body with hormones, creating overpowering responses to imagined threat. In using language and thinking and in chronicling events, he gained mastery over his thinking processes until he was able to use his *understanding* to balance the rush of emotions.

Writing and stories also directly engage imagery because language is a powerful method for creating images. In Mike's case, the use of imagery allowed him to add emotional elements to his intellectual understanding of what he had experienced; to balance the left and right hemispheres of his brain. The left hemisphere mode is linear, sequential and analytic, while the right recognises spatial relationships, sensory impressions, overall patterns and a range of subtle stimuli which bypass the left hemisphere (Williams 1999). Deikman (reported in Williams) suggests that multifaceted patterns provided by rich, traditional stories present left and right hemisphere information simultaneously, allowing the usually dominant left hemisphere to process material of its own type and reducing its interference with information that can be received by the right.

In telling his story of therapy to me Mike shows how he links his right and left hemispheres so successfully these days:

Kim: ...*and if you were to think about that [the therapy] in terms of an image?*

Mike: *Goodness me [long pause] – you see you ask me that question and a string of adjectives come into my mind that are quite different so it obviously wasn't one event...*

Kim: *Well stay with the adjectives and see what happens.*

Mike: *Scary... [long pause]. Sometimes it felt like a flower opening and sometimes it felt like someone trying to break into a walnut.*

As Mike began to write he began to feel, but for him it was necessary to write to the person directly rather than *about* the person, in order to make this connection with his feelings. Stephen also wrote a letter to his grandfather and this direct contact allowed a powerful breakthrough of anger – something he might have taken much longer to achieve by talking or writing *about* it.

Writing gives clients something to do between sessions and thus engages them in a collaborative process. Change is a conscious process and requires effort. When I asked Stephen about what the writing had meant to him, he wrote:

> Writing the diary in such detail helped me to remember what had been said in the sessions. I was desperate; I needed help; so I wanted to make the best use of it. I was very conscious of the time I had taken out 'to sort myself out', and so I wanted to make effective use of it. Keeping the diary was a way of doing so. I also felt guilty about the money I was using on myself, that I couldn't really afford – the money that Mike had given me. This was further incentive to get my money's worth!

Gillie Bolton (1999) expands on the therapeutic potential of creative writing and provides suggested exercises.

Types of Stories

Arthur Frank (1995) describes three different kinds of stories: restitution narratives; chaos narratives and quest narratives.

The *restitution narrative* is a modernistic, mechanistic view of fixing something to how it used to be (as perhaps in the case of an illness and return to health). The narrative is a response to an interruption in the person's life and the end of the story is a return to 'just before the beginning'. However, there was no way Mike and Stephen wanted things to go back to just before the beginning – because their abuse had happened from such an early age they had no sense of a life without it. So theirs was not a restitution narrative.

The *chaos narrative* is the opposite of this: its plot imagines that life can never get better. These stories are as anxiety provoking as restitution narratives are soothing. They are hard to hear. The tellers of such stories are said to be 'wounded storytellers', but those who are truly living chaos cannot put their stories into words. To turn chaos into a story is to have some reflective grasp on it; reflection requires at least some small distance, thus removing the teller from the centre of the chaos. So in the telling, there is a mediation of life events. In true chaos stories there is only immediacy and no mediation. The body is imprisoned in the frustrated needs of the moment. In telling his story to me, Stephen helped to place himself at a small distance from the chaos. It helped him to gain control; chaos feeds the sense that no one is in control. Ultimately chaos is told in the silences that words cannot penetrate and clients may need to work with drawing or clay before words are possible; but chaos stories need to be honoured before a client can accept care: 'To deny a chaos story is to deny the person telling the story, and people who are being denied cannot be cared for...they cannot be participants in empathic relations of care' (Frank 1995, p.190).

First we need to become witnesses to such stories, and to witness them we need to sit with them and accept them as they are – not needing to drag the client out of the chaos to relieve ourselves of the sense of being 'out of control'. It is a very great temptation to try to 'sort people out' when they come in a state of chaos, but chaos cannot be transcended – only accepted for what it is, until new stories can be created. Moving on may be desirable because neither client nor counsellor wants to remain in the pit of 'narrative wreckage'; but to attempt to move the client on denies what is being experienced in the moment and therefore compounds the chaos. Pennebaker (1993) supports this view with his research findings:

> Holding a coherent narrative to explain a traumatic or upsetting experience may not always be healthy at the beginning of therapeutic writing sessions. Movement towards the development of a narrative is far more predictive of health than having a coherent story per se. The construction of a story rather than having a constructed story, then, may be the desired endpoint of writing and, by extension, some therapy. (Pennebaker 1993, p.546)

Stephen began to write about his chaos and the uncontrollability of his life; he began to draw his images and flashbacks and began to gain control. As he wrote down or drew his flashbacks, he began systematically to desensitise himself to the images. In allowing himself to spend a restricted amount of time (just enough to attend to keeping a diary), which included time to pay attention to the images contained within his dreams and flashbacks, Stephen began to create a framework in which he could contain them. By externalising his words and images onto the page, he began to deconstruct the events of his life and the ways he had thought about himself and others (Freedman and Combs 1996). In the sessions with me he told his story orally again; re-experiencing and trying out his new constructions as he revisited his diary and drawings while receiving my support.

Little by little, through this process he began to order his chaos and transform his chaos story into a 'quest story', in which he met his suffering head on and began to use it, although his chaos remained as a background as he acquired his new voice.

I have described the three phases of the *quest narrative* in Chapter 6 as *the departure*, *the initiation* and *the return*. The quest story combines the telling with a *memoir*, which includes other events in the writer's life, as Stephen and Mike have done in Part 1. They fill us in on the background that led up to the time of our meeting through letters, poems and diaries and stories within the stories that they tell. Present circumstances require the telling of past events in order for us to contextualise our stories. There are powerful cultural forces that work against the telling: societial denial and family denial.

Quest stories may also become *manifestos* which require social action. Mike and Stephen's stories point up the need for social change; societal conditioning has caused the suppression of the truth about such suffering as they have undergone. This truth must be told if we are to break the seals of secrecy upon which child abusers depend. Without the secrecy and silence there would be no abuse; in a society where it was safe for children to speak out about these events, it would be unsafe for the abusers. Writers of such stories do not want to go back to the way it was before. They want to use the suffering to affect and change others and the society in which such events are allowed.

Both Mike and Stephen spoke in very personal terms about the sense of having discovered a 'new self' through the process of counselling. I believe the use of writing and creating narratives for their lives has enabled the co-construction of new selves. In my witnessing of the changes in both men, their change is affirmed – but these changes are about becoming 'who I have always been' – being newly connected with their own memories and experiences. The past is reinterpreted in the present and takes on a new meaning. In writing their stories Mike and Stephen were able to reassess their self-perceptions in terms of an updated view of what had actually happened to them.

Stories such as these can easily become 'escape' stories about 'rising above it', but the antidote to that pretence is the chaos story – we must not romanticise abuse. Mike and Stephen's story reminds us that they would prefer it never to have happened. Frank (1995) reminds us that the phoenix remembers nothing of his former existence as he rises from the ashes. An abuse victim does not forget once he has healed from the trauma. Renewal is never complete; he bears the scar in awareness and often with pride in order to remind others that they too can heal. Survivors only bear responsibility for surviving. The witness bears responsibility to inform others about what is usually denied or repressed, suppressed or unknown. The telling and witnessing of such stories provides us with a moral opportunity to set right what was wrong, or at least to know it for what it was. McLeod (1997) says; 'A story is not merely a chronicle of events. A story is an account of events set against a landscape of moral values. Narrative therapy involves the rediscovery of the "moral"' (p.153).

In writing down and thereby bearing witness to these stories I too have suppressed small portions of Mike and Stephen's stories for fear of making people turn away in horror. Bearing in mind that these individual testimonies are only a small fragment of a much larger whole, how can we remain detached and turn away? No doubt Mike and Stephen have also held back some of their stories from me and each other. There are some things that we keep hidden even from ourselves, for they are too hard to know. The more we tell, the more we make others and ourselves aware of the silence. Frank (1995) reminds us 'how much remains that can never be told is unknown' (p.138).

But witnessing is only one part of the relationship between myself and the reader; testimony requires that you enter this relationship and receive these stories: 'The listener must be present as a potentially suffering body to receive the testimony that is the suffering body of the teller' (Frank 1995, p.145)

These testimonies are complete in themselves but they require commentary if they are to be transformed into a social ethic. How is the reader affected by the story? How am I, the writer, affected by the story? And how much responsibility do I take for your responses to these stories? I can only take responsibility for my own responses to these stories. One of my responses is to protect you, the reader, from knowing all of it. I have to take responsibility for exploring why I need to do that and I will.

As I write this I realise that resistance to the lived flow of experience causes suffering and that people feel victimised when decisions are made about them by others. But in balancing the other aspects of what I have done in presenting these stories, I know that my testimony may be enough and that I can only testify from who I am; and I know I am not the hero in these stories.

Letter Writing
Negative feelings are most healthily expressed when they are directed to the person who has caused them. However, these are the very people who are often most difficult to confront. When a child is abused, the fundamental feeling is often one of fear; fear of being found out; fear of rejection; fear of the pain; fear of being out of control or controlled by another. This fear may block other feelings such as anger, disgust, shame, sadness or hurt. By encouraging clients to write letters, we can enable them to direct their words to the perpetrator, without having first to overcome the fear of meeting them, literally or metaphorically, face to face. Letters can remain private, or might be brought to the session to be shared. For someone who has had their privacy invaded, this might be the beginning of a realisation that they can choose whether or not they allow another person to share in their private world. The process of deciding might highlight that privacy is different from secrecy and that privacy is a human right.

Many people begin to deal with their abuse after the death of the abuser – it is often only at this time that clients feel safe enough to face it. But some may believe that it is too late to do anything about it once the abuser is dead. These people face yet another double bind. Offering a way of dealing with the unfinished business through writing letters can be a huge relief once the client has adjusted to the idea. Initially they might find the thought of writing to a dead person bizarre, but once they start, even if they do not believe it will work, they can begin to experience the potential power of the tool they have in hand. Sometimes behavioural change needs to come first; something that behavioural psychology has long recognised. But behavioural change is not enough in itself – the underlying feelings also need to be addressed, as well as the thoughts and beliefs that go with them. The sense of powerlessness is thereby diminished, simply by accepting that there is a way of working, in private or in the sessions, with unresolved feelings.

Stephen's distress was overwhelming and explosive when he first came. He needed to find a focus and a way of containing his thoughts and feelings. He was also full of shame especially as he had 'allowed' the abuse to go on for so long. The hardest thing for him to face up to at that time was that he had been 18 years old when he had finally said 'No' to his grandfather. He saw himself as an equal adult and therefore responsible. It was very important to him to connect with his victimisation as a child who had been programmed from infancy to behave sexually with his grandfather. Chronologically he was a young adult, but emotionally and sexually he had become frozen in time.

So I suggested that he might write a letter to his dead grandfather. I often suggest that the first letter should be written with a large, fat felt pen on a large sheet of flipchart paper. The very physical act of using these large tools allows for a release of energy. With a large sheet of flipchart paper the client usually has to get down on the floor, a position that helps him reconnect with the 'child within'. I might suggest that sentences might not come easily and that words might be enough – and there is an example of this on page 31 as Stephen began to experiment after the first counselling session. I also felt he needed something that he could do for himself in between sessions, to introduce the idea of self-support alongside the support he was receiving from me. This was particularly important as I had a two-week holiday break coming up and he would need to support himself in my absence.

It was between sessions 3 and 4 that the cork which had been loosened by writing down words on a large sheet of paper finally came loose and exploded – releasing his powerful expression of feeling towards 'Grampy'. He began writing at 10.00 pm and finished at 4.00 am! It was like running a marathon overnight; the exhilaration of the release of years of pent-up emotion carried him forward with great momentum, while at the same time relieving the pressure that built up behind the 'cork' (see Appendix 1).

Both Mike and Stephen wrote letters to their grandfather and to other significant people in their lives. The most significant person, of course, was the 'child within' who had suffered in isolation for so long and who, for the first time ever, had allowed the outside world in.

Poetry and its Uses

> Poetry is the response of our innermost being to the ecstasy, the agony, and the all-embracing mystery of life. It is a song, or a sigh, or a cry, often all of them together. Thus we are really all poets. (Angoff 1994, p.xi)

Poetry, as a tool for healing, provides a means of self-expression and personal growth, whereas the focus of poetry as art or literature is the poem itself. It is important that we explain to clients that they do not need to write for the sake of art but for healing and that we are all capable of writing poetry. Often poems written as healing become art and poems written as art can be used for healing. But we may need to release the restrictions adults place upon themselves that are left over from schooldays, when they received 'marks' for writing poetry and essays. It is the use of language, rhythm, metaphor, sound and image that creates healing, not literary excellence.

Longo (1999) reminds us that the word therapy comes from the Greek *therapeia* meaning to cure through dance, song, poem, drama or the expressive arts. The god of healing, Asclepius, was the son of Apollo, god of poetry, medicine and the arts – all historically entwined. My previous training as an occupational therapist (OT) built upon these ideas and embedded in me the value of creativity: arts and crafts, puppetry, clay work, dance, play, music and drama. This training emphasised the holistic approach to rehabilitation and healing, much as Jung proposed in his work, bringing into harmony body, mind and spirit through approaching the person holistically. So as a counsellor I bring these ways of working as a natural extension of myself as an OT.

I have loved writing and reading poetry since I was a very small child; the rhythm and imagery soothed me in times of distress and has helped me to express some of my deepest experiences. Poetry allowed me to *feel* my thoughts and images, and to *image* and *think* my feelings (Stainbrook 1994). Long before I entered my own therapy I had written poems that were healing, carrying messages from my unconscious to my conscious mind. The unconscious seeks meaning which can heal the troubled mind and soul. A symbol serves as a compression of meanings. When I look back now at some of my childhood poems I recognise the meaning of the symbols that I was unaware of at the time of writing.

Over the years I have come to respect the place within me from which poems come – and believe that there is such a place within all of us. For some people it is easy and natural to find a creative source that teaches us about ourselves and the world in which we live. In the silence, as we try to find words and form, we begin to define ourselves. I wrote the following poem many years ago, just after I began my training as a counsellor and shortly after I had begun my own therapy. It shows how I was beginning to observe myself and the movement from observer to subject – this may have been a way of coming to terms with my alienation from self as I began to increase my self-awareness at the beginning of therapy:

Myself

My self is who I am,
the one I know myself to be,
or two or three
or more;
the dark, the light
criss-crossed shadows;
the agony
and ecstasy.

My self is who I'm not,
the one the others see,
there and then,
yesterday,
the outside of the onion,
peeled away,
layers and layers
and tears.

My self is who I'll be,
In my becoming, when I grow,
Fluid, changing
moving on.
Metamorphosis continuous;
butterfly spreads
and dries its wings

and flies.

At a later stage in therapy, as I began to awaken to myself and integrate my repressed memories – as though I had been sleeping for a hundred years – I wrote the following poem:

The Awakening

Mists
shroud the dawn
heavy hanging, cloying
drowning the pores of living breath.

Earth
is sleeping, deathly
silent, half-aware life
within, safe and unlived.

Unwelcome
shafts pierce, cleaving
apart the tight-wrapped
arms of night, defending.

Light
dazzling, forcing
sight in half-closed eyes
breaking the silent seals of sleep.

And
then the pain,
limbs unfolding, hurting,
stretching, testing untried ground.

I step
uncertain, risking
terrifying exploration, straightening
tortured twists and crooked spine.

Upright,
ignore the pain again,
swaying full bodied in the sun,
suffusing easing warmth, constant as tomorrow.

Reaching
for the sky, head held high
embracing future winds that blow,
spirit free, exposed, brave...awakened.

Later, as I began to allow myself to feel joy, tentatively and for the first time, another poem emerged that captured and anchored the feeling, making it more solid:

Renewal

There's a floating effervescence that
comes from deep inside,
a rising well of
energy within my being.
The rainbow moving window
of my bubble
bounces, lifting,
resting, touching lightly down.

Drunk with this spirit
I smile at life
and others see the light

> switched on inside,
> shining through
> the outer layer of my soul.
> 'Come and see,' I want to say,
> 'look quick, before it goes.'
>
> I hold my bubble gently
> lest it burst too soon,
> trusting in the caring
> of my hands.
> Blowing lightly to keep afloat
> and moving
> this wonderful ball of light
> that is me.

Poems can, in a similar way, help us to notice the process of change and monitor our progress. Longo (1999) says that the process of creating and writing poetry down 'attaches us to the greater part of ourselves, to all that is whole and good and beautiful. And when we feel ourselves as not alone in the world, but a part of and integrated with all that exists, self-esteem grows' (p.1). Poems can be short – a few lines even. They aim for the core issue in a distilled manner. Lerner (1994) quotes Myra Cohn Livingstone, who says: 'Poetry humanizes because it links the individual by its distilled experience, its rhythms, its words to another in a way which no other form of communication can. Poetry also helps to ease the aloneness which we all share in common' (p.xi).

When I first propose the idea of writing a poem to clients, I often discover that they have found this way for themselves already. Some have written poetry as a kind of self-therapy for many years; others have never considered that they might have the ability, like Stephen. He wrote to me in response to my question about what the poetry had meant to him:

> The poetry! Thank you Kim; was it a *whim*! Or part of a plan (a plan I think). That helped me a lot; my emotions were raw and open and it poured out. I am still amazed and pleased that I was able to write that stuff. Despite the pain I was coming *ALIVE*. To emotions and feelings; tasting the air; colours were/are brighter; seeing the world with new eyes. The poetry was all part of that dramatic change in me.

He used the following poem to express his lowest point in therapy:

Lead

> Weighed down
> Under a blanket of lead.
> Encompassing, all over me
> Breathless,

> I feel half-dead.
> Energy, strength and power
> All sapped, drained away.
> I don't like it here
> Please don't make me stay.
>
> I feel so helpless
> Out of control.
> Optimism, hope, cheerfulness,
> I no longer extol.
> Gone away,
> Replaced by fear.
> Unemployment, debt, homelessness,
> All feel so near.

Human suffering arises out of an imbalance or conflict in the integration of feeling and cognition (Stainbrook 1994). Stephen uses the poem to ventilate unacceptable feelings, emotionally laden ideas and conflicts, thereby unfolding them to the observing part of himself so he can know about them more fully and reorganise his thinking. He is letting go of his old self that has kept him trapped in the past, but the fear of what those changes might mean is terrifying and he is not sure he can cope.

The client can use the poem to look at himself from another viewpoint – once he has written down his conflicts they stand separate and clear. In this way poetry can create clarity from which insight might arise. He may then recognise his own responsibility for where he is in his present life. At the same time he can work to find a way in which he is more comfortable with himself and his feelings about himself (Heninger 1994).

Poems can be used as a projective technique to say something about the writer's needs, desires and feelings. He can reveal himself without getting caught up in the fear of self-exposure. The poem acts as an indirect way to stimulate his self-understanding through exploring different parts of himself. Finally, poems can help us reach the deepest, most spiritual part of our being. Mike's poem on page 97 serves to integrate his spiritual self as he speaks from his centre to the suffering child within.

CHAPTER 11

Writing to and from the Inner Child

Inner Child as Metaphor

Metaphor has been described as 'the magic wand that enables pattern to be communicated' (Williams 1999). Metaphor is a way of communicating what is abstract – that which we perceive or know (tacitly or intuitively), but for which we have no direct translation into words. I have written about my experience of using the metaphor of 'The Iceberg' as a means to communicate a deeply felt sense, during one stage in my therapy. It was a way of speaking my truth from within. Williams describes this kind of truth:

> Metaphorically speaking, the idiom in our own language is precise: our truth is 'naked', indivisible, inexpressable; it lives in another dimension. To enter our company or our society in this world of words and expression, the pattern of truth must be clothed. And her clothing is metaphor. (Williams 1999, p.20)

The clothes (or metaphors) we use to dress our truths can vary in order to meet our needs at that time. I offered Mike (the walled-in, hermetically sealed client – his own metaphor) the clothing or metaphor of 'the child within'. On reflecting on his experience of counselling, Mike described the process as 'growing up – yes, actually that's what the whole thing was really – the part of me that hadn't grown up – growing up'.

Mike recognised that his development had been distorted and in some ways arrested at an early stage and that, in many ways, he still felt like a child. So it was through the use of letters to and from his 'child within' that much of his healing occurred. He has given me these letters to include in this book. It can be seen that through these letters Mike addresses his cognitive and emotional development – he explains to the child what has happened to him in a compassionate and caring way. During this process Mike is reconstructing his reality – he adjusts his thinking and understanding, which enables his feelings of compassion, love and care for the hurt part of himself to flow. In this way, he reduces shame, guilt and anger and releases himself from the powerful negative self-concept and mistaken belief system within which he has been trapped.

I suggest that the adult and the child begin to communicate with each other through writing. The adult sees himself as a 'friend' to the child. This works better than being a 'parent' – especially as the parent may have negative connotations. One useful model for exploring these internal dynamics is the Parent–Adult–Child (P–A–C) framework of transactional analysis (Berne 1961). This model uses these metaphors to describe the three separate ego states that Berne proposes each of us holds within. The Parent ego state is said to have been laid down during the first five years of life, in response to the messages we receive from the first authority figures in our lives, usually the parents. These messages will contain both nurturing and critical, controlling aspects. The Child ego state consists of our free child (as we were meant to be, and contains our spontaneity, feelings, creativity, sexuality and joy), as well as our adapted child, which has been restricted by social constraints and the type of parenting we have received. So a child who has been fortunate enough to have a healthy balance of control, criticism and nurture will have internalised a healthy Child. A child who has internalised negative, critical, judging parenting adapts by becoming needy and clinging or angry and fearful. The Adult ego state has the function of taking in the responses from the Child and the Parent states, which it processes to create a rational, balanced response. So we need all three states (P–A–C) available to us to form healthy relationships and live in harmony with ourselves and others.

If our childhood experiences have been damaging we may cut off the Child ego state which contains much of our distress; we do not want to be aware of our hurt. But by 'walling-in' our adapted Child we also cut ourselves off from the positive aspects of our free Child. In the absence of our spontaneity, creativity and joy, the Parent ego state may dominate our Adult much of the time and we might be experienced as judgmental, critical, humourless, heavy and dull. But what is suppressed often becomes most voracious and from time to time the Child might emerge, suddenly, forcefully (with equal force to that which is used to suppress it) and perhaps even destructively. Our adapted Child, full of anger, fear or neediness, can emerge when least expected.

So there is very little Adult to be seen anywhere. We are either in the grip of our outrageous and badly behaved Child or heavy-handed, dominating Parent. In writing letters to the Child we need to engage the Adult – as the friend who is not Parent. By encouraging this, the client begins to discover his Adult, recognise and control the negative aspects of the Child and Parent. The positive aspects of his Child and Parent can then be harnessed and a greater balance created between all three aspects. First we have to help the client overcome his fear and judgement and maybe even dislike of the Child.

The client is advised to write as the friend (Adult) with his dominant hand to the hurt Child and from the Child with his non-dominant hand back to the Adult – thus connecting and accessing both hemispheres of the brain. Mike began to reframe his experiences intellectually, thereby letting go of his critical judgements of himself. He addresses the Child within by his childhood nickname; from the manner of his language it can be seen that he is writing to a very young child. He begins to reframe the child's experience of himself as 'bad' and gives him permission to feel his emotions; reflecting them back and naming them, just as I was doing with him in the sessions. He also begins to acknowledge the part that his societal and family conditioning has played – 'boys should not cry'. He models a different kind of masculinity – one that is expressive, gentle and caring. He began to write to his Child between sessions 7 and 8. Up to this time Mike had been seeing me weekly – apart from a break of three weeks between the third and fourth session when I was away on holiday.

Monday 19th November

Dear Mickey,

I am sorry that I've not been in touch with you for such a long time. I've been so busy with so much that I've let myself forget all about you and I feel very sad about that.

I know you have been very unhappy. You must have been feeling really frightened and muddled about what's been happening to you. Its really important that you understand you are *not* responsible for a grown-up's behaviour. Grown-ups have to look after children, not the other way around!

So you see, when Grampy touched you like that, like children shouldn't be touched, it is bad. But it is Grampy who is being bad – not you. No one has ever explained to you about these things before, I know, but I am explaining it to you now. Everyone has private parts of their body, and of their life. These parts are not secret or nasty – just private – that means they are only for you, and very precious to you. One day when you are a grown-up, you may choose to share those private parts with another grown-up whom you really love, and that is OK. But children's private parts should not be touched by any grown-ups (apart from when they are very little and have to have their nappy changed, and washed). So when Grampy says it is a special way of loving you, and tells you it is a secret, he is being very bad. But you are *not* being bad – he is the Grampy and he knows it is bad; he is meant to look after you and keep you safe; you didn't know about these things, did you, so you haven't been bad.

And you know when Grampy gives you his special cuddles because Mum and Dad have been arguing, and you are frightened of Dad, that is extra specially wrong of him, because he is using your being afraid.

I know you get very angry sometimes, and grown-ups tell you it's naughty and you shouldn't. But you know it is alright for you to be angry with Grampy – I am too – because what he does is very, very bad. I know you are frightened to tell on him, and I understand that – it would be better if you did, because then other grown-ups might make him stop, but it's OK, I realise you are too frightened.

It's OK to be frightened too – I know you think that Dad wants you to be strong and a good fighter and play football and everything and that he thinks crying, and being frightened is sissy – but it's NOT. Everyone gets frightened sometimes, that's OK; and you have got lots more to be frightened about than other boys and girls – so it's OK to be frightened. I'm a grown-up and I'll make it safe to be frightened – we'll stick together and get it sorted out.

And you're sad aren't you, very, very sad I think – I know I was sad when I found out what was happening to you. It's OK to cry and be sad, you know. I think we could practice doing it together, you and me, being sad and frightened and angry. Because you don't need to be lonely anymore – I've found out what's happening to you and it'll be OK. It happened to me too, so I understand. You needn't be lonely any more because I'm with you, we can be sad and frightened and angry together.

I must stop writing now, because my own little boy will be home from the shops soon. I'll write again soon; please write to me too.
Love
Mike.

Figure 11.1 is the letter back from the child, Mickey.

Figure 11.1

19th November

Dear Mike

Thank you for writing to me. It has made me cry a lot your letter. I thought I was all alone in the world. I am glad that I've got a friend. I feel very bad sometimes, I know people don't like me 'cause I'm bad and fat, please help me,

Love from
Mickey

This is you looking after me

XX

Write to me again soon.

Just after writing this letter Mike takes three weeks' break from work, after much persuasion from me. He has twice weekly sessions with both myself and Sarasi during this period as he gives himself over to the process of healing. This is the stage at which he feels 'the cork begins to loosen in his bottle' and he feels very needy.

Just over a week since his last letter, Mike writes to his child again. He begins to recognise that when he is feeling very wobbly, it is the child within that is in need of support. At this time Mike is trying to deal with feeling very rejected by his father:

28.11.95

Dear Mickey

I just felt the need to get in touch with you today. I know that you are feeling very frightened at the moment and that you feel you are not loved or cared for. This must be very scary for you. But I'm here and I will make things safe. I'm scared too you know, but I'm a grown-up so if we stick together we'll be able to sort things out. You know, when it feels like people are rejecting you it may well be that what's happening is not to do with you at all! Sometimes grown-ups are very busy people and have their minds on other things; sometimes they are tired, or are cross about something that's nothing to do with you at all – that doesn't mean they don't love you, or don't want you. It's funny but I had to explain that to my own little boy just last night. But I was able to tell him that he was wanted and loved, and give him a cuddle. I wish I could give you a cuddle now and make you feel safe. (I stop and cuddle cushion).

I love you and I promise I won't let you down anymore. We'll sort things out and get you to feel safe.

Lots of love
Mike.

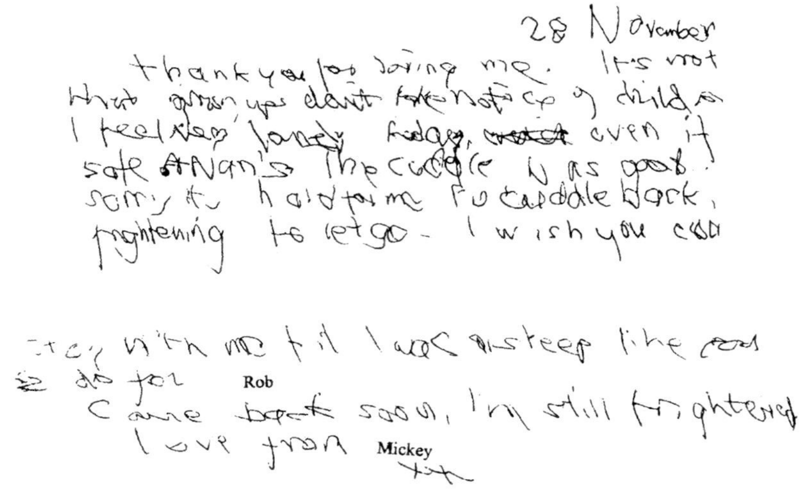

Figure 11.2

I had suggested that Mike visualises the child at these times and uses a cushion (or a big pillow) to represent him. I encouraged Mike to take the pillow and sit it on his knee, or lie down on a bed and cuddle the pillow, while using the senses to imagine the weight of the child, the softness of his skin, the warmth of his body, and to listen to what the child might be saying (Figure 11.2).

28th November

Thank you for loving me. It's not fair that grown-ups don't take notice of children I feel very lonely today even if I'm safe at Nan's. The cuddle was good. Sorry it's hard to me to cuddle back, frightening to let go. I wish you could stay with me 'til I was asleep like you do for Rob.

Come back soon, I'm still frightened.

Love from
Mickey XX

In the child's response, Mike's ambivalence about attachment is evident in that he likes the cuddle, but also recognises that it is hard to give a cuddle in response, while also being scared of letting go. The letters become more frequent as Mike's life becomes more tumultuous – his family is struggling to come to terms with the disclosures that lead to ever more disclosures.

There are signs of a shift in the age of the child to whom he is writing – the language is more adult and seems to be addressing issues about his changing body – something that comes with adolescence.

Monday, 4th December 1995

Dear Mickey,

I've just been looking at your photograph and felt I should write to you. It has taken me a long time to contact you I know, and I'm sorry for that. I'm afraid I've not liked you until now and that must have felt very unkind; but now I realise that of course it was fear of seeing myself in you that has come out as dislike. I am so sorry, so very sorry for that. Of course I know what is going on in your life and what a turmoil you're in. Oh, I know you don't see it that way, but you know, all that anger you feel has a cause and the cause is Grampy. You are *not* to blame – *he is*! You look around and wonder what its like to have sexuality awaken in its own time – Oh how much he has deprived you of!

In the picture you look so sad, so awkward in that body of which you should be so proud and with which you should be so excited. And who is there for you to turn to? No one, I know. Isn't that sad that you can't turn to your parents – but he's taken that too hasn't he? I love you, please realise that. I am here for you in your sadness and despair – I will help you, I promise; but try to let go and let me know how you are feeling.

I must close now, but please write soon.

Mike

The letter back from the child, the following day, makes it very clear that he is at the stage of adolescence. The handwriting is rounded and joined-up. He is distressed about being disliked by his peers; his body and his fear begins to emerge. Even Grampy does not like his bodily changes – paedophiles do not like to see any signs of puberty, sometimes going so far as to shave a child's pubic hair to keep them as children for as long as possible (Figure 11.3).

Mike reacts quickly as he recognises Mickey's need for reassurance and containment. However, it is clear that most of the young boy's self-esteem is related to being 'helpful' and 'caring'. In this letter we begin to hear about Mike's spiritual life and the importance of God and the Church.

Tuesday

Dear Mike, [Chapel]

I'm sitting here in the trying to think what to write to you! I'm sitting here, in my place as a form-prefect, felling very sad. I feel that no-one likes me. I know that some of these youngsters are a bit fond of me but that doesn't really count, does it? The teachers, well, some of them, are pleased with my work, but I think that's for their own benefit, perhaps. Well, I'm no good at sport and all that macho stuff am I? And I don't fit in with my family, do I? Especially, they tease me about my "posh" accent and they don't understand about school and stuff. I just don't fit. I get so fed up at home, Mum and Dad argue and Stephen runs off, and I feel lonely and frightened. Can I kill myself? No, it's wrong I know. I'm not like the other boys at all, and I've got the worst spots in the whole school now. Dad keeps on about them, saying I don't wash and telling me I've got to put a hot flannel on my face. I do, it doesn't work. He doesn't like me, does he; he never tells me anyway.

The only one who likes me is Him, he's always telling me I'm handsome, but he doesn't like my beard; he wants his little boy back.

But he would wouldn't he, because of what he does to me.

I am so sad and so lonely, no-one loves me for me.

Please help me, please look after me; I'm frightened, of him, of me, of Dad, of people finding out and knowing.

yours sincerely

Mickey

Figure 11.3

Same day.

I've just read your letter, and it's worried me very much. You are a good lad, you really are. You're caring of others aren't you – look how you feel so responsible for that class of noisy boys that you are here with! You care about the world, and what's happening in it. You care about God and the Church and so on. And really your spots aren't that bad and you're really not bad looking. And you're likeable you know. People who treat you like an adult do like you – the teachers do I'm sure – even if you are helping them keep their reputation up! Most of all I like you. I love you – please remember that. Enjoy your school days – they are good. Don't let him take them away from you.

I am very, very angry indeed, but with HIM not you – and don't you forget that. Must close for now but I'll write soon.

Mike

Stories for the Child Within

As the client discovers and strengthens his Adult, I encourage him to become the good parent to himself, always bearing in mind the time when the client will leave the counselling relationship and become self-supporting. One way of doing this is to suggest that the client writes a story for the Child within; a story which contains 'the moral' that the child most needs to hear. There is a lovely storybook that I enjoy reading to my small grandson which is called *I Love You Just The Way You Are* (Miller 1998). It tells the story of a small bear called Bartholomew who is sometimes very grumpy and badly behaved, but in spite of this George, his adult friend, loves him. The moral of this story is 'unconditional love'. I suggest to clients that they might write the story that their child within most needs to hear. The timing of this task is often when I am going to be away for a few weeks and the client needs to find the carer within himself.

The story might be written as a fairy tale. Listening to and writing fairy tales makes us travel back into our imaginary world of childhood and, with the conscious or unconscious co-operation of the client, it may become a way of entering into a state of altered consciousness. During abuse, children often enter such states as a way of dissociating from what is happening. People speak of 'leaving the body' or 'switching off', to keep the abuse compartmentalised and thereby to preserve one part of the self from harm. Children sitting around the teacher's feet in the classroom listening to a fairy story can clearly be seen to be lost in 'a world of their own' – daydreaming and imaging the pictures in their mind's eye. It is therefore sometimes necessary for the adult survivor to re-enter such a state for the healing integration to occur.

Fairy stories and the metaphors contained within them activate a series of psychological associations and start the mind working at an unconscious level, without the paralysing interference of conscious thought. This can open up a healing space that has special value because metaphor represents the language of the right brain and allows the client to expand into the unknown part of themselves to connect with 'gifts not yet exploited' (Godin and Ooghourlian 1994, p.189).

Bettelheim (1976) explains that fairy tales have therapeutic value because they allow the client to meditate about what the story reveals about himself and his internal conflict at a given time in his life. Fairy tales may be rewritten to convey personal, metaphoric meaning; the metaphor can trigger identification with the 'hero' of the story.

Mike and Stephen created the new fairy story of their lives (Chapter 1) which starts with the old fairy story of happy families. They have created an ending that is in line with the reality they have now accepted, although they know that some of their family have retreated back into the original fairy story – having been unable or unwilling to rewrite their own life stories. Mike and Stephen recognised that they had been living in a family fairy story, which was part of a closed, rigid system of beliefs that blocked anybody seeing the reality of their lives. They laughingly refer to a new fairy story, 'The Elephant in the Living Room', as a way of describing being in their family of origin now. Everybody can see the elephant but nobody mentions it – at least now everybody knows it is there! I referred to a previous conversation when I met with Mike and Stephen to begin discussing this book:

Kim: *Mike has talked about this elephant that sits in the middle of your living room...*

Stephen: I've met him, yes.

Kim: *You know the one?*

Stephen: Yes – he was there for most of our lives.

Writing Letters From the Adult

Mike writes a letter he has been postponing for a long time – his letter to God. In this letter he begins to separate inappropriate guilt (about the abuse) from appropriate guilt for his behaviour towards others. Although he recognises the cause of his behaviour, he still needs to take responsibility for it if he is to break the cycle of abuse. He wants to ask for forgiveness for his wrongs to others. He also wants to be able to forgive the wrongs that have been done to him.

Clients who have a relationship with God and the Church often need to address the issue of forgiveness. The concept of God the Father can create difficulties if their experience of 'father' or indeed 'grandfather' has been abusive. The internalised image of 'father' is tainted and spoiled. Stephen, unlike Mike, had fallen out with God because of the damage that had been done to him. His grandfather was a staunch member of the Church and symbolised hypocrisy and betrayal, which Stephen associated with his feelings of having been betrayed by God. Clients need to be allowed not to forgive; we should not expect people to forgive those who have not acknowledged what they have done, made amends and asked for forgiveness.

Moving too quickly towards forgiveness can be an avoidance of anger and fear, either for the counsellor or the client.

Gramps had previously asked Mike for forgiveness, having made a half-hearted apology, while at the same time justifying his behaviour and appearing to have no real understanding and empathy for his victims. Mike had attempted to forgive him but did not have it in his heart to do so. In his letter to God Mike asks for forgiveness for his own aggressive behaviour towards his wife and children:

Friday

God,

I've been putting this off for some time, but I know I need to make contact with you over this. Of course you know, but I need to tell you: I was sexually abused as a child, from very young until my late teens. As you know I have felt very guilty about it, but I realise now that this is not something to feel guilty about.

I feel very damaged by my childhood – so much of my psychological and emotional development has been arrested. I am moved very much by other's sins and I pray that you will give me grace day by day to forgive.

Most of all I need to say how bad I feel for all the damage that my screwed up life has done to others. It takes me a lot of courage to write this down. Especially, I feel so sorry that my repressed anger has hurt others, particularly Ellen and Judy. I feel desperate that I have not been able to show them that emotions are OK. I have transmitted that problem down the line I know. I ask you with all my heart to show me how and give me the strength to make amends. I do love Ellen and the children so much, and I am so sorry for all the damage that has been done. Please help us to love one another.

I am sorry too for all the other things I have done wrong, which are as a consequence of the abuse. You know them all I'm sure. I don't suppose there's any way of me making up for everything and I look to your love emblazoned in pain on the cross. That is the only way to atonement for me; and to offer my own pain. It has taken me a long time to realise things in my life which I have long neglected intellectually. I can only offer myself to you 'in dust and ashes'. I know now in my heart the importance of your Fatherhood, help me to keep that.

Lord, please help me to deal with all the calls on my time and to make time in the day for me and for you.

Give me the grace to forgive, to listen, to acknowledge; day by day, minute by minute.

Mike's internalised sense of God grants him forgiveness:

My son, be still. Be at peace. I love you now and always. I am here for you whenever you want me. Trust me, and it will be alright. See the good in yourself as well as the bad. Remember that you will find me at home in your loved ones as much as anywhere else. Be still, be at peace.

CHAPTER 12

Bodywork

There are some experiences that can never be written about – they just are. So in this chapter I am aware that I cannot do full justice to the topic of bodywork, because it is an experience and the very nature of 'experience' is elusive.

A Toe in the Water

Had I not been given a gift voucher for an aromatherapy massage many years ago, I might not have ever had subsequent experiences. Being a war baby and therefore unable to waste anything, I eventually had to use the voucher and took myself off, with some trepidation, to face the 'unknown' behind the doors of the 'massage parlour'. Unfortunately massage parlours have all sorts of unsavoury connotations attached and I found myself glancing furtively over my shoulder to make sure nobody was watching as I entered.

It was an amazing experience but I was not to repeat it for another six or seven years. In the meantime I had grown more and more convinced that talking therapy was not going to 'reach the spot' for me, although it had brought me a long way. But I was suspicious and untrusting and did not know how to find someone to whom I could entrust my body. A respected supervisee eventually gave me a name which I held on to for another year or so. Eventually I took the plunge and this was how I met Sarasi.

Up to My Neck

I worked with Sarasi using breathing, deep massage, visualisation and catharsis. It was a powerful and important experience that helped me connect with body memories, imprinted before I was able to use language or cognition to code my experiences. The work enabled me to gain control of my dissociation by making it conscious, recognising what the triggers were and thereby being able to change habitual patterns laid down in my childhood as a way of coping with my fear, but now redundant. I claimed my body for the first time in my life. I began to feel as though my body belonged to me and I began to enjoy being inside it. It was through this work that I managed to separate out myself from the 'merged' relationship I had with my husband, and Sarasi supported me through the terrifying changes of being alone for the first time in my life. Through this work I began to understand true intimacy – to feel the fear and reach through it to a physical, emotional and sexual closeness that was not based upon dependence or need, but on desire and choice.

I had had a complicated relationship with my body for a long time. As the only female in the family I had always felt something of a 'freak' – especially as the message within my home was that maleness was equated with superiority and strength and femaleness with weakness. My mother was frequently ill and I was usually the one who was kept off school to care for her. On the whole I was quite a healthy child and pretty tough too – for a girl. I tried hard to prove that I was as good as or better than the boys, better at fighting, racing on my bike, climbing lamp-posts and jumping from the swing as it reached its highest point. On the whole I lived quite dangerously and got away with it.

My Body Remembers

I remember one day writhing in pain on the floor (I think I must have had colic) and my mother standing over me laughing and saying, 'Every picture tells a story' – no sympathy or caring, just derision. But when I was about ten years old something happened that made me realise that being ill provided me with the kind of care and attention that I had not received in any other way. On this occasion I had developed a pain in my stomach and my father was present; he made quite a fuss about it, calling in the local doctor. Before the doctor arrived I had for the first time realised that my mother was a bit worried about me and my father was quite frantic. I had never experienced this kind of concern before. The doctor pressed my stomach and suggested that I might need checking over at the hospital. A few hours later I was in bed in a hospital ward full of other children and my parents had supplied me with comics. The following story was one I wrote based on my time in the hospital. I wrote it in the third person, about a little girl called Marion.

> *A few days went by, each day the doctor came and pressed her stomach.*
>
> *'Does it hurt?' he'd ask. She wasn't sure any more so she said, 'Sometimes.'*
>
> *The doctor was nice and seemed to like her. He shook his head and said to the Sister, 'We'll keep an eye on her for a while longer then Sister' and Sister smiled back at him, as if in some secret conspiracy. Marion imagined that they were really her mother and father and that a wicked witch had taken her away from them at birth. They were so pleased to have her back they had decided to pretend they were her doctor and nurse so that they could see her whenever they wanted to. She would play along with that until they could find a way of having her with them forever.*
>
> *There was a black girl in the next bed who was always in trouble with the nursing staff. She used the bed as a trampoline and her long skinny legs flew in the air as she bounced down on her bottom. Marion was delighted with her. She had never before met anybody quite so free in her behaviour and when Natalie told Marion that she was pretending to be*

ill because it was nicer here than in the Children's Home where she lived, Marion marvelled at her cleverness. Marion never knew the point at which she decided to say the pain was still there after she knew it had gone. She had been brought up to tell the truth, so she easily convinced herself that she did still feel a pain in her stomach from time to time, and indeed she did. Each time she thought about going home her stomach began to hurt. Then they started to talk about an operation to remove her appendix; grumbling appendicitis they called it. Marion watched closely to see what happened to other children who had appendicitis and she discovered that they were taken from the ward on a trolley and on the way to the operating theatre the ward sister asked 'Have you had anything to eat today?' Apparently it was necessary to say 'No'; so when the day came for Marion to be taken on the trolley past the Sister's desk and she was asked the question she answered 'Yes, I had my breakfast.' She was taken back to her bed and the operation was postponed. But this could not go on forever and eventually the operation was performed. She had overheard the staff nurse telling her father that they had found a healthy appendix when they opened her up, but they had removed it anyway.

But the stay in hospital had taught Marion that there were places in the world where she could be cared for and worried about. The price to pay for that safety was pain; the pain she had suffered post-operatively had been a fair price for the reward. But in the end it could not last forever and she had returned back home where things went on in much the same way as before.

The Body Speaks

So that began a pattern which I used throughout my life. I had no way of communicating my need for care and attention so my body communicated it for me. It was not a conscious decision – it is only in recent years that I wrote the above, having come to understand more of my story. So illness became the only way of resting from the relentless hard work that I used to escape from myself and attempt to prove to the world that I was 'good enough'. However, it brought me no real rest or comfort because somewhere inside myself I felt really 'bad' whenever I was ill. So I fought against it and made myself really ill in the process.

When a child is abused they know at some level that something 'bad' is happening. Because a child is completely dependent on the adult, they cannot allow the 'bad' to be located in the adult. A child needs a 'good' parent upon whom they can depend; their survival requires it. It may be the case that the adult is also someone who is 'good' in other spheres of the child's life. The father who plays with the child, buys them an ice-cream, gives them treats, might be the same father/grandfather who abuses them. Gramps had 'a jolly, red, round face, and a mop of white hair. He told lots of funny stories, and made everybody laugh. And everybody loved him.'

So the 'bad' cannot be given to the adult, but it has to be contained somewhere if is not to become overwhelming – so the child takes in the bad and makes it his own.

The emotions are split off and contained within the 'nightime self' – out of contact and awareness. In this state of dissociation my 'bad' became associated with my body and my body became my enemy. So I punished my body with illness, unnecessary surgical operations and investigations, and I felt more and more alienated from 'it'. Many of my later operations and investigations were centred around abdominal and gynaecological complaints – the parts of my body that held the unconscious body memories that I was to discover much later, after a hysterectomy. Davies and Frawley (1994) note that 'specific abuse memories are often encoded in specific somatic states that recur with regularity, and particularly at times of acute distress'; and that 'invasive medical procedures (like addictive acts of self-abuse) represent reenactments of the painful, intrusive sexual abuse' (p.50).

Somatisation

So my unconscious emotional distress became somatised (expressed through my body) and my need for care, attention and rest was sought through illness. However, my real needs were not being met because while they were out of my awareness I was not able to articulate them directly. So the split off dissociated parts of experience can be manifest through somatic disorders. Sadly, doctors do not seem able to help; they might respond to the symptoms but not to the underlying cause. Having investigated the symptoms and found no pathology, some doctors treat patients as malingerers, 'hysterics' or hypochondriacs. Further pain is caused to the patient who may be shamed in this process – thus the initial abuse is re-enacted over and over again.

In general, society is less ready to acknowledge and respond helpfully to emotional rather than physical complaints – there is still a degree of stigma attached to being mentally or emotionally vulnerable. This is particularly difficult for men who have been taught that toughness and invulnerability are indicators of masculinity. Physical symptoms more frequently attract sympathy and care (Wilkinson and Bass 1994).

Psychosomatic disorders

Another way of the body responding to unconscious material is by developing psychosomatic disorders – this is a way of describing a pathological condition that is caused or exacerbated by emotional or psychosocial factors. These conditions are usually related to stress. I have already described the condition of post-traumatic stress disorder as an outcome of sexual abuse during childhood. The abuse creates a trauma that is experienced as a stressor holding the body in a state of chronic tension and hypervigilance, which can become acute when activated by triggers that remind the person of the original trauma. These may become manifest as panic attacks, phobias, flashbacks and nightmares or they may be held as low level stressors causing chronic problems such as headaches, stomach ulcers and irritable bowel syndrome and may adversely affect immune functions and general health. As the original trauma is healed the psychosomatic disorders also heal.

Additionally, there is a growing body of concern about the increased health risks associated with a history of childhood sexual abuse. A study in the USA (Felitti 1998) involving 9500 people found that the risk of smoking, severe obesity, physical inactivity, depressed mood and suicide attempts increased 'as the number of childhood exposures (to abuse or dysfunctional households) increased'. Study participants whose childhoods ranked among the most difficult had more than twice the rate of heart disease, cancer and chronic bronchitis compared with individuals whose childhood was reported to be the least troubled. The increased risk of sexual disease among those who have coped with their childhood by engaging in high-risk sexual activity (perhaps re-enacting their abuse), whether homosexual and heterosexual, has also been reported. Increased use of alcohol and drugs is often found among trauma victims who attempt to increase their capacity to dissociate and remain numbed from feeling the painful experiences of childhood.

Hysteria

Hysteria was described by Freud as a way that intolerable psychological experiences were converted into physical symptoms – a historically female condition. Later 'shell shock' was the name given to the version of the same disorder seen in men during World War I. Men came back from the front suffering from blindness, paralysis, etc. with no apparent pathological cause. Similar symptoms can be found among many abuse survivors today. I have met several who have spent at least a period of their lives wheelchair bound, sometimes mistakenly diagnosed with multiple sclerosis. Others have been diagnosed as epileptic, having suffered 'fits' and been given medication. Greig and Betts (1992) reported that there is a growing suggestion of a causal relationship between non-epileptic seizures (pseudo-seizures) and sexual abuse. The nature of the disability often relates to the nature of unresolved conflict. For example, a stammer or inability to speak may relate to having something to say that is impossible to articulate, such as a child who is being abused by a close family member might experience.

Body Therapies

Reichian

Body therapy is by no means new. Freud said in 1923 that 'the ego is ultimately derived from bodily sensations'. Later, his student Reich (1949), who criticised the slowness of analysis in creating change and its taboo on touch, founded body psychotherapy. He believed that people develop muscular armouring during childhood in order to avoid painful emotions. For example, a child who carries too much responsibility may develop rounded shoulders, as if 'carrying the whole world on his shoulders'; or a boy who has been taught to have a 'stiff upper lip' and not to cry might develop tight muscles around the mouth and tension in his neck and shoulder muscles when he feels like crying.

This armour may serve a useful purpose during childhood, but its persistence into adulthood blocks the natural flow of energy, limiting the capacity for pleasure (Hull 1997). Reich believed that by manipulation of these muscles a loosening of tension occurs which will allow the release of the emotions contained within them.

He saw these blocks as a way of preventing 'forbidden impulses' from erupting from within us. He pointed out the amount of energy that was wasted in suppressing these impulses to cry, rage, shout, dance, or whatever we were inhibited from doing during childhood. When we inhibit our output, our energy is low and we inhibit our input accordingly, by breathing shallowly and cutting ourselves off from experiences. His technique for raising the energy level in the body was to encourage the person to take in more energy, perhaps by deep breathing, and to increase the discharge of energy by expressing deep feelings or by allowing the 'orgasm reflex'.

This reflex occurs when the body is open enough to release the flow of waves of energy that pass through the body – such as occurs during love making and orgasm. Reich believed that the ability to fully experience release through orgasm was an important sign of the health of the organism. He saw sex as the main outlet for the release and regulation of the high energy level of the healthy person (Ernst and Goodison 1981).

Reich's belief in sexual freedom of expression created a rupture between him and the analytic community in Europe. He then moved to the USA where he died in prison of a heart attack. He had produced a device which he stated could be used to cure people by absorbing orgone energy collected from the atmosphere. The device was banned by the US Food and Drug Administration and Reich was imprisoned for ignoring the ban. His present-day followers are medically trained and still adhere to his practices.

Reich (1951) understood how, as a Western society, we had become repressed and inhibited by our subtle conditioning; that males must be strong, not cry, suppress tender feelings; and that as females we were taught to suppress our assertive and aggressive instincts – much as I have described earlier. He was particularly concerned about the repression of sexuality and the manner in which a child has been taught to suppress its natural sexual curiosity. He saw that children were taught to deny and fear their bodies and their instincts and how that could lead to a fear of life itself.

Reich believed that it was only through a positive relationship with our body that we could feel self-respect, connect with our power and take responsibility for our life. It seemed to him that what was considered normal within our society was greatly at odds with what he believed to be our full potential. It was against such attitudes in society that body therapy had to work. The same struggle continues today.

Bioenergetics

Alexander Lowen (1967) was a student and patient of Reich and in the 1950s and 1960s he developed Bioenergetics with John Pierrakos. Bioenergetics works from the belief that 'we are our bodies' and that our physical expressions serve our way of being in the world. Lowen placed less emphasis on sexuality than Reich, seeing it as only one of many basic bodily drives including moving, breathing and feeling. I watched Lowen work during a demonstration at a conference in Hamburg in 1995 and I was impressed by the energy of the small man. He worked on the stage with a woman whom he 'grounded', by having her feet firmly planted on the ground, shoulder width apart. Having one's feet firmly on the ground is central to Bioenergetics. Then he asked the woman to lean backwards over a 'breathing stool'. As she expanded her diaphragm and breathed deeply the woman's legs began to shake uncontrollably and my understanding is that in that shaking the energy is released. However, Lowen was careful to point out that the *release of emotions* is not an end in itself, but part of a process of reintegration. Once we have overcome our terror and 'let go', that gives us the power to decide *when* we want to let go and when we do not. He called this 'self-possession':

> The containment is conscious and voluntary which presupposes an ability to let go. If one can't let go because the holding is unconscious and structured in the body, one can't speak of containment as a conscious expression of the self. The person doesn't contain: he is contained. (Lowen 1976, p.298)

It all looked extremely uncomfortable to me as an observer and I decided that my work with Sarasi was much more soothing. However, meeting the man and reading his books left a powerful impression on me. He must have been in his eighties at the time, still lecturing and giving workshops; if he practises what he preaches, he is a marvellous advertisement for the work.

Gestalt

Fritz Perls was another student of Reich. Perls's Gestalt psychotherapy (1969) focused on what was happening in the present, unlike Freud's work which was focused on the past. He was influenced by the existential school of philosophy. He moved away from interpretation, intellectualisation and rationalisation towards experiencing what we experience in the moment. He introduced the idea of 'closure' and finishing off 'unfinished business' in order to make an experience fully rounded and whole. He also encouraged 'filling in the gaps' of our experience, by recognising and taking back our projections, by becoming aware of the tensions in our bodies or the parts of ourselves symbolised through our dreams.

Gestalt therapy stresses the unity of all experience and healing is understood to occur through bringing together the unnatural splits between parts of ourselves and our world. A technique that is commonly used in this process is creating dialogue between two split parts, by placing them outside ourselves and exploring what is contained within each split off part. If the feelings are explored fully, there may be integration as the two parts come together. These may be conflicting parts within ourselves or parts of ourselves that we have projected onto others and disowned.

Perls saw therapy as a process of growing, of increasing in wholeness as we reclaimed all aspects of our experience in response to listening to the wisdom of our bodies. In Gestalt therapy behaviour is not interpreted as neurotic, but examined so that the person begins to understand how the patterns might be serving us or working against us; showing us alternative options in the process.

Integrative approaches

Body therapists work from the premise that the body has a wisdom beyond our everyday understanding, although there are scientists who have in recent years found ways of explaining this wisdom in terms that are scientific and logical (Pert 1998):

> My research has shown me that when emotions are expressed – which is to say that the biochemicals that are the substrate of emotion are flowing freely – all systems are united and made whole. When emotions are repressed, denied, not allowed to be whatever they may be, our network pathways get blocked, stopping the flow of the vital feel-good, unifying chemicals that run both our biology and our behaviour. (Pert 1998, p.273)

More recently bodywork has drawn from a variety of disciplines and integrated them into a new whole; postmodernism has reached the body! Integrative Body Psychotherapy, founded by Jack Rosenberg and Marjorie Rand, combines Reichian and Gestalt principles with yoga, dance and acupuncture, among other traditions (Hull 1997).

Biosynthesis

During the 1970s David Boadella created Biosynthesis, a somatic therapeutic method. He sought to integrate a tradition developed out of Freud's work by Reich, Lowen and Boyesen with another which focused on pre-natal experience; and a third, which is linked into the Object Relations School and Lake's work with regression therapy, which was initially used with LSD and later with breathing.

Biosynthesis is a process therapy which recognises the uniqueness of the individual and the variety of developmental paths that underlie our formation of self. The person is seen as multi-dimensional and the distinct levels of impression and expression are understood to be interconnected life fields of experience. Because polarity is a central concept in Biosynthesis, one person's nourishment can be another person's poison. Principle polarities are: inner work versus outer work; rising or sinking energies; active versus receptive; regressive versus progressive, and the play of interactions between verbal and non-verbal communication systems.

In working with the variety of human individuality, the therapist sees a range of polarities in his choice of approaches and is guided by the client's responses as to which side of each polarity to give preference to at any given time. In the dance of energies between therapist and client, self and other, the personal bio-drama of the person seeking help becomes highlighted, so that the latent meanings become embodied and a person gains help to respond to the dynamic of the inner ground guiding his journey.

Some people have criticised traditional body therapies as too forceful, pushing against defences and blocks in a way that can be experienced as re-traumatising. In response to this Ron Kurtz developed Hakomi which draws from Buddhism and Taoism. This involves using gentle and physical probes to elicit core beliefs held within the person that limit their life. For instance, if somebody believes that 'I will always be let down by people I trust', they might be asked to fall backwards into the therapist's arms, thereby experiencing the opposite of the premise they are holding. This method advocates self-reflection that produces change through increased awareness, rather than the effort involved in cathartic methods such as Reichian therapy.

So having outlined some of the ways of working with the body I will go on to consider some of the challenges when therapists attempt to integrate the Cartesian split between mind and body by working together to provide an holistic service for clients.

CHAPTER 13

Collaborative Working

Values and Beliefs

Needless to say, as with any other form of counselling and therapy, it is important that practitioners are suitably trained and that those of us who choose to work collaboratively explore together what we can do and what we are not trained to do. There are some fundamental differences in philosophies that can create problems between collaborating therapists. It is important to have a shared belief system concerning how change occurs, the use of supervision and the ethics of working with vulnerable people. Shared beliefs are also important between the therapist and the supervisor. Penny Henderson (2000) comments that 'the supervisor needs to have a developed set of beliefs which do not undermine this work, and do support it'. She adds that, as far as it is realistic, the supervisor needs to help to make it safe by rigorous attention to assessment of the client within the context of the work and by clarity about the therapist's limits and her own. It is clear from this that a supervisor who views the client in 'modern' terms (McLeod 1997) will have difficulty in managing to support the worker. Seaburn *et al.* (1996) note that the key ingredients in any collaboration in the field of health are:

1. The quality of relationship between the collaborators.

2. The commonality of purpose in working together.

3. Having perspectives on the work that are not mutually excluding (especially about understanding about the nature of the change process).

4. Clear, open communication with sufficient understanding of each other's language.

5. Geographic location that creates enough opportunity for communication to occur between collaborators.

6. Having a clear business arrangement that allows for the acknowledgement of a flexible hierarchy which depends on who is the key worker at any given time.

Working Together

Achieving all of this is not always easy; the very fact that workers have chosen different approaches usually indicates some differences in beliefs. However, I believe that if these differences can be brought out into the open, in order to recognise how they might either enhance or become a problem in the shared work, they can be creatively used and contribute to the growth of both workers and clients. It is often at the edges of boundaries that most creativity occurs. Hull (1997) comments on the lack of dialogue between the more traditional talking therapeutic schools and the field of body therapies and sees this as preventing the development of a common language. She reports a comment by Johnson who states: 'It's been very hard on a large level to get people together to do serious dialogue on casework. We need to get beyond sectarian dialogues and focus on healing the person' (p.7). She also reports a comment by a spokeswoman for the American Psychological Association, which has no official position on body psychotherapy: 'no-one here knows much about it'.

I am frequently asked to recommend a counsellor, therapist or appropriate helper to someone seeking to work on themselves, which is something I find very difficult. I can only know what I have experienced and what I have experienced may not be the same for another person. So my trust in and knowledge of Sarasi was because I had experienced the value of working with her first hand – for myself. Others have to establish their own ability to trust. But it was clear from what Stephen and Mike said that through their trust of me they were able to risk trusting their bodies to a stranger; not only a stranger, but someone who worked in ways about which they were cynical and mistrusting. In helping them across that threshold, by telling them of my experience and pointing out that it was mine and theirs would be different, that I was able to help them make a choice by giving information. This is a very powerful position and I found myself feeling quite scared of the responsibility they had handed me as they spoke about it in our research conversations. But I accepted that I had a responsibility towards them to ensure that they found trustworthy help while knowing that they would still have to face their own struggle with trust.

In postmodern times, 'schoolism' within counselling and therapy is being recognised as restrictive and holistic and 'integrative' approaches are becoming the norm. If we focus on our client's needs and not our own (which may be to preserve ourselves from 'contamination', to stem the threat of extinction or survival), we might do best to think about how we can work together more effectively. It may also be that our own fear of working through the body may make us disinclined to think of it as useful for our clients. David Boadella (1988) challenges the limitations of what we might offer to our clients: 'A good therapist with a limited technique will have a good effect on a client in a limited area. Thus a good verbal therapist may help a client to very important insights yet neglect crucial areas of somatic change' (p.164).

From time to time I have found myself struggling with feelings of insecurity as I have listened to my clients talking about the value of the work they are doing with Sarasi. A little voice inside my head sometimes whispers: 'She's much better for them than you are.' She tells me that sometimes the same little voice speaks to her, undermining her confidence as clients praise my work to her. This is something we need to acknowledge and explore. There is, of course, potential for splitting and by holding the split and letting clients know that we talk together, we usually manage to avoid that. If clients express concern or conflict with Sarasi, I will encourage them to talk to her about it; she does the same if they have negative feelings about me. We need to acknowledge the jealousies that spring up between us and the imbalance of power that sometimes occurs. Like any relationship, we need to dialogue and address the conflicts if the relationship is to be healthy.

There are some clients for whom collaborative working might not be helpful. Some clients need to be contained by one person and may feel too disturbed by the idea of working across two therapists at the same time. One client told me that she had experienced my suggestion of working concurrently with Sarasi as being told that she was 'too difficult' for one person to manage. In supervision I realised that my counter-transference had indeed been about feeling that she needed two 'good parents'. She had been abused by both mother and father, and there were times when I felt I was not enough for her. She helped me to realise that being held by one 'good enough parent' was exactly what she wanted and needed. She was also a 'hermetically sealed-in' client with whom I found it very hard to make contact for a considerable period of time. However, she refused to be 'fobbed off', as she described it, and stayed with me to a fruitful ending. It may be that at some time in the future she will decide for herself to use body work – and that will then be right for her.

Boundaries

Boundaries are always a live issue between us and with our clients. Overlapping relationships need to be constantly examined to explore how they might be affecting us and our work. It is crucial that our clients are held within firm and safe boundaries until such time as those boundaries become internalised. Internalised boundaries allow for further flexibility but unthinkingly adhering to boundaries might, in the longer term, prevent our clients from gaining a real understanding of their purpose. Boundaries that are rigid and automatic can become a repetition of the way in which the client has coped in the past – a way of compartmentalising areas of their existence in order to gain control. Boundaries might be useful ways of describing, naming, defining differences and what is 'self' and 'other', but 'when you establish a boundary so as to gain control over something, at the same time you separate and alienate yourself from that which you attempt to control' (Wilber 1979).

A boundary line both separates and unites but it is most often at the edges, where the overlaps occur, that the most useful and interesting things happen. It is in those moments of overlap between waking and sleeping that we allow our unconscious thoughts, feelings and images to emerge. In moments of existential contact with our clients, the rich clutter of deeper experiences has the opportunity to arise and become conscious through symbols, metaphors and ideas. A boundary line marks off an inside and an outside; the opposites of inside and outside do not exist in themselves until we draw a boundary line. Wilber (1979) describes a boundary as a potential battle line, an area of conflict. If we treat boundaries as 'real', we may then imagine that the opposites they create may be irreconcilable, separate, forever set part.

All of the above applies to differences in approaches to the work with clients, as well as our relationship as providers of an holistic service for them. It also applies to the boundary issues for the client where the boundary of his body is the skin, the outer layer of his body that has been touched in ways that have been damaging to his sense of self. The contact of flesh upon flesh during massage creates an overlap between two bodies that is non-sexual, soothing and healing. But it is in those moments of contact and overlap that unconscious feelings emerge and dissociation occurs. We begin to connect our sensual body with our emotional body.

People who have been sexually abused have had their boundaries ignored and invaded. Part of the healing through body therapy is enabling clients to choose whether or not they will allow themselves to be touched. If clients are reacting automatically to programmes that are out of date, they are not choosing – they are being controlled by the past. However, clients usually need help to make that choice. Raine (1999) comments on the violation of a person's most basic human need – the right to control one's own body:

> By destroying my ability to control my own body, he [the rapist] had made my body an object. I lost a sense of it as a boundary of self, the fundamental and most sacred borders. A self without boundaries is like a weak country that has been overrun by a stronger one. Once the borders are violated and the invader is entrenched, inhabitants can do little more than go into hiding and hope for outside aid. Touch that respects bodyright is healing; it restores the autonomy and authenticity of the self. (Raine 1999, p.163)

Part of my ongoing assessment of clients and evaluation of the work is deciding when it might be appropriate to consider complementing our work with body therapy. There are some clients with whom I do not talk about it as an option at all. For some people touch can be too confusing. Breaking down rigid emotional patterns can lead to disintegration or even reinforce avoidance – using the work, unconsciously and intra-psychically, as a repetition of past behaviours.

Confidentiality is an important issue that is understood and agreed between myself and the client. When working with another therapist it is important that we work together and this means gaining the client's permission to discuss the work. Counsellor's sometimes lose sight of the fact that confidentiality is for the protection of the client and not an end in itself. In many settings it is not possible or desirable to stick to what most counsellors would think of as the 'normal' rules. For instance, in a GP setting, counsellors need to keep the doctors informed about clients; not necessarily about the content of the work, although sometimes, when it is in the client's interest and with the client's full knowledge and permission, that too. What is important is that the contract is clear and negotiated with the client – and permission given.

I normally gave Sarasi an outline of the client's issue and the reasons for the referral on to her, although as we became more familiar with shared working I left the client to do that for themselves. Clients often brought back from her sessions experiences that needed to be reflected upon and understood in order to explore their meaning and assimilate fully. Sometimes material that came up in sessions with me was picked up in the bodywork sessions and in that way we built on the process – filling in the gaps in experiences.

So body therapy invites us to 'come to our senses', as Perls (1969) said; but it is not suitable for everybody, just as I believe talking therapy is not suitable for everybody. Many people would say that body therapy or any form of touch should not be used with survivors of sexual abuse. Generally speaking, I believe survivors of sexual abuse need bodywork more than do those who have not experienced sexual abuse. During abuse, whether physical or sexual, many people cope by 'leaving the body'. This is a description of dissociation often heard by those of us in this field of sexual abuse and often when physical abuse has been experienced without sexual abuse. As I have said earlier, this may become an automatic response to anything that unconsciously reminds us of the abuse. As clients begin to talk about their abuse I have sometimes had an uncanny sense that there is a fog between us or even that they are elevating in the chair. (I risk saying that even though you might be thinking I'm mad, but some of you will know what I mean.) As they begin to get closer to the feelings, the clients begin automatically to dissociate. Breathing becomes shallow or ceases for long periods, the eyes may close or glaze over, the client 'spaces out' and may become vague or silent.

My Story of Bodywork

During massage I began to notice myself dissociating – consciously aware of the experience for the first time. As Sarasi's hands moved over my body I felt the seduction of dissociation; I wanted to space out – it was a very powerful pull, a kind of warm blanket offering comfort and escape. She noticed me dissociating (holding my breath, growing stiller) and called me back into my body – saying 'keep the breath going Kim'. I didn't want to – I refused and I escaped. Time and time again the same thing happened, until eventually I began to feel safe enough to risk finding out what it would be like to stay in my body and feel my fear. She worked hard to keep me there, on the table, and eventually I was able to stay and enjoy the sensation of being touched, soothed and massaged from within my skin. The fear was not about 'here and now' – it was old fear that was programmed into me at an early age. Those programmes needed updating if I was to live fully in the present and reclaim my sensuality, sexuality and power.

At other times my body felt pain or tightness in certain areas. By paying attention to these bodily sensations, with Sarasi asking perhaps: 'If your shoulder could speak, what might it be saying right now', led into memories, feelings, forgotten distant experiences that I had held within my tissues. She encouraged the exaggeration of movements (as in Gestalt therapy) – using the voice to make a sound connected with the movement; visualising, creating images that symbolised the stuckness or the pain. Sometimes I needed to rage, kick, thump or scream – catharsis, to allow my energy to flow by freeing myself of buried pain and anger; always ending with a soothing massage, a relaxation of my body and connection with my loving compassionate, caring self.

Stephen's Story of Bodywork

When Stephen began to gain some control over his flashbacks and make sense of his experiences, I sensed he needed something more than I could provide. His needed to connect with the power of his body, to experience the cathartic release of his rage, to overcome his physical shame and to gain autonomy and control of his body. After six sessions with me he made an appointment to see Sarasi. I asked Stephen during a research interview how he had experienced our collaborative work:

Kim: So when I first started talking to you about bodywork, what was that like?

Stephen: Sheer terror! But I was so vulnerable – so willing to try anything you suggested because I trusted you completely by then, that I was willing to give it a go. But I was so repressed about that type of thing, a bit cynical about it really – I had the wrong idea of it all. . . . I was a bit prejudiced about that type of thing – I freely admit that. I wish I hadn't been.

Kim: But it didn't stop you?

Stephen: It didn't stop me – I was so raw and open I was willing to try anything

Kim: So you put an enormous amount of trust in me. I notice myself getting a bit scared inside myself when I realise you were so open to being abused I guess – you know – if I hadn't been trustworthy – or Sarasi hadn't been trustworthy – you were handing yourself over totally.

Stephen: Oh yes, very vulnerable – extremely. Into the unknown – I think part of that was that I was so desperate. I felt not that far away from death if you like – I was thinking at times that death was a better alternative than how I was – so I thought 'if I'm feeling like that I'll try anything'.

Kim: Death through suicide?

Stephen: I don't actually think I would have had the courage to do anything; but I wanted to be dead some of the time – yes, but that's two different things. I didn't think about doing it – but I wanted to be dead. Yes, I felt that bad – I thought it was hopeless – especially about work finding out – no way out until you gave me a way out.

Kim: I gave you a way out?

Stephen: You helped me to give myself a way out...

Kim: By...?

Stephen: Listening, talking and introducing me to Sarasi.

Kim: Right. So you took that really big important step and you trusted me totally — you'd give it a go — cynicism and all.

Stephen: Yes. Especially with a name like Sarasi — mystical overtones and all. I was very nervous that first time — stood in my underpants absolutely terrified [laughs]. Not now — I feel very fortunate to — did you read how I'd written up those sessions?

Kim: Those two sessions you wrote up were very powerful — the second session when she climbed on your back...

Stephen: Yes, that made me angry. Yes, I thought 'what is this woman doing this for...'

Kim: As I was reading that and thinking about whether or not to include that in the book... I was wondering how somebody, who was in the same place you were in before you went to Sarasi — with those kind of attitudes — I wonder what they would make of that.

Stephen: It might put them off.

Kim: I was thinking — there was a potential for you to be abused — as there was when you walked across my doorstep, or into any kind of therapeutic relationship. I was wondering if you could look back now — was it the right time for you to be referred for that kind of work — bearing in mind how scared you were — how vulnerable you were...

Stephen: Absolutely spot on — I'd say now. Yes, it was a big part of everything. Yes, it changed me really — it put me in touch with bits of myself I'd never previously been in touch with. Before that, because of what happened I suppose — I was staid, up tight. I wasn't fully functioning on all cylinders really but it was a time when I needed to change dramatically to survive. It gave me new tools, new ways of coping, being able to feel, to use my emotions, to feel things... To feel things in my body — to feel things like the birds in the sky, simple things. I was beginning to see things more clearly — like I said in my poems — it was like being in a haze before.

Kim: And you feel that was largely down to the bodywork?

Stephen: Yes, definitely — well it was the two of you working together — you seemed to be on the same side — with the same purpose.

Kim: So it was important that we were working together?

Stephen: You are so different but you were working to the same aim... My health and recovery.

Kim: Was it confusing to be working with two of us at the same time.

Stephen: No, not at all — 'cos I had this impression that you knew each other really well and that you got together in the background and decided what to do. It was good that you were so different — it was different ways of approaching things. I was using my brain and thought processes and my emotions with you, but it was very physical with Sarasi — I felt like a big lump of whale anyway then and I needed to become alive.

Kim: You see I'm thinking that some people reading your diary – some professionals might say – 'Woah – I don't know about that – exposing somebody who has been sexually abused to that kind of thing.'

Stephen: I didn't see it like that – in a way it was reassuring. After my initial embarrassment and fear – it seemed reassuring that somebody female would want to even touch me, after what had been done to me – after what I'd taken part in. I was so full of shame, guilt and disgust with myself I didn't think anyone would want even want to be with me – at that stage. It was reassuring – somebody nice and kind like Sarasi. It just felt comforting; especially a comforting massage. It was a bit scary at times; I needed to get lots of anger out as well. When you helped me to turn it to anger, I needed somewhere safe to unload it. It was very important – the part Sarasi played – crucial – if that stayed in me I would have been more stuck for longer

It was very cathartic. It was like having a baby if you like [laughing] – unloading so much – very, very powerful. I was having dreams – did you read the dream about the trip to the seaside? I was amazed how I woke up and I wrote it down really quickly so I'd remember it. It seemed really symbolic to me at the time. I thought: 'Crumbs.' It was like watching a TV programme – 'I've got to write this down it is so important.' That was fuelled by the work with you and Sarasi. It was crucially important.

Kim: What about the sexual aspect of the touch and the nakedness and all of that – and sex being something that…

Stephen: Well – she was getting me to simulate having sex at times. Well it was pretty scary at the time, a bit uncomfortable to start with. But I trusted her – I was open to anything really. I was so vulnerable – I just trusted her and put myself right into it. I had to because I went in a bit cynical – I knew that. It took me the first session to get somewhere; I knew I really had to let go, to get into it. I knew that if I didn't let go completely, then I wasn't going to benefit from it – so I just let myself go completely.

Kim: So you really went with the process and trusted it. So how did you know that Sarasi wouldn't abuse you?

Stephen: What – sexually? [Disbelieving.] Well, I trusted your judgement for one – you knew her so she must be alright. For a start I didn't think anybody would want to sexually abuse me…

Kim: Even though you had been sexually abused?

Stephen: Yes, but that was by a dirty old man wasn't it?

Kim: Right, right. So it might have been very different if the bodyworker had been a man.

Stephen: Yes, I don't think I could have done that – so I felt I was quite safe – I never thought she would – it never really crossed my mind.

Kim: You did record in your diary that she actually said to you on that first or second time that she would not do anything sexual to you.

Stephen: Yes, I don't remember at the time – it was a long time ago. I remember having to make those pelvic movements and I felt uncomfortable doing that to start with. But then Sarasi asked you to do uncomfortable things to tip you over into the stage of getting somewhere didn't she?

That was part of her skill, and at the time I thought: 'what the hell am I doing this for', and then realising that it was because she was wanting me to get angry sometimes. So even though I was very hard to work with, I expect – I was very lumpish – difficult to get going, but she did that very successfully... I feel I missed a lot by not doing it earlier. But I'm a lot more open about things now... A lot more understanding. I think it has done me good. I had a lot of anger. I'm a lot more tolerant to anything really – less judgemental, less rigid in my thinking – yes. Less staid, staid and rigid than I was. That was a survival mechanism.

Kim: Sure. It sounds like you are more open to experience now.

Stephen: Yes – that's right. Yes, good and bad –

Mike's Story of Bodywork

As a 'walled-in, hermetically sealed' client Mike needed to be helped to dismantle the wall. His body was very rigid, overweight and he suffered from irritable bowel syndrome. He had begun to discover the 'treasure chest' of his feelings. I 'winkled' away through his bodily sensations to find a chink in the wall and loosen a few bricks so that he might begin to think about what it was like to be able to peep through to the outside world. Once he had a peep he could decide whether or not he wanted to make real contact.

Mike had the advantage that Stephen had begun the bodywork before him and he was able to see some of the changes that were occurring. He talked to me about his early cynicism – especially coming from the world of traditional medicine:

Mike: *I can't remember how far in front of me Stephen was, but I think he was the first one to broach it – 'Oh guess what she said to me...' [laughs] and me saying 'oh you be careful Stephen' or something like that... I can remember being alongside him in the process of him deciding to go. I was asking him 'What does she mean? What sort of thing are we talking about?' But then of course Stephen went – so I was expecting you to ask me.*

Kim: *Yes, I remember you saying something like 'I've been waiting for this.'*

[Lots of laughter.]

Mike: *'I've been waiting for this.' Yes, I was scared about that. I think Stephen had already started to go by this stage and I was asking him: 'What happens? What does she do?' and he just wouldn't tell me and I used to get quite irritated with that – neither of you would really tell me what it was about and yet both of you were telling me it was OK, it would be good for me. I took a long time to go didn't I – to ring her.*

Kim: *Yes, you did. I think I was quite surprised when you came in one day and said, 'Well I've made an appointment.' Because I think I had almost expected that you wouldn't do that.*

Mike: *And then I spoilt it by enticing Sarasi into not doing any proper bodywork.*

Kim: *Did you – what did you do?*

Mike: *We were doing visualisations – I remember one afternoon sitting in that room of yours and you saying, 'Well I can do visualisations too.' [Lots of laughter.] 'Shall I show you?' And we did* one which I still use... It was something about finding a nice warm sunny place – to find a place of calm.

Kim: Yes. Oh I know what was going on for me – I think I was thinking 'that wasn't why I suggested you go and see Sarasi'.

Mike: *[Laughter]* So the next time I went to see Sarasi I said, 'Kim said I've got to ask you for a massage.'

[Laughter]

Kim: I sound like a controlling, bossy woman.

Mike: Well you were quite right, weren't you? Because what I was doing with Sarasi, in retrospect, was exactly what I had been doing by delaying making the appointment – avoiding the point when I'd take my clothes off and lie on the table.

Kim: But when you think about it – it was pretty amazing that both of you did that – you really must have had a huge amount of courage.

Mike: Yes. *[Pause.]* But I certainly wouldn't have come anywhere within worlds of someone like Sarasi if it hadn't been for you pointing me. At least with you there were connections at my professional level, even if they were sceptical, whereas there was absolutely no connection with Sarasi at all.

Kim: A different kind of world altogether. And I imagine knowing and seeing what was happening to Stephen – even if you didn't know the content of what was going on – in some way that must have been communicating something positive to you.

Mike: Oh yes. I do wonder – well I wouldn't have met you if it hadn't been for Stephen – but I wonder if Stephen hadn't been saying 'let's go for it' – I wonder if I would have. And I wonder – it's just come into my head as I'm talking – I wonder how much of it was 'Well I'll go and see what she does because I will be protecting Stephen in case there's something peculiar going on.'

Kim: Really? *[Pause.]* So tell me about the bodywork. One of the things I'm very conscious of is that there is a lot of scepticism out there about such things and a lot of suspicion – especially when we come to talk about body work with people who have been sexually abused. Some therapists would go so far as to say you should never **touch** people who have been sexually abused.

Mike: Well – I've seen that in books myself. Well yes, all of that. What is this Kim and Stephen are telling me to do? I must have been petrified I'm sure. I don't think I would have recognised it as that at the time.

Kim: How did you manage to get past that point?

Mike: I think it was because by that time I had got into such a relationship with you – which I would have said was trust at the time but, looking back, it was me being the child and you being the parent looking after me... I knew I'd end up doing it when you first mentioned it.

Kim: But you weren't going to go easily *[laughter]*... without a fight.

Mike: I don't see how that could have worked without that transference relationship. I knew that I was doing it. I wouldn't have known how to put it into words – I knew that I was putting myself in your hands...

We go on to talk about how the work slotted in with his counselling:

Mike: *Well you'd got me as far as recognising that I was frightened – very frightened. I just could not see what of – again I may be compressing something that took a long time. But yes, I was frightened of this and that and the other in the present, and that seemed reasonable. I remember when you were explaining about existential fear, there was one part of me – the intellectual part – saying 'this is a lot of eyewash isn't it' and the other part of me saying 'Yes, this fits.' That was really important. By which time I was seeing Sarasi and that was one of the points where you working together was important. By that time I was having massages a lot – so I felt that was a place I could go and be hugged if you like.*

Kim: *Yes, be held physically in your fear and come through it.*

Sarasi's Story about Doing Bodywork with Mike and Stephen

Sarasi had been an important person in Mike and Stephen's journey and both of them wanted her voice to be included in this book. I too felt the story would be incomplete without hearing what the work had entailed from her perspective. I invited her to contribute and she begins by introducing herself:

I originally trained as a teacher of Educational Drama, Improvisation and Theatre and Laban's Art of Movement. I worked in London as a performance artist for five years, becoming involved in the Personal Growth movement of the 70s and 80s. I lived and worked in therapeutic communities, training in Deep Tissue Massage, Neo-Reichian Breath and Bodywork, Bioenergetics and Tantra (sexuality work). I also qualified as a Yoga teacher and began leading workshops in Women's Co-Counselling and Sexuality, Dance and Expression, and Breath, Massage and Meditation.

I have been a therapist for 20 years, running a private practice and leading workshops in Germany, Australia and now in England. In the US I trained in Alchemical Hypnotherapy and Ericksonian Hypnosis. I am also a Master Practitioner of NLP (Neuro Linguistic Programming) and a John Bradshaw Accredited Therapist (Inner Child work). I spend two months of the year at the Osho Commune International, Poona, India, where I concentrate on my own inner work and also come in contact with the latest meditative therapies from all over the world.

Both Steve and Mike had the same intense longing to be free of their past. They were two very different people and in the work I had to use very different approaches. In essence I felt very touched by both of them.

When Mike came to me he was very afraid of his own violence and rage, afraid of causing damage to others, afraid of unfamiliar places, afraid of being rejected by his wife and family and of experiencing his own emotions and being out of control.

He wanted to connect with himself as a child. There was a tremendous sadness about the lost innocence of his childhood, the loss of love, friendship, the natural development of his sexuality. He told me how he had hidden behind his books, his intellect, but had really always longed to be able to play run, sing, jump and laugh with the other children. There was a deep loneliness in him – his abuse had cut him off from other children, even from his own son whom he longed to be able to play with without the fear of physical contact. The abuse had not only cut him off from people but also from the love and acceptance he so badly needed. There was a tremendous sense of having lost himself; the little boy driven by the desperate fear of being discovered had hidden himself almost completely.

Initially I spent a lot of time creating safety and trust. Together we built a very compelling sense of how he wanted his life to change. This was important. I wanted his longing to be the driving force during the difficult times ahead; I knew the bodywork would be very risky and challenging for him. Mike wanted to be reminded that he had a body and feelings. He wanted to get inside himself to access his rage at what had happened to him. There was a deep embarrassment about anything to do with his body. The first time we came to the massage Mike commented that he had never been touched in a non-sexual way before, so loving touch without sex was unknown to him and very threatening. His courage and the risks Mike took in entrusting his body to me were enormous. I felt humbled by the vulnerability of this huge man, who hardly fitted on my largest massage table.

The massage was not only a source of relaxation and comfort, it also provoked all the rage and frustration held in his very tight, loaded musculature. As I massaged deeply into the constricted areas of his body, inviting him to intensify his breathing, he began to release the memories, unexpressed feelings and emotions that had been held there. I encouraged him to move, to kick, to punch, to push and to shout out. He found it quite hard to give himself permission to make noise so I encouraged him to raise his voice, to shout and to vent his feelings of rage, disgust and tremendous hurt.

I remember one session when I gave him an exercise to express himself in gibberish – just unintelligible sounds; I remember it was very embarrassing for him, but it was working. He joyfully reported later that he had enjoyed playing unashamedly with his son; things were definitely loosening up and moving along. Another session he exploded so totally in anger, hitting the end of the massage table with a pillow. With a resounding crack one of the struts of the massage table splintered into smitherines. We collapsed in fits of laughter. The 'gentle giant', as he had called himself, was a furious, passionate, roaring giant. My massage table still bears those proud scars of that session to this day.

The later massage sessions with Mike became what I can only describe as deeply spiritual experiences. The whole room filled with a deep calm and a great sense of peace. It felt as if we were bathed in light. How ironic that his body, so misused and violated, should now be the vehicle of such a tremendous sense of Godliness and peace. What could so easily have been a breakdown, had been transformed into a breakthrough. This part of our work together was complete – what a perfect ending. It was 19 sessions all in all. I came to work with Mike again two years' later – but that's another story.

Sarasi and I had a conversation about her work with Stephen.

Sarasi: With Stephen, I could recognise that he was longing for a safe container in which he could express all the rage that was visibly exploding from his body. The bodywork provided him with an opportunity to express and offload all the rage and hurt – there was a lot of emotion. He didn't need the same preparation as Mike, as his emotions were much more accessible.

Kim: How did you help him to do that?

Sarasi: One of the ways was massage. For instance, his shoulders and his back contained a lot of tension and as I massaged the muscles he began to experience all that tension, frustration and held-in emotion. As soon as I see or hear that something is being provoked, I set up a dialogue with the body, accessing whatever emotions or memories are contained there. In his diary, Stephen wrote about me climbing on his back [laughter]. It wasn't quite like that. When he connected with the rage towards his grandfather, I helped intensify it by increasing the pressure of the massage and using my body weight. Basically, I was offering some bodily resistance so that he could physically throw his grandfather's presence off his back. It was also difficult for him to use his voice and I had to work through a lot of inhibitions to activate his vocal expression. I would encourage him to use words like 'Get off my back!' or 'I hate you', so that he could express what wasn't expressed at the time. There was always the aim in mind to bring in some kind of healing or resolution, so that he could complete the session really loving his inner child.

Kim: In terms of the collaborative work between us – I thought it might be useful to focus on that because we don't hear much about it. As you know there's a lot of scepticism out there and there's a lot of people sticking to their own particular way of working. And, as I've written and I know you agree, it's not necessarily always helpful to the client to hold those kind of boundaries. But what did you see as useful for these particular clients about us working together.

Sarasi: I think – in a sense it was very, very safe because they had a very strong, double holding. For instance when Mike said: 'Kim thinks I should have a massage today' – it moved things on faster than I would naturally go on my own. Being a person-centred worker I would probably pay attention to their resistance – but your input gave me an impulse to go faster than I normally would – to take more of a risk. I knew with two of us they were really held; so we covered work much faster and it probably went a lot deeper through having two very concentrated workers working with them.

Kim: That's perhaps the very thing that some people might criticise – that maybe the work was too fast and that defences may be pushed aside. For instance as you've just said – 'Kim thinks I should have a massage' – but maybe you are actually thinking that's not where the client is at the moment – maybe there is also a danger of crashing down some of those defences in a way that is not helpful. This is often a criticism of bodywork in general – isn't it?

Sarasi: I would always check to make sure that they actually wanted it themselves – often they would ask through the medium of 'Kim' – and probably vice versa. And I always checked it inside myself. If there was a 'no' on either side, I wouldn't carry out the request.

Kim: So you would never override anybody's defences and you would need to know for yourself that they were ready to let go.

Sarasi: Absolutely.

Kim: And the fact that they were communicating that message to you from me – at some level – would give you an indication that at least part of them – and you were checking about the rest of them – was actually offering themselves to do that.

Sarasi: I'm actually very careful about that. I know it doesn't work unless it's coming from the client.

Kim: **Sent** clients don't work [laughter].

Sarasi: Exactly.

Kim: Only those who are there and working of their own volition.

Sarasi: Yes, it's coming from them and their readiness.

Kim: So those messages that we passed between us were more indicators of where the client seemed to be ready to go.

Sarasi: That's right, potentials. And I would always carefully check it out to make sure it was really right for them. Generally it was, usually it was spot on and it kept the work alive and moving forward. It was a bit like having 'feedback' from outside.

Kim: Yes, that's a good metaphor actually. Like one of those feedback machines. 'What's the response coming back to me here?'

Sarasi: And it usually confirmed my own sense of what was needed.

Kim: Your own feedback mechanism...

Sarasi: Yes, and it kind of prompted me, 'Yes, come on – let's go for it.'

Kim: I was thinking about the way Stephen wrote his wonderful diary – the way he exploded onto the page and the obviously powerful impression that those first few sessions of bodywork had made on him. I was also thinking that the way he wrote them down – in a diary form – may have caused some people to raise eyebrows. In fact I spoke to him about this and he himself admitted that it might put people off. I just wondered what your response was when you saw the way that it had been reported, knowing the work from the other side. Is there anything you want to add to that to give a wider view for the reader?

Sarasi: When I first read it I couldn't recognise some of it. For instance, asking him to take his clothes off – it sounded very cold and clinical – climbing on his back – stretching his legs but I understood that was how he remembered it rather than an accurate transcript of how I work.

Kim: All the subtle bits about making it safe and the pace at which you work – he hadn't included that.

Sarasi: Yes, I work more through invitation or suggestion. Only with the actual anger work do I become more directive.

Kim: You help people to face it, go into it and get the most out of it.

Sarasi: Yes, anger work requires a more provocative role. Another part in the diary that I couldn't recognise was when Stephen said that I asked him to 'simulate sex'. I couldn't quite think what he meant – then I realised it must have been the pelvic bouncing and bioenergetics I did with him. I wondered what people would think –'what is she doing?' [laughter].

Kim: So it was actually the pelvic movements that he was interpreting as simulating sexual activity. What was the reasoning behind those movements?

Sarasi: Both Reichian therapy and bioenergetics recognise that a lot of tension, fear and anger can be held in the pelvis because – especially if you've been sexually abused – these are the areas that often get frozen, cut off and held in what's called 'body armouring'. Often there is very little movement in those areas, and when you start to activate them you can begin to release the emotions that are trapped in there. There's the 'jellyfish' where you open and close the legs very slowly whilst breathing in the abdomen... I think you wrote about that...

Kim: Yes, the legs begin to shake and there's a release through that shaking.

Sarasi: Yes. So with the pelvic bouncing, the kicking and hitting, all the mattress work, well it's a natural way that children tantrum – so you are giving the body permission to do something that it naturally does. These days I mostly don't lead so much because I notice, when I do a breath session on a mattress, that people naturally go into release movements – so then I just amplify what's already happening. They start naturally lifting their pelvis up and so then I will say 'Hold the mattress and make that bigger. Let out a sound or say "No" as you do that, or "Fuck you", or "I hate you" as you do that.' And they go into that naturally which is much better – I prefer that because it is more organic and the same with the kicking and the hitting. If we were forced sexually against our will and made a victim, then all that hate, revenge and anger remains held inside the body. It is very important to take back the power that was lost at that time. The beauty of this work is that it really frees and empowers our sexuality again. We can reclaim all that lost naturalness and innocence.

Sarasi ends on a powerful note of hope. Many survivors of childhood abuse believe themselves to be condemned to a future without the potential to reclaim their sexuality, joy and freedom. When we work together with body, mind and spirit the client has the best hope of healing we, as workers, can offer them.

John McLeod (1997) comments on the interaction between therapy and culture. He relates the development of therapy historically to the development of society. In the traditional era people's problems were dealt with collectively, within the community. In modern times the person was viewed as an 'autonomous bounded self' and their problems were dealt with in privacy behind the doors of the counselling room – for those who could afford it. In postmodern times the cultural position of counselling and psychotherapy is beginning to shift, as part of a broader movement characterised by globalisation.

One of the most striking developments within counselling and psychotherapy has been the erosion of the influence of major schools of therapy and their gradual replacement by an integrated approach created by individual practitioners committed to the value of pluralism rather than 'fixed truths'. McLeod (1997) adds that 'the colonialism of mainstream psychotherapy is increasingly challenged by voices from other cultures, and from traditions previously submerged within the dominant culture' (p.21). Counselling and psychotherapy, as well as society as a whole, have had to change to accommodate the voice of feminism, the influences from the changing political scene, the impact of alternative and complementary approaches to healing and influences of religions that have become more assimilated into our global community. For the counselling community these changes may be almost too soon – the profession being so newly formed.

So counsellors who have been trained to think in 'modern' terms and see their clients as only 'autonomous bounded selves' may find it hard to think about integrated working and collaboration may be even more difficult. People do, of course, need the safety that privacy offers in which they can discover the core of who they are, but if we are to think about people holistically we need to help our clients to expand to outside the counselling room, supporting and challenging ourselves and our clients to embrace our roles in the wider world of which we are a part.

CHAPTER 14

Stories Within Stories

As Mike and Stephen told their stories I heard other, half-spoken stories within them. In this chapter and the two that follow, I will attempt to focus on some of them – particularly those that are related to their gender. I believe that social conditioning in a patriarchal society creates particular problems for males who have been sexually abused in childhood. To be a 'normal' male means to aspire to leadership, to be competitive, aggressive and tough; to be responsible, to be sexually active, knowledgeable, potent and a successful seducer. The burden inherent in these expectations is clear.

Denial

Generally speaking, there is no longer the widespread denial that children are sexually abused, although it is only within the last twenty to thirty years that the feminist movement enabled women to break through the silence that had surrounded it. It was over a hundred years ago that Freud delivered his lecture to the Vienna Society for Psychiatry and Neurology (1896), during which he spoke of his belief that childhood sexual abuse was at the root of psychological disturbances in some of his adult patients. As a result of this lecture he was ostracised by a society that was not ready to hear what he had to say. He wrote of his pain following the alienation from his colleagues: 'I am as isolated as you could wish me to be: the world has been given out to abandon me, and a void is forming around me' (quoted by Masson 1984, p.104).

I am powerfully struck by the similarity in what happened to another doctor, Mike, 99 years later, when he tried to disclose his own childhood abuse and the rejection he experienced by his family:

> And now tonight Stephen has recounted his conversation with Mum, in which she said she'd decided to have no more to do with me or my family, and that she appeared to have gone over to Dad's attitude – how many more rejections can I take?

Nowadays there is a greater willingness to accept that girls may be at risk of sexual abuse by their fathers and other males, but resistance still exists when it comes to the idea that boys can also be abused and that women can be abusers. Studies of paedophiles show us that they frequently have multiple victims who are often exclusively boys. In recent years a clearer picture has begun to emerge as we hear of boys in children's homes, boarding schools and other institutions, who have undergone systematic sexual, physical and emotional abuse. Many institutions have become a haven for paedophiles, offering them protection and ready access to their victims. Closed systems – whether they be families where children are taught 'we don't talk about family matters outside the home', residential communities such as schools and hospitals, or local organisations such as boys clubs, sports clubs, scouts or churches – all offer opportunities for child abuse.

Some of the denial is related to the expectation that being male excludes the possibility of vulnerability or victimisation. Male survivors are therefore often imprisoned by patriarchy, which ignores the realities of their sexual abuse. This leads to isolation and loneliness. Even during his training as a doctor Mike had not been educated about the possibility of male abuse: 'The fact that boys could be victims, let alone grow into adults having to cope with their past was unthought and unspoken. No wonder I felt alone.'

In the face of such denial, men who have been abused by males have no frame of reference, no way of defining the event, no language with which they can speak about their abuse, except that of homosexuality. Mike writes of his own struggle as he decides to end the activity that his grandfather had programmed into him from infancy: 'All that I see, as I sicken with myself on the way home, is that my sin is twofold – to have sex, and to have sex with a man…understanding only that I myself had done wrong!'

He had gone through medical school without any challenge to his attitudes and he had been practising as a GP for several years when the realisation dawned, that what he had experienced was abuse. Even then he was not able to seek help and the need for secrecy drove him to visit adjoining towns – so great was his fear of being seen looking along the shelves of the bookshop for self-help literature.

Too often male survivors deal with their abuse 'like a man', by denying their feelings in respect of their victimisation. The response of male survivors reflects the values and norms by which they have been socialised. The dissonance created by their socialisation often causes male victims to remain silent in their shame; or to identify with the perpetrator ('I was responsible'), as a way of psychologically defending himself from acknowledging his powerlessness. Mike had never allowed himself to think of what had happened as abuse: 'My sexual past had never seemed other than something for which I was responsible; even if, to my shame, I had been unable to control it.'

Sometimes the abuser indoctrinates the child to believe they are responsible because they had 'enjoyed' it. This is a typically distorted belief that allows the adult abuser to deny the damage he is causing to the child and persist with his abusive behaviour. When Mike, as a young adult, confronted his grandfather about his abuse,

Gramps attempted to hand over responsibility to his victim: 'He said he had only done what he had done to me because I enjoyed it!'

Other messages given to their victims by abusers are further evidence of their distorted thinking. There are those, like Gramps, who consider that sexual contact between children and adults is not harmful. When Stephen attempted to talk to his grandfather about the abuse after it had stopped, he described what he had done as 'perfectly natural'. This attitude prevails among paedophiles currently and I believe has been encouraged by scientific research. An early Kinsey report (1953) stated that 80 per cent of the children in his sample had been 'emotionally upset or frightened' by their sexual contacts with adults. He saw this level of feeling as similar to that which children would show when they see spiders or insects or 'other objects against which they have been socially conditioned'. He went on to say: 'It is difficult to understand why a child, except for its cultural conditioning, should be disturbed at having its genitalia touched or disturbed at seeing the genitalia of other persons, or disturbed at even more specific sexual contacts' (Kinsey *et al.* 1953, p.121). He describes the 'current hysteria about sex offenders' as the possible cause of 'serious effects on the ability of many of these children to work out sexual adjustments some years later in their marriages'. Kinsey thereby implies that if children were conditioned to see sexual contact between adults as normal then no harm would ensue.

It has recently come to light that Kinsey used paedophiles who were known by him to be actively engaging in abusing very young children to collect data for the research. His attitudes to sex and the ways he manipulated his fellow researchers into sexual activity with each other and himself causes me to question the validity of his research. As the dominant male in the research team, he may well have abused his power for his own sexual gratification. As his research became seen as the definitive text upon which the societal norms of sexual behaviour have been deduced, this may have led to dangerous acceptance as 'normal' behaviours that may have been perpetrated by paedophiles and others caught up in a range of self and other abusive behaviours.

However, there is some evidence to suggest that the ways adults, both parents and professionals, respond to the child's victimisation can cause further damage. It is very clear from Mike and Stephen's stories that a great deal of additional pain was caused to both of them by the ways their parents handled their disclosures. After Mike's initial disclosure 'things seemed to close down. Little more was said'. When it was opened up again by Stephen's disclosure, Mike felt blamed and punished: 'It's apparently my fault that Dad has told his siblings, my fault that he, and now Mum have cut themselves off from me and mine.'

Gender and Sex Roles

Mike and Stephen's father had brought them up to follow in the expectations of the society in which he had been raised. I imagine his father, their abuser, had fed the same messages to him – perhaps as a way of defending himself from acknowledging his internalised homophobia. In his letter to his father Mike displays his father's attitudes towards him: 'I tried so hard to be "manly" for you – but no. I didn't like football and fighting and so forth (small wonder I suppose).... When I used to want to pop round to the girl down the road to play house and dolls with her, that made you angry didn't it?'

Any sign of what might be considered 'effeminate' behaviour is frequently not acceptable for boys – often more unacceptable to fathers rather than mothers. I believe this is a reflection of a man's need to conform to the stereotypes laid down by patriarchy, which values masculinity over femininity. The fact that girls are allowed to play 'boy's games' or wear 'boy's clothes' without fear of censure supports this argument. A girl can be referred to as a 'real tomboy' without any shaming involved, but a boy who is perceived as 'effeminate' is usually labelled as a 'namby pamby', 'sissy', 'mummy's boy' or suchlike; such labels always bearing negative, shaming connotations. So any behaviour that is stereotypically perceived as feminine is frowned upon and disallowed in males. This includes many of the 'softer skills' that contribute to intimacy between father and son, or indeed between any two males. As Mike began to understand the damage caused by socialisation to himself and his father, he grieved angrily for what 'might have been' in his letter to his father. As the letter unfolds, it becomes clear that Mike's father had perceived his eldest son's behaviour as unacceptable and had frequently rejected him – the quote above from his letter, indicates that somewhere underneath his rejection may have been the fear that his son was 'homosexual'.

When Stephen announces to his parent's, some time after Mike's disclosure to them, that he too had been a victim of his grandfather, his father's response was, 'Oh no, not you as well.' When Stephen asks, 'Did you not wonder about me after you knew about Mike?', he responds: 'Mike I can understand; his behaviour fits, but your doesn't?'

Stephen was the compliant child who behaved in ways that conformed to his parents' expectations of what it meant to be a boy. When he was upset he went off on his bicycle and disappeared for hours. But Mike had wanted to play with his little girlfriend's dolls house and suffered rejection – his rejection led to rebelliousness, leading to further rejection. Angry and aggressive behaviour may 'turn off' compassionate responses in others. As he told his story, Mike began to understand his need for his relationship with his grandfather and how, in the emotional absence of his father, he had valued the attention, listening and conversation that was not allowed at home. 'Why had I learned not to talk about feelings, or bodies, or sexuality at home? No, I had to go up to Gramps for that sort of conversation – and it came with strings attached!'

Stephen also spoke of the attraction of the attention he received from Gramps and how it made up for 'lack of interest and love from others...it was somebody giving me time and attention – sadly. And I think he knew that. Looking back on it.' Sexual abuse rarely occurs without a degree of emotional abuse or neglect within the parental relationship. Paedophiles are finely tuned to such children and will often look out for signs that a child will welcome attention from an adult – whatever that attention might consist of.

Many of the men I have spoken to about their families' attitude to sex indicated that it was ignored, non-existent or referred to negatively. There was no arena for discussion of normal sexual development or any way of satisfying a healthy curiosity about sexual matters in a safe environment. Sex was a taboo subject – denial, repression or suppression does not allow a healthy discussion of what should be a natural part of a child's education. As Mike and Stephen's family began to lift the shroud of secrecy around the abuse, other cousins, who had also been abused by Gramps, referred to 'being sent to fetch the coal' by their parents whenever anything to do with sex came on the TV.

Homophobia

Homophobia can influence the parents' attitudes to the sexual abuse of a child; some parents have been known to confess that they 'worried that something like that had been going on' but were afraid to enquire in case their worst fears were true. When asked about their 'worst fears', they admitted that it was that their son was homosexual and they were relieved to discover that 'it had only been sexual abuse'. So their homophobia prevented them from taking action that would have protected and helped their son (Etherington 1995).

Patriarchy cultivates homophobic fear. Condemnation of homosexual behaviour is deeply rooted in history and traditions of the male-dominated institutions and religions. Orthodox Judeo-Christian teachings are unequivocally antagonistic. Hostility towards groups or minorities whose habits and ideas are different from one's own is an almost universal human characteristic; prejudice against gays is just one example. Their very existence challenges fundamental assumptions about life's purpose and the natural order of things.

Pronouncements by medical authorities in the past have been influential in promoting homophobia by equating homosexuality with psychopathology, degeneracy or moral turpitude. Although Freud challenged these assumptions and indeed saw it as part of normal sexual development, his followers were still insistent upon them many years later. It was only in 1980 after much protest and lobbying that the American Psychiatric Association voted to remove homosexuality *per se* from its diagnostic manual of psychiatric disorders (APA 1980, DSM-III).

Many male victims fear that they will be judged as a homosexual – thereby denying their victimisation. The victim may be blamed for his homosexuality rather then the offender for the offence. A male victim may focus on feelings related to his inability to defend himself, and therefore his lack of 'manliness' and failure as a man. Having failed to protect himself from the abuse, he may overcompensate for his anxiety by macho behaviour to re-establish his perception of himself in a strong male image. Stephen used pornography in his attempt to reassure himself about his heterosexuality:

> I was scared of being gay if you like. As I got older, and understood more – I was thinking – 'I'm not gay despite what he's doing to me'; but then I thought, 'Well, I must be because he is doing these things to me.' And then it was reassuring – especially the pornography at school – buying magazines and stuff – it reassured me that I had very strong heterosexual urges and – yes, I read it and looked at it, used it.

Mike went even further and found himself a fiancée as proof that he was not gay. Internalised homophobic attitudes also create problems in forming or maintaining intimate relationships with other men. Mike describes his attitudes to men during his young adult years: 'I wondered vaguely if I was homosexual but as I was so awkward in the company of men I did not see how this could be put into practice!'

Too often men assume emotional intimacy is female behaviour and this may make it difficult for them to align themselves with any attributes that appear to define them as 'sissy'. Fear of appearing weak, needy or frail (all considered female attributes stereotypically) contributes to avoidance of intimate self-disclosure. Mike describes how he coped by forming friendships mainly with women: 'I found few friends and all of them were women; I hovered about the other men, rather in awe, but finding no companionship.'

The implications of all this for males who have been sexually abused by other males are clear. How can victims risk exposing themselves to questions about their sexual involvement with a member of the same sex while they and others have been indoctrinated within a homophobic society? Furthermore, the attitudes of society, which are introjected by the victim, will increase the likelihood that, once victimised, the victim will not be able to form intimate relationships with non-abusive males. Such relationships would provide him with an opportunity to mediate the effect of the abusive relationship and allow him an alternative learning experience out of which the seeds of his healing might emerge.

Dominance and Control

Apart from the parental and peer pressure to conform with male stereotypes, there is a much broader pressure within which these attitudes operate; that of the larger socio-political context of patriarchy which has been defined as 'the manifestation and institutionalisation of male dominance over women and children in the family' (Lerner 1986, p.239).

There are many and frequent references to stories about 'dominance and control' throughout Mike and Stephen's story. In many ways the rules of our patriarchal society indicate that a high value is placed upon control. Alongside that is the message that control is normally a male prerogative – indeed it is part of being a 'proper man' who is stereotypically 'the dominant species'.

Women and children in our society are encouraged to be passive, thereby conditioning them to accept the position of being controlled. Strong women are defined as 'aggressive' and strong children as 'rebellious'. The fourth commandment indoctrinates children to 'Honour thy father and thy mother'. Struve (1990) sees teaching a child absolute obedience as grooming the child for victimisation. Having a compliant child is seen as being a good parent. Mike and Stephen's father was a very controlling man but his behaviour affected his two sons very differently. Mike's response to feeling controlled was that he became angry, fearful and quietly rebellious. Stephen's behaviour as a child was compliant and passive. Part of being a good parent is, of course, being in control of our children and thereby protecting them, until such time as they no longer need us to do that for them. Gradually, as children grow and develop, little by little, we enable them to take more and more control of their lives. Control brings power and with power comes responsibility.

Traumatic experiences, particularly those that begin at a very early stage of the child's life and are repeated over time, may result in 'learned helplessness' (Seligman 1975). This refers to a state in which the person becomes extremely passive, depressed or even suicidal, or to a situation in which he attempts to over-control and regain power by constricting feelings of vulnerability and powerlessness by splitting them off. But split off feelings can nevertheless control us unconsciously; by becoming self-aware we can learn to control them rather than be controlled by them.

When a child has been controlled by an adult in ways that are destructive to his well-being, he feels powerless, and beneath powerlessness lies fear and rage. The usual response to fear is either 'flight or fight'. We run away, hide or become paralysed by our fear or we lash out against those we are frightened of.

Stephen reacted with a 'flight' response. Mike's response was to 'fight'. Rage that is uncontrolled can create havoc, both for the child and those around him. Rage that is over-controlled can create deep-seated and long-term psychological and relational problems for a child. Sometimes rage is both 'acted out' on others and 'acted in' on the self, thereby causing problems in all areas of life. Mike talked of his frequent suicidal feelings, as he turned his anger in on himself, that began during adolescence and carried on into adulthood. As a doctor he had access to drugs and he collected enough to have at hand when the urge to escape through suicide became too strong to resist. Fortunately, alongside that, he had a strong religious belief that may have protected him.

Male children frequently act out rage that stems from powerlessness. They have the additional burden of the expectations of their gender stereotyping. Powerlessness is anathema to maleness. They have no language to express their vulnerability, nor any frame of reference for understanding their experience, having been taught that males are not victims; males are powerful, sexually dominant and in control.

It is hardly surprising that men in our society have the highest rate of convictions for violent and aggressive behaviours; men carry out 90 per cent of all convicted acts of violence. In school 90 per cent of children with behaviour problems are boys. Men make up 95 per cent of the gaol population. The leading cause of death among men between 12 and 60 is suicide: in 1996 in Britain there were 6000 suicides (over 75% by men). There has been a 71 per cent increase in suicide among young men in the past ten years: they are now three times more likely to kill themselves than women. Boys aged between 10 and 15 are three times more likely to be involved in violent crime than girls, and ten times as likely to commit drug offences. Men are three times more likely than women to be dependent on alcohol (*Observer Magazine*, 20 June 1999).

Stephen had kept his experiences secret and to a great degree out of his awareness for most of his adult life. He had compartmentalised the abuse and thereby had it well under control. But suddenly he had been catapulted into the limelight. He felt exposed and terrified: 'I had lost control of it...a truly terrifying experience,' Stephen said, as his secret began to emerge. He had not arrived at the disclosure through his own readiness, but rather as an inevitable consequence of Mike's.

Men and Work

So men have been taught to be independent, tough and powerful. They have also been taught that they have responsibility for others, especially their dependant wives and children. Messages such as 'take care of Mummy while I'm gone' serve to train boys to believe that being male invests them with power over and responsibility for females. Part of this responsibility is to provide for those who depend upon them.

Status created a problem for both Mike and Stephen. As men with respected roles within society they felt the extra burden that exposure might bring. They assumed that to maintain their respect within the dominant culture they could not define themselves as victims, especially as sexual victims. They additionally felt that their sexual identity would be questioned if it were known that they had experienced sexual activity with another male.

In his first contact with me Stephen wrote in his letter about the importance of finding somebody to talk to with whom he could feel safe, and that safety would require that it was somebody unconnected with his working environment. When Mike heard that Stephen had found a 'safe' person, he still could not allow himself to see that he might also ask for help: 'I still didn't see it as something that could practically be available to me. The fact was that my professional position rendered enormous difficulties for me in seeking help.'

When I met Stephen he was taking two weeks' holiday from work; it was however not a holiday but a way of avoiding 'going on the sick'. Stephen was not fit for work and when he was due to go back I struggled to help him acknowledge that he was still unwell. His reluctance to ask for sick leave was tied up with his fear of disclosure. He did not know how he could explain his need to be absent without exposing his abuse: 'Kim suggests I should not go to work when my two-week holiday ends in three days' time. I PANIC, what can I do about work? I can't tell them; I can't trust them; I will lose my job.'

Mike has a similar struggle that is compounded by the fact that he is a doctor. Bennet (1987) describes how the 'persona' of the doctor can often conceal the true nature of the person. Society projects onto the persona of the doctor, giving him all the power of one who has the ability to defy death. We need the doctor to be powerful; the doctor may need us to project our power if they have little awareness of their own. However, the powerful doctor persona can also become a burden when the doctor himself is in need of help. Mike's describes the fear he felt as he made a decision to become 'the patient':

> I was desperately in need of taking time out of work in order to deal with my past, yet how does a doctor 'go on the sick' whilst retaining privacy from his colleagues? There is a culture of 'grin and bear it' among the medical profession which is far from healthy for us, or for our patients, although it seems expected of us by society at large. Well, after much soul searching, and nagging by my counsellor, I did take the plunge and allow myself some space. The courage it took to implement will only ever be known to me.

Stephen worked in the Prison Service, although he had trained as an orthopaedic nurse. This was a macho, tough environment where he perceived that weakness would not be tolerated.

Within the psyche of the doctor or nurse there are the polarities of 'healer–patient' (Bennet 1987). The 'healer' represents power, skill and knowledge while the 'patient' represents weakness, fear and helplessness. The two roles are never truly separated. The healer contains within him an element which is 'patient' and the patient an element which is 'healer'. The 'healer' element was dominant and the 'patient' element latent in both Mike and Stephen. But the latent weakness and helplessness was there, although not consciously accepted. It is only through conscious acceptance of both aspects that the 'wound' can be integrated and the person experience wholeness.

Both men found it hard to identify with the 'patient' role. This is not unusual among men generally, but for men who have defended themselves from knowing their vulnerability as victims of childhood abuse, the difficulty is exacerbated. Serious concerns have been expressed about men's inability to adopt the sick role –

especially men of working age. Statistics show that men live on average six years less than women. It is often women who take responsibility for men's health, sometimes to the extent that women visit their doctors to ask for medication for their husbands. The reluctance of males to ask for help, even during childhood, is evident from the statistics drawn up by Childline. Four times as many girls as boys call Childline, but when they call boys tend to report more severe problems.

The culture of patriarchy extends into the workplace. Any man who appears weak, either physically or emotionally, runs the risk of being judged negatively by his bosses. However, many men never allow themselves to take that risk and therefore never discover that their assumptions may not be borne out in fact. I held my breath and crossed my fingers as I encouraged both men to take time out; I became the woman who took responsibility for their health. Neither was fit to work and I knew that unless they faced the 'patient' within they would miss an opportunity which might not come again. I also feared for their safety and long-term health. Both men worked in responsible systems where any mistake would prove costly to themselves and others. Young hospital doctors frequently report how their fatigue and inability to concentrate put patients at risk. They have challenged the long hours that they are expected to work. Consultants, trained in a previous generation, declare 'We had to do it so why can't they'; much in the same way as men who beat their children say 'it didn't do us any harm' – and choose to remain ignorant of the cycle of abuse they are perpetuating. Mike talked about how difficult it was for him to ask for time off:

Mike: *I had this problem of not being able to go to the doctor and get a sick note... Because if one of the colleagues goes sick, the first thing every body wants to know is: 'Why – what's wrong with him?' You and I seemed to spend hours talking about it because I think you could see how important it was for me to make a bit of space for myself. I can remember driving home sometimes thinking 'I wish she'd give up on it.'*

In the end I had three weeks away. But that was partly them – 'We'll let you take a few weeks off' – not 'How many weeks do you need to take?'

I remember I had been to see the one partner and he'd said: 'Why don't you take some time off after Christmas?' And this other partner, Ian, collared me in a corner just off the reception area, having just discovered that I'd blocked out this three weeks and saying: 'What's all this about?' and me being conscious of all these people around – pinned up against the wall like a butterfly.

I said something like 'I've got some childhood stuff to work through'; and him backing off and saying, 'Oh, all right.' I have this vague feeling that his wife has had some similar dramas in her life. Hints have been dropped by third parties – that maybe Ian would understand because of that.

Stephen's story tells how he struggled to differentiate between privacy and secrecy: 'We discuss what I might say to people at work, that I can be honest BUT maintain my PRIVACY.' He had worked through his guilt about 'living a lie' and wanted to find a way that he could relate honestly to people which did not leave him feeling exposed. His abuse had created problems in knowing how to discern whom he could trust and who was untrustworthy. Much of the necessary developmental work he needed to undertake in therapy focused on his struggle with 'going on the sick'; he updated his learning and experimented with real life issues. As one person acknowledges their vulnerability, it then becomes possible for others; but it has to start somewhere:

> Sam from work calls. It's great to see him. We go out of the way into the roof…I tell him everything in general terms. He is very supportive, understanding; he discloses something very personal he has never told anyone before.

As Stephen prepared to return to work he began to find ways of communicating with others without exposing himself to an uncomfortable degree: 'Only a couple of staff probed at what had been wrong with me, so I told them I had been dealing with a personal problem and left it at that.' His new-found assertiveness allows him to let his boss know how his 'macho' behaviour creates problems in trusting him:

> I explained to him that I would like to be able to tell him about what had happened to me but that I was worried that he might have a laugh and a joke about it later, as I had seen him do with other people's problems. He laughed nervously, said he hoped he knew when to be serious and confidential. Assured me that what I said would go no further.

It seems from the above that Stephen is developing his skills of intimate relating. In a recent conference paper Michael Carroll (forthcoming) referred to a quote by Jourard (1968), which describes some of the difficulties for men in creating intimacy:

> Men are difficult to love. If a man is reluctant to make himself known to another person, even to his spouse because it is not manly to be psychologically naked, then it follows that men will be difficult to love. That is, it will be difficult for a woman, or another man, to know the immediate present state of the man's self and his needs will thereby go unmet. Some men are so skilful at dissembling…that even their wives will not know when they are lonely, bored, anxious, in pain, thwarted, hungering for affection, etc. And the man, blocked by pride, dare not disclose his despair or need. The fear of intimacy has held men in terrible isolation and loneliness.

However, having made useful preparation for his return to work, Stephen became fearful again of staying away any longer; his fear drives him to return too early and his lack of readiness becomes obvious as he loses concentration and makes a serious mistake. He realises on his first day back that he is not ready for the responsibility the job involves: 'I feel nervous, I only know three of the inmates well, otherwise I'm out of touch… I just about remember how to do the paperwork and allocation.'

After a prisoner under his charge escapes Stephen rapidly reverts to his old role of taking the blame, beating himself up, having little or no compassion for himself:

> In retrospect I fully realise how stupid I am for…coming back to work before my powers of memory and concentration were back to full power. I am a stupid fool, I just want to hand in my notice and get a boring, simple job because I can't cope, I'm not up to it. How can I though, I'm trapped, we need the money, now more than ever. What am I going to do? What if the escapee died or kills someone.

However, with support he is able to take the learning from what has happened and reframe the experience usefully. He learned to affirm himself, to accept that mistakes are part of being human and that he has been working in a dangerous and difficult environment for far too long. Through this painful process Stephen comes to accept that he no longer wants to work in this environment and he returns to orthopaedic nursing as a career. The pressure of being the breadwinner created huge obstacles for him. His wife was unable to work because of ill health and a change of job meant a reduction in income. His responsibility for his family conflicted with his personal needs – it was a brave and personal battle that he fought over many months.

Stephen had not been free to learn as a child, dealing as he was with surviving the abuse. Mike had survived by burying himself in his schoolwork and used that as a way to shut out his knowledge of the abuse. So Stephen had identified himself as 'non-academic' and had set his sights lower than his real potential. This was reinforced by family messages that Mike was the 'clever one'. One of the spin-offs of Stephen's decision to change jobs was that he decided to go back into education and attempt to better his career prospects by gaining further qualifications. Through the writing and finding his creativity he was able to imagine a better life for himself. He has gone on to achieve a senior grade within his chosen profession.

CHAPTER 15

More Stories Within Stories

Secrecy and Shame

The 'shroud of secrecy' operates from the underlying norm that sexual information is dangerous and corrupting (Lerner 1986). Therefore considerable energy is spent in maintaining a shroud of secrecy over all things sexual. This contributes to a global anxiety about sexuality which discourages most people from discussing sexual matters openly. Such an atmosphere creates confusion, distortion and fear. In our culture, sex is often linked with shame and our response is to hide what is shameful.

Shame is related to male conditioning. If men are meant to be 'in control', then anything that demonstrates their lack of control is shaming. Men can feel shamed for feeling needy, for being vulnerable, wanting to be protected, cared for, held; most of all for being a victim. But it is only when they can acknowledge their victimisation that healing can begin. If there is no victim, there is no hurt, no need for healing and care. During the first few months both Mike and Stephen were trapped within the shame and fear of exposure that meant they only had each other, and myself, with whom they could feel safe enough to examine their experiences closely. Once they had begun to face up to their victimisation and loosen the grip of shame and secrecy, they were able to confront other members of the family. In most cases, as in this one, it is really important that clients are secure in their knowledge that they were not responsible before they confront others. To seek to confront other family members without this security exposes the victim to further damage. In this case Mike had taken the hardest step alone. When he had initially disclosed, he did not have the additional support of knowing that his brother had also been abused. I asked Stephen what it meant to him to discover that he was not alone as a victim:

> The whole world changed. I felt a sick, sinking feeling. It put my abuse into a whole new larger picture. I felt able to be angry for Mike's sake (but not for my own at that stage – only guilt and shame). It unscrewed the lid on the jar. Knowing about Mike allowed me to be angry and to hate Gramps – it released the brakes on the roller-coaster ride to the point when I contacted you…when I realised about the others in the family I was devastated – the implications and legacy of what he had done to us all struck home. My story became broader – dealing with the traumatic

consequences – secrets, lies, pain, destruction for all the family and my relationships with them.

Their father's need for secrecy and control overruled his ability to recognise his sons' distress or to care for them as victims. His own need was paramount – in a different way this paralleled the behaviour of his own father, the abuser, who had also overruled his grandsons' needs by meeting his own. But this time Mike and Stephen fought back; they had each other. They had acknowledged their victimisation and, in doing so, they had begun to put the shame where it belonged–back onto the abuser and onto their parents who had failed to protect them from abuse.

It is important to separate out blame in this process. When we blame somebody we may fail to take responsibility for ourselves; our focus is on them and not on ourselves. If we can give back responsibility rather than blame, we can release ourselves from shame and express our rightful feelings, thereby taking our power and joining with our sense of self.

When Stephen disclosed to his father, having previously disclosed to his mother, he was very careful to ensure that they knew he did not blame them and that he loved them both. His father was able to acknowledge his feelings of guilt because he did not need to defend himself from an attack: 'Dad says: "It's MY FAULT, I FEEL GUILTY". He says it was his job to recognise these things in children BUT he still FAILED us.'

Stephen's father reacted dramatically, having several angina attacks, but on the whole was able to deal with the disclosure, while at the same time expressing his devastation: 'More angina attacks; asks for glass of water. We're worried he's going to have a heart attack.' As the information sinks in it becomes harder for him and he starts to lose sight of his son's victimisation as he begins to react to his own unconscious sense of powerlessness. Stephen notes: 'Stella reminded me that when I disclosed to him, he had said: 'You will work through this but I never will.'

Stephen had not been able to address his anger towards his parents, especially his father's dominating behaviour. He still related to his parents as the compliant child – not allowing his wife to express her anger towards them either. To some extent this kept him safer than Mike during the early period of disclosure. Mike wanted to express his anger to his parents, especially his father who was unable to deal with the additional feelings of guilt and shame that ensued, or his sense that he was no longer in control of the family secret. He needed to blame others in order to relieve his feelings.

It is often the case that when abuse is disclosed there is a need to blame. There seems to be a need for a scapegoat. Social workers often fulfil this role in our society and more recently counsellors have taken on the role. Their father attempted to cast me into the role of scapegoat: 'Counsellors are a waste of time – their own lives are usually a mess – they need counselling themselves.' Having admitted to myself the partial truth of his statement, I did not need to defend myself from his attack. Ugly scenes surrounding such cases as the killing of little James Bulger show us how some people need to split off the shadow within and project it onto somebody else – perhaps as a way of avoiding knowing the darker aspects of themselves. As a society we all have a responsibility when these events occur – how do we allow ourselves to ignore the fact that James's killers were themselves abused children that we as a society had failed to protect?

Mike and Stephen's father used various defence mechanisms to protect his fragile ego. He appeared to want to protect others from knowing rather than protect the 'victims', but of course he was actually trying to protect himself from what seemed unbearable. But Stephen began to relinquish his role as the compliant child. He presses his father again – confronting him with his responsibility, as he seems unable to confront himself. His father brings in reinforcements as he feels Stephen's insistence: 'He told me people he had spoken to also thought it was not a good idea to tell other people!' His father's pain at the disclosures is almost palpable and he seeks more ways to free himself from something that he cannot avoid dealing with any longer:

> Dad told me it all could have been better managed if we had told him before Gramps died. I explained that would have been impossible for me at the time, as it was repressed; I was afraid of discovery; afraid of the consequences for me and for DAD. He said it would have been easier to deal with it then, so I replied: 'What, with us going to the police; him in prison getting beaten up?'
>
> 'Uncle Adam agrees with me,' he says. He goes on and on about the consequences of what we had now started, 'the ripple effect'; 'pulling the carpet from under people's ordered lives', etc, etc.
>
> So I asked him if it would have been better if we had kept quiet?
>
> 'Oh, no,' he says, 'but by telling loads of other people like Wendy, Stella's Mum and Dad you have left me with no choice but to tell everyone else on *my* terms.'
>
> Also he says that he and Mum are now talking seriously about separation. I ask if that is my fault! 'Oh, no BUT if all this wasn't happening...'
>
> He would, of course, deny it, but I got the FEELING that he was blaming me for the mess HE now finds himself in; losing his father and his sons, the family; and for the break-up of his marriage; that it would have been better for me to keep quiet, or at the very least, hand over complete control of the situation to him to deal with how he felt best suited HIM.
>
> This feels like blame from my father BUT I know I am not guilty. Even so, it hurts; I am close to tears.

This theme continues even as it becomes gradually more and more obvious that the abuse has permeated through the family. Each time another family member discloses, their father attempts to defend himself further, trying like King Canute to stem the tide and the inevitability of the momentum of what must have felt like an erupting volcano. Stephen tries valiantly to reframe the experience for him: 'Dad comes to the phone. I tell him I am pleased to hear the family are supporting each other. He doesn't see it like that, STILL thinks it would have been *better not to involve the rest of the family!'*

The more his father thrashes around trying to free himself of the pain, the more clear becomes the picture of the family and how impossible it would have been for any of the victims to name the abuse. Even as adults, Mike and Stephen are being emotionally battered or blackmailed on all sides. Their father tries to manipulate their feelings, blaming their mother, dramatically leaving home, hinting at suicide, having angina attacks and physically attacking Mike and Ellen. Their mother also swings back and forth trying to find some solid ground – sometimes blaming her sons, sometimes her husband, sometimes being blamed herself, and finally Stephen helps her find the solid ground, the fact that she can no longer avoid: 'She says she wants to find someone who will take responsibility for all this. I ask: "Do you mean me or Mike?" "Oh no," she says. I tell her: "There's only one person responsible for this, isn't there?" She says, "Your grandfather, but he's dead".'

Their father is longing to retreat back into the familiar safety of denial: 'It's important we get back to normal!' he demands, graphically portraying his inability to recognise that 'normal' was never how it should have been.

The fear of exposure erupts within the wider family as more abuse emerges; others join with their father to put pressure on Mike and Stephen. But the counter-pressure also increases from other victims who join forces with them, having found a voice through Mike and Stephen's courage. Mike stops and takes account of the damage his grandfather has caused:

> I now know of admissions of abuse or attempts at abuse by my paternal grandfather of three of his five children plus his daughter's fiancé; myself and Stephen; two other male cousins (not brothers) one of whom witnessed the other, the second of whom is reported to have declared himself as 'in the clear'! Three other male cousins have said no, three female and one other male cousin have not been asked = so far eight admissions.

As they continue to refuse to accept the blame – even though at times Stephen reports, 'Mike now full of doubt about if he was right to start all this off' – their father begins to accept their feelings. This is a very clear example of how, when we refuse to accept or take on responsibility for other people's feelings, they will eventually have to know them for their own and may then be able to empathise with others.

This stage is a powerful turning point in the family's healing. They are now able to help their father, in the way they have been helped, to separate out inappropriate guilt from appropriate guilt. Yes, he is guilty of failing to protect them, but he is not the one responsible for the abuse. He then has to come to terms with the fact that his father is an abuser. By holding on to the guilt himself or putting it out on to others, he had been protecting himself from the loss of his own image of 'father'. He is also protecting himself from knowing that he, like his children, was powerless to do anything about it; and from knowing that he too has become his father's victim. His father has abused his trust, betrayed him and damaged his children. This is what he has to face – his father's 'fall from grace' which allows him to accept his own fall from grace: 'You were right and I was wrong – it's hard for me say that but I admit it.' In feeling his own victimisation he too can begin to heal.

Stephen has been the solid, mostly unwavering buffer throughout this storm. The fact that he had his brother alongside, as well as myself, during the whole period of disclosure meant that he was able to hold on to his convictions. Mike, having faced so much of this alone in the early part of his recovery process, found it harder to hold on. His writing shows how he needs to keep on reminding himself of the fact that 'I was sexually abused as a child', almost as though he needs to convince himself over and over again. At this stage, I believe that Stephen had not been able to release himself from the fear of his anger towards his father (or mother), although he had been able to express his feelings towards his grandfather. His need to protect his parents and for him to avoid their rejection and anger was still paramount. He had, however, been able to stand up to his father about current issues, adult to adult. His Child's anger towards his parents was still unexpressed.

Mike had not at this stage reached a point of real empathy with the abused child within him and there were remnants of self-blame that may have been blocking him from feeling secure. On 12 November 1995 he watched a TV film and listened to young men who were abused by a choirmaster during their childhood. Mike was reluctant to watch the film – his 'Child' fear still prevented him from getting too close to its cause. He noticed while watching how he felt 'sad at the pain of those men – but strangely I find it difficult to see the pain of the boys'.

It is a week later that he begins to write to the child within himself and begins to face his fear. So at the time this furore was erupting within the family (during September and October 1995), Mike was still in the grip of the unconscious fear of his Child. Stephen had faced some of his fear at this stage and was more connected with his Adult – he was therefore more secure in his position although the Child dread was still around. The voices of both Adult and Child can be heard in his diary on 4 October 1995: 'Despite all this, I am sure it is right for all this to come out, and hope and pray that everyone will progress to be free of his legacy. I am still scared that something terrible will happen though.'

Victim–Perpetrator Dynamic

A broad spectrum of theories on the issue of victims becoming offenders has been put forward that are based on clinical impressions to empirical data (Freund, Watson and Dickey 1988; Hindman 1988; O'Brien 1989). O'Brien's empirically derived theory suggests that a significant percentage of males who were sexually abused as children will become offenders. Moreover, he states that the gender of the perpetrator will affect the selection of the gender of the next generation of victims. However, Gerber (1990) extrapolates from his own experience, which is more in line with what I have found, when he says:

> As boys and men have a growing social permission to come forward and identify themselves as victims of sexual molestation and sexual assaults, we will see an increasing number of males referred who have not acted out sexually against others in response to their victimisation. (Gerber 1990, p.153)

Only two of the twenty-five men in my own study went on to become paedophiles, although ten admitted to acting out sexually during their childhood and adolescence in ways similar to their own abuse (Etherington 1995). Most of the theories that support the 'victim becoming offender' view have come from studies of convicted offenders and this fact inevitably lends bias that renders the research questionable in terms of generalisation. The reality is that those studies showed that men who are convicted offenders have frequently experienced childhood abuse themselves. This is *not* to say that men who are sexually abused go on to become offenders (Groth and Hobson 1983). As more and more men come forward we will have a clearer picture – it will not help men to come forward if we have made up our minds about the issue in advance. There needs to be further research into mediating factors before we can really understand why some victims do not offend and why some do.

I believe the fear around this issue is also related to the societal stereotyping of males as sexually aggressive and proactive and females as passive. What is also emerging at the present time is the recognition of female abusers. Females had abused over half the men in my previous study. In a society that teaches children that women are passive in relation to sexuality, there is no frame of reference for boys who are abused by women.

However, the effects of research have lent an additional anxiety to men's experiences of having been abused. All the men I have counselled have, at some stage of the work, faced the fear of their own potential to abuse others. Of course, all of us have within the potential to abuse, but for these men the idea can be particularly difficult to face. As Mike watched the TV programme mentioned previously he names his fear; he is 'angry and very, very frightened at how much the abuser looks like me! How can I stand this, I want to get off this ride now.' Nine weeks later Mike wrote of the new level of pain he experienced as this fear came into focus again:

> New Year's Eve 1995
>
> Well, I thought I was having a holiday from pain, but here is another burst!
> First the good – Ellen asking me for a massage, twice – excellent, the best thing for ages. But we've not really had a chance to build on it – more cuddles, less hostility, but still tiredness or business intervenes.

An angry outburst as I was dozing in the chair – still an issue between us – myself on guard, an angry reply and went to bed – fell asleep. When I woke it was to find Rob and Judy in bed with me (awake) and Rob complaining that he was being squashed between us. Only half awake I was aware of him fetching Ellen and her ordering Judy to her own room in a very angry voice. I sent Rob to his room to be fair (tempting as it was to keep him with me so as to avoid Ellen).

I woke to find him back on Ellen's instructions and Ellen in his bed.

I apologised to Ellen when she woke and she said she wanted to discuss something (progress, progress; find the good in it). She told me she loved me but had had a panic about trusting me with the children. Icy calm (in control or repressed?), I tried to reassure her:

(i) re: invalidity of arguing from abusers to generality;

(ii) re: the issue of acknowledging one's own abuse giving one the power to recognise abuse by oneself.

I was trying to apply the latter to me but Ellen perceived it as directed to her. I bring it back to me – our children are safe with me because I have acknowledged my own victimisation. I know it, but Ellen is not reassured. I acknowledge that I feel this applies to Ellen herself in relation to Judy and that is why I should like her to have counselling. Ellen: 'No I don't want to, I can't afford it'; 'I haven't got the time'; 'Perhaps I'm scared'; 'Is it any wonder we don't get it together if I feel I can't trust you with the children?'

I'm off to do calls, but when I have a quiet moment a wave of emotion comes over me – scared, angry, sad. I try to push it down but can't really manage it. I ring Ellen and tell her a little – she acknowledges it briefly but we pass quickly on to practical subjects.

I need to share this again, I need her to see my pain. I am angry, angry, angry with my abuser – still it hurts me; angry especially as I thought I had achieved so much. Angry I suppose, a little, with Ellen – no reason why; she has told me of her feelings and that is a good thing. But it hurts. Scared that I will lose the children – yes, that's it mostly – and Ellen but that's less so.

I was abused as a child, he damaged me badly, my emotional development was garbled and arrested in many ways. I am angry about that. But I have progressed, I have used my intellect and will to go back and learn things. I'm not perfect at practising them but I have learned the skills. I know that I'm not a risk to our (or any) children. These are my feelings; Ellen's are her own. I do not have to deal with hers – just let her express them. And she has – this is potentially a healing thing and she has connected it with sex – a breakthrough possibly.

Time and patience. I love her, but it is hard to trust – that must be so for her too. We have not learned to trust when we were little, so it is not surprising.

Oh, God, help us please to love unconditionally.

The same issue comes up during Stephen's story when he admits to thinking that his own father may have abused his child, Joe: 'Stella has just voiced her unspeakable thoughts that I have also been pushing to the back of my mind. Is Joe's behaviour like it is because of anything Dad has done?' His father raises the subject himself:

> He says: how did you let me take Joe away for the weekend? You must have been worried!! I tell him it's because I trust him, and don't associate him with abuse. He says he has even wondered if I've been abusing Joe because of the way he is! Then I spilled out: 'YES, these last few days I've wondered about YOU abusing Joe as well.' He replies that he has not and never would. I believe him and say 'Good, *'cause I would have killed you if you had.*' He accepts this and says since he heard about Mike he has been afraid of getting too close to his own grandchildren.

During our research interview Stephen tells me a story about a recent incident in which he felt he had been suspected of abusing his daughter. His daughter, who was at the stage of studying for important school examinations, was having difficulty sleeping at night. She went to her GP to ask for some medication. The GP (the same one Stephen had gone to when he was suffering from PTSD who had been very helpful and understanding) referred the child to a psychiatrist. Stephen was upset about it and went to ask the GP why this had happened without reference to her parents. He came away with the distinct impression that the GP's over-reaction was based on the fact that he knew her father to be an abuse survivor and therefore, in his book, was perhaps an abuser. Stephen was in a double bind – if he refused to allow his daughter to attend for a psychiatric assessment it might have been interpreted as him trying to prevent disclosure to someone outside the family. If he did not intervene, his daughter could be subjected to unnecessary psychiatric intervention. Stephen dealt with this by explaining to his daughter what he felt the doctor's anxieties were based on and allowed her to make the decision whether or not to attend. She was of an age when she was able to make such decisions for herself.

So Mike, Stephen and their father have all, at some stage, been suspected of child abuse. I believe it is important for us as counsellors to enable clients to face this issue. Many men are fearful of raising the subject in case it is seen as an indication that they are abusers. A child who is abused learns about both roles, victim and perpetrator. By exploring both capacities within us, we are better able to integrate them and thereby take control. There is often something in our behaviour that has remnants of our abuser's behaviour; it is not always sexual behaviour that is abusive. If we control others by our behaviour, act out our disowned anger, fear and sexuality, we can be experienced as abusive by others. Friedrich (1995) hypothesised that being in touch with the memories and pain of maltreatment in childhood provides a powerful deterrent against repeating abusive acts in adulthood. This is something with which I would wholeheartedly agree and is often the focus of the work I do with adult survivors.

Victim–Persecutor–Rescuer Dynamic

The victim–persecutor–rescuer is played out over and over again in families where children are abused. This triangular dynamic usually refers to behaviours that are adopted within groups. The three positions are fixed or switched around so that different people adopt the roles which are self-maintaining. We can usually recognise a role that is fairly fixed or familiar. People who enter the helping professions are frequently 'rescuers'. We step into the breach when we observe somebody being victimised – coming between the victim and the perpetrator. When we do this we can then become the victims, as either the victim or the persecutor attacks us for interfering.

Mike and Stephen were rescuers; their mother, the victim; and their father, the persecutor. The three men in the family swing backward and forwards between rescuer and persecutor but mother stays firmly stuck in victim. Women in our society, especially women of her generation, have been socialised by patriarchy into accepting the status of victim. During the 1960s and 1970s this began to change as the feminist movement gave women a voice and they began to recognise how they were being victimised by society and by men. They found new resources upon which to call and joined forces to support each other. However, women of their mother's generation often missed out on all this change. They had gone before and had become entrenched in their roles, not having had the freedom of the women of later generations. Their mother was financially dependant; she could not imagine how she could survive without their father, even though his dominating manner at times felt unbearable. Her sons had watched as she passively accepted her role and her husband's behaviour towards her, and they felt helpless. She called upon them frequently for help and support and they had always responded, thereby maintaining her in her helplessness.

All this began to change as they started to recognise the unhealthy family dynamics. As they begin to express their anger and sense of betrayal, the triangle swings and at times their parents try to hand them the roles of perpetrator and victim. But Mike and Stephen refuse to accept the roles and eventually refuse to become entangled in their parents' familiar 'games'. When somebody refuses to play the game, the game has to end. Refusing is sometimes seen as an aggressive act.

Mike's story describes his parents' inability to deal with his anger as he attempts to express his feelings about the abuse. His father responds with aggression and rejection and his mother behaves towards Mike as if he is the aggressor and she is his victim.

Haaken (1998) reflects on this dynamic within families: 'Sometimes knowing is anxiety provoking because it unsettles prior beliefs, ideals, or self-perceptions. And sometimes the act of looking and seeing itself is unconsciously associated with aggression and the violation of taboos' (p.10). She also comments on the role of the eldest child and asks why one remembers while the other did not? 'Does the eldest child remember as a form of justification of his own rebellion?' Is it possible that the younger child conforms so fully to the dictates of the adults that he has no independent vantage point from which to reflect on his life or autonomy, even in what he allows himself to remember? As the younger child, Stephen would have learned about the cost of not conforming as he watched Mike interact with their father. He may have decided to avoid similar treatment and keep on the right side of Dad, no matter what the cost to his sense of self.

CHAPTER 16

Traumatic Sexualisation

Finkelhor and Browne (1986) described traumatic sexualization as the shaping of a child's sexual feelings and attitudes in a manner inappropriate for the child's level of development. For example, traumatic sexualisation may produce concerns about a homosexual identity in a young male molested by an adult male; sexual dysfunctions; overall confusion about sexual matters; and interpersonal relationship problems.

Homosexual 'identity'

It is clear from what has already been said that Mike and Stephen were confused about their sexual identity in response to their abuse. When boys are sexually abused by other males, fears about homosexuality are common. The experience of a homosexual act contradicts the child's understanding of sexual relationships. A victim may worry that he is homosexual; that there must have been something about him that was recognisably homosexual for him to have been singled out by another male. In seeking an explanation for why he was selected, self-blame and guilt are common responses. A male may attribute his selection to a particular aspect of his appearance, his speech, his clothing or any other personal characteristic that might be perceived as effeminate and to have contributed to the assault. Through perceiving himself in this way the male victim may blame himself for having attracted the abuser. If he does not actively resist the molestation this may be taken as further proof of his lack of masculinity. He may be sexually aroused which creates further conflict in his sense of sexual identity and he may define himself as homosexual.

He may fear that the abuse experience will make him homosexual and that others will think he is homosexual. Not only do male victims worry about these issues, but their parents and others related to the victim may also be affected by these fears. Parents of molested boys frequently asked about the possibility of this outcome.

Identity Confusion

The more closely the victim is psychologically identified with the perpetrator, the more intense and exacerbated are his sexual identity issues. Significant males, such as fathers and father figures, play a large part in the formation of the psychosocial identity of young males. When sexual abuse occurs between a boy and a psychologically close male, the victim is likely to be left with a confusion about his sense of self-identity as related to his identity struggles with the offender. This struggle may be conscious, causing severe distress and confusion, or unconscious and therefore integrated into the self-identity; the victim becomes psychologically identified with the aggressor. Such internalised messages as 'Like father, like son' and 'I am my father's son' may contribute to these sexual identity confusions.

In this situation a child will make the psychological adjustments that lead them to believe that the abuse is a consensual act. Neither Stephen nor Mike was in a position to consent – or to refuse their consent. Consent requires that the person is fully informed about the nature of what they are consenting to. As children they were not in a position to understand such information even if it was offered, and of course it wasn't – any discussion about sex was taboo within their home. Consent also requires that the person is able to refuse; as children and adolescents neither of them was in the position to refuse. The inequality of power and dependency in the relationship negated any possibility of refusal.

Most people understand that a small child is not in a position to say no when an adult abuses them. What is harder for us to understand – and this was very true for Stephen and Mike themselves – is why, as young men of 16, 17 and 18, they were not able to say no. The fact that the abuse had continued into late adolescence and young adulthood was a source of deep shame for both men; it also reinforced their view of the behaviour as homosexual. Stephen hid the fact that he was 18 when it stopped even after he had overcome the shame of admitting his victimisation: 'Mike and I tell each other what happened to us. BUT I don't tell him how old I was when it finished.' It was nearly two weeks' later that he was able to admit this to his brother – even knowing that Mike had been 18 when he had stopped his own abuse.

Effects on Sexual Development

What neither of them was able to recognise was that children who are sexualised at such an early age are traumatically stuck in the addiction created by the arousal that overwhelms them and does not allow them to move on. It is often very hard for adults working through their abuse to admit to having been aroused and there is often judgement for those that do. When Stephen told his mother he had enjoyed it at the time, she reacted badly – making him feel guilty and responsible. The word 'enjoyment' is often confused with 'arousal'. What children feel is arousal and not pleasure. Arousal is a healthy and normal response to being sexually stimulated – it is important to separate out these two words if the adult is to be helped to reclaim his rightful ownership of his sexual feelings. Ejaculation is also confused with orgasm; ejaculation is a physical outcome of sexual stimulation, while orgasm is how the person feels emotionally. It is possible to have one without the other (Zilbergeld 1995).

This confusion is clear when Mike writes in his letter to his grandfather: 'Of course I enjoyed it – you'd been training my sexual responses since I was practically a toddler.' The child is trained by the adult to behave sexually – much as a dog can be trained to perform tricks. Mike recognises this too: 'How did you get me to do it to you – I really don't remember – it was always there; just a learned response I suppose, like Pavlov's dogs.'

Once the child reaches puberty and can ejaculate, the experience takes on a whole new meaning. The powerful physical sensations during ejaculation fix the addiction in a way that traps him. Stephen recognises something of the trap he is in: 'I can't break the habit of ejaculating with you. WHY, OH WHY, OH WHY?'

The abuse is like a drug – the addiction is every bit as powerful and we would not expect an 18 year old to walk away from heroin or cocaine, having been addicted from early childhood. Why then should we expect someone who has been sexually addicted to walk away from the abuse before they were able to recognise and meet the underlying need for attention, affection, privileges and gifts – the rewards that are received in return for sexual favours? Mike displays the addict's response of self-disgust after the craving has been met – the cost of short-term gratification is a growing long-term loss of self-esteem. The physical need for arousal that has been engendered in the child is also part of the addiction; so like drug addiction, there are both physical and social aspects of the addiction of sexual abuse.

Even his physical response is marred by its addictive quality. Addictive sex brings no sense of satisfaction. The boy becomes aroused by stimulation; arousal is followed by ejaculation but this is not followed by resolution as in the normal sexual response pattern. There is no relaxation but rather a sense of frustration that takes the boy back to the beginning; to the craving for a new arousal – hence the fruitless search for more that drives the boy back again into the addictive behaviour: 'I remember telling you how odd and shameful I felt after ejaculating, ha! And asking if you felt the same – no you didn't really understand did you?'

The use of pornography has been associated with compulsive masturbation. Stephen describes how as a very small child he is shown pornographic images by his abuser. Stephen notes, 'I was unshockable after that wasn't I?', referring to the book his grandfather owned. Paedophiles use pornography to create arousal in children, to normalise the behaviour and to instruct them in specific sexual activities. I asked him about what part pornography played for him:

Stephen: Yes he had this book – I remember in the very early stages – he brought this book home from work – cover off, paper back. I was very, very young when I read it and it was most explicit pornography you could think of. He used to let me read that – give it to me to read [pause] which was a terrible thing to do wasn't it? Of course because I was so young I found it absolutely fascinating. I reread it all the time, whenever I got the chance – it was more interesting than the Beano and 'hey, I can read this stuff – it is forbidden but I'm allowed to read it ... 'Cos it was forbidden and naughty and it got me aroused I suppose. I think I was reading it very early on, when it first started. I remember seeking it out, wanting to read it the whole time because I was so fascinated – I remember that book: 'School for Sex'.

Kim: And then later, you found some pornography under your father's bed.

Stephen: I did yes. It wasn't the first I'd seen. I'd seen some at school, with my best friend and among the choirboys – I was in the choir [laughs] and my fellow chorister – his Dad was in the army – he got some extremely hard stuff from his Dad from Germany. That was the most explicit I've ever seen – as I was only 8, 9, 10 or 11 it made an impression on me – a heterosexual impression on me really. 'I'd like to do that.'

Kim: So it sounds as if you are saying it was quite helpful.

Stephen: Yes, in a way. I was thinking, 'When I grow up I'll be normal – do things like this. I won't always be queer like this.'

Kim: So you thought you were 'queer'?

Stephen: I was in turmoil. I was afraid – but then I enjoyed the... I mean I went back voluntarily. I kept going back to see him all the time – I enjoyed the sexual stimulation.

He trained me from a very early age. Then I was going home and masturbating to pornography as well – I was addicted to sexual release, over and over and over and over and over again – so that I was tired from doing it so much – I'm still trying to break away from it now – I want sex too much now really. And I think, 'Is that because of what happened to me?' And then when I think of pornography – I think 'Oh dear, poor women, having to do this' and then I think 'Some people say they want to do it', and I'm all confused about it now. Certainly, I think it helped me. But I can see that it can also be an abusive... thing.

Kim: Well in a way you could say that it fed your addiction – it kept you in a state of arousal, interest, heightened sensitivity to sexual imaginings.

Stephen: Yes it was a way of getting ready for when I had the chance to do the real thing properly for real and not with him. In a way it was a way of preparing to be able to break away I suppose.

Research into sexual compulsiveness or addiction described by Hunter (1990) shows that 37.1 per cent of men and 65.2 per cent of women members of Sex Addicts Anonymous reported that they were sexually abused as children. Many other compulsions are also noted as well as sexual addiction; compulsive eating, drug and alcohol abuse are among those often noted. In Hunter (1995) useful innovations are described for the treatment of compulsions and addictive behaviours manifest as outcomes of childhood sexual abuse.

Compulsive masturbation can become a way of re-enacting the abuse – not by abusing others but by abusing themselves. The re-enactment is of the victim role but this time the abuser is also the victim. Raine (1999, p.193) explains: 'Re-enactments are emotionally driven attempts to master the overwhelming too-muchness of the traumatic experience. The compulsion to re-live is an attempt to master the terror, helplessness, and rage of "mortal danger".'

Relationships with Others

Sexual abuse interferes with the ability to form other intimate relationships. A child is isolated from normal friendships for fear that the secret might emerge; or he may be rejected by other children because of his precocious sexual knowledge or behaviour. Mike's first experience of dissonance was at a very early age: 'I remember telling about my sexual fantasies in the playground at primary school to a rather loud boy who told some of the others and who then shunned me – that must put it back to under seven years of age.'

In his letter to his grandfather he rages: 'You stopped me from having any real friends as a child. You evil bastard. I had no one but you.' Even the two brothers were kept apart, neither knowing of the other's abuse: 'My brother and I had never really been close. I had never understood why, but was not really surprised that we had little contact.'

In adolescence the sense of isolation grew – this being a time when young people need to be included in their peer group as part of their identity formation and separation from home. But their grandfather wanted them to remain tied to him. He filled the role normally taken on by a best friend – he was their confidant on sexual matters. Paedophiles psychologically identify with their victims. The boy appears to represent what the offender feels himself to be sexually and/or psychologically: an immature male. Boyhood may represent a return to a developmental stage of unfinished business, or a point of arrested development. Men who are sexually drawn to boys may have no satisfying peer or adult relationships and do not desire them, or they may have regressed to boys from a primarily heterosexual relationship (as in this case). The psychological nature of their sexual involvement with boys is better described as narcissistic rather than homosexual (Groth and Oliveri 1989).

Mike recalls his thoughts and feelings in his letter to his abuser. The horror of his growing realisation at what the abuse had cost him in terms of a normal life: 'All this time when other boys were beginning to explore their sexuality – you deprived me of that too. What should have been a gradual awakening in my teenage years had happened to me, in its perverted, strange way, years before. You sick bastard.'

Stephen manages to escape for a while at the age of 15 when he forms a relationship with his first girlfriend but after a while the relationship ends:

> Unfortunately she moves on to more mature males and I am out of luck… So after a few glorious months you get me back you BASTARD, as I am under your spell and in a HABIT. But I FEEL MORE GUILTY about it. I know for sure it is wrong but can't STOP.

Even when they manage to break free into marriage the effects are still there. Adults who have known the passive side of the abuse dynamic will often seek out partners who help them re-create the known and familiar ways of relating. In their adult relationships both men fluctuate between being the rescuer, the one who protects the family from the world, and the victim, as they allow their wives to treat them in ways that erode their self-esteem further. Mike's marriage was under severe strain by the time I met him. In fact his first experience in counselling had been through family therapy and Relate, the focus being on the relationship between himself and his wife, and her relationship with their daughter. Mike was so amazed that anyone would find him attractive, in view of the way he felt about himself, that he was bowled over when he fell in love.

Stephen's marriage, on the surface, seemed more successful, but as he began to change the 'marital fit' altered and problems began to emerge. So when somebody comes into counselling and their partner does not, it can change them so fundamentally that the marital 'fit' is no longer comfortable. Stephen had been compliant – 'anything for a quiet life' was a familiar phrase on his lips. As he began to change he became less compliant and conflicts emerged in the relationship. We talked about this in reviewing his counselling. I commented on the changes he had made:

Stephen: Changes. Yes. You can certainly say that.

Kim: You were a different person – you met your partner as this previous person – you met each other's needs and you changed and she hadn't changed – and that created a turbulence...

Stephen: Indeed. Yes. Things weren't what they were, equilibrium is disturbed.

Kim: You were no longer this person who thought that his life was only there for other people's needs.

Stephen: Yes, worrying about other people too much and what they'd think. Complicated by the fact that Stella became ill which made her needs, her expectations, even greater, immense.

Kim: She became very needy. Just as your expectations of what you were giving out to other people were trying to reduce – bad timing really... for that change to happen.

Stephen: Yes. She was really supportive at the start.

Kim: Very supportive, yes

Stephen: But that changed...yes.

Kim: And now?

Stephen: Up and down – difficult times and better times. She likes to become angry and irritable and take it out on me and whereas before I would have accepted it, now I don't – I tell her. And that causes problems – still. Things are a lot better than they were. Things have improved a great deal over the last year – we've come a long way. We are learning to live with each other more, accept each other. I say a lot more upfront about how it feels, I try and communicate – more. I think we are getting there.

Kim: Yes. And it's healthier from the sound of it – even though it's more uncomfortable at times.

Stephen: And for myself – I think I've learned to accept that everything isn't going to be perfect – a very hard lesson to learn. After all these changes that took place in me I just wanted – I thought: 'Oh life could be so good now; I want everything to be perfect – to live life to the full; to grab it; to be wonderful.' And then when it couldn't be, that was frustrating as well.

But since these years have elapsed, I haven't gone back to accepting things like I did, but accept things in a different way. By aiming for the best I can get within a certain set of circumstances. That means I have to accept Stella the way she is, with her faults; and she's got to accept me with my faults, and it's never going to be perfect, but I'm going to try and make the best of what there is. And that means making changes on both sides.

Kim: And it means conflict?

Stephen: Yes, conflict and compromise. It does.

Kim: None of those things are comfortable for any of us.

Touch

Another important aspect of relating to others is through touch. As a society we suffer from sensory starvation, a lack of non-sexual touching (Zilbergeld 1995). Our tactile sense is the first to develop and without touch a child will fail to thrive or even die. Touching can mean the difference between life and death for the infant and fortunately most parents realise this. However, fairly early on, there is a sharp decline in the amount of physical contact between adults and children, particularly from men and particularly to boys.

The child's training about touch starts early; one of the first commands we instil in our toddlers is 'don't touch'. Many men can barely recall times when they have been held or touched during their childhood. Boys fare far worse than girls. Their mothers stop touching them at an earlier age for fear that they will experience it as sexual (masculinity being equated with sexuality). Some mothers fear that touching too much will make a sissy of their sons – fathers often criticise mothers with this warning. Fathers who have been socialised within a homophobic society that instils them with fear may not touch their sons at all after infancy. As the father is the role model for a boy, he will grow up to recognise that it is not 'manly' to touch and he may interpret touching and hugging as outside the realm of acceptable behaviour among males.

Girls' sensuality is also developed through a variety of means; the type of clothing they are permitted to wear, soft, silky, frilly materials. Girls are permitted to use perfumes, grow their hair long, use perfumed shampoos and take time and pleasure in brushing it.

Boys are taught that contact is more acceptable through sport and rough and tumble games. There are no taboos against touching while wrestling, boxing or being rough in other ways. Men rarely hold or cuddle their sons, but they can be seen to roll around on the floor, wrestle or throw them about. There is a tacit acceptance that boys will be sexually active and, providing that it is heterosexual sex, there is often a blind eye turned; not so for girls who are warned of the dangers and cautioned against sex play. The most acceptable form of touching for adult males is through sex. So boys grow up knowing that wanting sex is acceptable but wanting to be held, loved, or to know they are not alone is unacceptable.

CHAPTER 17

What Helps?

Mediators

The effects of sexual abuse are undoubtedly variable and research has shown that there are factors which mediate and factors which protect some children from the more devastating effects that may be felt by others. Some of the ways children have protected themselves are explained through psychoanalytical theory in terms of defence mechanisms (Bowlby 1973; Freud 1946; Osborne 1990). These theorists suggest that the use of psychological defence mechanisms which protect the developing child's fragile ego from disintegration and help them to survive can become problematic when carried into adulthood, preventing the adult from reclaiming memories, connecting with feelings and affect, causing automatic avoidance and aggressive behaviours.

Researchers have found that the presence of someone in whom to confide and who is supportive appears to be important in helping individuals overcome the effects of abuse and may be one factor which breaks the cycle of abuse (Egeland, Jacobvitz and Sroufe 1988; Gilgun 1990; Wyatt and Mickey 1987).

It is very clear that the mediating relationship for Mike and Stephen was with their Grandma. Stephen reconnects with his grandmother during the bodywork and uses his memories of her to support him whenever he is feeling low. It is through her memory that he begins to understand feeling loved and loving:

> On the way home I feel drawn to Grandma's grave. I tidy the grave, and while Joe has a look round, I spend some quiet moments thinking of her, and how she has been in my thought *helping me*, even though she is gone. I talk to her, tell her I love her and miss her.

As Mike begins to open himself up to feeling through writing, he is reminded painfully of his grandmother. I am struck by the immediacy of his feelings – a sign that he is really undoing the effects of dissociation:

> Yours is the house with good memories, and even where he contaminated it, that can't spoil it. I wish I could be there now, in your front room with the red curtains with the regency stripes; with the sun shining in through the windows; warm and safe and comfortable; and with you, always beavering away at something, cooking or

cleaning; and best of all, telling me stories about the old days, of your youth and your squabbles with your family, of your days in service.

Other mediating factors in their story are their ability to self-soothe by means of using spirituality, intellect, nature (Stephen usually goes off on his bike into the countryside). Both men also have powerful imaginations – a child can escape his painful reality by creating a world of his own.

Counsellor's process

As I have been writing these stories within the stories, I have noticed myself feeling distanced from the material. I ask myself – why? It feels like a parallel process; patriarchy creates distance between men and women. I feel heavy hearted as I write these words and I realise that I have been defending myself from feeling while writing these stories relating to the influence of patriarchy on the lives of men who have been sexually abused.

Patriarchy is in the very air we breathe; it is hard to catch hold of, but we know it's there. As I collected the experiences of these men and placed them within the context of male socialisation, I have felt something akin to the oppressive atmosphere that precedes a thunderstorm and sadness envelops me. I feel sad to think that such additional burdens have been placed upon boys and men by our society. I feel sad for myself as a woman, who also feels the impact of such conditioning. I feel sad as the mother of sons who might have had to struggle against their maleness, instead of being able to celebrate their gender. I feel anxious for my grandsons in case all this is too slow in changing. I don't want to feel hopeless and despairing, but it's hard not to. Is there really change afoot?

But then I begin to realise that some of the sadness I am feeling is about my own years of denial; the denial that still exists within my own family of origin; the need for my brothers to avoid discussion of our childhood and our relationships with our parents. They want to 'leave the past behind' and get on with living. I know I could not leave the past behind and get on with my life until I had faced my memories and experiences. Their inability to deal with it limits my ability to deal with it; but I have also found some family members who can acknowledge part of what it was really like for us.

Some of my sadness is being reminded of the harm that was caused by my strict indoctrination into gender and sex roles. Being the only girl I carried the 'feminine' within the family. I was dressed by my father in clothes that he wanted for me – so that he could show me off as 'his' little girl. As a child I felt 'owned' by him – his pride in his possession did little to ameliorate the loss of my sense of belonging to myself. I remember my older brothers, sent away from home aged 8 or 9, to the all-male environment of a military boarding school and dressed in rough khaki while still children.

I recall my younger brother, at the age of 4, being dressed up in my clothes, a ribbon tied into his curls, and being laughed at by my mother because he liked to play with my doll's pram, and took my walkie-talkie doll to bed for his afternoon nap. I recall an older brother who was constantly derided and humiliated by my father for being a 'mummy's boy', and the implicit homophobia within that label. I think of the warnings that my mother gave me that 'men are only after one thing' and to 'steer well clear of them', and her reluctance to accept any of my boy friends into the home without a fight from me.

I feel the hurt and anger of being misunderstood and my reality negated when I attempted to tell a brother about my abuse and his rejoinder, 'Well, don't tell me you didn't enjoy the attention he gave you'; a message that tied in with the one from my mother that I was the lucky one: 'You had everything you wanted; you were the apple of his eye; you could twist him round your little finger.'

I recall the shame I felt as my breasts developed and my brothers teased me – throwing my bra to one another out of my reach as I tried to peg it on the clothes line. I feel angry when I think about the secrecy around sexuality within my home: I remember the terror I felt as I found myself bleeding – not knowing what it meant and assuming that I had something seriously wrong with me. Later, when I did eventually find out from my friends what was happening to my body, my mother telling me, 'On no account must you let your brothers see sanitary towels.' Even today when I hear my sons refer to their wives' 'time of the month' or see tampons openly on display in their bathrooms, I feel an anxious tightening in my stomach and the fleeting judgement introjected all those years ago.

I feel ashamed as I recognise the role of 'victim' that my mother modelled for me, which I adopted for far too long; and how difficult it has been to correct the manipulative behaviour she taught me as she sent me to meet my father from the pub with the injunction 'get him into a good mood'. I feel the shame of the abuser role I have sometimes adopted in my relationship with others, seeking to control them as I attempted to defend against my sense of powerlessness. I feel compassion when I think of how my need to control others, rather than be controlled, had for many years closed me off from freedom, choice and creativity.

I acknowledge that I have survived and more than survived, I have done well. Even as I write this I feel the old familiar tug of 'don't blow your own trumpet my girl'. But I will affirm myself; I have done well. My father gave me the gift of education, language, words and music and I thank him for that. He carried his own wounds into our home; wounds from his childhood, his education by the notoriously violent Christian Brothers in Ireland at that time; and the effects of the emotional and physical wounds he sustained during World War I. My mother gave me an escape into reading novels, a glimpse of other ways people lived their lives that taught me how mine could also change and gave me hope. My brothers taught me how to fight back and when to know I was beaten.

One special half-brother has always had a corner of my heart. He was my father's youngest son by a previous marriage who was 19 when I was born. He had always treated me as though I was his child, never forgetting my birthday during childhood, always magically knowing about and providing me with the present I most wanted. It was on his arm that I walked down the aisle at my wedding. His was the model of 'father' that balanced my experience and he was the man who gave me a positive experience of maleness as a child.

He brought me a walkie-talkie doll back from Italy at the end of the war when I was 7 years old. Such dolls were very rare at that time. That doll was very important to me – it had real hair and was dressed in clothes made by the dressmaker who made my own; she used the same material and patterns for the doll's clothes as she did for mine. My younger brothers played with the doll more often than I did and eventually they tore the hair and the head off and severed the arms and legs. My father took me, with the doll, to the doll's hospital and repairs were made – but she was never restored to her former glory. Later, the doll's re-severed head was used to terrorise me as I lay in bed at dusk. My brother crept into the room and suddenly brought the head, hair in disarray and eyes poked back in its head, from behind his back. I screamed. My father appeared on the scene and brutally beat my brother. I became known in the family as 'dangerous to play with'. As far as I am aware, to this day my brothers identify my father's 'protection' of me as something for which I was to blame.

What has helped me most has been my ability, even as a small girl, to find people to support me. My Guide Captain, Fran, who taught me that I was a leader; my English teacher, Sister Mary Magdalen, who read my poems and gave me a prize for them; the Scottish lady, Mrs Johns, who owned the corner shop, called me 'Rose o' my heart' and gave me sixpence for 'going on her messages' on a Saturday morning. Then there was God, of course, and my guardian angel. I went into the church on my way to and from school all through my early years and I lit a candle and talked to God. Considering our teaching – about sin, hell and punishment, etc. – I think I managed to find a way to make God what I wanted Him to be and not what I was told He was. He was always my friend and still is, although I rarely go to church to find Him; mostly I find Him within people, in the meeting of souls and the sharing of the darkest nights. As a teenager I cycled three miles to mass before school in hail, rain or snow: I can hardly believe it when I look back now. But I do not doubt that I might not have survived without all that support.

As an adult I found other good supports: my dear friend, who was my GP and who became like a brother to me, and his wife who became my sister; all my counsellors, who have held me through the pain of recovery – in spite of sometimes being kicked in the process, as I thrashed about trying, like Mike and Stephen's father, to free myself of the pain. Good friends who have offered challenge and support. But best of all, somehow I managed to find a good man to help me through my healing. Now, as I write this, I feel my spirits lift as I think of the reality of my own experiences of being with the men in my life now: my husband who has supported my growth, who 'feeds and waters' me while I write this book – who tends me like a wilting flower when I am in need of sustenance. I think of my youngest son, a creative, gentle young man; his two older brothers who take a full part in the care of their tiny sons, showing them a different kind of masculinity, bathing and feeding them, playing with them, cuddling them, massaging them, teaching them. They have become husbands who value equality in their relationships, respect women, other men and themselves equally. They know how to communicate their feelings and deal with conflicts in their relationships. I think of the new daughters I have found in my daughters-in-law – welcome female energy that I have been starved of for too long – and I am grateful.

As a small girl the story of the vestal virgins always caught my imagination; the idea that they always kept a lamp alight, night and day, somehow appealed to me. This image has returned to me as I write today and I think about how I used to light the candles in church. I think I have always felt that a flame has constantly been kept alive within me. I am reminded of the first sense of freedom I felt, the summer after my father died when I had just turned 16; my first Girl Guide camp and sitting around the camp fire as the sun went down, mugs of steaming cocoa, friendship – feeling safe, singing one of my favourite campfire songs:

> This little guiding light of mine
> I'm gonna let it shine.
> This little guiding light of mine
> I'm gonna let it shine.
> This little guiding light of mine
> I'm gonna let it shine,
> Let it shine, all the time.
> Let it shine.

CHAPTER 18

Endings

My Story About Endings

This final chapter of Part 2 is, appropriately, about endings. As a beginning counsellor I worked long term with a client who taught me a great deal about endings. I learned the hard way – and so did he. Ours had been a very deep relationship; he had been separated from his mother as a small baby and placed in an isolation ward in hospital. His illness had left him severely disabled and he had been taken from the hospital, where he had lived until he was 3 years old, straight to a residential school for children with disabilities. While at the school he was regularly and sadistically sexually abused. I worked hard with him and I loved him deeply – he healed many of the wounds of childhood during counselling, but there were some that did not heal. I worked carefully, over a long period, towards an ending, which I knew would be painful for both of us. I did not know just how painful his experience of abandonment had been until the day we ended. He ended in the only way he knew – he felt all the feelings of that small child whose mother drove away and left him at that school. He raged at me and clung to me. I felt all the pain of the abandoning mother and of the abandoned child.

I have reflected so often on that ending, trying to understand what I might have done differently. He had expressed his feelings about separation so many times in the years we had worked together, but they were still there and he felt them again on leaving me. For a long time I felt anxious about taking on another long-term client – fearing the possibility of such a thing ever happening again.

Since then I have had the experience of having been in long-term therapy myself and have learned that some of the value of the work is in helping clients come to terms with the disappointment that nobody can change their past and that counselling is not a magic cure – we cannot 'fix' what is wrong. What we can do is give a 'good enough' experience that will allow the client to take in some of the caring and love that may not have been available to them in earlier parts of their lives. I have also learned that people end in the way they need to, and that sometimes their way is not how I would choose. I cannot control the endings. I can only prepare for it and explore past patterns and how it might be possible to change them, while accepting that sometimes it is not possible.

The depth of need within the client reflects the degree of deprivation or neglect in their early relationships with caregivers. I wrote in Chapter 6 about attachment behaviour and how clients develop an 'internal working model' which impacts on later relationships. Dependency issues arise within the therapeutic relationship and when made conscious clients can explore their feelings in the present that may be related to their experiences in the past. Separation pain is the cost of attachment; the pain of loss is the price we pay for feeling love.

When I take on a new client I am always aware of the ending. I try to introduce the idea of endings in the first session, including in my written contract that I see counselling as process having three phases: a beginning, a middle and an ending. Initially I suggest we work together for six sessions, at the end of which time we evaluate the work and find out what is needed. It may be that enough has been achieved in that time; it may be that the client needs referring on; or that we can establish a longer term counselling relationship. If the latter choice is made, I ask clients to give notice when they feel the ending is approaching, so that we might pay attention to the process. So the client is made aware at the start of therapy that this relationship will end. He is kept aware of this during ongoing evaluation sessions when the issue may be raised again. From time to time I try to introduce the idea of a future without counselling, working sometimes in a narrative or solution focussed way (DeSchazer 1991; White and Epston 1990), asking future oriented questions such as 'When the time comes for you to end counselling, how will you know – what will be different?' It is sometimes difficult to balance this while at the same time allowing the client to experience a dependable relationship and one in which their dependency needs are experienced and worked through.

I have experienced many endings since that first painful one – and they are all unique, as are the relationships of which the endings are an important part. I usually ask the client some weeks in advance how they would like to end; thus giving them time to think about it and decide what would be meaningful for them. In planning it, we give the ending its rightful place in the process. Sometimes we have celebrated with a small glass of champagne. Sometimes we have exchanged goodbye letters such as those used in cognitive analytical therapy (Ryle 1990), letters that plot the relationship, reviewing how the work and our relationship has developed. These are often powerfully moving gifts to one another that honour the depth and importance of our time together.

Mike brought me a book as a parting gift, *The Return of the Prodigal Son: A Story of Homecoming* (Nouwen 1994b), symbolising what the work had meant to him, linking the themes of homecoming, affirmation and reconciliation and the challenge to love the father and be loved as the son. However, I found out much more about Mike's internal process as we ended through our research interview – the internal processes that had not come to light before and I wondered how often this happened with other clients.

Stephen's parting gift to me was a tape of his own music, written during the latter part of the time we worked together. I accepted it gratefully as an acknowledgement of my part in his discovery of his creativity and a sharing of the joy and pleasure that had come through so much pain and despair.

Ritual is an important part of ending for many people through which they can connect with the deepest and most fundamental aspects of themselves. Maggie Fisher and Brother Francis (1999) suggest that the energy which flows through this process is archetypal and 'at an individual level, ritual can provide symbolic expression of a deep internal energy which forces its way into consciousness to enable transformation' (p.56).

For Mike and Stephen their rituals became a rite of passage, part of a journey towards their centre that goes on into the future as they leave me behind. Mike called the counselling process 'growing up' and I remember feeling very much as I had done when I waved goodbye to my sons as they left home for university, one by one. In my interviews about their counselling I asked Stephen and Mike about the endings.

Stephen's Story About Ending

Kim: *So what about the ending – the ending of our relationship.*

Stephen: *Yes. In an ideal world I would have liked to have carried on. I was very aware that I had taken a lot of time off work. It seemed to come to an end partly because I was getting myself back together, I wanted to get going again – to get back to normal if you like. It was quite a long time I took off wasn't it?*

Kim: *It was nine weeks and two days [laughter] according to your diary.*

Stephen: *Was it?*

Kim: *And then you had two weeks' holiday.*

Stephen: *And then I went part-time, three days a week…*

Kim: *You went three days a week and four days a week, for a while…*

Stephen: *So it was about six months out altogether – I think that was at the back of my head. I think it was about right. I think I was realising that if I kept seeing you, then my marriage was going to come more and more into focus as the problem for me now. The focus was changing from the abuse into my present difficulties and I thought: 'This is too big, a hot potato. I can't really get into this – it's too much. If I do I might not be able to deal with it right now.' Looking back, yes, I think that was it – what do you think?*

Kim: *I can see what you mean –*

Stephen: *I think I was a bit afraid to go too far into therapy at that time.*

Kim: *You needed to gather some strength before you faced…*

Stephen: *I'd been through a lot already…and I couldn't quite manage that then.*

Kim: Yes. So partly there was the time element – you felt you wanted to go back to work, there was partly the money element, but there was also lurking somewhere underneath 'well, I don't know I that I'm ready to go on and look at that particular thing at this particular time'.

Stephen: Yes. I felt I'd come through the abuse...

Kim: ...dealt with the abuse

Stephen: ...and how I was changing and so in a way – at that stage it was safe to talk about that because we were at the end of it – but we had to move on to something else then. Yes, and I'd done something very important in changing jobs safely, which was a great relief and a big thing to do – so that was two huge things that happened. When we had our initial verbal contract – that was one thing we talked about wasn't it? To allow myself time to get back together – a beginning and an end. So I think I could see the end coming up.

Kim: So you were getting ready for it in some way.

Stephen: And I knew if I carried on, maybe I'd also get too dependent on you. Having somebody very kind and wise, and affirming there to talk to all the time is very nice – I'd like to catch you in a corner and talk to you [laughing] – I knew it was probably time to – I was wanting to draw it to a close in a way as well.

Kim: Yes.

Stephen: In some ways not, but in some ways I thought it was the healthy thing to do.

Kim: But it felt right – on all sorts of levels at the time.

Stephen: Yes... it did ...but it's like any parting. I really missed coming to see you for a long time. When I got stressed I thought 'see Kim'. But it was good to have to Sarasi to go and see. I go and see her every now and again – sometimes there's a fifteen-month gap – but if I desperately need to see her, I just ring up out of the blue and I'll go and see her and it feels really comfortable.

By the time we reached an ending Stephen had returned to his original place of work, gone through the traumatic experience of the escapee and the investigation that followed and had then decided that he wanted to move to a less stressful work environment. The personal changes he had made were destabilising the 'marital fit' and this became more and more the focus of the work. Stephen did not want to face this at the time and he was able to keep himself safe by not doing any further counselling at this time. Just prior to the ending he had begun to bring his guitar to sessions and play tunes that he had composed. It was as if he wanted to give me a special kind of gift – a product of his newly discovered creative self.

I found these sessions very moving and deeply appreciated his gifts to me. I also felt that he was very ambivalent about ending: on the one hand feeling he needed to, because he knew if he stayed he would stray into territory that was too risky for him at that time, the financial burden upon him and his need to return to work; but on the other hand it was as though he had not had enough time fully to experience the caring. We both knew that he might continue to see Sarasi and use bodywork when he needed a 'top up'. I think when we said goodbye we both knew that we would meet again.

Mike's Story of Ending

Mike's ambivalent attachment showed right to the end. We had reached a stage in our relationship where I sensed a shift was beginning to occur. We had spent some time in something of a 'parent–child' relationship, although the adolescent was certainly around much of the time! I ask Mike about how he experienced our relationship and as he starts to think about it he says:

Mike: *...actually quite a powerful part of it is the latter part of it. I think we're probably talking about the ending and a sense of having, or beginning to have, a more adult relationship between the two of us.*

[Pause]

Kim: *You were talking about the relationship and how, towards the end, it felt like there was a difference – that something changed in our relationship. How did that happen?*

Mike: *It felt as if I was learning skills...*

Kim: *Communication skills?*

Mike: *I think it was internal – before I could communicate to you that I was feeling a feeling, I had to understand it in here [indicating himself] – to feel it. I'm harking back to that old thing you know – beginning to connect the two.*

Kim: *Yes. I had a sense that there was a time when I invited you into a different kind of relationship. I said to you something about 'We almost have a choice point here when we could work to an ending or we could take the risk of entering into a more intimate relationship, where you talk to me and I talk to you about "here and now".' A bit like we're doing now. Do you remember that?*

[He shakes his head]

Mike: *No – that's not to say it didn't happen of course.*

Kim: *I think you went away and thought about it and then you came back and said 'yes'. You made a decision. You don't remember that? We started using immediacy in the relationship. You had begun to recognise your feelings and to articulate them, but there was a lack of spontaneity about it – you could rehearse and you could think about things and come and talk about them, much more so than you had. Initially, getting you to talk had been like drawing teeth [laughter]. I think I said that to you once – do you remember? I would invite you to talk about something or open up something, and you'd answer with some sort of closing down statement and I would sit hoping and waiting for something else to come.*

[Laughter]

Mike: *It must have been so painful.*

Kim: *It was really hard for me because of the kind of person I am – but you'd got past that stage and you were rehearsing – you were thinking about things you could come and talk about...*

Mike: *Like 'on Tuesday night I felt angry about something'...*

Kim: *Yes. And 'we had this conversation and she said this and I said that'; and what was happening with your mother and what was happening with your father. It was all 'out there' and I had this sense that the bit that was missing was the really immediate feelings – 'what is happening now, what are you feeling now, what are you thinking in response to what I'm saying?' It was about bringing you up-to-date in the moment I think. I have a fairly clear memory of that being a turning point and I think that's the point that you're now referring to when you talk about us having 'an adult relationship'.*

Mike: *No. I don't remember this at all but as we're talking about it I feel quite scared inside so I feel sure you're on to something that's real, but I just can't remember it.*

Kim: *We were in my new consulting room at that time.*

Mike: *I'm conscious of the move of location – that when I was there I was grown up, but quite where the transition came I don't remember.*

Kim: *At that time we did some chair work with your mother. There was a recognition that your mother was out there and not here – and that was also part of your movement. When we started to speak more immediately to one another – that was when you spoke much more about your spirituality – that was partly to do with you me asking you about the 'you and me' stuff.*

Mike: *I do remember that being significant. When I realised that you had a spirituality and you invited me to talk about what that was like for me. [Too quiet]*

Kim: *I remember all that quite vividly because I remember thinking, 'Ooh I'm taking a bit of a risk here.'*

[Laughter]

The above conversation describes how we moved into a new kind of relating when Mike became aware of having an adult-to-adult relationship with me which was essential before we could end. We went on to end about one month after the above period. The conversation that follows clarifies for me exactly what happened when we ended – something that I had felt vaguely uncomfortable about when it happened. I was quite surprised when Mike suddenly announced one day that he was ready to end:

Kim: *I remember the ending.*

Mike: *I remember when I bounced in and announced it.*

Kim: *Announced it – is that how it feels? What's your memory of it?*

Mike: *It seems like me saying, apropros of not very much, 'Well I think it's about time I put this down.' And wondering what you'd say.*

Kim: *What did you think I'd say?*

[Long pause]

Mike: The week before we'd been talking about Mum and it was a bit of an unresolved issue – in fact it's only been resolved recently, as you know. I remember when I announced that I thought it was time to finish, I was conscious of thinking that you felt that this was important and my feeling that 'Yes, it is unresolved but I'm not sure it's that important and anyway...'. And I suppose I was wondering if you would say, 'Don't you think we ought to do another couple of sessions?' – or something like that. And me being fairly conscious in fact that I wasn't trying to avoid talking about mother, but that it didn't seem like a big issue to me. Yes, that's the scene. And then being slightly shocked when you said 'Yes, alright.'

[Loud laughter]

Maybe I wanted you to fight a little bit.

Kim: To be a little bit reluctant about letting you go?

Mike: Yes.

Kim: We didn't actually end in the session when you came in and announced that you were ending.

Mike: No – I think it was 'Well, lets make the next one an ending.'

Kim: Yes. I remember there was more than that. I think we talked a lot about the ending.

Mike: Oh yes, it was more constructed than that. In the middle somewhere, I was very worried about the ending. I think this was at the point when I realised how dependent I was on you – and I suppose I started talking about it: 'I can't see there's any end to this', but really what I was saying was 'please don't leave me'. I remember you saying something like 'well don't worry, when the times comes, it will seem obvious', and me wondering if that was true because, as far I could see, I was going to feel like this for ever and ever.

Kim: Yes.

Mike: And when it did become obvious thinking, 'Yes, she was right.'

Kim: And you did know. And was it right?

Mike: Yes. I suppose I did have that sense that you felt there was some unfinished business.

Kim: Yes. I can remember having slightly mixed feelings. I remember feeling that your decision was something I did very much agree with, and this whole business about enabling you to be autonomous and to know that what your 'self' knows is right for you is right. You had shown that all the way through. It may have been more about the abruptness of the ending.

Mike: It seemed abrupt to me. I remember thinking afterwards 'that was abrupt wasn't it? I wonder if – oh well'.

Kim: My sense is that I may have been wanting to hold you just a little longer in the ending because of being a bit anxious that you were avoiding the feeling of the ending by doing it quickly.

Mike: Oh really.

Kim: Yes, you know: 'I'd better not hang around for long because it could hurt.' I don't know I might be wrong about that.

Mike: Yes, I think you are actually. [Sounds hurt]

Kim: That would be my question 'Is this an abrupt ending because it's right – that is where the client is?' or 'Is it an abrupt ending because of some kind of avoidance?'

Mike: I remember feeling surprised that it was so abrupt and I remember consciously experiencing the sadness and also a slight sort of rejection that you had given in so easily to me suggesting it. I thought 'Oh well – she'll string it out for another couple of weeks.' So, yes, I was a bit miffed and very sad and yet it felt totally positive – that it had been constructive and helpful.

Kim: So hadn't you intended to be so abrupt?

Mike: No.

Kim: But you announced it.

Mike: Yes, but I had announced it as something to be argued against – and you just agreed with me... [laughter]... I thought, oh shit. Because it had been a worry to me about how it was going to end. I think...

Kim: That's lovely [laughing].

Mike: I thought – you'd said 'Don't worry about it – it'll be alright on the night sort of thing' so I thought you had some master plan to rely on. So I had my faith in this master plan and I just thought 'Well, let's try and push her into bringing this master plan into effect'...

[Both falling around laughing]

...and actually that was it – one more session and we were off.

Kim: The master plan was 'he will announce it and he will know when he's ready, and he's done it – so he must be'.

Mike: But I was.

Kim: You were. Yes, you were.

I think I would have said to you 'when would you like that to be?' and I was probably surprised when you said 'next week' or whatever.

Mike: Maybe you asked me that and I thought 'what am I supposed to say to this?'

Kim: I would normally have said 'when do you think that should be?' and then worked to that point. Bearing in mind that I might have expected it to take three or four sessions as I'd had a fairly long relationship with you.

Mike: It did seem slightly abrupt.

Kim: It seems we were both a bit unaware of what was really going on.

Mike: But I'm not sure that was a bad thing. We did talk about it.

Kim: We did, yes. I would have been quite anxious to talk about it if we only had that one session to do it in.

Mike: Isn't that strange.

Kim: And when you finished?

Mike: When I finished... [pause]. It seemed so abrupt – I mean what we've been talking about was abrupt – and yet there didn't seem to be anything abrupt in the rest of my life. It wasn't 'Oh good, now I'll get on with my life' – because that was a process that was already happening. [Pause.] It was just: 'OK – wasn't that a really rich experience – it's finished and isn't that sad. She did get rid of me a bit quick though.' [Laughter]. It felt – maybe this is a bit corny – there was almost a sense of: 'I've now had a real relationship with somebody and its come to its natural conclusion — that's interesting — I've never had one of those before.' There was that level of it, although of course it was a strange relationship. But there was a sense of 'well if I've done that once I can do it again' — relate to somebody I mean.

Kim: Yes.

Mike: And there was the other bit — sorry I'm changing the subject a bit. To soften the landing a bit, I do remember Sarasi sitting me down and saying, 'I'm not quite like Kim about endings you know. They're not so important to me, so if you want to give me a ring and come back for a massage, that's fine' — and that was important actually, her saying 'she's funny about endings' — not that she said those words...so that helped to...

Kim: You knew you had someone who...did I actually say that you couldn't do that? I don't remember that.

Mike: I think you'd been fairly clear about how important it was to have an ending.

Kim: I can imagine in those circumstances I would think so, and that would be something to do with dependency I think.

Mike: Again I wasn't quite sure who you were trying to protect. That's the assumption that crept in again.

Kim: Protect from...?

Mike: A dependant relationship. I was very conscious of that around the ending. Because I remember saying something to you at the end: 'I'm pretty certain that this is the adult me talking to the adult you.'

Mike had spoken all the way through our conversation about how he had felt confused about whether or not I was trying to protect myself from his dependency. My recollection is that I was not, indeed I was much more aware of his discomfort and ambivalence about having such strong dependency needs. However, what he may have been picking up at the ending was *my* need for a good ending — about which I may have been anxious because it was announced so suddenly. I did not want to keep him any longer than he wanted to be there and I truly believed he was able to judge when he had had enough. In retrospect, maybe my anxiety had caused me to miss the fact that he actually wanted to be held just a little longer in the relationship. I was so grateful for this research conversation. Without it I would never have known something that seemed very important for us to understand. I am very struck by the interpersonal process that can add depth to our understanding if we can access it.

Of course, paradoxically, maybe at a deeper level we both knew that we had not really ended. Later Mike came to me in a new relationship as a supervisee and now he and Stephen have reconnected with me as research participants. It may be that in my ultimate avoidance of painful endings I have forever kept them in relationship with me by writing this book. I am reminded of Irvin Yalom's words at the end of the book he wrote with his client Ginny about their work together:

What did I do to prevent Ginny from leaving me? This book has insured that Ginny never will become a half-forgotten name in an old appointment book or a lost voice on an electromagnetic band. In both a real and symbolic sense we have defeated termination. (Yalom and Elkin 1974, p.232)

PART 3

The Researcher's Story

Put simply, I believe that intimate knowledge is likely to teach us more than distant knowledge. Personal knowledge is likely to change us more than impersonal knowledge. Knowledge gained with our eyes and ears wide open is likely to be more valuable than that acquired when we are conceptually and procedurally blindfolded. (Mair 1989, p.2)

CHAPTER 19

The Swamp

In a land not very far away from here there lived a good King who ruled his people strictly but fairly. In his youth he had married a Queen who loved him and who had born him three princes. The oldest prince had married a princess and they had gone to live in a distant land to learn about the customs of that country so that some day they would return to the land of their birth with greater knowledge and wisdom. The second prince had also travelled in other countries where he had met a princess whom he had married and brought back to his own country. Together they had built a small palace in the northern part kingdom where they lived happily with a baby son who brought his parents and grandparents great happiness and joy. The third prince, who was much younger than his brothers, had become a wandering minstrel and travelled the land playing his music in great houses. He lived for each day and thought little about the future.

The King was much concerned with his Kingdom and spent long hours travelling, working hard and raising money to improve the land and build new cities. His Queen was left alone for much of the time and, now that her children were raised, had time for herself. Every day she visited the marketplace where the people had become used to her and did not stand on ceremony. She sat in the cafés and talked with the people and one day every week she opened the palace doors to anyone who wished to call on her. That way she heard the whispers. She heard the women talking of a place deep in the forest where a dark swamp had swallowed children, and the people were afraid. The Queen talked to the King about it but he laughed and said, 'Don't go filling your head full of that nonsense, My kingdom is a warm and sunny place and my people are content.' The Queen listened to what he said and went back to the people.

'You must not think about such things,' she said to them, 'the King will provide safety for you. You must do as he does and think only of the good things.'

But the people were not satisfied and the Queen began to dream of the dark swamp that swallowed children and was troubled. One day she visited a wise woman and told her of her dreams. The wise woman said, 'How do you know the place of your dreams is the same swamp?' And the Queen went away and thought about that question. There was a place inside her heart that recognised the swamp and she saw pictures of the dark water surrounded by trees that dipped their drooping fingers in the bog.

She did not talk about this to the King who went about his work unaware of his wife's distress. The Queen visited the wise woman every week and little by little she pieced together her memories of the swamp and she knew.

One day she was sitting in her parlour, with her door open to any caller, when a passing traveller came before her. The traveller was clad in well-worn clothes that were patched but were obviously of good quality. He sat beside the fire with the Queen and said 'I have travelled many miles to this country but I know not why. On the way I heard tell of the Queen who was much loved by her people and who had been troubled by her dreams.'

The Queen told him her story. 'I want to find out more about the swamp and what happens to the children who are taken there. I cannot go myself, the King will not listen and refuses to accept that the swamp exists and my Princes are away in other parts.'

The traveller said, 'Madam, if you will permit me, I will go and find the swamp and when I have learnt all there is to know, I will return.'

The Queen was moved by the traveller's willingness to face the unknown and warned him, 'At one time it was believed that the swamp only took females but now there is a rumour that males are taken too. The King has a library in the tower. You should go there and read to find out what you can before you set off on your journey.'

So the traveller read all the books in the library and found something there about girls who had been taken by the swamp. There was nothing about the boys.

When the day came for him to set out on his journey the traveller said farewell to the Queen who gave him her blessing and warned him, 'Stay away from the edges if you find the swamp – it is a dark and dangerous place.' She gave the traveller her silver flute to soothe him and sent him on his way.

The traveller journeyed into unknown lands asking on his way if anyone knew of the swamp. People turned away from him, avoiding his eye. Some questioned why he should want to find his way to such a place and others tried to distract him by saying, 'Why not stay here in this warm and sunny place?' But he was determined and struggled on his way, remembering the Queen's distress and her stories of the children who had vanished.

Eventually, one evening, just as the moon was rising, he found the swamp. The dark waters lay still and deep and the edges of the swamp were thick with weed. No birds called from the trees, no insects played across the surface. The swamp was dead, lifeless. The moonlight cast pale shadows across the ground and the traveller watched and waited until morning.

When morning came the traveller decided he would build himself a house in the trees so that he could watch and wait in safety and he busied himself all day. He saw nobody and sang quietly to himself as he worked to keep his spirits up. When night came he climbed into his tree house and slept.

Several weeks went by and the traveller saw nothing. No animals came to drink from the water. Nobody approached. During this time he had walked around the swamp taking care to keep away from the edges. He began to recognise some of the plants that grew there.

Some of them were poisonous although they could also be medicinal when used correctly. The more familiar he became with the swamp, the more he realised that he did not need to be so fearful and that he was probably seeing little from the tree house. He decided to camp down beside the water's edge. He had brought a pair of thigh-length waders and considered treading carefully in the water. He had a large fishing net with which he could scoop out some of the mud and examine the contents with his microscope.

He began to feel more relaxed and in the afternoon he sat in the sun and played the Queen's flute. The clear notes of the flute sounded across the swamp and the traveller sat with his back against a tree, his eyes closed, enjoying the warmth of the sun on his body. He played like this for an hour or so and when he opened his eyes he was astonished to glimpse a group of children sitting a few metres away from him. On opening his eyes the children disappeared. The traveller rubbed his eyes and wondered if he had been dreaming. He walked carefully around the swamp and gazed into the surrounding trees. There was nobody there.

Each day at the same time the traveller played his flute and each day when he opened his eyes he would catch a glimpse of the children. After some time the children stayed longer, as if they had learned to trust that he would not harm them. Until one day a little boy came up closer and sat beside him. The traveller dared not speak for fear of frightening the boy away. The other children watched and waited. The little boy put out his hand and the traveller placed the flute into his small dirty palm.

The little boy began to play. The traveller sat and listened. The music began quietly, halting and tentative at first. And as the boy grew more confident the music swelled and notes of great beauty fell from the silver flute. The boy's eyes filled with tears as he played; melancholy reached the depths of the traveller's soul as he listened. The music told of the boy's life, his pain, his fear, his betrayal, the music went on and on until the traveller thought he could bear no more. At last he put out his hand for the flute and the boy stopped playing. His eyes were dark and heavy when he passed the flute back to the traveller. The other children sat silent and watchful as the traveller walked away into the forest. He could bear no more.

The traveller walked for hours, not knowing where he was going but wanting to put as much distance as he could between himself and the swamp.

'Why did I come here?' he asked himself. 'I was happy enough on my travels. I should have just kept walking.'

And as evening fell he stumbled back into the clearing he had made for his camp. He was back where he had started from earlier that day. He could not seem to leave the place. All paths led back there. The children had gone and once again the place was empty of all life. The traveller stood and looked over the water and felt a heavy weariness wash over him. He lay down on his groundsheet and wanted to sleep forever.

But morning came once again and the traveller woke. He lay thinking about the boy's music and felt a longing to hear it again. Now at a distance from the sound he could recognise the richness of the music. He stood at the edge of the swamp and called out, 'Where are you. Please come again and play your music to me. I will listen this time and will not stop you.' But there was no sound. He sat beside the tree and played his flute, eyes closed, expecting to open them to the sight of the children gathered around his feet but they did not come.

Two days went by and still the children did not come. The traveller decided he would go into the swamp and find them. He donned his thigh-length waders and took his large fishing net.

Tentatively he stepped into the water and felt the mud sucking at his feet, holding them hard in its grip. He hesitated, fearful. Then another step, and another. Suddenly a small creature darted from the weeds across his feet and disappeared. He did not recognise it, so fast did it move. He trawled his net into the weeds and pulled it back towards him, water dripping from the mud-filled mesh. He stirred up the bottom and waited. A few small creatures darted in and out of the weeds. He stood and waited, watching and waiting until night fell.

The traveller woke in the night. Something had disturbed his sleep. He crept from under his blanket and looked out across the swamp. There, in the moonlight, he saw them. There were hundreds of boys, some of them were drunk, laughing and swaying as they clung together. Others were stoned; their heads inside plastic bags, sniffing glue. Others were beating the bushes aimlessly, destructively, just wanting to hit out. A few of the bigger boys were forcing the little ones to touch them sexually; the little boys were crying, trying to pull free. One boy had lit a fire and was wafting the flames, trying to catch the forest alight. Another boy was curled up in pain, holding his stomach and crying out for help. Another was wheezing, gasping for breath. The boy who had played the flute was sitting watching the scene, large tears rolling down his cheeks. Two boys were sitting at the edge of the swamp, pulling legs off a frog, laughing hideously at the creature's pain. A fat boy was stuffing his mouth with food whilst a small skinny boy watched. In the bushes another boy was vomiting, his fingers down his throat. The traveller could just see two small boys clinging together and shaking with fear as they tried to hide away.

The traveller rubbed his eyes and stared. It was like an image of hell.

And then from the centre of the swamp arose the creature. It crawled up onto a grassy hummock and sat there. A great walrus-like creature, its head swaying back and forth as it surveyed the scene of its making. The traveller stared hard, trying to make out the shape of the creature in the half-light. The creature turned its head to stare at him and as it did he saw that it had two heads. The head at the front was male and the head at the back was female.

After a while the great creature slid from the hummock into the water and disappeared into the darkness. The boys seemed to wake as if from sleepwalking. One by one they trudged towards the swamp and followed where the creature had disappeared.

The traveller sat all night shivering at the horrors of what he had seen. Something had to be done about this. He had seen so much, but who would believe him? All this was going on and nobody seemed to know or care very much about it. He would have to write to the Queen and let her know what he had seen. Perhaps she would find a way to help these children and warn others. Perhaps she might even influence the King so that he could use his powers.

And with the images still fresh in his mind's eye the traveller sat down, took out a large pad of paper, picked up his pen and began to write...

(written in 1998 by Kim Etherington)

CHAPTER 20

Research Process

> Where to begin?
> I begin with an idea, and myself – I have a purpose, a curiosity and a will.
> I know others who want to join with me. I have awareness of the experiences I have shared with those others and I have some questions about what it all means.
> It is enough for the beginning.

Philosophical Considerations

There are so many decisions, so many choices to be made at the beginning – some choices are excluded early on because of who I am, because of how I like to work and what I believe in. I am not setting out to prove or disprove a hypothesis, to collect data across large numbers of people, to collect standard deviation statistics representing units of variability, or to verify the presence of cause and effect relationships between variables. I don't think like that and even as I write it down I begin to warn myself that I am in danger of losing myself in theory – and maybe my readers as well. Some people, who do think like that, believe that scientific methods are the best ways of gaining knowledge. They also believe 'that knowledge can be founded upon, or grounded in, absolute truth…that knowledge is "about" something external to the knower, and can present itself objectively to the knower' (Combs and Freedman 1994, p.269). This way of thinking has been described as 'modernist', 'positivist', or 'structuralist':

> In science, it is the worldview in which people believe it is possible to find essential and 'objective' facts that can then be tied together into overarching, generally applicable theories that bring us closer and closer to an accurate understanding of the real universe. In the humanities, it is the kind of humanism that seeks to develop grand, sweeping, meta-narratives about the human condition and how to perfect it. (Freedman and Combs 1996, p.20)

Postmodernists (and myself) have a different view of reality. I believe that we construct our reality within the social and cultural contexts of our lives – meaning exists but is influenced and limited by social contexts. This is very much in tune with my values and the values that underpin person-centred counselling as described by Carl Rogers and developed by Brian Thorne (Lynch 1996), and the existential approach (Frankl 1963;

van Deurzen Smith 1988). This means that I trust and value each person's uniqueness and difference; that I offer respect and empathic understanding, and that I enter fully into the relationship as myself. These values have developed out of my own experiences of therapeutic relationships.

My own journey over the last twenty years has taken me across a bridge from the 'modernist' view to postmodernism – although I did not understand it in those terms at the time. In my 'modern' era I believed that I needed to look outside myself for answers about the way I should understand myself, other people and the world in which I existed. I had been brought up to value other people's opinions and ideas and to discount my own. My upbringing within a male-dominated family, within a patriarchal society, meant that I had been well trained to ignore any sense of knowing anything for myself and that thinking about myself was 'selfish'.

However, all my life I had been aware of carrying a knowledge within me – a sense of 'tacit knowing' (Polanyi 1967) – and this 'knowing' drove me forward to find a way of making that knowledge explicit. But discovery requires the ability to trust in one's own experiences, self-awareness, understanding; having an internal locus of evaluation and a willingness to enter into a process rooted in the self (Moustakas 1990). My own life experiences had damaged my ability to trust myself (and others), to develop self-awareness, to understand or to feel any confidence about my powers of evaluation. More than anything, however, my fear had blocked my willingness to explore myself.

So my road to knowledge required me to overcome all of those obstacles and somewhere, I suppose, I did have enough self-trust to keep going. I had begun to work through a 'tacit knowledge' that I had been abused during childhood. I recognised that I knew more than I could tell and in more ways than I could tell, and I did not know how I knew. Each time I thought I had come close to 'really knowing', the knowledge slipped away into a protective fog of denial. On trying to talk to other members of my family, my reality was questioned, even denied; thus throwing me back into the fog of confusion and lack of self-trust. In spite of this, I had arrived at a place where I could manage to rest with my 'not knowing', while at the same time knowing enough to make it possible to do the work of healing. During that time I was able to fill some of the gaps by 'drawing from the mystery and sources of energy and knowledge within the tacit dimension' (Moustakas 1990, p.94). It was only in 1998, at a family funeral, that my 'tacit knowledge' became fully explicit. I discovered that my abuser had also abused another member of my family. The relief of validation shook my internal sense of self and created a period of destabilisation. At last I knew – really knew! That external validation of my own truth allowed me to value and trust myself in a way that I had never been able to do before.

So as a postmodernist I do not discount 'modern' thinking. I see it as one part of the story – one way of viewing reality and one that is quite useful in pursuing criteria of validity, control and predictability. But that view, taken separately, is no more 'real' or 'true' than many other ways of understanding the universe and its truths. As a postmodernist I am more interested in differences than similarities. I am more interested in individual stories than in grand generalisations. I value 'local knowledge' (Geertz 1983) while trying to understand myself and other people in relation to the rest of humanity.

So my reality and that of others is socially constructed, through dialogue and narrative: 'the experience of self exists in the ongoing interchange with others...the self continually creates itself through narratives that include other people who are reciprocally woven into these narratives' (Weingarten 1995, p.289). As a counsellor I listen to people telling their stories and, in the telling, I am aware that a self is being formed. As a researcher I am also listening to people's stories and in that telling yet another self is formed. There is a proliferation of self-stories now – people appear on TV bringing their personal stories into our lives; autobiographies are written by people who want to tell their stories – ordinary people are given a voice and in that process reclaim themselves. Each of these stories is grounded in some form of 'narrative wreckage' (Frank 1995). Postmodern times both produce the wreckage and the means of reclaiming. A postmodern storyteller writes to discover what other selves are operating in a story that is the writer's own, but that writer is several selves. In this book I am a storyteller who is also a researcher, who is a counsellor, who is also a survivor and also a mother of men and a grandmother. Many of my selves are present in the work and other selves are created as I work.

Qualitative methodology provided me with a means to engage with Stephen and Mike and listen to their stories. My postmodern views enabled me to stand back and examine a wide variety of choices that are open to me. My intention was to explore the journey that Stephen and Mike have undergone, what it means to them and what part I played during that journey. I wanted to capture their experience and my own and the ways we make sense of those experiences.

Qualitative Methodologies

Qualitative research methodologies draw upon several traditions and are more fragmented than quantitative methods. Denzin and Lincoln (1994) include phenomenology, hermeneutics, ethnography, feminist methodology, naturalistic research, heurism, grounded theory, discourse analysis and 'new paradigm' methodology in their weighty, in-depth and interesting tome. McLeod (1994) has written a very accessible book on *Doing Counselling Research* which is as good a place as any for Masters level students to begin. His new book on practitioner research in counselling (McLeod 1999) takes the student further into the field.

Denzin and Lincoln (1994) introduce the idea of the researcher as 'bricoleur' – master of all trades, someone who mixes and matches, takes from a variety of methodologies to create something uniquely suited to the researcher and the study. This approach suits me as an integrative counsellor who has taken from many counselling approaches to create a method of counselling that is my own. I do not intend to describe any of those methodologies in great detail, but rather to give an idea of those that have informed my work and from which I have gathered ideas. I will begin by describing the methodology I used in my previous research (Etherington 1995) and go on to describe the methodology I used to create this book. In this way I can share how my methodology suited the particular study, how my thinking has developed since undertaking my first major research project and my present understanding of the uses of different methodologies.

My Methodology Then

I described the methodology I used for my Ph.D. as 'feminine'. This was a qualitative methodology that was concerned with relationship between the researcher and subjects, which valued meaning and experience and sought to collect men's stories of their experience of sexual abuse during childhood. I drew on phenomenology (Polkinghorne 1989) which resulted in qualitative data described by Geertz (1973) as a 'thick' description of the world or experiences of the individual or group under investigation (McLeod 1994).

A phenomenological approach as described by Moustakas (1990) uses subjective experience as a source of knowledge; both the subjective experience of the participant and the researcher and valuing the uniqueness of each contribution. Researchers within this approach do not usually have a first-hand involvement in the phenomenon under investigation. Phenomenology focuses on the *essence of experiences* under investigation rather than retaining the *essence of the experiencing persons*. The research concludes with definitive descriptions of the structure of the experience which are distilled into a presentation that loses the person within the description (Moustakas 1990).

I did not call my methodology 'feminist', but I did draw upon feminist methodology, especially in respect of the importance I attach to recognising the power imbalance inherent in the relationships between researcher and research participants. One of the principles of feminist research methodology has been to challenge relationships based on power and control (Kelly 1988). Methods employed in feminist research aim to reduce the power imbalance between researcher and participants while acknowledging the fact that imbalance will always be present. The denial of the researcher's knowledge and skills, in order to attempt to minimise the imbalance, will not lead to a sharing of power but rather to a denial of its existence. If I acknowledge and claim my power, I am then in a position to share it – in sharing knowledge, I am sharing power (Foucault 1980).

Feminist methodology emerged in the 1970s as an increasing number of feminist academics undertook research in response to their growing criticism of the 'gender blind' research mainly undertaken and written from a male perspective. Feminist methodology draws on the practice of consciousness raising in stressing the importance of women's experiences of oppression in order to change it (Kelly 1988). However, men are also oppressed when they do not conform to the norms that underpin patriarchy; men who do not fit societal stereotypes – male survivors are often among that group (Etherington 1995).

Around the same time (1970s), feminists began to recognise and write about the inherent power held by the dominant discourse of traditional scientific research. Feminist research methodology arose out of the need to create a balance between masculine and feminine ways of knowing. In sharing information about the research and how it would be used, and giving participants more control over their material, feminists acknowledged the power inherent in knowledge itself.

Traditional science has been described as 'incredibly masculine' (Heron 1981). Mitroff (1974) saw the scientist as supporting traditional masculine values (aggression, power, authority, scepticism, etc.) and as unconcerned with subjective experiences. Orthodox research is deeply embedded in the culture of science and traditionally universities value intellect, external knowledge, cognitive assessment and objectivity in research and analysis. These have also been described as traditionally masculine values upheld within the larger socio-political context of patriarchy (Lerner 1986). Feminist research methodology challenged all of that.

Counselling, traditionally a female dominated discipline, places high value on feelings, knowledge from within, meaning, synthesis, process, interpersonal skills and self-awareness (Johns 1998). These might be described as traditionally feminine values. In an ideal world we need both modalities – something Jungians have described as a 'marriage between the masculine and the feminine' – that respects the values of both, and about which I have written elsewhere (Etherington 1998). Counselling research, also a comparatively new and emerging discipline, at its best, demonstrates how the masculine and the feminine principles can be upheld.

Kelly (1988) emphasises the importance of linking experience to the theory that underlies it, partly as a response to previous feminist writers who prioritised experience over all other considerations (Stanley and Wise 1983). My previous study sought to develop new theories and relate existing theories to the experiences described by the men using a grounded theory approach.

Grounded theory is a methodology that can be used in both qualitative and quantitative studies (Strauss and Corbin 1990). Theory emerges from the data collected – whatever the means of collection, for example, questionnaires, interviews, diaries, etc. Researchers look to the data to find emerging themes and patterns and constantly compare these themes and patterns with additional data as it is collected (Glaser and Strauss 1967). As different and perhaps opposing themes emerge, further questions can be applied to the data to deepen the understanding and explanations that are forming. Theory is formed through the interpretations made by the researcher. Hermeneutic inquiry is based on the researcher attempting to interpret a text (maybe a research interview) from some framework of meaning in order to provide an explanation (McLeod 1994).

As a woman exploring a man's world of experience I might also have been seen to be conducting ethnographic research; usually undertaken by a researcher who enters a field as an observer – a method traditionally employed by anthropologists studying different groups and societies. Hammersley and Atkinson (1995) suggest that the researcher using ethnographic methodology should treat the culture as 'anthropologically strange...in an effort to make explicit the presuppositions he or she takes for granted as a culture member. In this way it is hoped the culture is turned into an object available for study' (p.9).

However, I did not see myself as an 'observer' and I did not feel entirely a stranger to the male culture. Indeed, because of my upbringing it would probably be fair to say that the world of women was less familiar to me than the world of men. Even today with the recent birth of my third grandson (no grandaughters and no daughters), the female world still seems elusive. Maybe I am a participant observer.

Accounts of such research are filtered through the author, although ethnographers are increasingly using reflexivity on the self of the researcher in their writing rather than the role of the researcher (Hertz 1997). Ethnographers have traditionally been aware of the effect of the researcher on the environment in which they are researching, but less frequently has it been part of an ethnographer's remit to include how they themselves are affected by going into that environment. In counselling research there is a growing recognition of the way the research develops and changes the researcher's self (Grafanaki 1996; Speedy and Etherington 1999).

Reflexivity is at the heart of feminist methodology and increasingly other methodologies as well. 'It permeates every aspect of the research process, challenging us to be more fully conscious of the ideology, culture, and politics of those we study and those we select as our audience' (Hertz 1997, p.viii). Reflexive feminist ethnography encourages us as researchers to display the full interaction between ourselves and our research participants in our writing, so that our work can be understood not only in terms of what we have discovered, but how we have discovered it (Reinharz 1979; 1992).

So my 'bricolage' (Denzin and Lincoln 1994) for my previous study included aspects of phenomenology, feminist methodology, reflexivity, grounded theory, hermeneutics and ethnography. I would describe the main methodology as phenomenology as I attempted to describe the *essence of the experience* while losing the individual participant within the group – in order to maintain their confidentiality and anonymity. My 'self' was included although bracketed off from the participants' data. I used semi-structured interviews to collect the data which were transcribed and returned to the participants for purposes of triangulation, using a feminist power sharing, relationship approach. The data was analysed and interpreted from psychodynamic, sociological and social learning theory frameworks and new theory was formed from within the data using a grounded theory approach.

And Now

As my knowledge and experience have increased and I have moved towards the philosophy of postmodernism and the social construction of realities, I have become more at home with the greater inclusion of the researcher's self in the research. There is a tension, however, in balancing our inclusion of self with avoiding the label of 'self-indulgent'. This view, of course, is coloured by the values of the reader. A modernist may view the inclusion of self as distracting or even unnecessary, whereas a postmodernist will value knowing the researcher's process as a way of placing themselves in relation to the work and their understanding of it. Rennie (1992) makes the point that 'reflexivity modulates action…too much reflexivity leads to inaction, while too little reflexivity leads to action without direction' (p.21).

One anonymous piece of feedback I received on offering this book as a proposal to a publisher (not this one) was a concern that it might be 'navel gazing' and 'not very scholarly'. Mykhalovskiy (1997) wrote about his own devastating experience of having his Ph.D. failed and described as a 'self-indulgent, informal biography'. He analyses these charges and points out that, in his view, 'the abstract, disembodied voice of traditional academic discourse was a fiction, accomplished through writing and other practices which remove evidence of the text's author, as part of concealing the conditions of its production' (p.232). He observes that only those who believe that the inclusion of the researcher's self contaminates the work would describe such writing as 'self-indulgent'.

Students frequently tell of their difficulty in understanding the more traditional forms of academic research writings. Sometimes it seems that such academics are writing only for themselves. My own view is that we have a responsibility to write about our research in a way that makes it readable and engaging and, for me, that means personal. If I am to be personal in my writing I must be personal in my relationships with those who participate in the research. I want to create a 'working alliance' in which we are working together and each gaining something from the process. This means I have to engage with participants at an early stage in the process and continue with that engagement throughout.

New paradigm research, described by Reason and Rowan (1981), also views reflexivity as an important aspect of the co-operative approach which seeks to go beyond the split between subjective and objective. They encourage researchers to develop the ability to become critically subjective; a quality of awareness in which we do not suppress our primary subjective experience, nor allow ourselves to be overwhelmed by it; rather we raise it to our consciousness and use it as part of the inquiry process.

New paradigm methodology is wide ranging, from action research, which is often used in educational research and has as an intended outcome some kind change of policy or practice (Reason and Rowan 1981); to co-operative inquiry in which the researcher negotiates every stage of the process with the participants; to reflexive and narrative techniques (McLeod 1997; Reissman 1993).

Heuristic methodology is one in which we seek to obtain 'qualitative depictions that are at the heart and depths of a person's experience – depictions of situations, events, conversations, relationships, feelings, thoughts, values, and beliefs... Such qualitative methods enable the researcher to derive the raw material of knowledge and experience from the empirical world' (Moustakas 1990, p.38). Heuristic methodology is different from phenomenology in that it encourages personal connection and relationship to the topic; it leads to depictions of essential meanings and its significance to the researcher. Rather than producing a distillation of the structure of the experiences under investigation, as in phenomenology, heuristic research may lead to a creative synthesis derived from the knowledge gained, including tacit and intuitive knowledge, integrated into a meaningful whole. The researcher must be open to new learning and begin from a place of 'not knowing' so as to learn more (Moustakas 1990)

Hillman (1983) described heuristic methods as seeking to empower, accept and affirm the participants; honouring individual's contributions and engaging them as partners in the research, thereby seeking to minimise the imbalance of the power relationship; and mitigating against difficulties that might be experienced in the dual role of researchers who are using past clients in the research.

So I have chosen a heuristic methodology which is described by Moustakas (1990) as having six phases:

- initial engagement
- immersion
- incubation
- illumination
- explication
- creative synthesis.

I will describe these phases in greater depth as the process unfolds. Since writing this chapter I have come across John McLeod's (1999) term 'practitioner-researcher' which describes almost exactly how I see myself. He sees practitioner research to be that which is undertaken by practitioners for the purpose of advancing their own practice. I do indeed have this as my main aim – although it is not the only one, and I have described my other aims in Chapter 1. McLeod lists some of the key characteristics of practitioner research in counselling:

- The research question is born out of personal experience and a 'need to know'.
- The goal of the research is to produce knowledge that makes a difference to practice.
- Throughout the research, the investigator uses his or her reflexive self-awareness to gain access to the underlying or implicit meanings of the study.
- Each research project is relatively limited in scope, to fit the realities of the time and resources available to someone who is primarily a practitioner.
- The researcher actively addresses the moral and ethical issues associated with the combination of researcher and practitioner roles, and with the process of inquiry into the experience of perhaps vulnerable or fragile informants.
- The research is designed in such a way as to enhance and facilitate the counselling process.
- The researcher retains 'ownership' of the knowledge that is produced; the findings represent subjective, personal knowing as well as objective, impersonal or factual knowledge.
- The results of the research are written and disseminated in ways that are consistent with the principles and values of practitioner research outlined above. (McLeod 1999, pp.8–9)

He explores the practical implications of the above statements in the chapters of the book (McLeod 1999). I would recommend this as essential reading for students of practitioner research in counselling.

CHAPTER 21

Ethics

Principles

Having reflected on my methodology based on my worldview, my values and my beliefs about how we gain knowledge, I needed to consider the ethical issues that may arise from within the research process. Counsellors are trained to work within an ethical framework and to adhere to a code of ethics that is designed to ensure that the risk of doing harm to our clients is minimised. However, our training should do more than provide us with access to a code of ethics. We need to have spent time struggling with our own understanding of how that code applies in a variety of situations in which we may find ourselves as practitioners. Guidelines usually emerge in response to ethical dilemmas that arise from practice. The British Association for Counselling (BAC) code of ethics for practitioners has been updated and continually reassessed in the light of changes in the field. New technology and an ever-increasing range of occupational opportunities have meant that new considerations have emerged, such as the use of computers to store information and employment of counsellors within surgeries or the workplace.

Counselling research has increased in volume during the last ten years but only in recent years has a separate code of ethics for monitoring research in counselling been drawn up (BAC 1996). These guidelines were drawn in response to a growth in the numbers of research studies being undertaken, questions being asked and complaints being made. When I did my previous research study no such guidelines were available and I found myself struggling to find my way through 'the swamp', wishing heartily that I had such a guide. Looking back now I can see that I might have done some things differently and, having learned the hard way, I hope to be better prepared this time round.

Research ethics have been largely built on those from the field of moral philosophy, a major discourse in its own right. Medical, educational and psychological studies of ethics have guided the establishment of counselling ethics and are based on a set of ethical principles (Beauchamp and Childress 1979; Bond 1993; Kitchener 1984). Those principles are:

1. *Beneficence* – doing good for others – and perhaps sometimes knowing what is best for others. This requires the researcher to take authority in situations when they perhaps become aware that participants, through lack of awareness, might be exposing themselves to harm.
2. *Non-maleficence* – doing no harm. This may mean putting the needs of the research project secondary to the needs of the participants. Issues related to the safety of participants include confidentiality and awareness of outcomes of the research.
3. *Autonomy* – respecting the rights of others to make decisions for themselves. However, decisions and choices can only be made with *fully informed consent*. This means more than signing a consent form. It means allowing people to review their decisions as the study progresses and they become clearer about what the choices might entail.
4. *Fidelity* – being fair and just. This is a particular issue in studies that use 'controls' and researchers may decide to withhold treatment options (maybe counselling) from particular groups. We have to consider carefully the ethics of choosing whether or not to take part in studies using these approaches.

At face value these principles may seem straightforward and relatively easy to apply. However, there may be instances when two or more of these principles are in conflict. I raise this point later and illustrate it through my conversations with Stephen and Mike about 'truly informed consent'.

In counselling research the general aim of the study may be to do good, but the very process of interviewing people about sensitive material may stir up difficult and unwanted feelings which some may experience as 'doing harm' (Renzetti and Lee 1993). Most of these conflicts are also seen in counselling practice and counselling researchers may be familiar with these issues when they become researchers (Etherington 1996).

Power

Fundamental to most ethical issues in research are those concerning power; these are issues we also struggle with as counsellors in our relationships with clients. This is one of the many advantages counsellors bring when they become researchers. Many social scientists who have not had the benefit of counselling training have to grapple for the first time with these issues when they become researchers. Starhawk (1990) identified three manifestations of power as:

1. power 'over' (authority and control)
2. power 'with', (social influence and responsibility)
3. power 'from within' (the awakening of potential of the individual).

I recognise that I have experienced a struggle with all three of these manifestations of power in undertaking the research and writing of this book. Chapter 22 highlights the struggles with issues of authority, control, social influence, responsibility and the possibility of awakening potential power from within.

Egan (1994) also describes the 'social influence' potential of having power. He encourages counsellors to recognise and accept the power they hold within the counselling relationship in being perceived as 'attractive' and 'expert' and by doing so use it for the client's benefit. We carry that same potential with us as researchers – our role provides us with the power to choose whose voices will be heard and whose will not by the selection of our topic and participants. We have the power in the way we choose to analyse or interpret the meaning of the data we collect, and in our choice of audience for whom we write or present our research findings.

However, Speedy (1998) warns that 'power comes with fear', and if we are to accept and use our power we will need to face up to the fear that it might bring with it. She also drew attention to a three-dimensional model of ascribed, owned and disguised power, which she observed from her research on a group of female counselling trainers (of which I was one). I can relate those three dimensions of power to the researcher role: ascribed power, owned power and disguised power.

Ascribed Power

Power can be projected onto us by others through their perception of our role as researchers, thereby enhancing our status and depleting themselves in that process. This is a situation with great potential for abuse. Josselson (1996) warns of the power of the written word: 'I don't think we can underestimate the projected, imagined powers our apparent authority, which rests on our access to print, evokes' (p.67).

Owned Power

We can 'own' our power as a researcher, outlining our role and its limits and boundaries. When we acknowledge the power we hold in the role, it is then possible to share it with others. In being seen for who we are (including our powerfulness), we can genuinely respond to the situations in which we find ourselves. Power and authority used within a person-centred framework – having respect for ourselves and others and valuing the other person's feelings, opinions and rights – increases our potential for positive influence and genuine relationships with our research subjects.

Disguised Power

However, if disguised or disowned, power can be misused. Guggenbühl-Craig (1971) described the 'problem of the power shadow', when power is unconsciously used to disempower others. As researchers we have the power to choose which stories we report and which we leave out. Our interpretations are also a way of potentially disguising our power. However, participants as well as researchers can disguise power. Lieblich (1996) found that people she interviewed within a community used the subsequent book she produced to vent old grievances against others. She became a means for communicating between family members by people telling her about things that they knew she would report, as a way of telling others they did not want to deal with more intimately. I had a similar experience through the publication of my previous book.

Power is a word that often evokes discomfort – many people (especially women) link the word with abuse. However uncomfortable, we need to accept that we are powerful when we write about other people's lives. Josselson (1996) encourages us to worry about it:

> I would worry most if I stopped worrying, stopped suffering for the disjunction that occurs when we try to tell the Other's story. To be uncomfortable with this work, I think, protects us from going too far. It is with our anxiety, dread, guilt, and shame that we honor our participants. To do this work we must contain these feelings rather than deny, suppress, or rationalize them. We must at least try to be fully aware of what we are doing. (Josselson 1996, p.70)

Dual Relationships

One of the major ethical considerations we must face if we are to engage with our ex-clients for purposes of research is that of 'dual relationships'. This arises out of issues of imbalance of power between the counsellor and client, which is additional to the imbalance of power between researcher and participant. In a previous article I have explored some of the boundary issues and critical dilemmas for counsellors as researchers (Etherington 1996). These issues are undoubtedly exacerbated when our research is with our own clients.

I was very conscious of this issue when I considered the possibility of working with Stephen and Mike for this research. I had been supervising Mike on his work in the surgery for about a year when the work on the book commenced. We had therefore already struggled with some of the issues of 'dual relationships'. Since working with his abuse, many of the patients he met in the surgery had disclosed childhood sexual abuse. This is a phenomenon that is often observed in the counselling world. It is almost as if a signal goes out that attracts others to us who have suffered in similar ways to ourselves. Or is it that we are more aware, more attuned to recognise what we are seeing and through our 'empathic resonance' (Spiro *et al.* 1993) and thus enable others to feel safe enough to disclose? Mike had not broadcast to others about his abuse – a few of his colleagues were trusted with the information, but certainly no patients had been told. Mike discovered that he needed a special kind of support when dealing with these patients and took the responsibility upon himself to seek supervision. Three years had passed since he had been my client and I knew he was still working with Sarasi from time to time – so he had another therapeutic relationship. We continue to monitor the effects of our previous relationship upon the supervisory process and relationship.

However, it was somewhat different for Stephen. I had not seen him since he was my client (we had our last session in April 1996 and the research for this book began in 1999). Although he had an occasional visit to Sarasi when he needed, I felt he was probably still slightly attached to me as his counsellor. I knew the work had not continued long enough for him to have completely worked through some of his feelings of dependency on me. We had our first session at the end of August 1995 and had met, in total, 27 times by the end of our counselling relationship in April the following year (only eight months). Initially we had met twice a week for six sessions – until I had gone on holiday for two weeks. After this we met weekly until the beginning of February 1996, and then fortnightly during March and, after a month's gap, had our ending in April. In my terms this was 'brief therapy'. He had three sessions with Sarasi in September and then three sessions in December, three in January and three in February, two in March, one in April, one in May, another in September, one in March 1997 and another in October 1998 (total 19 sessions). It had been 'good enough' at the time, but the ending had been arrived at sooner than I considered ideal. There were other considerations (p.237–238) which brought the work to an end when it did. Although three years had elapsed, I sensed there would be some unresolved feelings to be dealt with. I raised the subject early in the first interview when we met to talk about writing the book (see Chapter 22).

Josselson (1996) explores some of the ethical issues concerned with using our ex-clients for research. She advocates that we should ask ourselves: 'Do you really feel like interfering in his or her life? Will you be able to live with the consequences of this encounter or intervention? Is it justified from the interviewee's own perspective?' (p.9). When clients have finished their work with us they may want to put the whole episode behind them and get on with the rest of their lives. However, my knowledge of Stephen and Mike led me to believe that they felt they would gain something for themselves through doing the research for the book. Shortly after Mike had agreed to take part in the process I asked if he had any anxieties and he said, 'Yes. My greatest anxiety is that you will change your mind about doing it.' When I asked why he thought I might change my mind, he replied that he was still uncertain about whether or not his story was worth telling.

Josselson (1996) warns us that in choosing clients to write about, we run the risk of aggrandising them:

> In fact we have aggrandized our participants – we regarded them as important enough to write about. But the experience of the grandiose self is always accompanied by shame and by an unconscious conviction of being in complete control of the Other, and this, I think, complicates people's experience of being written about. (Josselson 1996, p.65).

I think the anxiety expressed by Mike might have been related to the confusion of feelings attached to the idea of taking part in the research with me.

Gabriel (1999) has delineated some useful guidelines for minimising practitioner-researcher role conflict:

1. Provide clear information for participants about:
   (a) details of the research
   (b) informed consent
   (c) information on the possible consequences of participating on them, the relationship and maybe others too
   (d) researcher role as different from counsellor role.
2. By forming an effective research alliance by:
   (a) negotiating a clear contract with good boundaries
   (b) keeping a compassionate distance in the research role and not confusing the client by going back into counsellor role
   (c) outlining the tasks and goals of each
   (d) by striving to achieve a balance between impassioned and impassive responses
   (e) by considering any evidence of parallel processes
   (f) communicating limits to the relationship (e.g. what happens when the research is over?).
3. Have a clear policy on confidentiality:
   (a) point out the context of what is disclosed in the research interview is not subject to counsellor/supervisor codes of ethics
   (b) be clear about the limits of confidentiality and when you might have to discuss the information with others.
4. Cultivate self-reflexivity:
   (a) by regularly reviewing the researcher role/research process
   (b) by using supervisory meetings to do this
   (c) by using code of ethics for researchers and moral principles etc. for guidelines for consultation.

Participant and Data Protection

It is normally though not always the case that research participants wish to remain anonymous. This needs to be clarified early in the process. It is our responsibility as the researcher to explore the participants' attitudes to this. Sometimes we need to spend time exploring what it would mean to them to choose to allow themselves to be identified or not. Providing they are fully informed and have a real choice, it is the participant's decision.

Another ethical consideration concerns the decision about how we protect data during the process of research. When people hand over their personal diaries, letters and other documents it is essential that we honour them with care and protection. Material that is copied onto a word processor comes under the restrictions of the Data Protection Act. Any researcher working in a college or university setting or for any agency concerned with people, such as social services, general practice and voluntary agencies, will find that there is a designated person who is responsible for ensuring that the Data Protection Act is implemented. This person can give advice about matters concerning the confidentiality of data housed in this manner. Researchers working independently are required to register with the appropriate government department (providing the study is large enough).

Counsellors are required to protect client's privacy and information concerning them should be housed in a secure place. This is, of course, the same for research material. Identifying names and addresses should be kept separately from taped conversations, written material, etc. so if they fell into the wrong hands they could not be linked together.

One of the additional risks we take when we return transcripts to our participants was brought home to me at one stage of the process. I had posted some typed manuscript to Stephen and during the following night I dreamt that the envelope had been improperly sealed and had been opened by an official from the post office. The content of the writing (his letter to his grandfather) was very explicit about the abuse he had suffered. In the dream I was arrested for sending obscene material through the post. This really worried me and the following day I was on the point of telephoning Stephen to check if he had received the transcript when he rang me to thank me for sending it. But it did alert me to the additional danger when we send material of this nature through the post. It may well fall into wrong hands. I was aware that I may also have been experiencing something of a parallel process; the fear that Mike, Stephen and myself may have experienced about writing about this subject (and abuse victims in general) and the fear that by doing so we may be punished for doing something 'wrong'.

Research participants should be given information about what will happen to tapes, etc. after the study is completed. Sometimes they may be wiped clean by the researcher, after a period of time that is agreed, or they may be returned to the participant.

Ethical practice in research requires that we continuously monitor ourselves and our work through every stage of the process. The methods we use will reflect internal consistency between our values and beliefs. The following chapters will demonstrate my attempt to achieve and maintain this consistency.

CHAPTER 22

Research Methods

Several years had passed since the traveller returned from his journey. He had rested for a while and had settled down in a new part of the country. He was older and wiser. But he had never forgotten his journey to the swamp. It had been an important journey and he had returned from it a changed person. He had used what he had learned well and had taught others through his writing and teaching about the horrors of that dark place. Some people turned away saying, 'We don't want to hear about such things.' Or they joked saying, 'Why don't you just write a travel book – something we might enjoy reading.' Sometimes he met men who told him they too had been in the swamp and they wanted help to try and remember the time they had spent there so that they might forget about it. The traveller listened as they told their stories, until they did not need to tell them anymore. They said they were glad to find someone who was able to listen without turning away in horror.

Two of these men, who were brothers, wanted to join the traveller for a while – they knew their own route back from the swamp and they wanted others to have a map so that they too could find their way home. But they realised that there were many paths back and theirs may not be the one that others might use. They themselves had diverged from the path sometimes and taken byways not known to each other. But in the end they decided that their maps might be useful after all – if only to help people know that it was possible to find a way back. Others might later draw their own maps and eventually a whole book of maps might emerge.

So the three of them sat down together and began to talk about how they would produce a map that was clear enough to help others on their way. It needed to include directions about many different paths and some that might appear more difficult or dangerous than others; lists of equipment they might need for the journey; and information about what might happen on their return home.

At this point I would like to show some of the ways in which these tasks were undertaken. Moustakas (1990) writes:

> A typical way of gathering material in heuristic investigations is through extended interviews that often take the form of dialogue with oneself and one's research participants. Ordinarily, such 'interviews' are not ruled by the clock but by inner experiential time. In genuine dialogue, one is encouraged to permit ideas, thoughts,

feelings, and images to unfold and be expressed naturally. The inquiry is complete only when the individual has had an opportunity to tell his or her story to a point of natural closing. (Moustakas 1990, p.46)

Obtaining Truly Informed Consent

The following is a transcript of the first meeting between Mike, Stephen and myself, before there was any real clarity about what would happen. We had talked about the possibility of a book and they had expressed interest in contributing to it in some way. I had a publisher tentatively interested but I was leaving the proposal outline until the first meeting had occurred. We were starting from a place of 'not knowing' and beginning the engagement phase of heuristic research. I had set up the interviews at the university – a different venue from where they saw me as counsellor/supervisor. I believed this would help separate out the differences in our roles for this task. I had sent a letter to both men with some broad suggestions for discussion and this is where we began the process of gaining their informed consent:

Kim: *I wondered if you had any ideas about what this book will look like – whom do you imagine this book will be for, for instance?*

Stephen: *Either for victims of abuse or people who are trying to help them. I wasn't sure which.*

Mike: *I'd rather imagined it would be directed at counsellors et al. – but, seeing as I became a client through finding a book, it might well be for other people who do the same.*

Kim: *So if we could find a way of it being interesting and readable to both clients, counsellors, therapists, probation officers, mental health workers – whoever works with the client group and look at it from both sides? That's the sort of thing I had in mind – so my thinking was that it would need to be sufficiently theoretical but not to the detriment of its readability and its wider appeal. Yes?*

Stephen: *There's so little about men – that's why it was so surprising to spot your book on the shelf.*

Kim: *Yes, I don't think there has been a book written specifically about work with adult male survivors – so in that respect it would be really unique.*

[To Mike]... Did you have sense of what the shape or content of the book might be?

Mike: *No, I think I purposely tried not to think about that because when you first mentioned it to me I started to think along those lines, but then got into all those worries about whether the story might not be important enough to be told. [Laughs.] Since then I think I've laid that one to rest, but I'm not surprised that I've not undertaken too much organisation – I've had other things on my mind.*

[Mike had recently separated from his wife and set up in a house nearby so that his children have easy access to him.]

Kim: *Well, I've given it quite a lot of thought – I haven't come to any conclusions – but I've got a publisher who is interested – so that seems like a good starting point. I talked to Jessica Kingsley – she publishes quite a lot of books in this field.*

Stephen: Looking in the bookshops — there's loads of books for women — some of them were very interesting.

Kim: ...and parts are just as applicable. I thought this one should be as gender specific as possible. What makes it different to be a man recovering from this stuff?

Mike: I found reading the women's specific ones was very —'yes, this is really interesting and exciting' — but then suddenly a little bomb would go off — some sort of feminist (that's probably the wrong word) thing would appear — some anti-male remark...

Stephen: ...and then I'd say — just a minute — what about me?

Kim: Yes. So I think it's really important to think about this from the male perspective; and to acknowledge where they can overlap; and the whole problem of the experience of sexual abuse being seen as a woman's preserve which, in some ways, has made it a bit harder for men to acknowledge. In terms of this being done by you two and me — what were you thinking would be your input Stephen?

Stephen: I didn't really know — apart from being...

Mike: Going back to when you first mentioned it — I was thinking, 'Am I going to be writing here?', then it seemed to move on as we were talking. It seemed that you had it in mind to interview us, record us — I suppose that's partly why I suspended my burrowing.

Kim: Would you like to write something?

Mike: I'm not sure about that — probably the answer is, yes.

Kim: What kind of things could you see yourself writing?

Mike: Well, I suppose the very beginning — you know — finding the book — how to get into the system. That might be worth commenting on because I suspect counsellors may see the finished product in a way, when somebody is presented in the room.

Kim: Yes, and we have no idea how that person has struggled to get there.

Mike: I worry about being able to recover objectivity about it.

Kim: I don't think you need to be too objective. What I want is for this to be a kind of narrative — a story about therapy, so it can be as personal as you want it to be. I certainly wanted it to start before we met, and I was thinking about including your letter [to Stephen] because that's the bit where I came in really. The other thing I wanted to pick up on is the idea that each of your journeys has been an individual journey, and yet at times they've overlapped and you've shared parts of it together. That's complex and interesting in itself — because it's quite unusual really for a counsellor to work with two brothers who've had virtually the same upbringing — and had the same experiences of abuse with the same abuser — and yet you are two very different people. [Laughter.] I know you look very alike — but you are two very different people aren't you? I mean your work (therapy) — from my perspective — was different because you had very different needs.

[To Stephen] I did say a bit of this to Mike when we talked. But part of my anxiety is about not losing your uniqueness, your individuality and your confidentiality, because we can find ways to keep you non-identifiable as far as possible, without losing some of your really important particular features. But you two will know who is being talked about in this book, *perhaps in a way that nobody else will, except me, and I was just wondering if you'd thought that. I know there have been things that you have talked about quite deeply together, but I guess there are also things that you have kept really private and separate, and I don't know what those things are and I don't want to be...*

Stephen: From each other...?

Kim: Yes.

Mike: I'm not sure that I do actually [know] – which is part of the problem.

Kim: Right [all laugh]. There may be particular things that you've wanted kept very private and I think that's absolutely right – I guess we won't really know until we come up against those things.

Mike: I think I'd need to go over the material and think 'ah ha'... and maybe I'd need to go and talk to Stephen, but maybe I could say 'no, we can't put that in'. [Pause.] I'm not actually sure that I could write you a list of things that that would apply to and maybe there won't be.

Kim: No, no – but we need to ensure that your privacy is respected – from each other as well as the wider world. Just to have that awareness is really important as a starting point and to know that just because you have agreed to do this together, doesn't necessarily mean that you lose your own material – that you still have ownership of that.

Mike: I have been really surprised at how unfrightening it has been. I have been much less worried than I ever thought I would be about the world reading the story...and that's really surprising.

Stephen: I find it incredible. As you know, when I first came to see you I was terrified that anybody would find out. Whereas now, I think I'm in danger of going too far the other way – not like shouting from the rooftops – but I think I'll have to be careful. I feel safe with you...so

Mike: But from the times you've discussed with me about disclosing to other people Stephen, you've been fairly certain of your judgement.

Stephen: I think I have – yes. But I think it's because it was so difficult in the beginning – incredibly difficult – it seemed impossible. It's almost immeasurable. I just can't believe it really.

Mike: One of the things that I've been almost looking forward to is that – whatever I do now – even if I sit with my diary in front of me and go over it – in the end what comes out will be seen through the lens of now – the therapy and the recovery. Am I making sense? ... it won't be the same as just reproducing it as it happened.

Kim: No – it's a reflection – looking back over it isn't it?

Mike: Yes, and I suppose one interesting thing is to compare the two – the finished product – as it were.

Kim: Yes – you kept a journal did you – all the way through?

Mike: Oh well, I wouldn't say I kept a journal –neither was it all the way through but...

Kim: ...but you've got a kind of record... [to Stephen] and you have as well...?

Stephen: I've got everything, yes.

Kim: Wow – we must have known this was going to happen someday [all laugh].

Stephen: Well, I was actually coming to a point when I thought, 'What shall I do with all this?', because...

Kim: Have you thought of the idea of writing your own book?

Stephen: No, nobody would want to read it.

Mike: I have actually toyed with the idea.

Kim: Well, I suppose it doesn't have to be an either/or – it could be an 'and'. This one and later maybe your own.

Stephen: Going back to the last point – I think it would be good, from my point of view, to talk about it now, to look back and see how far I've come – to know how I've changed. I think it would be quite healthy to talk about it from a safer place.

Mike: [To Stephen] How hard did you find it to pick it up? Because I know where it is but I must admit I've thought to myself 'I ought to read that', but I haven't done it.

Stephen: I've read it three or four times when I'm feeling low sometimes – to see how far I'd come – to reassure myself, but erm – I find it is a bit uncomfortable. I was saying to Kim, I realised how much pain I was in when I was writing it by the style of writing – it was a different me. It was very interesting. I read it yesterday; just reading that letter reminded me how I was panicking. [Laughs.] It reminded me how scared I was; what a terrible place I was in; how desperate I was feeling.

Kim: Mmm. That's reminded me of the other thing that I wanted to bring into focus. The process of doing this may very well churn you up and open up things again, and I wonder what that would be like for you and what you would do then...?

Stephen: I feel like I'm ready for that. I think I could cope with that now – at this distance. I could deal with that now.

Kim: How about you Mike?

Mike: [Pause] Mmm. Yes I think so. I think I've demonstrated by recent events that I can mobilise support if I need to [pause]. And I suppose the fact that I'm not living with Ellen now makes me feel I am able to do these things. I dare say I'm projecting, but I suppose I feel more worried about you now [to Stephen].

Kim: But here we are now, moving into a different relationship when I'm not your counsellor. What would that mean if anything did come up? What might be your expectations of me if you got very distressed about something that was happening as part of the research process? I suppose my concern is – that if you needed counselling – I don't think it would now be appropriate for me to offer that.

Stephen: That would be OK.

Kim: [To Stephen] But I am also aware that you have financial limitations, that would make it hard for you to get counselling elsewhere. I just wondered if you had thought about that.

Stephen: [Mumble] ...talk to Mike [laugh] – it's exciting – just go for it.

Kim: So you have some contingency plans that might be possible? There are other options too that I can put you in touch with. There are other agencies where you can go for low fee or reduced fee counselling, but I think for me to get involved again with you as a counsellor – at this *point in time – would be too messy if we are contracting a different kind of relationship now. That's not to say that I don't expect this to be therapeutic, or that I'm not going to be able to be supportive as a researcher, and I certainly wouldn't leave you in the lurch and abandon you – either of you. But I think its important for you to know that this is a different kind of relationship.*

Stephen: Of course.

Mike: I suppose that was what I thought would be so.

Kim: That might be easier for you Mike – because we already have a different professional relationship in supervision – than it would be for Stephen who hasn't worked with me since I was his counsellor. So I suppose I just need to talk about that whole thing – being very conscious of the power that the counsellor has in the client/counsellor relationship. I know the client has a lot of power too – but from my memory of being the client, I certainly perceived the counsellor to have quite a lot of power, and I'm not sure what that's like for you now, seeing me again, after all this time in this different role. In this relationship we need to have a sense of more equality – you need to be able to say to me 'no, I don't want you say that'.

[Laughter]

Stephen: Right.

Kim: And I need to be able to say that to you too, without worrying about my 'clients' [laughter]. Does that make sense?

Stephen: Yes – balance it out.

Kim: ...and you know the nature of the relationship we have with our counsellor is often child/parent at least some of the time...

Stephen: That was certainly where I was coming from.

Kim: It might be quite difficult at times. So I am aware of that – are you? Did this occur to you?

Stephen: I hadn't really thought about it until you mentioned it. I know what you mean.

Mike: Shall I push you a bit then?

Kim: Yes.

Mike: Can I ask you how much you see this being three people working together, and how much you see us two helping you to write a book.

Kim: Yes. That's what the publisher asked me and I said that I would have to talk to you about this. I was thinking that it was me writing a book and you giving whatever you wanted to give as part of that process. If you wanted your name in there, then we would have to talk about that – my understanding was that you probably wouldn't. [Pause.] It feels peculiar in a way – because I think what we are trying to capture is your work, your process, my work, my process, but I want to put that into the context of the wider work that I do with men and I will be drawing on other material as well and I think I will be doing most of the work so...

Mike: I have a picture in my mind then – of we three together being a source...

Kim: Yes... but there is another source that I bring to this, which is my other research, client work, my own therapy. When I spoke to the publisher I said, 'I'm not quite sure whether this is going to be just these two men or whether it would be more "proper" to include others.' I was wondering 'what if there isn't enough material?'. But I don't actually believe that because there's a huge amount of material; and maybe it would be easier to anonymise you if there were more of you – but I also want to hold on to that.

Mike: It's just going to be harder to hide our identity...

Kim: That's right. So when I asked you if you had any sense of 'how' – I was really wanting to know if you had any ideas of how to manage that tricky process.

Stephen: ...of anonymity?

Kim: No – of keeping your two stories as the core and maybe also bringing in other material – other sources – we'll come to the anonymity business in a minute. So I'm playing round with that idea and I haven't got any answers yet.

Mike: I came to asking the question from the co-worker business – I suppose if in the end it is your book to which we are contributing a source – then the power relationship is going to be unequal...and that has to be faced up to in that sense...

Kim: Yes, insofar as that is true. But what I want is for everything that happens – as far as it is possible and practicable – to be upfront and agreed. So what I was hoping is, that I would interview each of you separately; I would then transcribe those tapes – I remember how that took at least six hours for each tape when I did it before – then I would send it back to you and you would go through it, and ensure that it was saying what you had intended it to say. And if there was anything in there that you did not want said, then you would have a chance to remove it – or to anonymise it. In that sense, the material would be given back to you to take ownership of and for you decide how and whether you wanted it used. If there were pieces that you said 'no I don't want that used', then you have the power to say 'no'. So in that sense the power would be... Yes, we have to face up to the fact that it would be my book and it would be my name on it and – although I would be prepared to talk about it if you wanted your name on it as well.

Mike: So it's not just sitting down and writing a book.

Kim: No. I've been imagining different ways of approaching it and I would really like to be creative about it. I'm very taken up with the whole idea of narrative as a methodology at the moment. A sort of story telling and actually something you said Mike has triggered me off. [To Stephen] Mike has talked about this elephant that sits in the middle of your living room...

Stephen: I've met him, yes.

Kim: You know the one?

Stephen: Yes – he was there for most of our lives.

Mike: I must say this is not original – I'm sure I saw it in a film – I can't remember who said it [laughter].

Stephen: We could call the book 'The Elephant in the Living Room'!

Kim: We could, couldn't we. I've been thinking about titles actually – and the trouble is – you've got to have something with key words, so that if people logged into 'sexual abuse', 'men', they would be able to find it in the title. 'An Elephant in the Living Room' – maybe we could have a subtitle.

Stephen: Yes.

Kim: I really like the idea of having it begin with something like 'once upon a time there was a daddy and a mummy and they lived in a little... I'd like you two to create that story – a fairy story that your lives would have been seen as by the outside world – do you know what I mean? It's going to be about how you healed from what happened to you. But we will have to say what happened to you – but what I'm hoping is that – if that fairy story was the prologue we would start the beginning of the book with something quite real. That's the fantasy, the illusion; that's what the outside world saw – but this is what actually happened. Not to put too much of that – I'm not saying we should pussyfoot around it – but not to go into too many details. At some point in the book – I'm not quite sure how to do it – I will need to go into the theory – but maybe that will be separate from your story in a way.

Mike: It's how to fit that into the narrative part of it.

Kim: Yes, yes and maybe they don't actually go together.

Stephen: Fantasy and reality – like at the funeral with everybody saying what a wonderful chap he was – in the church.

Mike: Yes, I don't remember all this.

Kim: That was before Mike said anything?

Stephen: Yes... [too quiet].

Mike: I'm quite fascinated with this narrative thing 'cos that's how it seems to be. I tend to look back and see it as a new product – that's not strictly true and yet it was a narrative – it was a journey that took time to unfold.

Stephen: Erm – I want to look after my own [anonymity] which would also mean Mike's – but I trust you to use your judgement. I don't think I would be very easily identified but that might not be so for Mike being a professional man.

[Laughter from all.] It's an old habit for the two brothers to always present the needs of the other and ignore their own.

Kim: So you think if a book was written about a [height and appearance] man who was a [his job] in a [place of work] who had [x] no of children... you wouldn't be recognisable?

Stephen: Yes, well that would be going a bit too far. I wouldn't want that for the sake of my children.

Kim: No – right.

Stephen: That's one extreme – the other extreme is missing what happened – but we need somewhere in the middle.

Kim: Did you have any thoughts about that Mike?

Mike: Yes I did and isn't it funny [mockingly] that I was more worried about Stephen than I was about me [laughter], because I was thinking: 'Well, who's likely to read this that I know' or 'Who would work out who I was?' I suppose I was thinking: 'Well if they've gone to the trouble to read this book (if the book is how I imagine it will be), then I probably don't mind them working out that it's me.' But that might seem very 'gung-ho'. I think you [to Stephen] have an over-inflated idea about the reading matter of GPs and the sort of ones who might read it.

Kim: I think what we mustn't lose sight of – is that you are very important in this – and the people who you care about are important.

Stephen: Yes.

Mike: Right – and then there's their confidentiality.

Kim: Yes.

Stephen: Needs a lot of thinking about.

[Long pause.] I think it's the first time they have really thought about other members of their family being in the public domain.

Kim: It's important to raise these issues you see – for you to really know what it means. One of the things that happened after the last book was published…

I tell the story about how people's life stories can be recognised by people who know them (even when written about anonymously), because of the uniqueness of the narrative; and how that can cause distress to others who may be included in that story, but who have had no part in the decision-making process – not having given their informed consent.

…so those two incidents have made me very cautious and I'm sharing that with you because I want you to know that we don't always know until it happens – even when we take as much care as we can at the time. And when you open that book and see your words and your story out of your control, in the public eye – it's potentially a very disturbing experience – and I think you really need to think about that.

Stephen: Yes. You've really made me think about it in a wider way now – thanks.

Mike: So I think that needle is moving further to the left now.

Kim: What's at the left?

[Laughter]

Mike: Towards changing things – identities I mean. I guess it's not just me in the end that I have to think about…

Kim: When you actually see that in print – it's a powerful medium for something that has been for so long very private for you, even secret and shameful – suddenly 'aaahhh!' And you've been through abuse and over-exposure and I didn't want to be a party to that happening to you again.

[Long silence]

Kim: So in a way I hope I'm answering some of your question about the power…

Mike: I suppose now I'm trying to ask myself how important are some of these identifying characteristics to the story.

Kim: Absolutely. But it's a fine balancing act.

Stephen: You don't want to be misrepresenting or lose the power of what you were saying.

Kim: One of the ways of disguising somebody is not so much what you change about them or take away from them – its what you give them. For instance if I said you had five children, or if I said you lived in a large house in the country – or I don't know – we could imagine all sorts of additional things which are actually not true.

Stephen: Rich – living in a mansion.

[Laughter]

We talk about some of the particular ways we might change their identity – what would be important to leave in so as not to lose the power of their stories.

Kim: So we don't have to decide today – these are just things I wanted to flag up – to begin that process of awareness of what this might mean. For instance – does Stella know about this book *[to Stephen]*?

Stephen: Yes.

Kim: So Stella will want to read it?

Stephen: Presumably – yes.

Kim: So what would Stella feel when she read some things that…

Stephen: Mmm. Perhaps I'll need to talk to her.

Kim: Yes, that's one way, but maybe there are things we might not be able to put in the book – you don't have to bare all.

Mike: I had thought of Stella as being a person who would know who I was.

Kim: Yes, of course. What about Ellen – what about your kids?

Mike: Well – they would want to read it if they knew of its existence I suppose. I hadn't thought that I would tell them – having said that they could find out …

Kim: The other thing I was a bit worried about – a possible dilemma – was the idea of secrets – the need to keep a secret.

Mike: Meaning that it would be healthier for me to tell them?

Kim: Not necessarily, but I don't want to re-create a situation in which you are forced to keep a secret again that might feel in some way not comfortable or…

Stephen: I think I have to bear in mind that it would not be appropriate for my children to read it now, but that in the future it might be. I'll have to bear that in mind.

Kim: Right – so when we are writing or reading this, you'll have to be doing it with lots of different eyes.

[Pause]

Mike: Yes, what you've done for me now, is to show me how complicated the anonymity side of it is going to be.

Stephen: Yes – I was looking at it in a too narrow way.

Mike: Yes, it's about other people as well as us

[Long pause in which I am wondering if I should offer them an explicit opportunity to withdraw at this stage.]

Kim: You might change your mind altogether.

Stephen: No. I've been thinking about the reasons for doing it and maybe the reasons for not doing it. What I said already is I think that to re-look at it again from this perspective will help me; the other thing is I want to help other people in the same situation, people who are victims. People like yourself are doing so much to help. I really want to give some of that back – I want to help. This is my chance. It was chance that you lived near enough for me to have counselling – even if it was quite a journey. I felt very fortunate and I don't think I've put anything back and I want to...

Kim: You don't have to put anything back.

Stephen: No, but I want to.

Kim: You want to.

Stephen: I feel – as I say – that it will be a 'safe help' for me – doing it.

Mike: [To Stephen] I don't know if you know, but that is something I have more or less said to Kim too. I sometimes have these guilt feelings that I should be starting a campaign but maybe this is a real, practical way – something I can do [too quiet]... There is another – can I change the subject?

Kim: Can we just finish this bit because I wanted to capture what you said Stephen – you said 'these are the reasons why I do want to do it' and then you said something about the reasons you don't...

Stephen: [Laughing] Yes – erm I think I can remember...

The tape was too quiet here, but when asked to fill in the gap Stephen said he was thinking of not wanting to return to the pain of the past – that was the reason he might *not* want to do it.

Mike then raised his concern about our different perceptions of each other's 'academic ability' – he was aware that Stephen had always deferred to him as the 'academic' member of the family and he wondered if that would be an issue for him as we discussed the book together. Stephen said he felt much more confident about his academic ability since his counselling and his return to studying.

Mike: But this is a peculiar situation isn't it? I don't mean just sitting in this room talking, but the project we're talking about involves disclosing things about one another to the outside world.

Kim: Yes, yes. There's also my need to disclose things as well – have you thought about that. I had thoughts and feelings when I was doing some of this work with you.

Stephen: [To me] I used to worry about you.

Kim: Did you?

Stephen: Yes — you used to say to me about it at the time. Most days when I was with you I used to worry about what it would do to you, having to listen to all that stuff *[too quiet]*.

Kim: Oh, yes. I think I knew you used to worry about me on that level. I used to worry about me too *[laughter]*...

...I'm thinking more about revealing my own process — what I was thinking, what I was feeling, what I was wanting to say that I didn't say sometimes because it wasn't appropriate.

Mike: ...or the things you did say that you wished you hadn't?

Kim: Yes, yes, you can tell me what they were.

[Laughter]

Mike: I'm not sure that I can. I remember noticing sometimes: 'I think she wishes she hadn't said that.'

Kim: Yes. I will probably say what made me feel anxious — if I can remember. I probably won't remember it all — it will be very interesting to be reminded and for me to look back.

Stephen: I wrote up every session.

Kim: I'm so glad you did.

Stephen: I think you asked me to — you suggested it — once I got started I couldn't stop.

Kim: That's great. I wonder if we could actually use that? *[Very tentatively.]*

Stephen: And I thought well...I'm paying all this money — I'd better get my money's worth.

[Laughter]

Kim: Well you did use that — it was very much part of your process at the time.

Stephen: Yes.

Mike: I think, yes, I haven't looked at it recently but I suspect I probably I did on occasion think: 'So many things happened in that hour I must write them down, otherwise I'll forget them.'

Stephen: It's such a good learning. I keep it on top of the wardrobe *[too quiet]*.

[Pause]

Kim: Yes. So maybe we've said enough for tonight because we have covered an awful lot and you're going to need to go away and think about it aren't you? And let it sink in and chew over some these things and maybe have some ideas about the answers to some of those potential problems?

Stephen: You asked us what we thought the book would be for, but I wondered what you thought.

Kim: Well, I thought virtually the same as you really. I want it to be a message of hope. I want people to know that terrible things can happen to people over a long period of time — the worst things — the most extreme abuse, and still they can regain their wholeness. And you know — it's a very peculiar thing isn't it — when people talk about 'going and getting some counselling' — they don't know what its really like behind the closed doors of the counselling room.

Stephen: I was reading my stuff yesterday. I actually rang Childline when I was desperate and was told 'you are too old for us to help' ...and yet that was the first thing that came to mind.

Kim: I thought I would try and write something. I feel as if I've shared a lot of my thinking with you and

[Pause]

...maybe you'd like to write a fairy story to start with – between you or one of you – the fairy story of the happy family – it doesn't have to be long...

Stephen: Can I write this down?

Kim: Yes. Do you want some paper? If you feel as if I'm asking you to do too much then please say so. I want you to get something out of this.

Stephen: If it just helps one person.

At this point we talk about money and I tell them about the amount I have received in royalties from my previous book. They are surprised how little that is and we go on to talk of the myth about making money out of writing. I do not expect there to be any profit from this book – as I am writing it in my freelance time, having no paid time to write or do research in my university post; indeed I would not expect to cover costs. There is some discussion of their anonymity being preserved (if their names were on the contract they would be known to the publishing company). However, this is an issue we will return to later, but at this stage I clarify that their motive for writing excludes an expectation of receiving payment. I go on to say what I will get out of it:

Kim: I suppose I will get the kudos that would come with that. I'm too old for it to be a boost for my career – but it will be very nice if people recognise something worthwhile in it. I think more than anything I will gain a sense of passing on to the next generation something worthwhile. I'm also very interested in the process of research and I feel as if this (what we are doing now, as we talk) is an interesting research process too. What I'd like to do, at the end of the book, is to reflect on the process of writing the book – so things like this meeting will be part of that. The way we've talked about confidentiality; anonymity; the ethical principles that underlie what we're doing; and this whole thing about 'not doing harm'; and 'how does the good outweigh the harm'; and what kind of freedom of choice do you have as collaborators in this – autonomy, power, ownership. Those things are what I teach MSc students and I would like this book to be a demonstration of that.

I think I also want to give you two something. I suppose I really do believe that this will also be a part of that continuing process of healing – that you might be doing some of the unfinished business. I also I think your story is really worth telling and unique. So I think that's where I'm coming from.

Mike: I wonder if it's as unique as you say. Yes, I know everybody's story is unique. I mean unique in being members of the same family.

Kim: Quite. That's what makes it important isn't it – it's not unique in that respect. There must be brothers and sisters and families all over the place going through something similar to what you experienced; but I think one of the great things is that you two have gained so much from each other and strengthened each other and yourselves in sharing that process.

I think of the differences now – in your relationships with your father and mother – between the two of you. Then there's all that stuff about the family – all those skeletons that fell out of the cupboard – in a heap, all at once it seemed.

[Laughter]

Mike: *I've never heard that expression before 'all the skeletons falling out of the cupboard' – that's absolutely spot on – you're very good with words.*

Kim: *There's a hell of a lot in there. So what do you feel about using additional material? I mean there will be additional material because I will have to relate this to counselling theory in some way – but maybe in terms of other men's stories.*

[Long pause.] I am aware of Josselson's (1996) warning about 'narcissistic injury'. I have made them 'special' by suggesting their story is important enough to be told and here I am now suggesting that others might also be important: 'Our participants are left to deal alone with... their injured or over-stimulated grandiosity and with their recognition that they are not in control of us. And being so close to the narcissistic core of personality organization, none of this can be easily discussed' (p.65). I want to find a way of discussing it so that they will not be left with it.

Mike: *Yes, I suppose if I'm honest I feel slightly jealous of it...*

Kim: *You don't want other men's stories?*

Mike: *...but that's being...*

[Pause]

Kim: *...[To Stephen] How do you feel?*

Stephen: *I got the impression it was only about our story; so if it is, it is and if it isn't, it isn't.*

Kim: *I wanted it to be about your story.*

Stephen: *It's fine with me – I feel protective.*

Kim: *You'd feel better if it was just your story?*

[Pause]

...I think what I can do is, when it comes to the more theoretical part, I could introduce some little vignettes...

Stephen: *Of course.*

I talk about why I might need to include other material – because of the issues that are different from their experiences; for instance 'false memory', childlessness, becoming an abuser, drug abuse, alcoholism, etc. I may not go into these kinds of issues as I covered them in my previous book (Etherington 1995), but, just in case, I want to raise it as a possibility.

Mike: *But in the end if you make us too central to it then it doesn't become useful... it just becomes a therapeutic process for us...*

Kim: *Yes, yes. So I don't want it to be less useful but I want to find a way of not taking away the centrality of your story. Neither of you have ever been in prison, for instance.*

Mike: Drugs, prison, prostitution – unless there are secrets I don't know about.

[Laughter]

Kim: [To Stephen] Are you going to tell him about your rent boy activities or do I have to tell him?

[More laughter]

Kim: That's the sort of thing I'm talking about. I'm just not quite sure how. Have you had enough now?

Mike: I haven't eaten yet.

Kim: Nor me. All right. Thanks for coming – I hope you've found it useful and interesting.

Mike and Stephen: Yes, yes.

Kim: You might feel quite churned up after this. *[Tape ends.]*

CHAPTER 23

Doing the Research

Interviews

Interviewing can be a method of gathering data for most kinds of qualitative research. However, if the research is to be a process of discovery and starts from a place of 'not knowing', those interviews are most helpfully in the form of conversations between participants and researcher (see Ellis *et al.* 1997). We can discover where it leads – we may find some surprises on the way, surprises that engage our creativity and spontaneity. We may also stumble across dilemmas that arise out of a relatively unplanned journey. We need trust and courage and openness to undertake such a journey and we need to choose our companions well. In my previous study I interviewed 25 men using a general interview guide, outlining some of the questions I wanted to answer. I used an open-question style and checked with the guide at the end of the interview to ensure nothing important had been excluded. In the main, I never saw or heard from most of them again although there were a few exceptions. I returned the transcripts to all participants and very few returned them with comments. Some had told me they did not want to receive the transcripts. This time I met with only two men, both of whom I had met before, knew quite well and they knew me. But their knowledge of me is limited – there is an unequal balance in these relationships. They have told me their painful stories, allowed me to come close to their hidden selves and trusted me. I know more about them than they do about me. The balance needs redressing in our new relationships. In a conversation I can be included as myself. They can listen to my thoughts and feelings, as I share more of myself.

Moustakas (1990) quotes Jourard (1968) emphasising that 'dialogue is like mutual unveiling, where each seeks to be experienced and confirmed by the other... Such dialogue is likely to occur when the [two] people believe each is trustworthy and of good will' (pp.47–48). We meet as often as we need to until the story has been told and understood in the telling.

All that is discovered through this process is depicted through stories: metaphorical stories, narratives, stories told through diaries, poems and conversations. Research material is usually interpreted and presented through the words of the researcher. I have presented Stephen and Mike's own words both in their different forms of writing and through the inclusion of the actual conversations we held. In order to present this material it has been necessary and important for all involved to see and be aware of the material written by each other. Trust therefore must also exist between participants.

Data to provide evidence of my experiences as a researcher is not limited to that which is obtained through interview, stories and texts gained from Stephen and Mike. If I exclude the practicalities of note taking, documentation of the order in which events occurred as the process unfolded, the informal contacts and communications between us, then the reader is presented with a partial account. So I have included further information in this chapter.

Order of Service

10.12.98

Letter to Stephen and letter to Mike proposing our collaboration.

27.1.99. Initial engagement

First interview with Mike and Stephen (Chapter 22) – transcribed and returned to both men who then corrected it, commented upon it and returned it to me.

3.3.99

Second interview with Mike and Stephen. Tape did not record properly! I had found the previously taped interview difficult to hear in parts, so this time I decided to use an extra flatbed microphone inserted into tape machine. Even though I tested it at the time and it seemed to be working, when I tried transcribing it I discovered that what had been picked up was a football match that had been on the radio at the time we met! I made notes of what I remembered from our meeting (below) and sent them to Mike and Stephen to check out if I had forgotten anything important or remembered anything incorrectly. They agreed with my account of that meeting.

> SECOND MEETING – NOTES
>
> We discussed where they were in their decision about anonymity. Stephen has told his wife and thinks he should tell his parents because he does not want to keep secrets. Mike does not want to tell his wife or parents. He thinks his wife may veto the work and he thinks his parents will be distressed by it all being brought out into the open. He is fearful that the support he has recently received from his parents might be withdrawn if they become angry again. Neither want to tell their children in detail at this stage although Stephen has recently told his teenage daughter about his abuse. Mike has already told both his son and his daughter. He thinks they may want to read the book one day – but not just yet.
>
> Stephen told a story of why he had told his daughter at this time. The GP has referred her to a psychiatrist because she is not sleeping and Stephen thinks that because the GP knows about his abuse he is adding two and two and getting five!
>
> We had a discussion about the pros and cons of telling parents; discussed the difference between secrecy and privacy and that there were always some things

parents weren't told about. What would it be like if they found out some time in the future and hadn't been told at the time? Stephen said, 'It's my story and I can tell it if I want to.' I said, 'It's also their story and they do not have a choice about whether or not it is told.' We decided that Stephen and Mike need to think about it and talk some more together about it.

NB. Parallel process with the disclosure of original abuse. We had a conversation that is almost parallel to the conversation in the diary about differences between secrecy and privacy.

Stephen and Mike had begun the 'Fairy Story' – both were remarkably similar. They would go and see if they could amalgamate them into a whole. I explained how I had described the shape of the book to the publisher and asked what they thought about it. Both seemed quite happy with the outline shape.

Mike had thought some more about how he could be disguised and decided that he would exclude some info that might make him identifiable. He might write another book from that perspective for himself.

Stephen gave me his diary which contains all the sessions at the beginning when he was in severe distress and having flashbacks. It covers the period up to just before he decided to leave the job. It includes his letter to his grandfather that he spent about four hours writing in the early hours of the morning. It can probably be used in its original state with a bit of editing. Graphically describes the post-traumatic stress condition he was in at that time and the whole family relationships disturbance that followed. It also demonstrates his growing empowerment. Highlights issues such as:

(a) How the child becomes the adult and how that is carried on into adult life and work.
(b) Describes actual abuse behaviours.
(c) Describes grooming process.
(d) Effect on developing sexuality especially around puberty.
(e) Confusion around orientation – need to prove heterosexuality.
(f) Shame, responsibility, fear, secrecy.
(g) Relationships with father/mother.
(h) Relationship with wife.
(i) Bodywork – first sessions with Sarasi – releasing shame and guilt.

We ended the meeting by deciding that the next meetings would be to begin taping interviews with them individually.

Explained how the research process would be captured as part of the book and highlight good practice about:

(a) informed consent – what does it really mean;
(b) confidentiality – complications when others are involved;

(c) whose story is it?

(d) power relationships with researcher;

(e) researcher's reflexivity and transparency;

(f) dual roles of counsellor/researcher – power issues.

Talked to Mike on the phone about tape not working. He said the meeting ended feeling more positive than last one. He thought that was because they had started out quite 'gung-ho' and then gone down with the realisation of what might go wrong. He said he was glad I had made them aware, because if I hadn't they might have felt betrayed later when things happened that they had not been prepared for. He said my term 'truly informed consent' felt like a very good one.

22.2.99

Copied Stephen's diary onto the word processor.

24.3.99

Interviewed Stephen about his diary and about the counselling process. Gave him the printed version of his diary. He gave me their 'fairy story' which they'd written together since our last meeting. Started transcribing this interview during following week.

17.4.99

Received printed version of the diary back from Stephen and a letter from him saying:

Sorry for the delay in returning the enclosed; it gave me quite a shock. Seeing it in print was quite frightening, and I had some doubt about it.

However, after consideration, and talking it over with Mike and Stella, please go ahead and use it as you like. Feel free to edit it if you want to. I have changed a few words to increase its anonymity.

20.4.99

Wrote to Mike to suggest that we might postpone his interview until after he has written his story so that I could interview him about what he had written as I had done with Stephen.

22.4.99

Started writing introduction.

1.5.99

Returned transcribed interview to Stephen for correction etc.

11.5.99

Received transcribed interview back from Stephen saying: 'I have read it through and made some of the alterations I want'. He answered some additional questions on an enclosed sheet – these were questions that had arisen for me during transcription.

Beginning of June 1999

Received Mike's story. Copied it onto word processor during the following week.

7.6.99

DIARY NOTES: IMMERSION STAGE

Woke at 4.00 am. Research going round in my head. Trouble is – the next morning I can't think of what I had been planning during my sleepless hours, so it's a bit of a waste of time really! I'll have to take my notebook to bed.

I think I'm in the immersion stage. Feeling a bit daunted by the size of the project – asking myself, 'Why am I doing it?' I don't really need the hassle – what am I getting out of it? I'm jolly glad I didn't get the funding for that research project now. I wonder if I'd feel differently if I was getting paid for the time I'm spending on this one? Won't ever know that now.

I feel as if I'm doing something I'm not very good at, at this point in the process: i.e. the organising side of it. When I try and arrange layers it all seems to get tangled. Which is the research data – it feels like it's all research data – maybe it is. I want to include every word that passes between us because of letting it be seen for what it really is, but will other people be bored by all the trivia that is caught up in all that? I am remembering being told to 'get to the point' when I tell stories – told that I ramble on – am I doing that again?

23.6.99

Interviewed Mike about his story and counselling process.

Mike gave me his 'diary' and offered me his 'letters to the inner child' material if I wanted to use it.

During the following week I transcribed tape and returned it to Mike for comment, correction, etc.

June–July: incubation stage

During this time I am aware that I am spending a lot of time thinking about the data, becoming more aware of the many layers, trying to categorise the meanings as they emerge and shift. I just keep writing. It seems the only way. Maybe later I can sort it more when things become clearer. Now that I've got most of the 'field data' I can see more of the whole picture. I have to wait a while to find out where/how I can introduce Sarasi's data.

I inserted some of Mike's letter material into his story to introduce some of the 'then' experience into his 'now' account. Sent this to him asking if he felt OK about the changes.

Mid-July 1999

Met with Sarasi to discuss her involvement in the research process – she went away to think about it. Rang later to say she would like to be involved and wants to use her name.

Four weeks later sent Part 1 and almost completed Part 2 to Sarasi so that she could contextualise herself within it.

August: illumination stage

There's a lot going on inside me at this time – I feel my awareness expanding. I'm learning new things about myself and the work – it's quite a hard time. I am still writing. Seeing things on paper helps. I go back over it time and again and listen to my 'voice' and see what I've said. I sit too long at the word processor and my neck aches.

19.8.99

Met with Sarasi to begin her input and made tape of our short conversation. She decided she would like to write something from her notes, with Mike and Stephen's permission.

20.8.99

Rang Mike and Stephen to ask for permission for Sarasi to use her notes of their sessions for her writing. They are both very pleased that she is going to write from her perspective.

2.9.99

Met with Sarasi again. She has written a piece about her work with Mike and will go away to write about Stephen. She prefers to use her own words rather than the conversational style of interviewing I had suggested. I am happy with that. It has made me aware that the type of interview we choose may be important to discuss in advance. Perhaps I've taken for granted that my naturalistic approach will suit people without that necessarily being the case. I'm getting anxious about the deadline approaching and needing to finish the writing so that I can print off some copies to send out to Mike and Stephen and some colleagues for feedback. I have to do that before I go away on holiday on September 14th. After that I will have a final meeting with Mike and Stephen to discover what they feel at the end of the process. I've begun to wonder how it will be for them to see and hear my process – will that be destabilising for them?

4.9.99

Received Sarasi's final copy by e-mail. Copied into script and sent her final copy to check again – returned it with a few minor amendments. She wants it to remain as it is with her own writing for the part where she discusses her work with Mike and the conversation between us in the part that covers her work with Stephen. She sees it fits with the general style of the book and provides a nice contrast.

5.9.99

Finished writing collaborative working chapter – only got the last chapter to go now but can't do that until I've sent it out and met up with Mike and Stephen.

7.9.99

Handed over a copy to Mike and one to Stephen – felt like a real ceremony.

12.9.99

Received a card from Mike saying 'Wow! Powerful stuff – thanks.' Handed a copy over to a colleague to read while I am on holiday and arranged for others to receive it in my absence.

14–28.9.99

Two weeks on a Greek island. Strange dreams some nights. Began to feel anxious about how it would be received as I flew home.

28.9.99

Letter from Stephen waiting for me on return. He has been deeply affected – especially by reading Mike's material which he had not seen before. It seems overall to have been a positive, if painful experience.

29.9.99

Colleague rang and gave me very positive feedback. I felt like crying with relief.

31.9.99

Took students for residential weekend – more positive feedback in message on my return home.

4.10.99

Last meeting with Mike and Stephen. Felt good. Now I can get on with the last chapter. No idea what it will look like at this point. Want it to capture the essence of our last meeting.

10.10.99

Wrote final chapter 'Where Three Streams Meet'.

11.9.99

Sent copies of final chapter to Mike and Stephen.

15.10.99

Both Mike and Stephen loved the last chapter. Stephen sent me a card saying that it had captured the essence of our last meeting. Mike said the same thing.

16.10.99

Checked with Sarasi to see if she would like her name on the cover of the book. She would. I will put this to the publisher. Write to Mike and Stephen to ask again about whether or not they wish to share the royalties and have their names on the cover of the book (their pseudonyms). We discussed this in our first meeting but as a lot of water has passed under the bridge since then I want to give them an opportunity to rethink that decision.

17.10.99

Phone call from Stephen to say he has talked to Mike and they both want things as they are, i.e. the contract to be between the publisher and myself and they feel that their names on the cover would be unnecessary.

19.10.99

Minor adjustments made to text in response to feedback received.

26.10.99

Printed off double-spaced copy and posted it to publisher. (Index will need to be completed when page proofs are returned to me.)

Right from early on I was writing. I think it is important to start writing something down very early in the research process – it almost doesn't matter what! To submerge oneself in the research process without writing may be a recipe for feeling overwhelmed at a later date and not knowing where to begin. A good way to begin is to think onto paper; perhaps beginning with a research diary, staying inside the process; logging feelings, images, thoughts, ideas, plans, meetings, conversations and dreams. All of this will keep the writing as part of the ongoing process.

Voices

My voice throughout takes many forms. In this section of the book I use my researcher's voice. At other times my voice has been heard as the actor in my own story, as participant in Mike and Stephen's story, and you have also heard my voice as storyteller. Sometimes I have found it hard to allow my voice to be heard; juggling with old 'programmes' that I have carried as a woman, that maybe I do not have anything really important to say; old programmes that I have carried as a survivor, after many years of silence, that there are things I still should not tell and that people do not want to hear. Many students tell me of their lack of confidence in using their own voice, sometimes for similar reasons but sometimes also because they have been programmed into believing that research only speaks in graphs, figures and numbers – the language of the dominant discourse.

Even having overcome all of that, there is still the dilemma of how to express my voice as researcher in the midst of a study designed to capture the experiences of others, as well as mine. How do I balance out fairly so that I am received as genuinely open while also taking care of myself, and at the same time as I try to take care of Stephen and Mike? This juggling act is captured by Clandinin and Connelly (1994): 'The researcher is always speaking partially naked and is genuinely open to legitimate criticism from participants and from audience. Some researchers are silenced by the invitation to criticism contained in the expression of voice' (pp.423–424).

There are times when voices have been only partially heard (a Freudian slip occurred as I wrote this – I wrote vices instead of voices!). In my presentation of the research data I have chosen which stories to tell and which to leave out. Sometimes I have been very conscious of this and I am sure that there may also be times when I have not been aware. For example, I have struggled very consciously with one small story and have wondered if and where I could find a place for it. The story concerned pornography.

As I talked to Stephen about pornography I found myself disturbed to think that pornography can actually be helpful. I ask myself how this comes to be the case? How is it that images which sexually degrade both men and women are helpful to a young boy in reassuring him about his sexual identity? I realised that during our counselling I had not spent any time looking at this issue. I wanted to understand, so I asked him about it during our research interview:

Kim: *The other thing that kind of took me by surprise – and yet I must have known about it at the time – but reading your letter to your grandad, I was very powerfully confronted with the role pornography had played in your abuse. And I don't think I had actually – maybe I've been defending myself a bit here – but I've kind of forgotten about that and it seemed like quite a big important part in a way... I was quite surprised at how much there was about that in your story. I just wondered, as you look back at that now – how you see that and what you think about it. You know, there are these arguments about whether pornography is good or bad aren't there – what's your view? How do you see pornography as part of what happened to you now?*

I found myself wondering how often I and other women who counsel men or research men's issues have unconsciously avoided something that we may not have wanted to hear. Is it just as hard for male counsellors to hear? Is it not hard to hear for some male and female counsellors? Even as I listened to his answer I found myself wondering if I could bring myself to report what he said – that pornography was helpful. Yet I really understood his point of view (see p.226).

Listening to the tape as I transcribed it, I noticed a hesitation in Stephen's voice as we had that conversation. I wrote to him and asked him how he had felt at that point. He replied saying: 'I felt a bit embarrassed. Felt you might be disgusted that I had found pornography positive and helpful.' In the above instance I caught myself in time – how many times have I not noticed when I have avoided something too difficult to confront? In presenting the data so fully I hope you, the reader, will be able to see the answer to that question for yourself. Using Interpersonal Process Recall (IPR) as a research tool (Kagan 1984) enables the emergence of these questions, taking the process deeper and closer to fully understanding the meaning of what participants say.

Kohut (1971) comments that what the client has brought out into the open, after a struggle with resistance, shame or fear, may not seem important to us and we may pay attention to different stories. This may only become apparent to the client on reading the text after we have written it, or even published it, if we have not kept an ongoing process of connection with them as the writing develops. By then it may be too late. They may feel too ashamed or embarrassed to tell us and they may be left alone to deal with their injury to the self (Josselson 1996). Giving voice to people whose stories have been silenced means that we must do more than empower them to speak out or write about their lives. It means that we must also share with them the power to define the form as well as the content of their communication (Houston and Kramarae 1991).

Transcribing

Lapadat and Lindsay (1999) comment on the fact that the process of transcription, although routinely used in qualitative studies, is rarely commented upon in the research literature. It seems to me that if we exclude this important part of the process we are in danger of misrepresenting the whole research process. When we listen and transcribe audiotapes of research interviews we will almost certainly be making choices based upon the theories that we hold. Each individual researcher makes a decision about whether or not to transcribe, what to transcribe, and how to represent the transcription in their presentation. If we do not make the process explicit the readers will have no way of knowing how to interpret the findings and presented data.

Transcripts that stand alone without having the context of the lives of the speakers against which to hear them can be 'an impoverished basis for interpretation' (Kvale 1996, p.167). Kvale comments that analysis of the data begins during transcription. I would agree and for this reason I believe that a researcher who does not undertake this part of the work loses the opportunity that transcribing presents us with.

When we listen to the tapes and transcribe them personally we have an opportunity to pick up on nuances, hesitations, pauses, emphasis and the many other ways that people add meaning to their words. It is a difficult and time-consuming task but I believe that the outcome is more than worth the extra effort. Not only does it help us to listen and hear more of what we might have missed in the moment, but it also gives us a chance to check that we have been ethical. The following is an example of what I mean by this.

As I listened to the taped interview with Stephen I became aware of several questions that had arisen out of listening to the tape. I wondered at one point if I had bulldozed him into agreeing to use his diary, so I wrote and asked him. He replied saying:

> No, I was just shocked that you wanted to use it all! I thought you would just use it for background information and make perhaps a few quotes. Didn't imagine that anyone would find most of it that interesting or readable – seeing as it was so personal. Also felt it might be a bit confusing with all the different names, etc.
>
> As I said in my last note to you, I was a bit shocked and worried when I first read it in print. I think it was the fact that I had hidden it away on top of my wardrobe, covered in dust, safe and secure away from the world. I was even thinking of destroying it, so that no one close to me would read the pain and trauma involved. However, after talking to Stella and Mike, they both reassured me that it could be anonymous, and both gave their permission to go ahead. Also over the weeks I have realised more that it does show the dramatic changes that I went through – especially losing the guilt, and releasing rage and anger and being able to change jobs. From that a reader may get some encouragement to start the process of healing. However, please feel free to edit it at your discretion.

So transcribing became one of the ways of ensuring 'process consent'. It is often during most meaningful moments of conversation that voices drop and may be indecipherable – an ongoing relationship with the participants allow us the chance to return the text to them and asking them to fill in the gaps.

Sometimes, just one word can change the meaning and if we hand this part of the process over to a typist we may miss out on these minor points. Transcribing takes a great deal of time; it takes even more time if the quality of the recording is poor. For this reason it is advisable to take the time, trouble and money to invest in good equipment and to run a preliminary test before we begin to tape the conversation. Even then, of course, we can end up with a football match instead of an interview (see my research notes!).

Having transcribed the conversations and interviews with Mike and Stephen, I returned them to check for accuracy and to allow them to censor anything they were not happy to have included. Mike was concerned about how inarticulate he sounded and wondered if this hampered the reader's enjoyment or understanding, something that is often questioned by researchers themselves. Until we see such transcripts we are rarely aware how much of the spoken language is made up of incomplete sentences and incorrect use of grammar or language generally. I agreed with both the men that I would make minor alterations, removing some 'erms' and 'ums' and 'you knows' etc., and any other small adjustments that would contribute to the flow of the reading without changing the sense or meaning. Of course these changes do make a difference to the data and require a further check by participants to ensure that the meaning is intact following the changes made by the researcher. I have used transcripts in their original form (with some editing as stated above) because I wanted the reader to have as much of a sense of Mike and Stephen's experience as was possible. I believe that my reporting of conversations (which is only my interpretation of what is said) is sometimes less useful than allowing the reader to make their own interpretation from their position as 'a fly on the wall'. However, there have been times when I have reported parts of meetings (often for the sake of brevity) or created a 'story' or metaphor (see Chapter 25) which provides a distillation of an experience and has a value of its own.

The time spent transcribing is an important part of the immersion phase of heuristic research – noting our feelings and responses, we can enhance the depth and quality of the research process. At the end of the day, however, it is important to acknowledge that transcripts are social constructions, retellings and re-creations of stories that have already happened and not a faithful copy of a static world (Lapadat and Lindsay 1999).

CHAPTER 24

Sorting Data and Writing

Explication Phase

As I write down the stories that I have gathered during this research process I am doing more than chronicling events. I have found it difficult to avoid some form of evaluation of how and why events occur. I have looked for the meaning of the events for those who have experienced them but I have undoubtedly also added some of the meaning with which I have imbued those events. Although I have avoided interpreting the actions of others in the story where possible, using their own words, it would be naïve to think that my interpretations have not sneaked in somewhere – sometimes perhaps more than I have realised.

However, by exposing myself throughout those stories and my own connections with the data I have given you, the reader, an opportunity to decide for yourself what effect my subjective bias may have had on this writing and thinking with Mike and Stephen's stories.

In transforming the 'field text', contained in Part 1 (Stephen and Mike's stories) and the texts contained in Part 2 (poems, letters, interview material) into 'research text', I have had to find a way to say what I want to say as the researcher. Clandinin and Connelly (1994), reflect the point I have made earlier about the researcher's 'signature' being written too strongly, resulting in over-subjectivity. But they also warn of the consequences of a signature being written too thinly, when other texts or theories 'sign the work', or we give away our researcher role to participants and their 'field text'. I have found this to be part of my struggle – wanting to present the 'field text' with all of its authority, power and voice, but also wanting to find a way of being in there as myself. This struggle started at my first meeting with Mike and Stephen when we began to plan the book (see Chapter 22).

I have gathered some of the strongest stories together under chapter headings in Part 2 that form themes and categories in 'grounded theory' terms. These stories are simply descriptive narratives of central phenomena of the study that, when analysed and related to theoretical frameworks, become the core categories. Strauss and Corbin state: 'The core category must be the sun, standing in orderly systematic relationships to its planets' (1990, p.124). Sometimes particular stories have been chosen consciously because they are areas that I believe will be of particular interest to my audience and which may not have been written about by others.

I have had to repeatedly ask myself 'What are we doing here?' This question has helped me sort out where to place what. In the first research conversation (Chapter 22) this too was teased out and it was clear that one of the main purposes of the research was to use our experiences as client, counsellor and researcher to educate and assist others, potential clients, counsellors who are working in the field (and other helping professionals) and counselling researchers. There was a moment when this was illuminated in that early conversation when Mike said: 'But in the end if you make us too central to it, then it doesn't become useful…it just becomes a therapeutic process for us…'

Although at times I felt that the field texts were adequate unto themselves, I have had to remind myself that I am not writing only for myself or my ex-clients. Fortunately, the further exploration of meaning within the research text can also be therapeutic and meaningful for participants and myself: 'Just as serving the self serves the community, so too serving the community in research texts also serves the self' (Clandinin and Connelly 1994, p.425). So through my addition of theory and the meanings I have found in their stories, I may be able to add cognitive elements to their understanding which they did not previously have.

Audience

When we write of experiences we connect with humanity – deeply felt experiences shared with others through narrative form are probably the closest we can come to knowing what it is to be human. I have shared my clients' oral stories through being with them as their counsellor. I have shared their written and oral stories through being with them as researcher and now I want you, the reader, to share them as an audience. So I speak to you directly, seeking a relationship with you so that you may engage with us in this process of education, possible transformation and even perhaps political change.

In Part 2 I have tried to find ways of presenting my findings about my ex-clients' experience of their relationship with me, the counselling process and what they have identified as helpful or significant in their process of healing. I have contextualised these findings within the process by creating a loose framework of beginnings, middles and endings. The other context I have considered as a major influence is the societal context of patriarchy and male socialisation within it. I have also linked their stories with theories through which I have understood their stories and the literature that informed me. I have gathered stories from within the 'field texts' – those were the stories I heard, not necessarily the stories the men told – you can read for yourself the stories the men told. McAdams (1996) points out that even their stories, their data, are not 'precisely the same thing as the implicit, inner narrative the person has constructed over their lifetime in order to make sense of it. The inner narrative integrates the reconstructed past with their perception of the present and the anticipated future – providing that life with a sense of coherence, unity and purpose' (p.131).

As I immersed myself in the multi-layered texts I had gathered, I waited until a shape formed in my mind. Once again, I just began to write and trusted myself to allow whatever was really meaningful to unfold. But what was meaningful to me may not only be what is meaningful to you. It was my background as a woman who was aware of the impact of the socio-political culture on myself, first, and then upon the men in my previous study, that helped me hear those stories in my own particular way. You may hear other stories because of who you are and your own experiences – somewhere perhaps we might meet and recognise ourselves in each other.

I had a strong image as I was writing this of myself going up an escalator that was coming down and of meeting myself face to face. My counsellor self met my researcher self – and we recognised each other as the same. We turned together to travel in the same direction, in a way that meant I did not have to work against 'the tide'. The tide symbolises traditional, positivist research that excludes subjectivity and seeks for 'proof' – the flow is towards experience as legitimate in its own right. This is what I seek to explore both as a counsellor and a researcher. As I met myself on the escalator the research–practice gap (Fourie 1996) closed.

Narrative

Narrative is both a form of inquiry and a phenomenon in itself (a story). Both are linked together in this study of experience. Experience is both temporal and storied (Clandinin and Connelly 1994). In Stephen's story there is a strongly temporal quality as he diaries his experiences of living through a particular time. There is a 'shape' to this time beginning as it does, slowly with few words recorded in the early part and growing ever larger as the plot thickens and builds as the story crescendos to a peak. Slowly the peak subsides, until it peters out, ending with: 'Day at the seaside with Mum and Dad. Went OK, didn't talk about it at all, good to have a break.'

Embedded in this story is his letter to his grandfather (see Appendix 1) which describes a different time, when he was being abused; this story too is shaped by time. In both narratives there are scenes, where the action takes place; plots, as the events unfold over his lifetime; and characters, the actors in the narrative. All through his story there are other stories, the story of the counselling process among them – these are so linked that it has been hard to separate them, even though there is little documented in comparison to what is going on in his family story at the same time. My story and Sarasi's story duck and weave in and out of the plot, and Mike's story too. All these stories create other stories of meanings; meanings of the separate stories in isolation, but also meanings of the stories in relation to each other. Behind all of this there is a larger life story.

Mike's narrative is stylistically different but the story is almost the same; the characters, the scenes, the events, the plot, all present – just as they are in his brother's narrative; the larger life story, the story of counselling and bodywork too, but a different point of view – another person's life experience. Mike tells his story from his present-day position. He is not living in his story as he tells it – except of course he is; for as he writes yet another story is created which is the story of 'now'. Inserted into his narrative are moments of 'then' – snapshots of his story 'in action'. I added those parts to his narrative from other material he gave me to use, to illuminate, to bring into focus, to sharpen the picture. In doing this I took some responsibility to recreate his story. I returned the script to him, asking if he felt happy about this before I went ahead.

They also tell stories of their experiences of counselling, body therapy and their relationship with me. I tell of my own experiences and my responses to them as their stories unfold. The bottom line of course is that the final account is only one person's view. Kreiger (1991) comments: 'The person most responsible for putting those aspects together would be held accountable for the work in the end' (p.53). Therefore I must take responsibility and acknowledge my own interests and I must not lose sight of the 'additional authority our words and ideas carry when transferred into the permanence of print' (Josselson 1996).

A story is full and rich, coming as it does out of personal and social history. People lead storied lives and tell stories of those lives; whereas narrative researchers describe those lives, collect and tell stories of them and write narratives of experience (Clandinin and Connelly 1994). Each story is unique and this very uniqueness creates the greatest problems in writing those stories for publication. The struggle to maintain my professional and personal integrity, the integrity of the client and of the story, has meant that I have had to bear Mike and Stephen constantly in mind, every step of the way, as well as Sarasi with her involvement. I have tried to imagine all of them reading what I am writing, what they might think, feel, want or not want, while at the same time being true to myself. Having such a personal relationship with both men and with Sarasi, over a period of time, has meant that I believe I probably understand what they might need, desire and demand from me and this work – if not, they are able to let me know. This, I believe is one of the many advantages of undertaking research with people we know.

Validity

'How do you know they were telling the truth?' she asked, looking down at the table in front of her. It was as if she found it hard to meet my gaze. I sighed deeply, wondering again why it was that this question was rarely asked when the topic of people's research was exploration of people's experience of loss, bereavement, stress in the workplace, teenage pregnancy, etc., but so frequently asked about people's experiences of sexual abuse in childhood.

'She' was a member of a medical ethics committee and I had been called before them to explain a study that I was proposing to undertake. I had presented my previous study (Etherington 1995) as the starting point for further exploration of a newly proposed research project (for which I did eventually get ethics committee approval but no funding). She went on to ask me if I had heard of 'False Memory Syndrome'. I pointed out that I had included a chapter on it in my previous book and that I was very aware of the subject.

'False Memory Syndrome' has given rise to a very productive resurgence of interest in studying memory, trauma and repression (Orr 1999). In this way I believe the debate will, in the long term, have proved helpful. However, the question raised at the ethics committee made me aware of yet another level of potential harm that accusations made by the 'false memory' lobbyists may have caused. If research is blocked because of a 'syndrome' that is based on a view which denies the existence of dissociative amnesia and repression, for which there is now a great deal of scientific evidence which has been reviewed by Brown, Scheflin and Whitfield (1999), how will society be helped?

There are valid concerns about the uses of some techniques or suggestions used by some therapists that may interfere unnecessarily with a client's process of memory recovery and I have written in more details about the subject elsewhere (Etherington 1995). However, those who are interested in this debate will benefit from the well-documented findings of a plethora of recent research studies that have been collated by Marjory Orr, the founder of Accuracy About Abuse which now has its own website (Orr 1999).

Objective truth is still seen as the benchmark for 'good' research in traditional establishments. The idea that people have experiences and that social science is founded upon the study of those experiences is based upon a particular philosophical belief about the nature of 'truth' and knowledge, as I have discussed at the start of this section of the book. As I explained there, I do not aim for generalisability or objectivity. That is the language of positivism.

In presenting two 'case studies' I have explored the stories of two brothers, both of whom suffered the same kind of abuse, from the same abuser, over the same period of time. In this sense the term 'case study' does not denote a methodology, but the 'subject' that is being explored. In studying 'cases' I am seeking out what is common and what is unique (Stake 1995). Neither of these men had ever truly forgotten their experiences but they had coped by denying their reality. They had not wanted to think about their experiences of abuse, so they had separated them out from the rest of their lives. I asked Stephen about a question that I had raised in an earlier interview:

> Stephen: I've been thinking about that since you asked me about it. It never really went away but it was very suppressed within me. I'm upset now that even after it stopped I continued our relationship – but only as a grandfather – which makes me angry now. I regret that I didn't do anything about it when he was alive and now I'll never be able to – writing the letter to him helped.
>
> It did come back to me on occasions. He used to ask me to cut his nails when he was older and the close physical contact was very, very uncomfortable. I used to try and avoid it. He'd ask me 'oh will you...' because I was a nurse, I suppose. I used to feel nauseous because of the close contact as I was touching him. I feel really bad because when our children were very tiny, like babies, I was always very cautious about leaving him alone with them. I'd never be overt about it, but if I had to go and get something – I'd kind of hang about. I don't think I was thinking that he would actually do anything – it wasn't even in my mind because it was so suppressed, but I know there was something very deep in my consciousness that wanted me to be careful.

The facts of these stories become clearer as they develop; each new disclosure added weight to the horror of the impact their grandfather made on so many people's lives. Even so, their stories are both the same and very different, because they are very different people. If I collected data from one or two hundred men who had suffered childhood sexual abuse, they would all be different – so even a large number of subjects would not provide generalisable data. I might send out questionnaires to two thousand men who had been sexually abused, but like Mike and Stephen's, their stories too would be unique and we could not take for granted that any of that data would be generalisable. So I am not seeking generalisability. I am seeking to represent two men's experiences as truthfully as possible so that you, the reader, can discover if there is anything that will touch you and inform you.

Their experiences of their relationship with me and their experiences of the counselling process are individual, personal and their own; validity is not in question. However, it would be naïve of me not to comment on the absence of hostility or anger towards me in their accounts of counselling. Hillman (1983) reminds us that what is told depends upon who is listening, as well as the moment in the storyteller's life. I wrote to Stephen saying that I was very aware that he had been unable to say anything negative about our relationship and that I felt it would be most helpful if he could let me know of anything that he had found unhelpful. He wrote back saying:

> Yes, OK then; only a small thing!! Occasionally you did come over as having a 'Christian' viewpoint which I found mildly irritating. At the time I just said 'Yes! Yes!' and was glad when you moved on. I think I found this irritating because of the strong associations religious Christian people have with abuse for me. [Grandfather was an active Church member.] Now looking back – I am happy for you to hold such views, envious even, and fully respect your right to your own beliefs. But at the time it hit a RAW nerve! (Oops sorry! I hope I haven't upset you!).

Different perspectives on the same experience add colour, interest and depth. They also emphasise the uniqueness of being human; they also allow for triangulation (observing the same phenomena from different viewpoints). When I ask myself about validity in relation to this work, what I want to know is whether I have made sense of this data in a way that is meaningful to my participants, that resonates with their truths and my own. I have endeavoured to present as accurate a representation as possible of my own understanding of the many layers of experience and information that I have gathered in a way that is coherent, well founded, credible and resonant with the experiences that have been shared with me.

But Denzin cautions that 'there is no way to stuff a real life person between the covers of a text' (1989, p.82). Stories are not real life as it is lived and experienced, they are simply stories and cannot present factual accuracy; they can only highlight problems of representation. By presenting many of my stories as first person narratives, I have represented the presence of multiple voices. Reflecting upon the reality that problems of representation cannot necessarily be solved through research will help me to be cautious about making any assumptions or drawing any conclusions from what I have written (Rhodes 1996). In being open and reflexive throughout this study I have been able to reflect the many ambiguities, contradictions and questions that are some of the products of this many layered account, as well as share the richness, colour and textures of the fabric from which lives are woven.

CHAPTER 25

Where Three Streams Meet

The sun was setting as the traveller reached the place where the three streams met and flowed into a wide and beautiful river. It was autumn and the dying golden sun reflected the warm colours of the leaves on the trees that grew along the bank. The summer had lingered late this year and the evening air still held the remnants of the warmth of the day. The traveller was glad he had chosen this place to meet the brothers for the last part of their task together. He had arrived early so that he had time to gather his thoughts before their meeting.

The maps had been drawn – each one separately – and another larger one had been created combining all three routes, the traveller having included his own journey. When he had created the whole, the traveller had sent it to the brothers to examine, comment upon and validate as true to the journeys that they had made. He had dedicated much time and energy to the work and had become anxious to know how it had been received. Would the brothers recognise their routes? Would the traveller's representation of their experience be true for them?

As he waited, the traveller thought again about the swamp with its lifeless water and as he looked out across the river he was glad that he was no longer in that place. The water here flowed fast and clear. Overhead, birds gathered on the branches of the trees; vast swarms of starlings, like charcoal smudges on the darkening sky, flew in to settle for the night, the chattering sound of their collective voices fading to silence like a large family of children calling to each other as they snuggled down beneath their duvets, gradually letting go of the day. In the silence he heard small plopping sounds as fish leapt to catch the evening insects that swarmed just above the surface of the water. A lone heron flew across the sun towards a large untidy nest that swayed dangerously high among tall trees. The traveller marvelled at its awkward elegance as it settled for the night. A moorhen trod daintily between the reeds at the water's edge.

The traveller perched upon a fallen tree and waited. The younger brother was the first to appear and they greeted one another; then the older brother slipped into the clearing and they began to talk. The traveller asked them, 'Speak to me of what has passed in the making of our map?'

And so the brothers spoke. They spoke of the sadness of remembering the swamp; of being almost overwhelmed at times; of poring over and over the map late into the night, unable to put it down, searching for signs of their own particular footprints, noticing the ground that had been trodden by all three and the ground that was their own. They noticed the places where they had rested on their journeys and the places where they had met with people on the way – and whether those people had been friend or foe. They spoke of their uncertainty of knowing what the outcome would be; the power of seeing the journey mapped out before them on the page and of realising that even the warnings they had received did not entirely prepare them for their feelings upon reading the final scroll. They spoke of their concern for each other and for the traveller, who had been caught up in their journeys and had shared his own.

The traveller asked, 'What lies beneath this concern that each of you has for the other?' And the younger man spoke directly to his brother:

> My concern is another word for my love,
> For showing how much I value you
> And how much I care.
> You alone know the place where I have been
> As no one else can ever know
> And you are precious in my sight.
> I love you.

His brother received the love with brimming eyes and he could not, for a moment, speak. The traveller felt the depth of this moment of intimacy and knew that the making of the map had brought them even closer than they had ever been before.

And the traveller asked about their pain and sorrow, 'What of regrets – about deciding to retrace your footsteps, and draw your maps?'

And they had none – even the memory of the suffering they did not regret. They had seen how far they had come and marvelled at their present strength despite the swamp. They knew their feelings now were memories of times before, long passed – even if they sometimes felt anew.

And then the traveller asked the question he had carried deep within his heart, knowing it must be answered before this night had passed.

> The journeys have been mapped
> The stories have been told
> And now we must decide
> If we want them to unfold.
>
> This day has not yet ended
> And soon we three must part
> Knowing with integrity
> The feelings of our hearts.

> *We three might build a bonfire*
> *Cast our map upon the flames*
> *Or send it out into the world*
> *And have no further claim.*

The brothers were silent. The powerful moment of decision had come. The traveller knew within his heart that whatever they decided he would honour. It would not be a sacrifice to him. The journey and the making of the map were the creation – and creation could never be undone. The paper was not the map – the map was indelibly carved on his heart and mind.

And first the younger brother spoke: 'I have thought long about this question and know that my story should be told; if only for one single soul who's lost upon the road and seeks to find a way home, that alone would be enough. But then again – I want every part of my journey to be known. Nothing left out. There may be those who want to find a way to find those boys to use them for their evil ways and if perchance they find our map, let them find within those pages what horrors they create, let them know this map marks every sin upon their souls – let it shout to them loud and clear of the damage they have done.'

*Then the older brother spoke: 'At first I thought I'd find it hard to claim the right you offered me to wield the censor's pen. But instead it is the other way around. I find it hard to **give** that right to anybody – although my brother's right is clear and must be honoured. Never again do I want to permit my voice to go unheard – nothing vetoed – the unspeakable must be spoken by those who know. I bear witness for myself and all those who have been silenced in the past.'*

The traveller nodded, saying: 'And to that witness I add testimony by the work that I have done.'

The three sat in silence and watched the sun sink over the horizon. The day was over. And then the older brother spoke again, directly to the traveller: 'And what of you my friend? What has it meant to you?'

The traveller sat deep in thought for a long time and pondered upon this question. And finally he spoke: 'My heart is full of gladness that the map has now been drawn and that you are both satisfied with my work.'

Then he thought for a while and spoke again, hesitantly, understanding the answer to the question only as he spoke. He spoke of brotherhood, of bonding, of solidarity. In the making of the map and in the inclusion of his own journey, the traveller had ceased to feel alone. These brothers also understood his pain, his aloneness; his fears – as he had understood theirs. To hear and understand and to be heard and understood – he felt part of a brotherhood into which his own brothers had never admitted him.

Their voices murmured on and on, the water carrying the sound. The moon hung over the river in the early night – a full harvest moon, pale gold; a single bright star dangled beneath it in a sky not yet dark enough for other stars to shine. A golden carpet had been unrolled across the water in reflection, like a pathway inviting them, leading them ever onwards.

The two brothers rose to their feet and opened their arms to enfold the traveller and all three embraced with love before going on their way. And the river flowed on and on.

APPENDIX I

Stephen's Letter to his Dead Grandfather

(Written on 3–4 September 1995 between 22.00 hrs and 04.00 hrs)

Well, your secret's out now. I've stopped playing the dutiful grandson looking after his old 'GRAMPY'. I don't know how I went along with it; but I suppose I do. I can't deny, I did like you, enjoy your company, and feel sorry for you in your painful end. BUT the part of you I liked was as a 'grandad'; a REAL grandad, that I needed. The same grandad that as a *little* boy I adored and trusted, as a kind father-figure who gave me treats and spoiled me – as REAL grandads do.

I kept quiet while you were still alive because I valued that real grandad part of you. I had shut out what we did together for all those years because I didn't want that DELUSION shattered. For my sake, for Stella's sake, Mum and Dad's sake, and all the family's sake. I could not have coped with the consequences of being discovered; that would have jeopardised all that I love and value. While you were dying I was terrified that you would say something about what we had done. BUT at your funeral I was choking with grief for ME; trying to stay in control.

The family all around me must have thought, 'Poor Stephen, he was very close to his Grampy'; not knowing quite how close. OR DID SOME OF THEM KNOW, OR had some of your sons, daughter, grandsons, granddaughters REASON to feel the same as me? Your glowing eulogy poignantly impressed the full church, where you were held in such high regard. All I could see was you and me engaged in perverted sexual acts. Filled with self-loathing and disgust, a part of me wanted to shout out, 'HEY WAIT, YOU DON'T KNOW THE FULL STORY, HE WAS A FUCKING PERVERT who from when I was about seven years old SUCKED MY COCK and taught me how to suck his bigger long stiff one, until hot sticky white stuff shot out.' With lots of practice I enjoyed having my cock sucked and the nice feeling it gave me. I was fascinated with your cock as well; it was amazing. YES, I really enjoyed coming to see you when I was a little boy. Going to the pictures, staying up late, watching whatever I wanted on TV, lots of chocolate; EVERYTHING I wanted. I suppose I didn't say anything because, well you don't talk about 'willies' do you. Other people might not think it is the right thing to do. It couldn't have been wrong though, COULD IT Grampy?

I am 7 you are 59. Everyone loves you, looks up to you; you are a hero; you were in the war. You tell funny stories about when you were in the trenches and needed a colander to drain the vegetables. You held up a tin helmet until the German machine gun's bullets had made holes in it. Wow! My own Grampy did all those things! Oh, and you need some company to cheer you up 'cause Gran has just died. You like me so much you give me a German soldier's document case you captured in the war. You must think I'm very special. So NO, you wouldn't do anything wrong.

Well, I'm getting good at making your cock get stiff now. My cock stands stiff now and you like rubbing it and sucking it. I get funny feelings when you do that, you reassure me that it's nothing to worry about and that SOON I will be able to shoot 'spunk'. I really look forward to that day. I'm getting more hairs around my balls and cock now, so it shouldn't be too long to wait now.

Well, you were right, you managed to make me 'come' – in your mouth. Wow, what a funny feeling. It was, frightening but I liked it. 'It was worth all the practice wasn't it,' you say. With more practice and tuition, you are soon able to make me come again and again. I'm pretty good at it now aren't I – better than you even?

I really look forward to having sex now. I can make myself come at home now; it's really easy. I use a tissue and flush it down the toilet – I don't want to make a mess; Mum might want to know what I've been doing. Sometimes it happens when I am asleep. It's called a wet dream I think. I'm really embarrassed though; it leaves a stain on the sheets. I don't want to be discovered.

Well, Gramps, I've started secondary school now. Some of the boys bring in magazines with pictures of naked women in them. You can see their tits and fanny and some of them even have their legs wide open, showing EVERYTHING. I couldn't see so much though because everybody was trying to see. I'd like to have a good look at one of those magazines, to see what it really looks like. 'What's it like Gramps, doing it with a woman.' (I feel a bit awkward asking you this, 'cos well, I realise you must have done it with my Gran, 'cause she was your wife wasn't she?) I feel a bit confused about this, and maybe feel it's not quite right. Still you tell me it's no good with women, that their cunts are horrible smelly things. I feel a bit awkward – is this how you felt about my Gran?

Some of the girls at school are really pretty and fun. They tease us boys; a few of them don't mind if we grab their tits, they just giggle and laugh. I really like the girls in the choir at church. Me and my mate Oliver, well we've had snogging sessions in the long grass in the churchyard. They are older than us, Gramps, very well developed. I even brushed my hand against one of their tits – I don't think she noticed. There's this new paper, 'The Sun', they show women's tits in it. I've managed to get a few. When I look at them I feel stiff, and I come very easily.

Something funny happened today, Gramps. Dad was bossing me around as usual; sent me to fetch something from his bedroom. While I was looking for whatever it was, I saw a magazine under his bed, like the ones the boys had in school. I was shocked. Why had my Dad got one of those? Surely my Mum can't be very pleased at him looking at pictures of other naked women.

I ask you Gramps if you can get me one of these magazines. You don't but you do let me read a book. It's called 'School for Sex'. It's a very tatty paperback, but bloody hell, it's really filthy. It's amazing, I didn't know men and women did those things. There's lots of men and women doing things to each other at the same time. You say it's no good with a woman, but I wouldn't mind trying some of those things when I'm older.

Oh by the way, Gramps, I don't think we should do it when Uncle Clive and Auntie Sue are in the next bedroom. They might hear us; people might find out. BUT I still like all the other things we do, like going out for treats, etc. I still like the sex *but* only when there's no chance of being discovered.

Well, Gramps, my curiosity got the better of me. When Mum and Dad were out I looked for Dad's magazine. It wasn't under the bed, but I found it in his cupboard. Cor blimey, you wouldn't believe some of the other magazines that were there! There's one, it must be Swedish I suppose, it shows everything.

I saw some more really good stuff. My friend in the choir, Freddie, well his Dad's in the army, and they have just returned from living in Germany. Freddie showed me this picture of an orgy, cocks, mouths in cunts, everything!

I feel bad about looking at my Dad's stuff now, but it serves him right for having it. I can't get those pictures out of my head though; I wank thinking about them. When you're tossing me off, or sucking me off, I think about doing it with a woman.

By the way Gramps, I don't want anybody to know about what we do. You scare me sometimes when you take risks. I didn't like it that time when I was younger, when you were rubbing my cock, when Mum and Dad were in the SAME ROOM! I was playing with my toys, laid on the floor; you had your arm over the side of the settee, rubbing my PENIS. I don't think you should have done that. I felt embarrassed that time in the cinema, when you put your coat over our laps and you played with me. WHAT if we had been seen, we might have been arrested or something.

A holiday in Ireland, what me! Great! Go on an aeroplane! I've never flown; come back on a ship! Wow! Well I enjoyed flying and seeing Ireland, but when you were doing things to me I was scared we would be discovered. When we were eating breakfast in the hotel I was thinking: 'What if those people knew what I was doing last night?'

I didn't like it on that holiday in Devon with Mum and Dad. They were in the NEXT ROOM. What if they had heard? No, we must only do it when we are alone. Uncle Clive and Auntie Sue will be moving out soon. It will be safer then.

I don't know why, Gramps, but I get very embarrassed at school when it's games. I feel really shy and try not to let anyone see my cock in the changing rooms or showers. Most of the others aren't embarrassed; they boast about how big they are and show off. I feel very awkward and self-conscious. I figure it's because I've got a small one. BUT looking back now I think it was because I was ASHAMED of myself.

A holiday in SPAIN! Why, that's abroad! Fantastic, but I won't want to do anything – you know. You say that's OK, that my cousin Bill will be coming as well, so there won't be sex. I enjoyed that holiday and felt safe because Bill was there.

Well, now you're on your own. Auntie Sue and Uncle Clive have moved out. I am able to relax more. I read 'School for Sex' while you make me come. It's about this time that you try to bugger me, you BASTARD. You tried to stick your cock up my arse but it wouldn't fit. I was in agony so you stopped. Then later I stuck my penis into you, but I couldn't do it because I was so DISGUSTED. This image still haunts me now. HOW COULD YOU DO THOSE THINGS TO YOUR OWN GRANDSON?

NOW I'VE LEARNED YOU WERE BUGGERING MY BROTHER AT THE SAME TIME! AND GOD KNOWS WHO ELSE. YOU FUCKING BASTARD. RIGHT NOW, WRITING THIS, IF YOU WERE HERE, I COULD KILL YOU, WITH MY HANDS. The other night I woke up dreaming I was strangling you.

REMARKABLY, I don't know how I kept this part of my life separate, shut away. NO THANKS to you, I do have many happy memories of my childhood, of good friends, and *normal* relationships. Although looking back, thanks to you, I was very shy, self-conscious and nervous in large groups of people, UNLIKE MY BROTHER.

YOU COMPLETELY TOOK AWAY, STOLE HIS CHILDHOOD AND I AM VERY ANGRY ABOUT THAT – I COULD SMASH YOUR HEAD TO A PULP FOR THIS if you were here. BUT YOU'RE NOT – YOU GOT AWAY WITH IT. YOU CRAFTY CUNNING BASTARD. YOU WERE SO LUCKY. DID YOU LIKE THE RISK, THE DANGER, YOU BASTARD. LOOK AT THE FACES OF YOUR CHILDREN, YOUR GRANDCHILDREN, YOUR WIFE, OTHER VICTIMS, CHURCH, GOD, etc.

To get back to telling you how I survived despite you, YOU PAEDOPHILIC PERVERT; I must be 14 now and I'm feeling guilty, disgusted, ashamed of what we do. I've got my own magazine now and I wank myself stupid, trying to reassure myself I'm not queer. BUT I CAN'T BREAK THE HABIT OF EJACULATING WITH YOU. WHY, OH WHY, OH WHY?

I fall madly in love with a choirgirl who is about 15. More snogging a few times, but it does not mean as much to her as it does to me. Then me and my friend Oliver become friendly with a few girls from school. We meet every dinnertime, supposedly to look after all the science laboratory animals. Oliver and I lust after the girls which I'm sure they realise. We meet out of school; I pair up with Susan. We go 'out together' for a few months. I fall madly in love. Lots of kissing and she lets me play with her breasts, but no further. She doesn't touch my penis but she knows it's stiff as I'm lying on top of her. This is mind blowing! I'm normal after all! Unfortunately Susan moves, and I'm out of luck. However, we remain platonic friends to this day.

So after a few glorious months you get me back YOU BASTARD, as I'm under your spell and in a HABIT. I FEEL MORE GUILTY ABOUT IT. I know for sure it's wrong but *CAN'T* STOP.

You're retired now, working part-time at the library. You bring home all the crude books you can find. I'm 15–16 now, feeling more and more ashamed and guilty and seeing you, then feeling sick immediately after ejaculating. I'm also wanking myself silly with the porn to prove to myself I'm normal.

I start work at 16. Our sex becomes less frequent. I meet new people at work. I realise I'm sick. I am full of guilt and shame, I want to stop. My Dad is horrible to me, which MAKES ME SEEK COMFORT FROM YOU; THE HABIT CONTINUES.

My body is in turmoil. I want to be NORMAL. I want to be FUCKED BY A WOMAN; TO BE CURED. I flirt with girls at work but I am shy. I realise I must stop it. SO I DO – AGED 18!

AGHHH – YOU BASTARD ?, 2, 3, 4, 5, 6, 7,? – 18 years!

So I tell you it's stopped and say ' No thank you' when you offer. I still see you often, but not for sex, just as my GRANDAD.

Maggie, a student, comes to work for the summer holidays in my office. She is older than me but is also very shy. We get on well. She also lacks confidence and self-esteem. We date, fall in 'love' and quickly progress to heavy petting in the car, and then for a few glorious months we discover REAL SEX. It's difficult at first as we are both virgins (although me not a PROPER one). WE do everything I ever dreamed of and I FEEL CURED; RELEASED FROM YOU.

Maggie goes back to college. I visit a few times, but we drift apart.

An old family friend, Wendy, knows of my problems with my father and meets me for a lunchtime drink once a week. She is a lovely person whom I admire and look up to. She is also very attractive, and I long for her to whisk me off and seduce me! I now feel very sure of my sexual orientation.

My disgusting experiences with you are going from my mind. I am NORMAL, I've had sex with Maggie – even took her to meet you (as a grandfather). You continue to make suggestive comments, but nothing happens. I agree to go on holiday with you to the Isle of Wight. We don't have sex but I talk frankly with you. I don't hold any grudge or anger, I just see it as having stopped. I ask you about what happened. You have no regrets; see it as perfectly natural. Tell me you were in love with another man before you got married. That it's perfectly natural. We leave it there and never discuss it again.

About a year later I meet Stella during my training. We fall passionately in LOVE and marry. My life is complete; I am happy, I've made it in despite everything. I've made it.

The memories are buried, gone, repressed. I don't even think about them. Stella thinks you are lovely, fun. I enjoy your company. I occasionally get a bit nervous if you say something suggestive. You ask me to cut your toe nails – this turns my stomach – the close contact, the touching, stirs up memories, but they pass. Then we all get back to playing happy families; lovely old grandad; dutiful grandson. I even let you *HOLD OUR CHILDREN*; I am a little wary, but the memories are so far under I only see you as a grandad now.

THAT MAKES ME REALLY ANGRY, I WAS LIVING A LIE. I WAS BEING DISHONEST TO STELLA and MYSELF. I couldn't face up to the pain of disclosure. I was going to take my secret to my grave. Anyway, it would be safe soon, just as soon as you died. JUST SO LONG AS YOU DIDN'T SAY ANYTHING.

[I stop here and draw my flashbacks – I am amazed. I draw one like I am looking down on myself and him on the bed. I notice that I had drawn myself as physically 'mature', and therefore GUILTY and RESPONSIBLE. So I drew another picture of myself as a small naked child standing next to HIM as a 59-year-old naked man to redress the balance.]

APPENDIX 2

Resource List

If you would like to find somebody to talk to about your own experiences of abuse you can use some of the contacts below as a starting point.

British Association for Counselling
1 Regent Place
Rugby CV21 2PJ
Tel: 01788 578238

The above organisation has a directory which includes information about voluntary organisations that provide counselling as well as details of counsellors who work in private practice. Many voluntary organisations use trainee counsellors, although some use well-qualified and experienced counsellors. If you telephone BAC they will send you a printout of the directory pages covering your area. It is advisable to check the qualifications, approach to the work, experience and whether or not they are in supervision and have had their own therapy. Choose a few to phone and visit for a one-off meeting to see if you think you could work with them. Think of a list of questions that you might like to ask a counsellor before you commit to a contract and see if their answers match your requirements and how they respond to being questioned.

Those listed in the BAC directory as BAC Accredited have had to go through a process of selection over and above that which is required by their training institution. However, there are some counsellors who have not gone through this process who are very good at the work. It is important that you choose someone, so try and meet a few before deciding.

Survivors of Sexual Abuse: this is a helpline which offers a free counselling service to both male and female survivors; they use both male and female counsellors. They also run groups in Hounslow, Harrow and Twickenham which are facilitated by survivors: Tel: 020-8890 4732.

Rape Crisis Centres, Mind and **SANE** are also useful starting places (see your local phone book).

Survivors: runs groups for men and offers individual counselling. Helpline available Tuesday 7–10 pm. Tel: O20-7833 3737. Address: PO Box 2470, London SW9 9ZP.

Childline: although primarily for children, they have some information about groups and counsellors for survivors throughout the country. Tel: 020-7239 1000.

MASH: Bristol helpline for men open Thursday evenings only. Tel: 0117-9077100.

DABS (Directory and Book Services): phone line for list of counsellors for abuse survivors and for information about useful books. 79 Copley Road, Doncaster, South Yorkshire DN1 2QP. Tel: 01302-768689.

Accuracy about Abuse:
    P.O. Box 3125
    London
    NW3 5QG
    Tel: (44) 020-7431 5339
    Fax: (44) 020-7433 3101
    Website: www.accuracyaboutabuse.org

An organisation set up to provide accurate information about those concerned about 'false memory'. They provide information about recommended books and research data (among other things). It now has its own website which contains all the backcopies of its newsletters. There is a lot of helpful information held here.

Bibliography

Ainsworth, M.D.S. (1989) 'Attachments beyond infancy.' *American Psychologist* 44, 709–716.
Alexander, P.C. (1992) 'Application of attachment theory to the study of sexual abuse.' *Journal of Consulting and Clinical Psychology 60*, 185–195.
Allen, L. (1990) 'A client's experience of failure.' In D. Mearns and W. Dryden (eds) *Experiences of Counselling in Action*. London: Sage.
American Psychiatric Association (1980) *Diagnostic and Statistical Manual of Mental Disorders*, 3rd edn (DSM-III). Washington, DC: APA.
American Psychiatric Association (1994) *Diagnostic and Statistical Manual of Mental Disorders*, 4th edn (DSM-IV). Washington, DC: APA.
Angoff, C. (1994) 'Preface.' In A. Lerner (ed) *Poetry in the Therapeutic Experience*, 2nd edn. St Louis: MMB Music.
BAC (British Association for Counselling) (1996) *Ethical Guidelines for Monitoring, Evaluation and Research in Counselling*. Rugby: BAC.
Barker, P. (1991) *Regeneration*. London: Penguin.
Bays, B. (1999) *The Journey*. London: Thorsons.
Bear, Z. (ed) (1998) *Good Practice in Counselling People who have been Abused*. London: Jessica Kingsley Publishers.
Beauchamp, T.L. and Childress, J.F. (1979) *Principles of Biomedical Ethics*. Oxford: Oxford University Press.
Bennet, G. (1987) *The Wound and the Doctor*. London: Secker and Warburg.
Berne, E. (1961) *Transactional Analysis in Psychotherapy*. New York: Grove Press.
Bettelheim, B. (1976) *The Use of Changement*. New York: Knopf.
Black, W. (1994) 'Why we need qualitative research.' *Journal of Epidemiology and Public Health* 48, 425–426.
Blaxter, M. (1996) 'Criteria for the evaluation of qualitative research papers.' *Medical Sociology News 22*, 1, 68–71.
Bliss, S. (1994) 'Ericksonian application in the use of art in therapy.' In J.K. Zeig (ed) *Ericksonian Methods: The Essence of the Story*. New York: Brunner/Mazel.
Bliss, S. and Wilborn, B. (1992) 'The art process in therapy.' *TCA Journal 20*, 3–8.
Boadella, D. (1988) 'Biosynthesis.' In J. Rowan and W. Dryden (eds) *Innovative Therapy in Britain*. Buckingham: Open University Press.
Bolton, F.G., Morris, L. and MacEachron, A. (1989) *Males at Risk: The Other Side of Sexual Abuse*. Newbury Park, CA: Sage.

Bolton, G. (1999) *The Therapeutic Potential of Creative Writing.* London: Jessica Kingsley Publishers.
Bond, T. (1993) *Standards and Ethics for Counselling in Action.* London: Sage.
Boulton, M. and Fitzpatrick, R. (1997) 'Evaluative qualitative research.' *Evidence Based Health Policy Management 1*, 83–85.
Bowlby, J. (1969) *Attachment and Loss: vol. 1. Attachment.* New York: Basic Books.
Bowlby, J. (1973) *Attachment and Loss: vol. 2. Separation.* New York: Basic Books.
Braun, B.G. (1988a) 'The BASK model of dissociation, Part 1.' *Dissociation 1*, 1, 4–23.
Braun, B.G. (1988b) 'The BASK model of dissociation, Part 2: Clinical applications.' *Dissociation 1*, 2, 16–23.
Brown, D., Scheflin, A.W. and Whitfield, D. (1999) 'Recovered memories: the current weight of the evidence in science and in the courts.' *The Journal of Psychiatry and Law 27*, 5–156.
Burgess, A., Hazelwood, R., Rokous, F. and Hartmen, C. (1987) 'Serial rapists and their victims: re-enactment and repetition.' Presented at the New York Academy of Sciences Conference on 'Human Sexual Aggression: Current Perspectives', New York City.
Campbell, J. (1972) *The Hero with a Thousand Faces.* Princeton, NJ: Princeton University Press.
Carlson, S. (1990) 'The victim/perpetrator: turning points in therapy.' In M. Hunter (ed) *The Sexually Abused Male vol. 2.* Lexington, MA: Lexington Books.
Carroll, M. (in press) 'Supervision in and for organisations.' In M. Carroll and M. Tholstrupp (eds) *Integrative Approaches to Supervision: Proceedings of the 1999 BASPR Conference.* London: Sage.
Charon, R. (1994) 'The narrative road to empathy.' In H. Spiro, M. McCrea-Curnen, E. Peschel and D. St James (eds) *Empathy and the Practice of Medicine: Beyond Pills and the Scalpel.* New Haven, CT: Yale University Press.
Clandinin, D.J. and Connelly, F.M. (1994) 'Personal experience methods.' In N.K. Denzin and Y.S. Lincoln (eds) *Handbook of Qualitative Research.* London: Sage.
Combs, G. and Freedman, J. (1994) 'Milton Erickson: early postmodernist.' In J.K. Zeig (ed) *Ericksonian Methods: The Essence of the Story.* New York: Brunner/Mazel.
Cook, J. and Fonow, M.M. (1986) 'Knowledge and women's interests: issues of epistemology and methodology in feminist sociological research.' *Sociological Inquiry 56*, 2–27.
Damasio, A. (1994) *Descartes' Error: Emotion, Reason and the Human Brain.* New York: Avon.
Davies, J.M. and Frawley, M.G. (1994) *Treating the Adult Survivor of Childhood Sexual Abuse: A Psychoanalytical Perspective.* New York: Basic Books.
Denzin, N.K. (1989) *Interpretive Biography.* Beverley Hills, CA: Sage.
Denzin, N.K. and Lincoln, Y.S. (eds) (1994) *Handbook of Qualitative Research.* Newbury Park, CA: Sage.
DeSchazer, S. (1991) *Putting Difference to Work.* New York: Norton.
De Vault, M. (1997) 'Personal writing in social research.' In R. Hertz (ed) *Reflexivity and Voice.* London: Sage.
Devereux, G. (1967) 'Unconscious meaning of research.' In G. Devereux *From Anxiety to Method in the Behavioural Sciences.* The Hague: Mouton.

Dolan, Y. (1994) 'On the treatment of sexual abuse.' In J.K. Zeig (ed) *Ericksonian Methods: The Essence of the Story*. New York: Brunner/Mazel.

Douglas, B. and Moustakas, C. (1985) 'Heuristic inquiry: the internal search to know.' *Journal of Humanistic Psychology 25*, 3, 39–55.

Dryden, W. and Yankura, J. (1992) *Daring to be Myself*. Buckingham: Open University Press.

Edgar, K. (1994) 'The epiphany of the self via poetry therapy.' In A. Lerner (ed) *Poetry in the Therapeutic Experience*. St Louis: MMB Music.

Edwards, A. and Talbot, R. (1994) *The Hard Pressed Researcher*. London: Longman.

Edwards, R. (1993) 'An education in interviewing.' In C.M. Renzetti and R.M. Lee (eds) *Researching Sensitive Topics*. London: Sage.

Egan, G. (1994) *The Skilled Helper*, (5th edn). Pacific Grove, CA: Brooks/Cole.

Egeland, B., Jacobvitz, D. and Sroufe, A.L. (1988) 'Breaking the cycle of abuse.' *Child Development 59*, 1080–1088.

Ellis, C., Kiesinger, C.E. and Tillman-Healy, L.M. (1997) 'Interactional interviewing: talking about emotional experiences.' In R. Hertz (ed) *Reflexivity and Voice*. London: Sage.

Ernst, S. and Goodison, L. (1981) *In Our Own Hands: A Book of Self-help Therapy*. London: Women's Press.

Etherington, K. (1995) *Adult Male Survivors of Childhood Sexual Abuse*. Brighton: Pavilion Publishing.

Etherington, K. (1996) 'The counsellor as researcher: boundary issues and critical dilemmas.' *British Journal of Guidance and Counselling 24*, 3, 339–346.

Etherington, K. (1998) 'Establishing a discourse between GPs and counsellors.' *Journal of the Counselling in Medical Settings Division of BAC 55*, 65–67.

Felitti, V. (1998) 'Childhood trauma tied to adult illness.' *American Journal of Preventative Medicine 14*, 245–258.

Finkelhor, D. and Browne, A. (1986) 'Initial and long-term effects: a conceptual framework.' In D. Finkelhor (ed) *A Sourcebook on Child Sexual Abuse*. Beverly Hills, CA: Sage.

Fisher, M. and Brother Francis (1999) 'Soul pain and the therapeutic use of ritual.' *Psychodynamic Counselling 5*, 1, 53–72.

Foucault, M. (1980) *Power/Knowledge*. New York: Pantheon.

Fourie, D. (1996) 'The research–practice gap in psychotherapy: from discovering reality to making sense.' *Journal of Contemporary Psychotherapy 26*, 1, 7–20.

Frank, A.W. (1995) *The Wounded Storyteller*. London: University of Chicago Press.

Frankl, V. (1963) *Man's Search for Meaning*. Boston: Beacon Press.

Freedman, J. and Combs, G. (1996) *Narrative Therapy: A Social Construction of Preferred Realities*. London: Norton.

Freud, A. (1946) *Ego and the Mechanisms of Defence*, vol. 2 (revised). Madison, CO: International Universities Press.

Freud, S. (1912) 'Recommendations to physicians practising psychoananlysis.' In J. Strachey (ed and trans.) *The Standard Edition of the Complete Works of Sigmund Freud*, vol. 17. London: Howarth Press.

Freud, S. (1955) 'Group psychology and the analysis of the Ego.' In J. Strachey (ed. and trans.) *The Standard Edition of the Complete Works of Sigmund Freud*, vol. 18. London: Howarth Press.

Freund, K.R., Watson, R. and Dickey, R. (1988) 'Does sexual abuse in childhood cause paedophilia?' Joint Study of the Department of Behavioural Sexology and the Forensic Division, Clarke Institute of Psychiatry, Toronto, Ontario, Canada.

Freyd, J. (1996) *Betrayal Trauma: The Logic of Forgetting Childhood Abuse*. Cambridge, MA and London: Harvard University Press.

Friedrich, W.N. (1995) *Psychotherapy with Sexually Abused Boys: An Integrated Approach*. London: Sage.

Friedrich, W.N., Einbender, A.J. and Luecke, W.J. (1983) 'Cognitive and behavioural characteristics of physically abused children.' *Journal of Consulting and Clinical Psychology 51*, 313–314.

Gabriel, L. (1999) 'Practitioner–Researcher Role Conflict, May,' Paper presented at BAC Research Conference. Leeds, Hilton Hotel.

Geertz, C. (1973) *The Interpretation of Culture: Selected Essays*. New York: Harper and Row.

Geertz, C. (1983) *Local Knowledge*. New York: Basic Books.

Gendlin, E. (1978) *Focusing*. New York: Everest House.

Gendlin, E. (1996) *Focusing-oriented Psychotherapy. A Manual of the Experiential Method*. New York: Guilford Press.

Gerber, P.N. (1990) 'Victims becoming offenders: a study of ambiguities.' In M. Hunter (ed) *The Sexually Abused Male*, vol. 1. Lexington, MA: Lexington Books.

Gergen, K.J. (1990) 'Social understanding and the inscription of self.' In J.W. Steigler, R.A. Sneider and G. Herdt (eds) *Cultural Psychology: Essays on Comparative Human Development*. Cambridge: Cambridge University Press.

Gergen, K.J. (1991) *The Saturated Self: Dilemmas of Identity in Contemporary Life*. New York: Basic Books.

Gilgun, J.F. (1990) 'Factors mediating the effects of childhood maltreatment.' In M. Hunter (ed) *The Sexually Abused Male*, vol 1. Lexington, MA: Lexington.

Gilligan, C. (1991) 'The psyche lives in a medium of culture: how shall we talk of love?' Paper presented at the American Psychological Association 99th Annual Convention. August 16th–20th, San Francisco.

Glaser, B.G. and Strauss, A. (1967) *The Discovery of Grounded Theory*. Chicago: Aldine.

Godin, J. and Ooghourlian, J-M. (1994) 'The transitional gap in metaphor and therapy.' In J.K. Zeig (ed) *Ericksonian Methods: The Essence of the Story*. New York: Brunner/Mazel.

Goleman, D. (1996) *Emotional Intelligence*. London: Bloomsbury.

Grafanaki, S. (1996) 'How research can change the researcher: the need for sensitivity, flexibility and ethical boundaries in conducting qualitative research in counselling and psychotherapy.' *British Journal of Guidance and Counselling 24*, 3, 329–338.

Greenhalgh, T. and Hurwitz, B. (1999) 'Why study narrative?' *British Medical Journal 318*, 7175, 48–50.

Greig, E. and Betts, T. (1992) 'Epileptic seizures induced by sexual abuse. Pathogenic and pathoplastic factors.' *Seizure 1*, 269–274.

Grierson, M. (1990) 'A client's experience of success.' In D. Mearns and W. Dryden (eds) *Experiences of Counselling in Action*. London: Sage.
Groth, A.N. and Burgess, A.W. (1979) 'Sexual trauma in the life histories of rapists and child molesters.' *Victimology: An International Journal 4*, 10–16.
Groth, A.N. and Hobson, W.F. (1983) 'The dynamics of sexual assault.' In L.B. Schlesinger and E. Revitch (eds) *Sexual Dynamics of Antisocial Behaviour*. Springfield, IL: Charles C. Thomas.
Groth, A.N. and Oliveri, F.J. (1989) 'Understanding sexual offence behaviour and differentiating among sexual abusers: basic conceptual issues.' In S. Sgroi (ed) *Vulnerable Populations*, vol. 2. Lexington, MA: Lexington Books.
Guggenbühl-Craig, A. (1971) *Power in the Helping Professions*. Dallas: Spring.
Haaken, J. (1998) *Pillar of Salt: Gender, Memory and the Perils of Looking Back*. London: Free Association Books.
Halpern, J. (1993) 'Empathy: using resonance emotions in the service of curiosity.' In H.M. Spiro, M.G. McCrea-Curnen, E. Peschel and D. St James (eds) *Empathy and the Practice of Medicine: Beyond Pills and the Scalpel*. London: Yale University Press.
Hammersley, M. and Atkinson, P. (1995) *Ethnography: Principles in Practice*. London: Tavistock.
Harber, K.D. and Pennebaker, J.W. (1992) 'Overcoming traumatic memories.' In S. Christianson (ed) *The Handbook of Emotion and Memory: Research and Theory*. Hillsdale, NJ: Lawrence Erlbaum.
Henderson, P. (2000) 'Supervising counsellors in primary care.' In S. Wheeler and D. King (eds) *Supervising Counsellors: Issues and Responsibility*. London: Sage.
Heninger, O.E. (1994) 'Poetry therapy in private practice: an odyssey into the healing power of poetry.' In A. Lerner (ed) *Poetry in the Therapeutic Experience*. St Louis: MMB Music.
Herman, J. (1981) *Father–Daughter Incest*. Cambridge, MA: Harvard University Press.
Herman, J. (1992) *Trauma and Recovery*. New York: Basic Books.
Heron, J. (1981) 'Human inquiry: a sourcebook for new paradigm research.' In P. Reason and J. Rowan (eds) *Human Inquiry*. New York: Wiley.
Hertz, R. (ed) (1997) *Reflexivity and Voice*. London: Sage.
Hillman, J. (1983) *Healing Fiction*. Woodstock: Spring Publications.
Hindman, J. (1988) 'New insight into adult and juvenile sex offenders.' *Community Safety Quarterly 1*, 4, 1.
Houston, M. and Kramarae, C. (1991) 'Speaking from silence: methods of silencing and of resistance.' *Discourse and Society 2*, 4, 425–437.
Howe, D. (1993) *On Being a Client – Understanding the Process of Counselling & Psychotherapy*. London: Sage.
Howe, D. (1996) 'Client experiences of counselling and treatment interventions: a qualitative study of family views of family therapy.' *British Journal of Guidance and Counselling 24*, 3, 367–375.
Hull, J.B. (1997) *Listening to the Body: Common Boundary*. Internet.
Hunter, M. (1990) *The Sexually Abused Male: Prevalence, Impact and Treatment*. vol. 1. Lexington, MA: Lexington Books.

Hunter, M. (ed) (1995) *Adult Survivors of Sexual Abuse: Treatment Innovations.* London: Sage.

Janesick, V.J. (1994) 'The dance of qualitative research design: metaphor and methodology and meaning.' In N.K. Denzin and Y.S. Lincoln (eds) *Handbook of Qualitative Research.* London: Sage.

Johns, H. (1997) *Personal Development in Counsellor Training.* London: Cassell.

Johns, H. (ed) (1998) *Balancing Acts. Studies in Counselling Training.* London: Routledge.

Johnson, R. and D. Shrier (1987) 'Past sexual victimisations by females of male patients in an adolescent medicine clinic population.' *American Journal of Psychiatry 1445*, 650–652.

Josselson, R. (ed) (1996) *Ethics and Process in the Narrative Study of Lives*, vol. 4. London: Sage.

Jourard, S. (1968) *Disclosing Man to Himself.* New York: Van Nostrand Reinhold.

Kagan, N. (1984) 'Interpersonal process recall: basic methods and recent research.' In D. Larsen (ed) *Teaching Psychological Skills.* Monterey, CA: Brooks/Cole.

Kahn, M. (1997) *Between Therapist and Client.* New York: W.H. Freeman.

Kardiner, A. and Spiegel, H. (1947) *War, Stress and Neurotic Illness (rev. ed. The Traumatic Neuroses of War).* New York: Hoeber.

Karen, R. (1994) *Becoming Attached.* New York: Warner Books.

Kaufman, G. (1996) *The Psychology of Shame.* New York: Springer.

Kelly, L. (1988) *Surviving Sexual Violence.* Cambridge: Polity Press.

Kemshall, H. and Pritchard, J. (eds) (2000) *Good Practice in Working with Victims of Violence.* London: Jessica Kingsley Publishers.

Kershaw, C.J. (1994) 'Restorying the mind: using therapeutic narrative in psychotherapy.' In J.K. Zeig (ed) *Ericksonian Methods: The Essence of the Story.* New York: Brunner/Mazel.

Kinsey, A.C., Pomeroy, W.B., Martin, C.E. and Gebhard, P.H. (1953) *Sexual Behaviour in the Human Female.* Philadelphia: W.B. Saunders.

Kitchener, R.S. (1984) 'Intuition, critical evaluation and ethical principles: the foundation for ethical decisions in counselling psychology.' *Counselling Psychologist 12*, 43–55.

Kleinman, A. (1988) *The Illness Narrative.* New York: Basic Books.

Kohut, H. (1971) *The Analysis of the Self: A Systematic Approach to the Psychoanalytic Treatment of Narcisstic Personality Disorder.* New York: International Universities Press.

Kohut, H. (1977) *The Restoration of the Self.* New York: International Universities Press.

Kohut, H. (1984) 'How does analysis cure?' In A. Goldberg and P.E. Stepansky (eds) *How Does Analysis Cure?* Chicago: Chicago University Press.

Kramer, P. (1993) 'Empathic immersion.' In H.M. Spiro, M.G. McCrea-Curnen, E. Peschel and D. St James (eds) *Empathy and the Practice of Medicine: Beyond Pills and the Scalpel.* London: Yale University Press.

Kreiger, S. (1991) *Social Science and the Self.* New Brunswick, NJ: Rutgeis University Press.

Kvale, S. (ed) (1996) *Psychology and Post-modernism.* London: Sage.

Lamin, A.D. and Murray, E. (1987) 'Catharsis Versus Psychotherapy.' Unpublished manuscript, University of Miami.

Lapadat, J.C. and Lindsay, A.C. (1999) 'Transcription in research and practice: from standardization of technique to interpretive positionings.' *Qualitative Inquiry 5*, 1, 64–86.

Launer, J. (1999) 'A narrative approach to mental health in general practice.' *British Medical Journal 318*, 7176, 117–119.

LeDoux, J. (1992) *The Emotional Brain.* New York: Simon and Schuster.

Lerner, A. (ed) (1994) *Poetry in the Therapeutic Experience.* St Louis: MMB Music.

Lerner, G. (1986) *The Creation of Patriarchy.* New York: Oxford University Press.

Levasseur, J. and Vance, D.R. (1993) 'Doctors, nurses and empathy.' In H.M. Spiro, M.G. McCrea-Curnen, E. Peschel and D. St James (eds) *Empathy and the Practice of Medicine: Beyond Pills and the Scalpel.* London: Yale University Press.

Lew, M. (1988) *Victims No Longer.* New York: Nevraumont.

Lewis, M. (1992) *Shame: The Exposed Self.* New York: Free Press.

Lieblich, A. (1996) 'Some unforeseen outcomes of conducting narrative research with people of one's own culture.' In R. Josselson (ed) *Ethics and Process in the Narrative Study of Lives,* vol. 4. London: Sage.

Lincoln, Y.S. and Guba, E.G. (1985) *Naturalistic Inquiry.* London: Sage.

Longo, P.J. (1999) 'Poetry as therapy.' *Sanctuary Psychiatric Centers' Information Network.* Santa Barbara: Internet.

Lowen, A. (1967) *The Betrayal of the Body.* New York: Macmillan.

Lowen, A. (1976) *Bioenergetics.* Harmondsworth: Penguin.

Lynch, G. (1996) 'What is truth? A philosophical introduction to counselling research.' *Counselling 7*, 2, 144–147.

Mair, M. (1989) *Between Psychology and Psychotherapy: A Poetics of Experience.* London: Routledge.

Masson, J. (1984) *The Assault on Truth: Freud's Suppression of the Seduction Theory.* New York: Farrar, Straus & Giroux.

Mays, N. and Pope, C. (1995) 'Rigour and qualitative research.' *British Medical Journal 311*, 109–112.

McAdams, D.P. (1996) 'Narrating the self in adulthood.' In J.E. Birren, G.M. Kenyon, J. Ruth, J.J.F. Schroots and T. Svensson (eds) *Aging and Biography.* New York: Springer.

McLeod, J. (1994) *Doing Counselling Research.* London: Sage.

McLeod, J. (1996) 'Qualitative approaches to research into counselling and psychotherapy: issues and challenges.' *British Journal of Guidance and Counselling 24*, 3, 309–316.

McLeod, J. (1997) *Narrative and Psychotherapy.* London. Sage.

McLeod, J. (1999) *Practitioner Research in Counselling.* London: Sage.

Mearns, D. and Thorne, B. (1988) *Person-Centred Counselling in Action.* London: Sage.

Mezey, G.V. and King, M.B. (1992) *Male Victims of Sexual Assault.* London: Oxford University Press.

Miller, A. (1990) *Thou Shalt Not Be Aware: Society's Betrayal of the Child*, 2nd edn. London: Pluto.

Miller, M. (1996) 'Ethics and understanding through interrelationship: I–Thou in dialogue.' In R. Josselson (ed) *Ethics and Process in the Narrative Study of Lives,* vol. 4. Thousand Oaks, CA: Sage.

Miller, V. (1998) *I Love You Just the Way You Are.* London: Walker Books.

Mitroff, I.I. (1974) *The Subjective Side of Science: Philosophical Inquiry into the Psychology of the Apollo Moon Scientists*. Amsterdam: Elsevier.

Modell, A. (1986) 'The missing elements in Kohut's cure.' *Psychoanalytic Inquiry 6*, 367–385.

Moustakas, C. (1990) *Heuristic Research: Design, Methodology and Applications*. London: Sage.

Moustakas, C. (1994) *Phenomenological Research Methods*. Thousand Oaks, CA: Sage.

Murgatroyd, S. and Woolfe, R. (1982) *Coping with Crisis: Understanding and Helping People in Need*. London: Harper and Row.

Mykhalovskiy, E. (1997) 'Reconsidering "Table Talk": critical thoughts on the relationship between sociology, autobiography and self-indulgence.' In R. Hertz (ed) *Reflexivity and Voice*. London: Sage.

Nouwen, H. (1994a) *The Wounded Healer*. London: Darton, Longman and Todd.

Nouwen, H. (1994b) *The Return of the Prodigal Son: A Story of Homecoming*. London: Darton Longman and Todd.

O'Brien, M.J. (1989) *Characteristics of Male Adolescent Sibling Incest Offenders: Preliminary Fndings*. Orwell, VT: Safer Society Press.

Ochberg, R. (1996) 'Interpreting life stories.' In R. Josselson (ed) *The Narrative Study of Lives*, vol. 4. London: Sage.

Orr, M. (1999) *Accuracy About Abuse*. London: Accuracy About Abuse.

Osborne, J. (1990) 'The psychological effects of childhood sexual abuse on women.' *Social Work Monograph*. Norwich: University of East Anglia.

Parker, L. (1998) 'Healing the wounded healer.' In H. Johns (ed) *Balancing Acts: Studies in Counselling Training*. London: Routledge.

Parks, P. (1994) *The Counsellor's Guide to Parks Inner Child Therapy*. London: Souvenir Press.

Pennebaker, J.W. (1988) 'Confiding traumatic experiences and health.' In S. Fisher and J. Reason (eds) *Handbook of Life Stress, Cognition and Health*. Chichester: Wiley.

Pennebaker, J.W. (1993) 'Putting stress into words: health, linguistic and therapeutic implications.' *Behaviour Research and Therapy 31*, 539–548.

Pennebaker, J.W., Colder, M. and L.K. Sharp (1990) 'Accelerating the coping process.' *Journal of Personality and Social Psychology 58*, 3, 528–537.

Perls, F.S. (1969) *Gestalt Therapy Verbatim*. Moab, UT: Real People Press.

Pert, C.B. (1998) *Molecules of Emotion: Why You Feel the Way You Feel*. London: Simon and Schuster.

Petrovich, M. and Templar, D. (1984) 'Heterosexual molestation of children who later became rapists.' *Psychological Reports 54*, 810.

Pinkola Estes, C. (1992) *Women Who Run With the Wolves*. London: Ryder.

Polanyi, M. (1967) *The Tacit Dimension*. London: Routledge and Kegan Paul.

Polkinghorne, D.E. (1989) 'Phenomenological research methods.' In R.S. Valle and S. Halling (eds) *Existential–Phenomenological Perspectives in Psychology*. New York: Plenum Press.

Racovsky, M. and Racovsky, A. (1950) 'On consummated incest.' *International Journal of Psychoanalysis 31*, 42–47.

Raine, N.V. (1999) *After Silence: Rape and My Journey Back*. London: Virago.

Reason, P. and Rowan, J. (eds) (1981) *Human Inquiry: A Sourcebook of New Paradigm Research*. Chichester: Wiley.
Reason, P. and Rowan, J. (eds) (1988) *Human Inquiry in Action*. London: Sage.
Reich, W. (1949) *Character Analysis*, 3rd edn. New York: Orgone Institute Press.
Reich, W. (1979) *The Sexual Revolution*. Farrar Straus and Giroux: New York.
Reinharz, S. (1979) *On Becoming a Social Scientist*. San Francisco: Jossey Bass.
Reinharz, S. (1992) *Feminist Methods in Social Research*. New York: Oxford University Press.
Reinharz, S. (1997) 'Who am I? The need for a variety of selves in the field.' In R. Hertz (ed) *Reflexivity and Voice*. Thousand Oaks, CA: Sage.
Reissman, C.K. (1993) *Narrative Analysis*. Newbury Park, CA: Sage.
Remen, R.N. (1993) *On Healing*. Bolinas, CA: Institute for the Study of Health and Illness.
Renee, D. (1985) 'Client deference in the psychotherapy relationship.' Paper presented at the 16th Annual Meeting of the Society for Psychotherapy Research, Evanston, Illinois.
Rennie, D. (1990) 'Towards a representation of the client's experience of the therapeutic hour.' In E. Litaer and R. Rombants (eds) *Client-centred Experiential Psychotherapy in the '90s*. Leuven: Leuven University Press
Rennie, D. (1992) 'Qualitative analysis of the clients' experience of psychotherapy: the unfolding reflexivity.' In S. Toukmanian and D. Rennie (eds) *Psychotherapy Process Research*. Newbury Park, CA: Sage.
Rennie, D. (1996) 'Fifteen years of doing qualitative research on psychotherapy.' *British Journal of Guidance and Counselling 24*, 3, 317–327.
Renzetti, C. and Lee, R. (eds) (1993) *Researching Sensitive Topics*. London: Sage.
Rhodes, C. (1996) 'Researching organisational change and learning: a narrative approach.' *Qualitative Report 2*, 4, 1–7 (http://www.nova.edu/ssss/QR/QR2-4/rhodes.html)
Rivers, W.H.R. (1918) 'The repression of war experience.' *The Lancet*, 2 February.
Roberts, H. (1981) *Doing Feminist Research*. London: Routledge and Kegan Paul.
Rogers, C. (1951) *Client-Centred Therapy*. London: Constable.
Rogers, C. (1961) *On Becoming a Person*. Boston: Houghton Mifflin.
Rogers, C. (1975) 'Empathic: an unappreciated way of being.' *Counseling Psychologist 5*, 2, 2–10.
Russell, D.E.H. (1984) *Sexual Exploitation: Rape, Child Sexual Abuse and Workplace Harassment*. Beverley Hills, CA: Sage.
Ryle, A. (1990) *Cognitive Analytical Therapy: Active Participation in Change: A New Integration in Brief Psychotherapy*. Chichester: Wiley.
Sacks, O. (1985) *The Man Who Mistook His Wife for a Hat*. London: Duckworth.
Sanderson, C. (1995) *Counselling Adult Survivors of Child Sexual Abuse*. London: Jessica Kingsley Publishers.
Schafer, R. (1981) 'Narration in the psychoanalytic dialogue.' In W.J.T Mitchell (ed) *On Narrative*. Chicago: University of Chicago Press.
Schon, D. (1991) *The Reflective Practitioner*. Aldershot: Arena.
Seaburn, D., Lorenz, A., Mauksch, L., Gawanski, B. and Gunn, W.B. (1996) *Models of Collaboration – a Guide for Mental Health Professionals Working with Health Care Practitioners*. New York: Basic Books.

Seale, C. and Silverman, D. (1997) 'Ensuring rigour in qualitative research papers.' *European Journal of Public Health* 7, 379–384.

Seiber, J.E. (1993) 'Ethics and politics of sensitive research.' In C.M. Renzetti and R.M. Lee (eds) *Researching Sensitive Topics*. London: Sage.

Seligman, M.E.P. (1975) *Helplessness: On Depression, Development and Death*. San Francisco: Freeman.

Sepler, F. (1990) 'Victim advocacy and young male victims of sexual abuse: an evolutionary model.' In M. Hunter (ed) *The Sexually Abused Male*, vol.1. Lexington, MA: Lexington Books.

Sgroi, S.M. and Bunk, B.S. (1988) 'A clinical approach to adult survivors of child sexual abuse.' In S. Sgroi (ed) *Vulnerable Populations*, vol. 1. Lexington, MA: Lexington Books.

Speedy, J. (1998) 'Issues of power for women counselling trainers.' In H. Johns (ed) *Balancing Acts. Studies in Counselling Training*. London: Routledge.

Speedy, J. (2000) 'Singing over the bones: an exploration of the relationship between counselling research and counsellor education.' Unpublished Ph.D. dissertation, University of Bristol.

Speedy, J. and Etherington, K. (1999) 'Personal development as an intended consequence of experiential training in qualitative research methodologies.' Paper presented at BAC Research Conference, Leeds.

Spiro, H.M., McCrea-Curnen, M.G., Peschel, E. and St. James, D. (eds) (1993) *Empathy and the Practice of Medicine: Beyond Pills and the Scalpel*. London: Yale University Press.

Stainbrook, E. (1994) 'Poetry and behaviour in the psychotherapeutic experience.' In A. Lerner (ed) *Poetry in the Therapeutic Experience*. St Louis: MMB Music.

Stake, R. (1995) *The Art of Case Study Research*. Thousand Oaks, CA: Sage.

Stanley, L. and Wise, S. (1983) *Breaking Out: Feminist Consciousness and Feminist Research*. London: Routledge and Kegan Paul.

Starhawk (1990) *Dreaming the Dark: Magic, Sex and Politics*. London: Mandala.

Stevens, A. (1990) *On Jung*. London: Penguin.

Strauss, A. and Corbin, J. (1990) *Basics of Qualitative Research: Grounded Theory Procedures and Techniques*. London: Sage.

Struve, J. (1990) 'Dancing with patriarchy: the politics of sexual abuse.' In M. Hunter (ed) *The Sexually Abused Male*, vol. 1. Lexington, MA: Lexington Books.

Summit, R.C. (1983) 'The child sexual abuse accommodation syndrome.' *Child Abuse and Neglect* 7, 177–193.

Terr, L. (1991) 'Childhood traumas: an outline and overview.' *American Journal of Psychiatry* 148, 10–20.

Tomkins, S.S. (1963) *Affect, Imagery, Consciousness: The Positive Affects*, vol.1. New York: Springer.

Truax, C.B. and Carkhuff, R.R. (1967) *Towards Effective Counselling and Psychotherapy: Training and Practice*. Chicago: Aldine.

Van der Kolk, B.A. (1987) *Psychological Trauma*. Washington DC: American Psychiatric Press.

van Deurzen Smith, E. (1988) *Existential Counselling in Action*. London: Sage.

Vasington, M.C. (1989) 'Sexual offenders as victims: implications for treatment and the therapeutic relationship.' In S. Sgroi (ed) *Vulnerable Populations*, vol. 2. Lexington, MA: Lexington Books.

Wasserfall, R. (1997) 'Reflexivity, feminism and difference.' In R. Hertz (ed) *Reflexivity and Voice.* Thousand Oaks, CA: Sage.

Watkins, W. and Bentovim, A. (1992) 'Male children and adolescents as victims: a review of current knowledge.' In G.C. Mezey and M.B. King (eds) *Male Victims of Sexual Abuse.* London: Oxford University Press.

Weingarten, K. (1995) 'Making meaning around experiences of sexual abuse.' *Family Process 34*, 257–259.

West, W. (1998) 'Critical subjectivity: use of self in counselling research.' *Counselling 9*, 3, 228–230.

White, M. and Epston, D. (1990) *Narrative Means to Therapeutic Ends.* New York: Norton.

Wilber, K. (1979) *No Boundary: Eastern and Western Approaches to Personal Growth.* London: Shambala.

Wilkinson, P. and Bass, C. (1994) 'Hysteria, somatisation and the sick role.' *The Practitioner 238*, 384–390.

Williams, P. (1999) 'Telling tales: the elusive power of stories.' *The Therapist 6*, 1, 18–23.

Winnicott, D.W. (1965) *Maturational Processes and the Facilitating Environment.* New York: International Universities Press.

Wyatt, G.E. and Mickey, M.R. (1987) 'Ameliorating the effects of child sexual abuse.' *Journal of Interpersonal Violence 2*, 403–414.

Yalom, I. (1989) *Love's Executioner and Other Tales of Psychotherapy.* Harmondsworth: Penguin.

Yalom, I. and Elkin, G. (1974) *Every Day Gets a Little Closer: A Twice-Told Therapy.* New York: Basic Books.

Yin, R. (1989) *Case Study Research: Design and Methods.* London: Sage.

Zeig, J.K. (ed) (1994) *Ericksonian Methods: The Essence of the Story.* New York: Brunner/Mazel.

Zilbergeld, B. (1995) *Men and Sex: A Guide to Sexual Fulfilment.* London: HarperCollins.

Subject Index

Abusive relationships 139, 227
Absent fathers 110
'Accommodation syndrome' 138
Accuracy About Abuse 299
Action research 259
Addiction 89, 180, 225 *see also* Masturbation, compulsive
  Sex addiction 225, 309
  Alcohol and drugs 180
Adolescence 126, 308–310
Adrenaline 141
Aggression 116, 208, 221
Alcohol/drugs 180
Alliance, working 124
Altered consciousness 173
Ambivalence *see* Attachment
American Psychiatric Association 138, 205
Amygdala 140–143, 154
Analysis 292
Anger work 35, 47, 196, *see also* Appendix 1
Animus 111
Anonymity 257, 266, 277
Armouring, body, 48, 180, 199
Arousal 224
Assessment 109–113, 116–7
  Client 109
  Client's assessment of counsellor 112–113, 117
  Self 109–111

Attachment 122–129, 236
Audience 295–6
Audio-tapes 267, 284, 293
Authority
  And voice 196–7,
  Printed word 263, 298
  Field text 295
Autonomy, 51, 241
'Autonomous bounded self' 199–200

BAC code of ethics 261
BASK model 149
Beginnings 29
Behavioural approach 119
Behavioural manifestations of abuse 149
Betrayal, of trust 122, 148
Blame 57, 92, 214
Bioenergetics 182, 198
Biosynthesis 183–4,
Body memory 143, 148–9, 176–9, 190,
Body psychotherapy 180
Bodywork 18–19, 96, 176–200 *see also* Stephen's Story
  Healing through the body 35, 48, 176
  Listening to the body 148
'The boon' 107–108
Boundaries 187–9
Brain changes due to PTSD 140–144
Breaking the cycle of abuse, 37, 174–5,
Breathing 18, 176, 181
Bricolage 257

Case study research 299–300
Categories 295
Catharsis 35, 47, 96, 153, 181, 190

Chaos 110, 155
'Chaos stories', 155
Child development
Child sexual abuse accommodation syndrome 138
The Church 174
  Attitudes to disclosure 66,
  Attitudes to abuse 95
  Forgiveness 174
Client's experience, *see* Stephen's Story and Mike's Story
Cognitive communication 115
Cognition/emotional development 115, 150, 165
Cognitive-analytical therapy, CAT 236
Cognitive processes 142, 150, 154
Coherence 152, 156
Collaborative working, 18–19, 185–200
Communication 115
Compliance 204, 207, 222
Compulsive masturbation 89, 225
Confidentiality 189
Conflict, in family *see* Stephen's Story and Mike's Story
Confrontation 79
Co-operative enquiry 258–9
Consent 224, 269–282, 293
  Informed 224, 269–282
  Process 293
Contempt 150
Contracting 114, 236
Control 57, 79, 118, 122, 139, 206–7

325

Convicted offenders 11
Coping, 230
  Intellectualisation 89, 131, 147–8,
  Somatisation 106, 149, 179–180
  Identification with the aggressor 145
  Compliance 222
  Accomodation 138
Core conditions 119, see also unconditional positive regard
Cortex of brain 140, 154
Counsellor as researcher 20
Counselling research 21
Counter-transference 130, 136, 148
Creative synthesis 259, 302–305
Creative arts in therapy 160
Crisis 106, 109, 114
Cultural forces 156–6
Culture of therapy 199
Cycle of abuse, 11, 59, 174

Data,
  Diaries 27–76, 267
  Interviews 112–113, 117–118, 128, 131–133, 140, 146–7, 237–238,
  Letters 175, 267
  Field notes 284–290
  Field text 295
Data analysis 295
Data protection 266–7
Deconstruction 156
Defences 197, 215
Defence mechanisms 230 see also Coping
Denial 125, 145, 155–6, 201–203, 216, 231,253

Dependency 127, 132, 241
Dependency needs 126–7
Depression see Suicide
Diagnosis 114
Dialogue with the body 197
Dialogue in research 283
Diaries see Stephen's Story and Mike's Story
Disclosing abuse 79, 117
Disclosure see also Stephen's Story
  Counsellor 117, 130
  Self 130
Disintegration 150,
Dissociation 111, 125, 148, 173, 176
Doctor's persona 209
Dominance and control 206
Dominant discourse 291
Drawing chaos 155
Drawing flashbacks 34, 310
Dreaming 50–51,
DSM lll 138
DSM lV 138
Dual relationships 21–22, 259, 264–266
Dynamics 217–222
  victim–perpetrator 217–220
  victim–persecutor–rescuer 221–222
  parent–adult–child see Transactional Analysis and PAC

Effects of abuse 146, 224, 230,
Ego 148, 230
Ego, fragile male 215
Ego states see Transactional Analysis, also PAC
Ejaculation 224–5

Emotional abuse and neglect 205
Emotional brain 140–1
Emotional memory 140
Empathy 119
'Empathic intunement' 121
Empathic resonance 264
Empathic understanding 113–121
Empathy, darker side 121
Employment 69–75
  Sick note 30
  Occupational Health 56, 74,
  Rehabilitation back to work 73
Endings 235–244
Epilepsy 180
Ethics 261–267,
  Autonomy 262
  Beneficence 262,
  fidelity 262
  informed consent 262, 269–282
  non-maleficence 262
  principles 261
Ethics and power 263–264
Ethnography 257
Evaluation,
  Ongoing 118, 236
  Locus of, internal 253
Existential-Phenomenological Perspectives 253
Existential school of philosophy 253
Explication 259, 295
Exposure, fear of 14, 68, 81
Externalising 156, 183

Fairy stories 23
'False Memory' debate 299
False reports 146
False self 106, 125

SUBJECT INDEX

Family dynamics 221 *see also* Stephen's Story
Father,
  Fear of 37, 82
  Image of, 174, 217, 233
  Fall from grace of 217
  Mike's letter to 82–84
Fear 82, 95, 96, 98
Feelings 30–32, 116,
  Shut down 139, 141
  Flooding 121, 139, 144, 154
  Language 148
Felt sense 107, 147–8,
Female survivors 90, 138
'Feminine' methodology 256
Feminism 9, 80, 199, 221
Femininity 9, 231,
Feminist research methodology 256
Fight/flight response 141, 207
Flashbacks 29, 139, 156, 310 *see also* Stephen's Story
Focusing 107, 149
Forbidden impulses 181
Forgiveness 84, 86
'Frozen face' 149

Gender
  Male abuse 9
  Masculinity 9
  Roles 14, 110, 204, 231
  Role conflict 83
Generalisability 300
Gestalt therapy 182
God, relationship with 233
God, letter to, 175
Goodbye letters 236
GP 18, 30, 73–74, 220
Grounded theory 256, 258, 295

Grounding in Bioenergetics 182
Guilt 35, 40, 49,

Hakomi 184
Hard science 21–22
Healing 107, 143–145, 169, 173, 234
Healer–patient archetype 209–210
Healing power of stories 173
Health 106
Hermetically sealed-in client 114, 146
Hemispheres, left and right 154, 166
'The hero's journey' 107
Hermeneutics 256
Heuristic inquiry 259, 269, 284–290
Homophobia 205
Homosexual identity confusion 78, 205–6, 223
Homosexuality 206
History of post-traumatic stress disorder 137 *see also* shell-shock
Hypervigilance 179
Hypochondria 179
Hysteria 137, 179–180

Iceberg, The 103–105
Identification with the aggressor 145
Identity confusion 223
Illness 106
Illumination 259, 288
Imagery 154
Images 106, 111, 133, 144, 154, 156, 234
Immersion 259, 287, 294

Impact of abuse on males 15
Impact of disclosure *see* Stephen's Story
Incubation 259, 287
Informed consent 114, 269–282
Initial engagement 259, 269, 284
Inner child 166
  letters to 167–173
  stories for 173
  as metaphor 165
Integration 107, 162–4, 173
Integrative approaches to bodywork 183
Intellectualisation 131
'Internal working model' 123, 236
Interpretation 295–6
Interviewing 257, 268–9, 283, 288
  Conversational 283, 288
  Semi-structured 257
Intimacy 177
Irritable bowel 149, 153
Isolation 94, 133, 145, 201–202,

Journey 107, 119, 144, 270

Knowledge
  local knowledge 254
  tacit knowledge 107, 253
  external 252
  as power 131

Left hemisphere 154
Letters 14, 155, 158
  To father 82, 155
  to the inner child 166–8
  from the Adult 174
  to God 174–5

to perpetrator 84–91, 158
  also *see* appendix
Limbic system 140
Local knowledge 254
Locus of evaluation 253

Male abuse 9, 214
Maleness 9, 110, 181, 201,
Male socialisation 201–234
'Marital fit' 228, 238
Masculine aspect 111, 256
Masculinity 9, 167, 181,
  202,
Massage 176–177,
  189–191, 196–7,
Masturbation, compulsive
  89–90
'mature independence' 120
Mediating the effects 220,
  230–234
Medical profession 18, 98,
  115, 117, 193
Medication 143
Memory 143, 299
Men, 11, 15, 16,
Men and illness, 209–210
Men and
  intimacy/vulnerability
  201–2, 204,
Men and work 208
Metaphor 150, 160, 165,
  174
  and therapy 150
  as healing 107, 160, 174
  inner child 165
Methodology,
  Qualitative 254–260
  Quantitative 252
Modernism 186, 199,
  252–3,
Mourning 96, 143–144
Multiple victims 61–65,
  216,
Mutuality 112

Narrating the self 296
Narrative 297–8
  methodology 259, 297
  as form of inquiry 259
  phenomenon of 297–8
  Plot 297
  Restitution 155
  Scene 297
  Self-stories 17, 254
  Temporality 297
Narrative therapy, 10
'Narrative wreckage' 156,
  254
Neediness 126- 129 *see also*
  dependency
Neo-cortex 140–141,
  143–144, 154
Neuroscience 140–144
New paradigm research 21,
  258

Occupational Therapist 21
Offender research 11
Oral stories 296
Orgasm 181, 225
'Orgasm reflex' 181
Over-lapping relationships
  187

Parent-Adult-Child (P-A-C)
  136, 166, 217 *see also*
  Ego States and
  Transactional Analysis
Paedophiles 10, 23, 171,
  201–202, 225
Panic attacks 179 *see*
  phobias
Parentification 73, 75
Passivity *see* compliance
Patriarchy 9, 18, 201–234
Pelvic bouncing 48, 198
Person-centred counselling
  154, 252,

Person-centred framework
  263
Phenomenology 257
Phenomenological research
  111
Philosophical
  considerations 22
Phobias 179
Physical response to
  emotions 147
Physical contact 188, 229
Physical illness 179–180
Physiological changes
  Through writing 153
  In trauma 137–144
Physiology of brain *see also*
  trauma
Pleasure *see* arousal
Pluralism 199
Poetry, healing power of
  159–164
Pornography 206, 225,
  291, 307
Positivism 252, 297, 299
Postmodernism 152, 186,
  252–3, 258
Post-modern storyteller 254
Post-traumatic stress
  disorder 50, 55, 76,
  114, 137–142
  history of 137–8
  diagnosis 55, 114, 138
  flashbacks 34
  secondary 111, 145
  physiology of 140–142
Power and control 122,
  207
Power, over 136, 207
Power from within 181
Power with 118, 292
Power 121
  Ascribed 114, 263
  Owned 263
  Disguised 263

SUBJECT INDEX

Shadow side 207, 263
Power/knowledge 131
Power in the helping
  professions 114,
  121–122,
Powerlessness 121, 145,
Practitioner-researcher 259
Pre-frontal cortex 140–143
Projection 116
Psychic numbing 114
Psychosomatic disorders
  179
Puberty 307

Qualitative research
  254–260
Quantitative methodology
  252
Quest story 20, 108, 156

Rage 138, 190, 207–8,
Rape 188
Readiness 198
Relationship problems 146,
  227
'Real relationship' 119,
  130, 133
Reality, social construction
  of 252, 258
Reconstructed self 153
Recovery
Re-enactment and
  repetition 226
Reflexivity 257–8
Reichian 180
Rejection 43, 83
Relationship, 227
  Real 119
  Reconstructive 130
  'security-giving' 131
  therapeutic 119
  transference
    counter-transference
    130–136

Relationships, dysfunctional
  139
The Researcher's Story
  247–305
Research methods 268–272
Research–practice gap 297
Research process 252–260
  Philosophical
    considerations
    252–254
  'order of service' 284
  heuristic process 259
  initial engagement 259,
    284
  immersion 259, 287, 294
  incubation 259, 287
  illumination 259, 288
  explication 259
  creative synthesis 259
Responsibility 298
Restitution story 155
Representation 301
Right hemisphere of brain
  154, 174
Ritual, endings 237
Roles,
  Gender roles, 14, 21
  Sex roles, 14,
Role-reversal see
  Parentification
'rough guide' for
  counselling researchers
  20

Safety 116, 124
Scapegoat 214
'Schoolism' 186
Science 21–2, 252
Secondary post-traumatic
  stress disorder 111, 145
'Secure base' 110
'Security-giving
  relationship' 131
Secrecy 15, 213

Secrecy, 'shroud of' 205,
  213
Seeking help 14, 80,
Seizures 180
Self of counsellor 119,
  231–234
Self,
  Physical 125
  Cognitive 125–126
  emotional 125
  multi-dimensional 152
  reconstructed self 152–3,
Self-assessment 5
self-indulgence 258
Self-in-relationship 119,
  124–5
Self, narrating the 17,
  152
Self as primary instrument
  16
self via poetry therapy 10
Self-care 173
Self-disclosure see also
  disclosure,
  counsellor's 117,130
  clients 14, 28,
Self-esteem 171, 225
Selves, 152
  'live in the face' 9
  many 152, 254
Sensitive topics 21, 24
Sensory memory 143
Separation 6, 18, 235
Sex Addicts Anonymous
  226
Sex roles 14, 204, 231
Sexual development 224
Sexual identity confusion
  126, 223
Sexual orientation 223, 310
Sexualisation 87–88
Sexuality 199, 224
Sexual stimulation 224–5
Sexual trauma 89

Shame 127, 131, 149–150, 159, 213
'Shell shock' 137, 180 *see also* Post-traumatic stress
'Sick' role, men's difficulty with, 98
Silence 15
Social construction of realities 20, 157, 254
'Social influence' 263
Social learning theory 258
Socialisation 181, 201–229
Societal denial 137, 145, 156–7
Solution-focussed approaches 236,
Somatisation 106, 149, 153, 178–9,
'Spacing out' 173, 189
Splitting 148, 179, 187,
Spirituality 164, 171, 196
Stephen's Story 27–76
Stephen's letter to his dead grandfather 306–310
Stereotyping 115, 206–7, 218
Stigma 131
Stories, types of 14, 15, 16, 155 *see also* Narrative
  Chaos 155
  Fairy 23, 173
  Restitution 155
  Quest 20, 108, 156
Stories 17, 152, 177 *see also* Narrative
  As communication of memories 17
  Constructing person's world 17, 152
  Reclaiming ourselves 17
  Fairy stories 17, 153, 174–5
  'as if' stories 17
  symbolism 17

finding our voice 17
stories as research 17
stories as testimony 17, 156–8,
moral opportunity 157
Stress 111, 153, 179 *see also* Post-traumatic stress
Structuralism 252
Subjectivity 258, 295
Suicide 95, 208
Suicidal feelings 55, 83, 90, 207
Supervision 134, 145
Supervisor 145
Survival 139, 157
Swamp, The 247–251
'Switching out' 173
Symbols 143–4, 160
Systematic desensitisation 156

Tacit knowledge 107, 253
'Talking cure' 150, 176
Tape recording *see* Audio-tapes
Tension 179, 181,197
Testimony 156–8
Themes 256
Therapeutic relationship 119–136
Touch 188,194, 229
Transactional analysis 136, 166 *see also* PAC
Transcription 292
Transference 130–134
Trauma 137–144
Trauma, healing 143–151
Traumatic memories *see* Flashbacks
Traumatic neuroses of War 137
Traumatic sexualisation 223–229
Triangulation 257, 301

Triggers 144, 176, 179,
Trust 122
Trustworthiness 122

'Unconditional positive regard' 106, 119, 173
Unconscious meaning of research 121
Uniqueness 16, 20, 176, 298

Validity 254, 298
Values and beliefs 256
Victims, multiple *see* Stephen's Story and Mike's Story
Victim–perpetrator dynamic 217
Victim–persecutor–rescuer dynamics 221
Victims becoming offenders 218–220,
Visualisation 150, 176, 194
Voice work, 196–7
Voices, many 290, 301
Violence 208
Vulnerability *see* Intimacy

Walled-in client 114, 146
'Where Three Streams Meet' 302–305
Witnessing 156–8
Work, men and, 98
Working alliance 258
Workplace 98
Worldview 253–4,
Wound 108
Wounded healer 106, 108,
Wounded storyteller 152, 155
Writing letters, 158
Writing up data 295–301
Writing 152–169
  as therapy 152–155

Poetry 159–164
to the inner child
165–168
as self-help 154

Author Index

Abel, G. E. 10
Alexander, P. C. 123
Angoff, C. 159
Atkinson, P. 257

BAC 261
Barker, P. 137
Bass, C. 179
Bays, B. 107
Bear Z. 20
Beauchamp, T. L. 261
Bennet, G. 115, 121, 209
Berne, E. 136, 166
Betts, T. 180
Black, W. 21
Blaxter, M. 21
Boadella, D. 183, 186
Bond, T. 261
Bolton, G. 17, 155
Bolton, F. G. 15
Boulton, M. 21
Bowlby, J. 123, 230
Bowlby, J
Braun, B. G. 149
Brown, D. 299
Bunk, B. S. 122
Burgess, A. 11

Campbell, J. 107
Carkhuff, R. R. 119
Carlson, S. 11
Carroll, M. 211
Childress, J. F. 261
Clandinin, D. J. 291, 295, 296, 297, 298
Combs, G. 156, 252

Connelly, F. M. 291, 295, 296, 297, 298
Corbin, J. 21, 256, 295

Davies, J.M. 146, 148, 179
Denzin, N. K. 21, 254, 257, 301
DeSchazer, S. 236
Devereux, G. 121
Dickey, R. 217
Dryden, W. 12

Egan, G. 263
Egeland, B, 230
Einbender, A. J. 125
Elkin, G. 11, 244
Ellis, C. 283
Epston, D. 236
Ernst, S. 181
Etherington, K. 10, 11, 14, 110, 116, 205, 218, 255, 256, 257, 262, 264, 281, 299

Felitti, V. 180
Finkelhor, D. 223
Fisher, M. 237
Fitzpatrick, R. 21
Foucault, M. 131, 255
Fourie, D. 297
Francis, Brother 237
Frank, A. W. 16, 20, 22, 102, 107, 120, 152, 153, 155, 156, 157, 158, 254
Frankl, V. 253
Frawley, M. G. 146, 148, 179
Freedman, J. 156, 252
Freud, A. 230
Freud, S. 120
Freund, K. R. 217
Friedrich, W. N 114, 123, 124, 125, 138, 220

Geertz, C. 254, 255
Gendlin, E. 149
Gerber, P. N. 218
Gergen, K.J, 152
Gilgun, J. F. 230
Gilligan, C. 123
Glaser, B.G. 256
Godin, J. 174
Goleman, D. 138, 140, 141, 144
Goodison, L. 181
Grafanaki, S. 257
Greenhalgh, T. 22
Greig, E. 180
Groth, A.N. 11, 218, 227
Guggenbühl-Craig, A. 263

Haaken, J. 221
Halpern, J. 120
Hammersley, M. 257
Harber, K. D. 153
Henderson, P. 185
Heninger, O. E. 164
Herman, J. 9, 137, 142, 143
Heron, J. 256
Hertz, R. 257
Hillman, J. 259, 300
Hindman, J. 217
Hobson, W. F. 218
Houston, M. 292
Hull, J. B. 181, 183, 186
Hunter, M. 15, 226
Hurwitz, B. 22

Jacobvitz, D. 230
Johns, H. 256
Johnson, R.11
Josselson, R. 263, 265, 292, 298
Jourard, S. 283

Kagan, N.292
Kardiner, A.137

Karen, R. 123
Kaufman, G. 119, 130, 131, 149, 150
Kelly, L. 255, 256
King, M. B. 15, 139
Kinsey, A. C. 203
Kitchener, R. S. 261
Kleinman, A. 22
Kohut, H. 120, 292
Kramarae, C. 292
Kramer, P. 121
Kreiger, S. 298
Kvale. S. 292

Lamin, A. D. 154
Lapadat, J.C. 292, 294
LeDoux, J, 144
Lee, R. M. 262
Lerner, A. 163
Lerner, G. 207, 213, 256
Levasseur, J. 120
Lew, M. 15
Lieblich, A. 264
Lincoln, Y. S. 21, 254, 257
Lindsay, A.C. 292, 294
Longo, P. J. 160, 163
Lowen, A. 182
Lueke, W. J. 125
Lynch, G. 253

Mair, M. 246
Masson, J. 201
Mays, N. 21
McAdams, D. P. 296
McLeod, J. 16, 17, 18, 21, 154, 157, 185, 199, 254, 259
Mearns, D. 12
Mezey, G. V. 15, 139
Mickey, M. R. 230
Miller, A. 19
Miller, V. 173
Mitroff, I. I. 256
Modell, A. 121

Moustakas, C. 21, 107, 253, 259, 268, 283
Murgatroyd, S. 114
Murray, E. 154
Mykhalovskiy, E. 258
Nouwen, H. 20, 108, 236

O'Brien, M.J. 10, 217
Oliveri, F. J. 227
Ooghourlian, J-M. 174
Orr, M. 299
Osborne, J. 230

Parks, P. 150
Pennebaker, J. W. 153, 156
Perls, F. S. 150, 182, 189
Pert, C. B. 183
Petrovich, M. 11
Polanyi, M. 253
Polkinghorne, D. E. 255
Pope, C. 21
Pritchard, J. 11

Raine, N. V. 116, 143, 188, 226
Reason, P. 21, 258, 259
Reich, W. 180, 181
Reinharz, S. 257
Reissman, C. K. 259
Remen, R. N. 102, 152
Rennie, D. 11, 12, 258
Renzetti, C. 262
Rhodes, C. 301
Rivers, W. H. R. 137
Rogers, C. 20, 119, 120, 121, 253
Rowan, J. 21, 258, 259
Russell, D.E.H. 9
Ryle, A. 236

Sacks, O. 26
Sanderson, C. 20
Schafer, R. 17
Scheflin, A. W. 299

Seaburn, D.B. 185
Seale, C. 21
Seligman, M. E. P. 207
Sepler, F. 138
Sgroi, S. M. 122
Shrier, D. 11
Silverman, D. 21
Speedy, J. 22, 257, 263
Speigel, H. 137
Spiro, H. M. 264
Stroufe, A. L. 230
Stainbrook, E. 160, 164
Stake, R. 299
Stanley, L. 256
Starhawk 262
Stevens, A. 111
Strauss, A. 21, 256, 295
Struve, J. 207

Templar, D. 11
Terr, L. 138
Thorne, B. 12, 253
Tomkins, S. S. 149
Toukmanian, S. 12
Truax, C. B. 119

Vance, D. R. 120
van Deurzen Smith, E. 253
Van der Kolk, B. A. 148
Vasington, M. C. 127

Watson, R. 217
Weingarten, K. 254
White, M. 236
Whitfield, D. 299
Wilber, K. 187, 188
Wilkinson, P. 179
Williams, P. 154, 165
Winnicott, D. W. 125
Wise, S. 256
Woolfe, R. 114
Wyatt, G. E. 230

Yalom, I. 11, 244

Yankura, J. 12

Zilbergeld, B. 224, 229
Zeig J. K.

Printed in the United Kingdom
by Lightning Source UK Ltd.
130072UK00001B/58-66/A